Red Arctic

Red

Arctic

Polar Exploration

and the Myth of

the North in the

Soviet Union,

1932–1939

JOHN McCANNON

New York   Oxford

Oxford University Press

1998

Oxford University Press

Oxford   New York
Athens   Auckland   Bangkok   Bogota   Bombay   Buenos Aires
Calcutta   Cape Town   Dar es Salaam   Delhi   Florence   Hong Kong
Istanbul   Karachi   Kuala Lumpur   Madras   Madrid   Melbourne
Mexico City   Nairobi   Paris   Singapore   Taipei   Tokyo   Toronto   Warsaw

and associated companies in
Berlin   Ibadan

Copyright © 1998 by Oxford University Press, Inc.

Published by Oxford University Press, Inc.
198 Madison Avenue, New York, New York 10016

Library of Congress Cataloging-in-Publication Data
McCannon, John, 1967–
   Red Arctic: polar exploration and the myth of the north in the Soviet Union,
1932–1939 / John McCannon.
      p.   cm.
   Includes bibliographical references and index.
   ISBN 0-19-511436-1
   1. Russia, Northern—History.   2. Arctic regions—Discovery and exploration—
Soviet.   3. Soviet Union—Territorial expansion.   4. Soviet Union. Glavnoe
upravlenie Severnogo morskogo puti.   5. Soviet Union—History—1925–1953.
I. Title.
DK501.5.M38   1997
947—dc21   97-13937

9 8 7 6 5 4 3 2 1

Printed in the United States of America
on acid-free paper

Acknowledgments

In the course of writing this volume, I have received encouragement and expertise from too many individuals and institutions to list completely. At least a few, however, deserve to be singled out.

Since this work grew directly out of my graduate research, my thanks go first to the members of my dissertation committee at the University of Chicago: Sheila Fitzpatrick, Richard Hellie, and Bernard Cohn. All three provided invaluable guidance and assistance in too many ways to say.

If there is a Russian studies group in North America that is more congenial and high spirited (or simply rambunctious!) than the graduate students of the Russian and Soviet History Workshop at the University of Chicago, I would be surprised to hear it. I was privileged to belong to the workshop from 1989 to 1994, and I would like to thank all my fellow members for more than half a decade of continuing advice, support, and friendship.

For sponsoring my archival research in Russia, my appreciation goes out to the University of Chicago, the Urals Branch of the Russian Academy of Sciences, the Russian State Humanities University (RGGU), and the European University in Moscow. I thank Veniamin Alekseev, Evgenii Logunov, Aleksei Kilin, Vladimir Shkerin, Sergei and Nastya Dubinskii, Sigurd Ottovich Shmidt, Vasilii Spiridonov, Vadim Mokievskii, Valentina Mokievskaia, and Alexander Teniakshev for their hospitality and assistance. I am also indebted to the Mellon Foundation for supporting the final stage of my dissertation work in 1993–1994.

Dozens of individuals have given me suggestions, alerted me to sources, or made helpful comments and criticisms about my work. Many of them are cited in the text itself, but I would like to thank especially Daniel Alexandrov and Mark Bassin for input, advice, and insight. Also important are the many graduate students and faculty researchers I had the good fortune to work with in the Moscow archives in 1992. In addition, my thanks go out to the participants—audience and panelists alike—of the various conference sessions in which material from this book has been presented. Of special note here are Lynne Viola, Roberta Manning, E. A. Rees, Douglas Weiner, Richard Stites, and all the student and faculty members of the Midwest Russian History Colloquium. For their assistance in the preparation of the final manuscript, I wish to extend my appreciation to the library staffs of Northeast Louisiana University and Norwich University, as well as to the reviewers and editors at Oxford University Press who worked on *Red Arctic*—especially Thomas LeBien, Jeff Soloway, and MaryBeth Branigan.

Finally, this volume is dedicated to my parents, John and Jan McCannon, who have provided me with a lifetime of support and encouragement. *Red Arctic* is also dedicated to my wife, Pamela Jordan, whose criticisms and suggestions played a significant role in the shaping of the book and whose love and companionship have made the writing of it (and all else I do) worthwhile.

Permission to quote from James Thurber's "The Greatest Man in the World," in *The Middle-Aged Man on the Flying Trapeze* (New York: HarperCollins, 1935), has been granted by Rosemary Thurber of Thurber Literary Properties. The map of the Soviet Arctic appears courtesy of Addison Wesley Longman, Ltd. Credits for the remainder of the illustrations are cited as they appear.

Portions of chapters 4 and 5 have appeared elsewhere. For permission to reprint sections of "To Storm the Arctic: Soviet Polar Exploration and Public Visions of Nature in the USSR" and "Positive Heroes at the Pole: Celebrity Status, Socialist-Realist Ideals, and the Soviet Myth of the Arctic," I am grateful to the journals *Ecumene* and *Russian Review*, respectively.

Contents

A Note on Transliteration

In its scholarly apparatus—in its notes and bibliography—*Red Arctic* adheres to a strict Library of Congress transliteration of the Cyrillic alphabet. In the text, however, I have devised a method of transliteration that is strictly my own. This system does not pretend to complete consistency but provides what I hope is maximum readability. First, I have eliminated all "hard" and "soft" diacritical marks (*except* when I first introduce a Russian term in a parenthetical gloss). I have chosen to render terms and surnames ending in *-skii* and *-kii* as *-sky* and *-ky* (hence, "Gorky" rather than "Gor'kii"). Although feminine endings remain as *-aia*, rather than *-aya*, I have opted to eliminate the double *i* from feminine endings such as those found in "Sofiia" (instead, "Sofia") or Mariia ("Maria"). One notable exception is the title of the newspaper *Izvestiia*, which I have allowed to stand as is. The consonant cluster "*ks*" will typically appear as "*x*" ("Alexei," not "Aleksei").

Names and words beginning in letters rendered technically as *E-*, *Iu-*, and *Ia-* are generally transliterated as *Ye-*, *Yu-*, and *Ya-* (therefore, "Yanson" instead of "Ianson"; "Yezhov" rather than "Ezhov"). The Russian version of "Simon" has been rendered as "Semyon," although the corresponding surname remains "Semenov" (however, "Fedor" and "Fedorov" rather than "Fyodor" and "Fyodorov"). Finally, to avoid having him sound more German than Russian, I have chosen to retain a strict transliteration of Otto Shmidt's surname rather than anglicizing it to "Schmidt."

Abbreviations

AKO	Kamchatka Joint-Stock Company
ARAN	Archive of the Russian Academy of Sciences (Moscow)
ARCOS	All-Russian Cooperative Society
Arktikugol'	Arctic Coal-Mining Complex (Spitsbergen)
ASO	Sakhalin Joint-Stock Company
ASSR	Autonomous Soviet Socialist Republic
BBK	White Sea-Baltic Sea Canal (also *Belomor*)
Dal'stroi	Main Administration for Construction in the Far North
DVK	Far Eastern Region
FAI	International Aviation Federation
GARF	State Archive of the Russian Federation (Moscow)
GASO	State Archive of the Sverdlovsk Oblast' (Ekaterinburg)
GATO	State Archive of the Tiumen' Oblast' (Tiumen')
Glavzoloto	Main Administration of the Gold and Platinum Industries
GOELRO	State Commission for the Electrification of Russia
Gosizdat	State Publishing House
Gosplan	State Planning Committee
GRU	Chief Intelligence Directorate of the General Staff of the Red Army
GUGVF	Main Administration of Civil Aviation (also *Aeroflot*)
GULAG	Main Administration of Corrective Labor Camps
GUSMP	Main Administration of the Northern Sea Route (also *Glavsevmorput'*)
IES	Institute of the Economy of the North
INS	Institute of the Peoples of the North
KARZ	Krasnoiarsk Aviation-Repair Factory
KIRP	Kolyma-Indigirka River Fleet
Komsomol	Communist Youth League
KSMP	Committee of the Northern Sea Route (also *Komseveroput'*)
kul'tbaza	cultural base
Narkomles	People's Commissariat of Forest Industries
Narkomprod	People's Commissariat of Food Production
Narkompros	People's Commissariat of Enlightenment (Education)
Narkomsnab	People's Commissariat of Supply
Narkomvneshtorg	People's Commissariat of Foreign Trade
Narkomvod	People's Commissariat of Water Transport
Narkomzem	People's Commissariat of Agriculture
NKVD	People's Commissariat of Internal Affairs (secret police)
Nordvikstroi	Nordvik Mining-Construction Complex

Noril'stroi	Noril'sk Mining-Construction Complex
Osoaviakhim	Society for the Assistance of Defense and the Aviation and Chemical Industries of the USSR
partorg	Party organization
Plavmornin	Marine Scientific-Research Institute
politotdel	political department
Politupravlenie	Political Administration
RGAE	Russian State Archive of the Economy (Moscow)
RGAKFD	Russian State Archive of Film and Photo Documents (Krasnogorsk)
RGALI	Russian State Archive of Literature and Art (Moscow)
RSFSR	Russian Union of Federated Socialist Republics
RTsKhIDNI	Russian Center for the Preservation and Study of Documents of Recent History (Moscow)
Sevekspeditsiia	Northern Scientific-Commercial Expedition
Sibrevkom	Siberian Revolutionary Committee
Soiuzpushnina	Soviet Fur Trust
Soiuzzoloto	All-Union Trust for the Gold Industry
Sovnarkom	Council of People's Commissars of the USSR
STO	Council of Labor and Defense
terupravlenie	territorial administration
TsAGI	Central Aero-Hydrodynamic Institute
TsGAIPD	Central State Archive of Historical-Political Documents (St. Petersburg)
TsGA RSFSR	Central State Archive of the Russian Federation (Moscow)
UBEKO	Administration for the Guarantee of Navigational Safety on the Kara Sea and the Mouths of the Siberian Rivers
VAI	All-Union Arctic Scientific-Research Institute
VDNKh	Exhibition of the Achievements of the People's Economy
VSKhV	All-Union Agricultural-Economic Exhibition
VSNKh	Supreme Council of the National Economy

Red Arctic

Introduction

One summer day in Moscow, as I was bringing my dissertation research to a close, I decided to combine business with pleasure by visiting the Druzhba ("Friendship") Theater. Showing that afternoon was a matinee of *The Two Captains*, the film adaptation of the famous novel by Veniamin Kaverin. In what was by far his most popular work, Kaverin depicts the adventures of a young man who grows up to become an Arctic pilot during the Stalin era.[1] The story itself was inspired directly by the central subject of my research: the real-life exploits of the Soviet polar heroes who stormed their way into the hearts and imaginations of citizens throughout the USSR during the 1930s. It was only natural, then, that I should take some time off from the archives and the Lenin Library to spend the day at the movies.

Although both the book and film were blockbusters in their own day, I had little faith in the ability of a black-and-white, Soviet-era workhorse like *The Two Captains* to hold its own in the new Russia of the early 1990s. Multimillion-dollar megahits courtesy of Stallone and Schwarzenegger were packing audiences into theaters across the country, and, thanks to modern technology and the less-than-vigorous enforcement of intellectual-property laws, videotapes of Hollywood's entire inventory from the previous two decades were available in kiosks on every street corner. The classics of Soviet filmmaking seemed faced with the dreary prospect of being piled away forever in dusty canisters on forgotten shelves. So when I entered the Druzhba, I was startled to find that the auditorium was almost completely full.

Reaction to the movie was beyond all expectation, and I quickly became more interested in my fellow viewers and their interaction with the film than in what was happening on the screen. From start to finish, children and adults alike applauded the hero, hissed at the villain, gasped during the aviation scenes, and audibly expressed deep satisfaction over the hero's successful wooing of his childhood sweetheart, all with rare gusto. And although I hardly needed further confirmation of the film's appeal, I found it after the last reel spun itself out.

As the lights came back up, a group of young boys, ranging from eight to twelve years old, approached me to find out just why a vaguely foreign-looking person had been scribbling notes into a booklet during the entire movie. After I explained that I was in Russia to write about Soviet polar explorers, the boys held a quick debate as to whether my dissertation was a worthwhile enterprise, concluding that, if one had to study history, the story of Arctic heroes was at least relatively painless as far as research topics were concerned. When I asked for their opinions about the movie, the boys' unanimous and enthusiastic verdict was that the film was "Klass!" or, roughly translated, "Cool!" Why? "Because of the airplanes," one said, going into a spirited imitation of a pilot in a cockpit, about to execute a diving roll. An older boy added, "It's a great story. Just watching it, I feel like a hero myself." A third voice piped up to tell me that the Arctic was the best part about the movie. So what did the rest of the impromptu Kaverin fan club I had inadvertently gathered around me think about the Arctic? All agreed that it was a land of excitement and bold deeds, and at least a couple declared that they wanted to become icebreaker captains or polar explorers. After a few moments, of course, the boys went their separate ways, answering the calls of their parents or going off on their own, all of them making the journey back from the realm of cinematic fantasy to the present-day reality of Moscow. After saying my goodbyes, I left my seat and prepared to do the same.

My experience at the Druzhba Theater, as well as the continued appeal of *The Two Captains*, can, no doubt, be explained in a number of ways. But to me, the incident was above all a striking illustration of how strong a hold the Arctic has on the modern Russian mindset. For as long as Russia has existed as a country, and particularly during the twentieth century, the Arctic has occupied a place of prominence in its national development. For the Soviet state, the Arctic was a matter of paramount importance. Possessing great strategic significance, comprising over one-fourth of the entire Russian landmass, home to more than two dozen nationalities, and containing the lion's share of the country's most valuable natural resources, the Soviet Arctic commanded the attention of the USSR's foremost statesmen and generals, engaged the minds of its finest scientists and economic planners, and attracted vast quantities of money, equipment, and sheer human energy. From 1920 onward, Soviet efforts to explore and develop the Arctic represented an unceasing endeavor, the results of which—both positive and negative—are still felt today.

The zenith of this perennial campaign came during the 1930s, when the USSR launched what was perhaps the most systematic and all-encompassing sequence of Arctic expeditions in the history of polar exploration. In little more than a half-decade, Soviet explorers, pilots, and scientists made history in the Arctic many times over. In 1932, the icebreaker *Sibiriakov* became the first vessel to cross through the Northern Sea Route—the fabled Northeast Passage—in a single navigational season. Two years later, Soviet polar aviators staged one of the most daring aerial rescues of the century by evacuating the stranded passengers of the ill-fated *Cheliuskin* from the ice floes of the Chukchi Sea. In 1937, the banner year for the USSR in the Arctic, Soviet pilots captured the world record for long-distance aviation two times in succession by soaring over the North Pole from Moscow to the United States. That same year, the USSR became the first nation in history to land aircraft at the North Pole itself and, as a result of the same operation, the first nation to establish a scientific outpost at the pole. In general, the Soviets boasted that their constant activity in the North had done more in only a few years to further scientific knowledge about the Arctic and bring infrastructural development to the region than had been accomplished in all the previous centuries combined.

The great drive to conquer the Arctic during the 1930s became one of the most stirring and memorable episodes of the Stalinist era; as such, it is the primary focus of *Red Arctic*. It should be said at this point that the emphasis of this volume rests on "Soviet" rather than "Arctic"; its main purpose is to examine certain questions about the USSR through the prism of the North.[2] Hence the time frame chosen for this study. Although the Arctic was a critical issue for the Soviet Union over the country's seven-decade history, it took on an overwhelming double significance during the 1930s. On one hand, the Stalinist regime reached a new stage in its economic development of the Arctic and sub-Arctic and faced crucial choices about how best to proceed with it. On the other hand, the Arctic came to play an increasingly conspicuous part in Soviet public life after 1932, as the widespread appeal of polar heroes made the North a central, even definitive, feature of Stalinist popular culture and propaganda. Neither of these two issues can be considered in isolation; as a result, *Red Arctic* will undertake to examine both in detail.

Polar Exploration and Soviet Political Economy

As the First Five-Year Plan drew to a close in 1932, the Stalinist regime found itself forced to consider its position in the Arctic closely. Not only was this a time of overall reorganization and rethinking in the economic sphere throughout the USSR, but new approaches to the Arctic itself were needed as well. The Soviets' declared goal of taming the North and transforming its icy, hostile wastes into a bountiful, productive powerhouse had been a daunting one from the moment Lenin and the Bolsheviks seized control of the government in 1917. Nearly 6,000 miles of Arctic coast, the majority of which was still inadequately mapped and largely unknown as late as the 1920s, stretched between European Russia and the Bering Straits. Political, military, and administrative absorption of the USSR's Arctic and sub-Arctic territories remained incomplete long after the Red victory in the Civil War. The nomadic native Siberians, the so-called small peoples of the North, had yet to be assimilated into the Soviet way of life. The economic enterprises of the North—fur, fishing, and timber—were not organized to the state's satisfaction. Most important, the Soviets had not yet gained full access to the breathtaking quantities of rich mineral deposits hidden throughout the circumpolar wilderness.

During the 1920s, the government assigned tasks in the Arctic to a dizzying assortment of committees, institutes, and people's commissariats. Despite the flurry of activity, however, administrative redundancy and bureaucratic conflict hindered Soviet polar work. During the First Five-Year Plan, the state attempted to remedy the situation by bringing a small transport agency to the forefront of Arctic exploration and development: the Committee of the Northern Sea Route (*Komseveroput'*, or KSMP). By the end of the First Five-Year Plan, Komseveroput had assumed the responsibility of coordinating the activities of the dozens of agencies involved in Arctic work. Komseveroput, however, was understaffed, underfunded, underequipped, and, above all, unable to satisfy the ever growing demands placed upon it by the First Five-Year Plan. By 1932, it was obvious that

Soviet efforts in the Arctic over the previous decade and a half had not yielded anywhere near all the results that the regime had hoped for. Soon thereafter, KSMP was disbanded.

Even in its demise, however, Komseveroput provided a model for what was to come, since the notion of keeping a highly centralized body in charge of Arctic affairs was attractive to the government. Consequently, of the two basic strategies for Arctic development adopted by the regime in the early 1930s, one involved the formation of an agency similar to Komseveroput in design but radically different in power and prestige. This was the Main Administration of the Northern Sea Route (GUSMP, or *Glavsevmorput'*), which ruled the Soviet Arctic almost single-handedly from its establishment in December 1932 until autumn 1938. The new agency's bland title belied its gargantuan nature; Glavsevmorput has been compared not inaccurately to a fiefdom, a semiautonomous republic, even a country within a country. Its charter gave it almost complete suzerainty over the 2 million square miles that lie east of the Ural Mountains and north of the 62d parallel, in addition to all the island groups in the USSR's Arctic waters. Over time, this bureaucratic juggernaut came to employ almost 200,000 workers; it received a yearly budget of over 1 billion rubles. Responsible for practically everything in the Arctic and sub-Arctic, from fish-oil canneries and Russian-language schools for the Siberian natives to coal mines and local theater troupes, GUSMP can be seen as one of the Soviet Union's greatest experiments in hypercentralization—at least in theory.

Although, in the end, much of its power turned out to be illusory, GUSMP became one of the largest and most unusual agencies in the USSR during the 1930s. Institutionally speaking, it plays the starring role in *Red Arctic*, which examines Glavsevmorput in a number of new ways. Although the Russians have written extensively about GUSMP, the agency faded from the attention of the West soon after 1939 and has since been a subject of interest to only a handful of specialists on the economy of the Arctic. Of the Western accounts that do make mention of Glavsevmorput, none has ever tapped into the wealth of archival material that has become available to scholars since the early 1990s. More important, no work, Russian or non-Russian, has ever provided a history of GUSMP as comprehensive as that contained in this volume: one based on detailed archival research, one free of politically motivated distortions, and one conscious of Glavsevmorput's role in the wider contexts of Soviet economic issues and, as described below, Soviet cultural trends.[3]

Although the Soviet presence in the Arctic was heralded until the outbreak of World War II as one of the USSR's brightest accomplishments, there was a darker side to it as well. Along with its establishment of GUSMP, the Stalinist regime chose to experiment with a second means of exploiting the resources of its circumpolar regions: the full-scale implementation of convict labor. Glavsevmorput itself was not untainted in this regard; archival evidence indicates that it, like all other major concerns involved with developmental work during these years, made at least limited use of unfree workers. But GUSMP was not alone in the Arctic, and it was a comparatively minor player in the forced-labor trade. The infamous GULAG apparatus began operations in 1930, and a good number of its facilities were located in the Arctic and sub-Arctic. The most prominent of these was the Main Administration for Construction in the Far North (*Dal'stroi*). Created in 1931 as an adjunct of Stalin's secret police organization (although not a component of the GULAG until 1938), Dalstroi was designed to locate and develop the dozens of gold deposits scattered throughout the Kolyma river basin, in northeastern Siberia.

The gold mines administered by Dalstroi went on to become the deadliest and most notorious prison camps in the USSR, and Kolyma remains one of the most frightful symbols of the brutality and repression that characterized the Stalinist era.[4] Furthermore, Dalstroi eventually assumed a dominant role in the overall development of the North. However, Dalstroi and the GULAG are, for the most part, subjects beyond the scope of this study. The GULAG itself was a massive, sprawling network whose reach extended to every corner of the country; it is not a topic suited for a work specifically devoted to the Arctic.[5] As for the Kolyma camps, Dalstroi did not take up its central part in the economic administration of the Arctic until near the end of the 1930s.

This is not to say that Dalstroi is without a place in the story that *Red Arctic* has to tell, for it and Glavsevmorput existed side by side in a relationship of intense rivalry. As the 1930s passed, Dalstroi grew into a major conglomerate; as it did so, it struggled with GUSMP, its nearest neighbor, for resources, territory, and power. In summer 1937, Glavsevmorput, already unable to shoulder the heavy burdens placed upon it by the state, began to lose ground to its competitor as well. Finally, in August 1938, Glavsevmorput was demoted for a variety of economic failures and deprived of its Arctic empire; Dalstroi inherited the bulk of that empire and went on to prosper until its own demise in 1956. In the long run, GUSMP outlived its enemy, but only as a ghost of its former self; from 1939 until 1970, the former ruler of the polar realm was relegated to a subordinate status within the Ministry of the Marine Fleet.

For all its supposed strength, then, Glavsevmorput was a giant with weak knees, buckling under pressures from within and without. Its place in Soviet economic-administrative history can be interpreted in one of two ways. Did GUSMP represent an abortive attempt on the part of the government to experiment with an alternate method of developing the Arctic—one that was less dependent on prison-camp labor than the GULAG? Or was it simply a parallel agency, created to provide transport and logistical support for a region that the regime intended to bequeath to the GULAG all along? Whatever the case, the end result is clear: Glavsevmorput was brought to ruin—or at least mediocrity—by a series of events discussed in chapters 2 and 6. Still, GUSMP's accomplishments cannot be ignored. As described in chapter 3, the agency had a number of outstanding successes to its name. And, more than that, the fact that the Russian Arctic has been brought under the sway of the rest of the country to any extent at all owes a great deal to Glavsevmorput and its efforts during the 1930s.

The Arctic as Popular Culture

Glavsevmorput's efforts in the Arctic were not connected solely with mundane matters such as production levels, shipping manifestoes, or transport dilemmas. There was much more: the heroics of GUSMP's explorers and aviators attracted the attention of the world and captured the affection and enthusiasm of the Soviet public. From 1932 to the beginning of 1939—the period commonly spoken of as "high Stalinism"—the Arctic and the men and women who worked there stood out as being among the brightest strands in the fabric of Soviet society and culture. They became great favorites of the Soviet media and played a highly influential role in both official and unofficial formulations of the popular culture of the USSR for almost a decade.[6]

That this took place was only natural. In one review of Soviet historiography, Stalinism is likened to "two towering and inseparable mountains: a mountain of national accomplishments alongside a mountain of crimes"; the author goes on to add that "the accomplishments cannot be lightly dismissed."[7] Indeed, they cannot, for it was that set of achievements—the Arctic exploits of the 1930s ranking among the most noteworthy of them—that helped to hold the Soviet nation together during an era of great stress and strain in a way that simple coercion could not have done. One of the central questions facing scholars who study regimes that have traditionally been termed "totalitarian" is how those regimes are able to command loyalty, or at least obedience, from their populations. Beyond that, how do "totalitarian" states mobilize, inspire, educate, and communicate with the people they rule? All these things lie beyond the ability of brute force, and they are too subtle to be explained by popular but clumsy terms like "indoctrination" or "brainwashing."

Many answers to these questions can be found in the domain of popular culture, and a number of authors in the Soviet-studies field have done profitable work in this area since the 1970s. Vera Dunham's groundbreaking study of how Stalinist cultural mores were transmitted through literature, Christel Lane's examination of the symbols and rituals built up around Marxist ideology, Nina Tumarkin's innovative investigation of the Lenin cult, Sheila Fitzpatrick's incisive analyses of the struggle between the intelligentsia and political authorities to define and create "Soviet culture," and Katerina Clark's thematic interpretation of the socialist-realist novel all fall into this category.[8] Since the late 1980s, the works of Richard Stites, Hans Günther, Régine Robin, Jeffrey Brooks, Rosalinde Sartorti, and others have expanded upon this body of literature, weaving a rich tapestry of cultural knowledge about a country that has been seen for so long by Westerners through almost an exclusively political lens—and allowing readers to view Soviet history not just from "above" or "below" but, as Stites puts it, "from the side" as well.[9]

Curiously enough, however, the place of the Arctic in Soviet popular culture has been consistently neglected, despite the fact that one would be hard pressed to read through more than a week of any major Soviet newspaper from the 1930s without coming across at least some reference to the country's polar adventures. Only a few works have made note of the Arctic heroics of the Stalin period, although general recognition of their importance has been increasing, if slowly, since the early 1990s. This book intends to provide the first thorough treatment of how Arctic-based culture—what this volume refers to as the "Arctic myth"—came to exist between 1932 and 1939, how it was created, and what it meant for the USSR.

The Arctic myth was a product of socialist realism, the hegemonic cultural framework of the Stalin period. "Socialist realism" in this sense refers not merely to the literary formula of the same name but to the overarching aesthetic that held sway over fact and fiction, fantasy and reality, and official doctrine and public attitudes from the beginning of the 1930s. Socialist realism's principal motifs are well known: the cults of Lenin and Stalin, a keen sense of patriotism, a great emphasis on technological and industrial prowess, and, above all, heroism. The Arctic culture of the high-Stalinist period embraced all of these themes and combined them with two other symbols of great potency: the North Pole, whose enigmatic mystique was age old, and aviation, perhaps the twentieth century's most triumphant expression of modernity. This blend was an extraordinarily successful one, and the Arctic became one of the most visible and appealing elements in a cultural environment already saturated with attempts to make every deed seem grand and epic.

For that reason, the Arctic myth has much to say about its times. As what anthropologist Clifford Geertz might term a "master fiction," Arctic culture was bound up with state ritual, major propaganda messages, political symbology, and official values, not to mention the various ways in which these items were read and interpreted by the public. The Arctic myth therefore lends itself well to a detailed thematic decoding of the socialist-realist worldview. How did the USSR see itself and the world around it? How did the Soviets conceive of the relationship between the individual and the Stalinist state? As a key facet of the socialist-realist worldview, the Arctic culture of the 1930s remains a tremendously useful —and largely untapped—resource in understanding how the state and ordinary people perceived these issues. In addition, since the Arctic myth prompted one of the most extensive media blitzes in Soviet history, it makes an excellent case study of how a Stalinist propaganda campaign was designed, produced, and received. Stalinist culture was the end product of a highly complex interaction that took place within the public sphere—among the state, the media, and the public, as well as a myriad of subgroups within each of these three broad categories—but the precise nature of that interaction remains something of a black box. Unraveling the mysteries still concealed within that box is a crucial task facing Soviet cultural studies, and *Red Arctic* aims to be a part of this ongoing line of inquiry. Chapter 4 addresses the various meanings of the Arctic myth, while chapter 5 discusses the means by which it was actually propagandized.

Defining the Arctic

One important note remains to be made: the precise meaning of the term "Soviet Arctic" and, with it, the terms "Siberia," "Soviet North," and "polar." Unfortunately, none of these phrases has a fixed, clear-cut meaning. Technically speaking, "Arctic" refers to the territory that lies above the Arctic Circle, or 66°30' North. But the Russians have tended to use the term much more loosely, often in reference to regions farther south. "Siberia" is an even more fluid concept. As one work notes, the region has "no history of independent political existence, no claim to a separate ethnic identity, no clear borders."[10] Obviously, much of Siberia can be labeled "Arctic," but much of it cannot. Likewise, much, but not all, of the Soviet Arctic is part of the Siberian landmass.

One solution is to refer to the area as "the North." But there is no more specificity involved with this term than with any of the others. "Polar" is equally vague and denotes a fairly small area surrounding the North Pole itself; even its more inclusive cousin "circumpolar" is too restrictive. Neither are official geographic designations for Siberia of much help. For one thing, boundaries changed constantly. During the 1920s and 1930s, approximately half a dozen large regions were mapped out in "the North." "Western Siberia" (*Zapadnaia Sibir'*) bordered the Ural Mountains. "Eastern Siberia" (*Vostochnaia Sibir'*) included the Kransoiarsk region and sometimes Yakutia. "Transbaikal" (*Zabaikal'ia*) consisted of the lake region and the area surrounding Irkutsk. The "Far (or Extreme) North" (*Krainii Sever*) included the Chukchi Peninsula, Kamchatka, and the Kolyma basin; at times, it referred to Yakutia as well. The "Far East" (*Dal'nii Vostok*, or DVK) included Sakhalin, Vladivostok and Khabarovsk, the Amur region, and sometimes Transbaikal. Regrettably, none of these labels provides a clear sense of where "Arctic," "North," and "Siberia" begin or end. Furthermore, none of them applies to the island groups of the Arctic Ocean—Novaia Zemlia, Kolguev Island, Franz Josef Land, Severnaia Zemlia, the New Siberian Islands, and Wrangel Island—or the Arctic territories that lie west of the Urals, in European Russia. To understand just how fluid the term "North" could be, consider the official delineation of the "Far North" proposed by the Soviet Russian Federation's (RSFSR) Council of People's Commissars in September 1931: all land including the Murmansk District; the Nenets National Region; parts of the Komi ASSR; the Yamal-Nenets National Region; the northernmost districts of Western Siberia; the Taimyr Peninsula; the Turukhansk Region; the Khatanga National region; several districts in the Buryat-Mongol ASSR; the Yakut Republic; the Chukchi, Koriak, and Okhotsk National Regions; Kamchatka; Sakhalin; and all islands in the Arctic Ocean and its adjoining seas. Taken together, this territory measures over 3.5 million square miles and ranges over a good portion of the map of Russia in a less than methodical fashion.[11]

Some sense of exactitude is necessary for an understanding of the Soviet Arctic; depending on how it is defined, "the Arctic" can comprise one-fifth, one-fourth, or even one-third of the entire USSR.[12] The most appropriate guideline for the purposes of this study is to equate "the Arctic" roughly with the territory controlled by Glavsevmorput: the 2 million square miles east of the Urals and north of the 62d parallel. If this is combined with GUSMP's "support zone," which extended south into the sub-Arctic and west into European Russia (including Karelia, the Kola Peninsula, the White Sea coast, and the Komi ASSR), the result bears a close resemblance to a standard definition of "Arctic" and "North" proposed by scholar Franklyn Griffiths.[13]

The terms most commonly used by *Red Arctic* to describe this area will be "Arctic" and "North." Some specialists, including Griffiths, recommend that "Arctic" be used only in reference to the oceanic littoral—the coastline, the waters, and the islands—while "North" be used to denote the larger territory on the mainland.[14] This author prefers a looser approach, and so, for all intents and purposes, "Arctic" and "North" will be considered interchangeable. "Polar" and "circumpolar" will also be used, but only to indicate areas that are above or near the Arctic Circle. In addition, "Siberia" will appear in certain contexts, if the term is suitable to the specific region in question.

ONE

Footholds in the North
The Russians in the Arctic, 1500–1932

At first glance, Russia's place in the annals of polar exploration seems incongruous. Nearly one-third of the country's 6.5 million square miles can be considered Arctic or sub-Arctic. With the world's finest furs and largest timber reserves, as well as a lavish abundance of mineral deposits, the entire region is a treasurehouse of fabulous proportions. The strategic importance of Russian's northern coast has increased steadily since the late 1800s. Over the course of almost five centuries, therefore, Russia has dedicated a tremendous amount of time and energy to the development of its northern domain. And yet the Russians are conspicuously absent from the pantheon of explorers popularly associated with the Arctic.

There are several reasons to explain this, including a distinct Anglo-American slant in the general historiography of polar discovery, as well as a pervasive unwillingness on the part of the West to acknowledge any kind of Russian achievement whatsoever during the years of the Cold War. But much of the silence has to do with the nature of Russian exploration itself. From the days of Ivan the Terrible to the beginning of the twentieth century, Russia's approach to the North can best be described as sporadic, with long stretches of neglect or ineptitude punctuated by occasional bursts of genuine progress. It was not without reason that, by the end of the nineteenth century, the rest of the world regarded Russian efforts in the Arctic with lukewarm politeness, if at all.

By the middle of the 1900s, however, the entire world recognized the Soviet Union as a dominant force in Arctic exploration. After World War II, the USSR emerged as one of the top nations in polar research and development, both in the Arctic and the Antarctic. In less than half a century, the Soviets had risen from mediocrity to preeminence in the polar community. It was during the 1930s that the USSR began in earnest to establish its formidable presence in the North. As the decade passed, the Soviets, despite setbacks and miscalculations, brought breathtaking changes to the Arctic wilderness. Their seamen tamed the legendary Northeast Passage—the Northern Sea Route, as the Russians called it—and turned it into a regular, navigable sea-lane. Soviet geographers charted the still-mysterious expanses of the Arctic Ocean; their colleagues in the natural, meteorological, and geological sciences amassed an invaluable stock of data pertaining to the Arctic environment. Outposts, factories, and cities appeared throughout the barren tundras of the North. Finally, throughout the 1930s the Soviets strikingly demonstrated their mastery over the Arctic with a series of high-profile expeditions by land, air, and sea that culminated in the conquest of the North Pole in 1937 and elicited admiration from onlookers the world over.

As dramatic as the changes it brought about were, however, the USSR's campaign in the Arctic was linked in many ways with what went before and cannot be considered in isolation. The purpose of this chapter is to place the polar exploits of the 1930s in their proper context. It begins with a discussion of Russian expansion into the Arctic between 1500 and 1800. It continues with the late imperial period, pausing briefly for a look at the "Race to the Poles"—a classic moment that influenced the Russians, even though they themselves took little part in it. Finally, the chapter examines the attempts of the Soviet regime to assimilate its Arctic hinterland between 1917 and 1932.

First Steps: Opening the North, 1500–1800

Although Russian settlement of the Arctic began as early as the eleventh century, with Novgorodian and Muscovite colonization of the north Dvina, the White Sea coast, and northwestern Siberia, systematic exploration of the region did not start until the mid-1500s.[1] The first forays were made by ships flying Dutch and English flags and seeking out new sea routes to the East. Venturing into the frozen waters of the North, mariners searched for the Northeast Passage, along the northern coast of Russia, and its better-known counterpart, the Northwest Passage, through the islands of the Canadian Arctic. Captains like Sebastian Cabot, Willem Barents, and Henry Hudson first tried their hands at the Northeast Passage but were able to go no farther than Spitsbergen and Novaia Zemlia. Still, the initial probings to the northeast were not fruitless. Richard Chancellor of England landed on the shores of the White Sea in 1553, traveled to Moscow, and negotiated a trade agreement with the court of Ivan the Terrible. The brisk commerce that sprang up between Russia and England over the next decades led to the 1584 founding of the rugged Arctic port of Arkhangelsk—one of Russia's most vital maritime outlets—on the mouth of the Dvina River.

For a route to Asia, the English and the Dutch looked next to the Americas. But after years of testing their skills against the mazelike waters of Canada, seafarers met with little success in their quest for a Northwest Passage. Furthermore, the importance of the passage itself was dwindling, as the Spanish chokehold on existing searoutes to Asia began to slip. Over time, the Northwest Passage became a navigational curiosity rather than an economic priority, and no concerted effort to uncover its secrets was made again for almost two centuries. And in abandoning the Northwest Passage, the nations of the West abandoned the Arctic almost altogether.

Not so the Russians, for whom the North was a far more immediate concern. There had always been Russians living and traveling there, but not until the sixteenth century did they begin anything resembling a deliberate attempt to absorb the Arctic. This effort was connected somewhat with Muscovy's new interaction with foreign traders in the White Sea but grew primarily out of its colonization of Siberia.[2] During the 1550s, Ivan the Terrible's victories over the Tatar strongholds of Kazan and Astrakhan opened up his realm's eastern frontiers, and high-volume expansion into the Asiatic half of the subcontinent soon followed. Leading the way was Cossack warlord Ivan Timofeevich Yermak, whose band of freebooters crossed the Urals in 1579 and established Russia's first footholds in Siberia by founding the cities of Tiumen and Tobolsk in 1586 and 1587.

By the middle of the following century, Russian soldiers, hunters, and merchants (*promyshlenniki*) had traveled the breadth of the Siberian landmass and reached the Pacific. By 1600, the Ob and Irtysh river basins were Russian territory. The Yenisei Valley followed in 1628, as did the Lena region in 1642. In 1648, Semyon Dezhnev rounded the northeasternmost corner of the Russian coast, becoming the first European to sail into the Bering Straits. As the years passed, movement into Siberia assumed ever larger proportions. For the most part, the Russians came to the North to make their fortunes, especially by trafficking in furs. But exiles and religious schismatics found their way to the frontier as well, voluntarily or otherwise. Moreover, the political and social turmoil of Ivan the Terrible's reign, not to mention the Time of Troubles which followed Boris Godunov's years on the throne, provided a powerful impetus for migration to the east, as did land hunger and other economic factors.

Having more Russians in Siberia, however, did not by itself translate into genuine control over the region. The Russian presence in this immense land consisted of a tenuous network of small wooden fortresses, called *ostrogi*, built mainly along the river basins. Among the most important were Tomsk (1604); Krasnoiarsk (1628); Yakutsk (1632); Anadyr (1648); Irkutsk (1652); and Nerchinsk-on-the-Amur (1654). Although many eventually grew into major cities, the ostrogi originally served only as garrisons, crude administrative headquarters, and gathering points for the fur trade. They were by no means numerous, and their links with Moscow were often weak.

Russian movement into Siberia led to a correspondingly increased presence in the Arctic. During the 1600s, growth in the North was driven mostly by economic concerns. Trade and fishing flourished in the Arkhangelsk region, and, for a short time, a second major port appeared on the northern coast, only five weeks' sail eastward. This was Mangazeia, founded in 1601 near the mouth of the Taz River. Mangazeia became Siberia's most dynamic center for international commerce and the fur industry—a hoarfrosted oasis in the Arctic. In 1619, however, the city's heyday came to an abrupt end when Tsar Michael, unsettled by foreign penetration so deep into his country's waters, shut down Mangazeia and redirected all northern trade back through Arkhangelsk. Still, Russian hunters, fishermen, and trappers went on with their ramblings through the Arctic, gradually threading their way along the entirety of the northern coast. By the end of the 1600s, the Russians had accumulated a considerable body of knowledge about the region, although much of it was more on the order of anecdote and folklore than concrete fact.

Things began to change during the eighteenth century, which brought with it a new inquisitiveness about the Arctic. During the last years of his reign, Peter the Great, the scientifically minded modernizer of Russia, initiated a wave of Arctic exploration that continued well after his death. In 1719, Peter sent teams of naval geodesists to map the Kamchatka Peninsula and the mouth of the Ob. It was in 1724, however, that he set the wheels in motion for what would eventually become the most ambitious battery of expeditions in the Arctic to that time. That December, Peter commissioned Vitus Bering, a Danish captain in Russian service, to determine whether or not Russia was joined to the American continent.

Bering returned from this first mission in 1730, having sailed through the narrow straits that bear his name, but without final proof that Russia and America were unconnected. Immediately, Bering petitioned Empress Anna to sponsor a second journey into the Arctic. This was the Great Northern Expedition, which grew into a mammoth undertaking involving over 3,000 men and lasting from 1733 to 1749. The scope of the project was staggering. Bering was requested by the Senate, the Admiralty, and the Academy of Sciences to chart the entire coastline between Arkhangelsk and Kamchatka; to conduct a comprehensive geographical, zoological, and anthropological survey of the whole littoral; to establish diplomatic relations with Japan (and, if possible, to move on farther southeast to search for "Gamaland," a mythical realm of gold and silver); and to travel east to Alaska, claiming any American lands not already belonging to Spain. The Great Northern Expedition was extremely costly in money and lives — Bering himself died of scurvy on his return trip from Alaska — and its results fell somewhat short of expectations. But it also yielded an unprecedented wealth of information about the Arctic and represented Russia's first real effort to gain a full understanding of its northern territories.

Furthermore, Bering's expedition did much to spur increased interest in the Russian Arctic. Mikhail Lomonosov, Russia's greatest Enlightenment-era scholar, became one of the region's most passionate spokesmen; pointing to the subcontinent's vast wealth and the strategic value of the Northern Sea Route, he proclaimed that "it is in Siberia and the waters of the Arctic that Russia's might will begin to grow."[3] Inspired by the expansion of the fur industry and the recent discovery of precious metals, explorers and traders streamed into the North; by the end of the 1700s, approximately one million Russians were living and working in Siberia. The Russians even went beyond their own continent, spreading into North America. In 1799, Emperor Paul granted a charter to Nikolai Rezanov's conglomeration of fur-trading enterprises, allowing them to form the Russian-American Company. For over half a century, the company attempted to create an economically viable colony in Alaska and the American Northwest, connected with what was intended to be a healthy, prosperous settlement zone in northeastern Siberia. But the state proved unwilling to support the company with the resources it needed to carry on with its work. Before long, the company was left to wilt on the vine, and by 1867, with the sale of Alaska to the United States, it was defunct.

The fate of the Russian-American Company serves as a useful illustration of the regime's conflicted attitude toward the Arctic during the imperial period. When it gave serious thought to the North, which was seldom, the state recognized the usefulness of the region and was perfectly content to allow private individuals to explore or develop it — at their own expense. However, the government was reluctant to make any sizable investment of its own. This pattern of diffidence continued for most of the 1700s and did not disappear; if anything, it grew and became a serious hindrance to polar work at a time when the Russians had a chance to start gaining a firm and permanent hold over the North. With only a few exceptions, the story of the Russian Arctic during the nineteenth century was mainly one of squandered opportunities.

The Arctic in the Late Imperial Period, 1800–1917

The eyes of the West turned once again toward the Arctic in 1827, when British officer William Parry launched the first major expedition designed expressly to sail to the North Pole.[4] Parry failed to reach his destination, but his voyage in the *Hecla* took him above the 82d parallel and set a "Farthest North" that remained unequaled for fifty years. It also sparked a race for the North and South poles that lasted more than eighty years and, along with the renewed competition to discover a Northwest Passage, beguiled the imaginations of millions.

The Race to the Poles quickly became an obsession in Europe and America, due to several factors. As nationalism became a political force in the nineteenth century, success in exploration served as a tangible index of a country's prowess in the international arena. Improved communications technology made it easier for an interested public to keep abreast with events in even the most distant points of the globe. Most important, polar exploration was perceived as the crowning glory of the modern era's Second Age of Discovery. During these years, the final "blank spaces" on the map (to borrow Joseph Conrad's famous metaphor)—the African interior, the Central Asian deserts, the Tibetan highlands, the Amazon basin—were gradually being filled in, and the Western public watched with fascination as the world's last frontiers and horizons disappeared. Exploration in general took on an epic quality, but the highest drama of all was reserved for the North Pole, and audiences remained breathless as a dazzling array of new heroes staged their repeated assaults on the very roof of the world.[5]

By the 1890s, the chief contenders in the Race to the Poles were the United States, Great Britain, and the nations of Scandinavia. In the end, the North Pole fell to the Americans, the South Pole to the Norwegians. Both races were hotly contested. In 1909, two Americans returned from the Arctic, each claiming to have been the first to reach the North Pole. Commander Robert Peary informed the press that he had driven in the "Big Nail" on 6 April 1909; his rival, Dr. Frederick Cook, asserted that he had done so almost a full year beforehand. Before Christmas, Cook, his story riddled with inconsistencies, was exposed as a fraud. But the scandal also cast doubt on Peary's claim, even though his sponsors, the *New York Times* and the National Geographic Society, stood by him firmly. The U.S. Congress had no wish to entertain the possibility that both men had lied, and, in 1911, it validated Peary as the first person in history successfully to travel to the North Pole.[6]

If the battle for the Arctic prize was controversial, the final sprint in the Antarctic was tragic. In 1911, two parties set their sights on the South Pole: one led by Sir Robert Falcon Scott of Britain, the other by Norwegian explorer Roald Amundsen, who had, in 1906, completed the first voyage through the Northwest Passage.[7] Amundsen's party reached the South Pole first, on 14 December 1911; a month later, on 16 January 1912, Scott and his men arrived at the pole, only to be greeted by Norwegian flags and a placard reading "Welcome to the South Pole!" Exhausted by their bitter defeat, Scott and his men encountered severe weather during their return trip, and every one of the five men on the last leg of the expedition died of starvation, including Scott himself. The world rejoiced at Amundsen's victory but mourned the loss of one of England's most celebrated heroes as well.

Russia took almost no part in the race to reach the North Pole—certainly one of the reasons that its efforts in the Arctic have gone largely unappreciated. In contrast to the quest for the pole, Russian work in the North appeared plodding and mundane. The image of a few lone men struggling to reach the top of the world made hearts quicken; geological surveys and botanical expeditions did not. Russian polar explorers were not without their successes during the late imperial era, but their achievements were overshadowed by the dash and daring of their Western counterparts.

To be fair, it can be argued that the Russians—with so much circumpolar territory of their own—possessed a more practical outlook toward the Arctic. Although the Russians followed the Race to the Poles with great excitement, they focused their attention primarily on those explorers whose work emphasized living and traveling in polar conditions for extended periods of time. The 1878 voyage of Denmark's Adolph Nordenskjöld in the *Vega*, the first vessel ever to complete the trip through the Northeast Passage, received much acclaim in Russia. Later, Roald Amundsen won high marks from the Russians for his three-year drift through the Northwest Passage in the *Gjoa*, as well as for his voyage through the Northeast Passage in the *Maud*, from 1918 to 1920. The Russians also appreciated the work of Vilhjalmur Stefansson, who spent five years in the Arctic, from 1913 to 1918, proving to the world that a nonnative could live indefinitely above the 70th parallel by adopting the lifestyle of the Arctic's indigenous peoples.

If the Russians had one undisputed favorite among Western explorers, it was Norway's Fridtjof Nansen, who combined courage and endurance with intelligence and scientific precision. Renowned for his career as an Arctic adventurer, Nansen also repatriated refugees for the League of Nations, coordinated famine relief for the International Red Cross (particularly in the USSR, during the outbreak of mass hunger in the early 1920s), and won the Nobel Prize for Peace in 1922. Although Nansen played a major part in the race for the North Pole, his main purpose was not to break records but to gain a better comprehension of the Arctic itself. From 1896 to 1899, Nansen attempted to drift to the pole in a vessel named the *Fram* ("Forward"). He never reached the pole, but his three-year meander through the Arctic waters allowed him to obtain invaluable data about meteorological and oceanographic conditions in the Far North. The Russians considered Nansen's drift to be the ideal method of exploring the Arctic, and his example played a tremendous role in shaping their approaches to polar research.

The Russians, of course, had their own work in the North. During the nineteenth century, small circles of Arctic enthusiasts—scientists, military officers, and financiers—began to form. Limited both in numbers and resources, these groups nevertheless made some progress in advancing the cause of Arctic development. Among the leading individuals were Count Fedor Litke, president of the Academy of Sciences; Alexander Sibiriakov, who provided much of the financial backing for Nordenskjöld's voyage in the *Vega;* gold-mining magnate Mikhail Sidorov; and Norwegian trader Jonas Lied, an acquaintance of Nansen's who became a Russian citizen. By 1882, the First International Polar Year, Russia had become tolerably well established in the Arctic community. Urged on by Admiral Stepan Makarov, the Russian Navy began to acquire a small fleet of icebreakers during the 1890s, starting with the 8,250-ton *Yermak.* In August 1914, pilot Yan Nagursky, in the *Pechora,* became the first person to fly an airplane north of the Arctic Circle.[8] A year later, Boris Vilkitsky became the second seaman to sail through the Northeast Passage, captaining the *Taimyr* and *Vaigach* from Vladivostok to Arkhangelsk.

Such accomplishments, however, had little to do with official policy. The Admiralty continued to send out the occasional mapping surveys it had begun in the late 1700s (Alexander Kolchak headed more than one of these before commanding a White army during the Russian Civil War); the Academy of Sciences subsidized a few private expeditions. Beyond that, the regime's support for work in the Arctic was minimal. The remark of one Petersburg official during the mid-1800s—"Nevsky Prospect alone is worth at least five times as much as all of Siberia"—reflects the low esteem in which the region was generally held by the government.[9] Near the end of the century, renowned scientist Dmitry Mendeleev, inventor of the periodic table and an outspoken advocate of developing the northern coast, penned a memorandum to Finance Minister Sergei Witte, insisting that "it is absolutely necessary to conquer the polar seas, especially for the direct economic benefit of Russia and humanity, but for the triumph of knowledge as well."[10] Heedless of Mendeleev's suggestion and similar advice, the government of Nicholas II continued to ignore the northern question and let the Arctic and sub-Arctic lie fallow. East of the Urals, state attention was devoted almost exclusively to the Trans-Siberian Railway, the construction of which began in 1891.

The perils of wrong-headedness about the Arctic became manifestly clear after the turn of the century. The most drastic consequences of Nicholas's northern policy were felt during the Russo-Japanese War of 1904–1905. The disasters that Russia faced throughout the war were compounded by the fact that its forces were hopelessly overextended. Since the government had never taken the pains to develop a useable sea-lane along the Arctic coast, the only means it had to transport troops and supplies over the more than 4,000 miles that separated St. Petersburg from Vladivostok was the horribly overburdened Trans-Siberian Railway. Even worse, when Zinovy Rozhdestvensky's Baltic fleet was called upon to reinforce the battered Pacific navy, it was forced—by the lack of a suitable waterway in the Arctic—to sail literally halfway around the world just to reach the war. When Rozhdestvensky's exhausted armada finally steamed into the Straits of Tsushima in May 1905, it was annihilated in what proved to be the last major action of the war—and perhaps the most humiliating defeat in naval history. A decade later, the desperate need for a northern seaway was illustrated yet again by central Russia's economic and logistical isolation during World War I and the Russian Civil War.

In the meantime, private exploratory ventures into the Arctic suffered dire results, due in great part to the state's failure to lend them support. Baron Eduard Toll's 1902 voyage in the *Zaria* ended in catastrophe on the New Siberian Islands. Two expeditions in 1912 also met with disaster: Vladimir Rusanov and the *Hercules* never returned from the Taimyr Peninsula, and only two members of Georgy Brusilov's fifteen-strong *St. Anna* expedition survived their journey. In 1913, Georgy Sedov set out in the *St. Foka*, hoping to reach the North Pole, but died of scurvy as he drifted northward.[11]

During the final days of the imperial era, therefore, there was an unmistakable sense of ambiguity about Russian efforts in the Arctic. Much had been done, and the triumphs of Nagursky and Vilkitsky on the eve of World War I were cause for some optimism. But the shocking failures of the Rusanov, Brusilov, and Sedov missions gave rise to a pervasive feeling of frustration and despondency. It is impossible to guess how this situation, left uninterrupted, might have changed: for better, for worse, or not at all. But as World War I, the revolutions of 1917, and the Russian Civil War swept away the old order, they brought about a remarkable metamorphosis in the Arctic as well. The new Soviet regime would usher in a new approach to the development of the North: one that, while hardly flawless, replaced lassitude and incompetence with energy and initiative. However, the two-decade transformation proved neither quick nor easy.

Building the North: The Soviet Arctic, 1917–1932

Like the rest of the new Russian nation that emerged from the broken remnants of the old regime by the 1920s, the Arctic underwent a severe baptism of fire for more than half a decade. Remote as the North may have been, it could not escape the warfare and political upheaval that raged throughout the country from 1914 to 1921. Global conflict, revolution, and civil war came to the Russian Arctic, effectively disrupting most polar work from approximately 1915 to 1920. And when the fledgling Soviet government finally turned its attention to the Arctic for the first time, it took a number of years to determine which goals to pursue there and even longer to decide how to pursue them.

War in the Arctic

Although military action there was limited, the Arctic was not an insignificant theater of operations during World War I. The German navy made passage through the Baltic Sea impossible, while Turkey sealed off the Black Sea to the Allies. This left the Arctic coast, with the ports of Arkhangelsk and Murmansk, as the only channel through which France and Britain could feasibly supply and aid their ailing co-belligerent.

The North became even more crucial during the Russian Civil War. Only a few months after seizing power, the Bolsheviks found themselves hemmed in by enemies from all directions. The British navy, in support of Nikolai Yudenich, prevented the Reds from venturing into the Baltic. Anton Denikin controlled most of the south and, with help from the British and French, closed off the Black and Caspian seas. To make matters even more difficult, the Bolsheviks lost their outlet to the Arctic shoreline as well. White commander Yevgeny Miller, backed by a contingent of British and American troops, gained control over the White Sea region. In August 1918, Miller occupied Murmansk and Arkhangelsk, depriving the Reds of their last links with the outside world. The Soviets fared little better in Siberia. The uprising of the Czech Legion in May 1918, followed by the initial military successes of Admiral Alexander Kolchak, who went on to establish a short-lived dictatorship in Siberia, placed huge portions of the subcontinent in White hands. Furthermore, 7,000 American soldiers and 72,000 Japanese troops poured into southeastern Siberia, occupying Vladivostok and taking over the Maritime Province and Transbaikal.

For months, Soviet territorial control was restricted to the central part of European Russia. Vulnerable and hard pressed, the Bolshevik portion of the country suffered cruelly under the iron blockade imposed upon it by the Whites and the Allied Powers. Every port was closed, and millions died of hunger, cold, and disease. For a short while, it appeared that the Whites would be able to win the Civil War simply by using the power of geography to strangle their opponents into submission.

But that time passed quickly. In autumn 1919, the Bolsheviks dealt crushing blows to Denikin and Yudenich. Meanwhile, Red forces relentlessly pursued Kolchak to the Urals and beyond. Proclaimed only a year earlier as the "Commander-in-Chief and Supreme Ruler of All the Russias," Kolchak saw his territory melt away in a matter of weeks. In November, the Soviets took Omsk; in December, they seized Novosibirsk (Novo-Nikolaevsk until 1926) and Tomsk, gathering up the wealth of arms, supplies, and gold bullion left behind by the retreating Whites. In January 1920, the Bolsheviks thrust even deeper into Siberia, retaking Irkutsk, one of Kolchak's key strongholds. In February, the Supreme Ruler himself fell into Soviet captivity and was executed for crimes against the Revolution.

Victory over Kolchak opened up the way to the conquest of the entire North. Red forces drove eastward, cementing their hold on the Trans-Siberian Railway, as well as the vital urban centers along the railroad. They reasserted their control over the great Siberian river basins that joined the Trans-Siberian with the waters of the Arctic Ocean. Then, with the threat of Kolchak removed, the Soviets turned to the northwest corner of Russia. By March 1920, the Red Army had driven Miller and his troops back to the White Sea coast, and, after having undergone a year and a half of devastating economic deprivation, the Bolsheviks finally reclaimed the ports of Arkhangelsk and Murmansk.

Not surprisingly, exploration and development in the Russian Arctic came to an almost complete standstill. A few attempts were made to keep polar work going, combat conditions notwithstanding. In April 1918, geologist Alexander Karpinsky, president of the Academy of Sciences, created a Collegium for Northern Research; in June, Yuri Shokalsky, head of the Russian Geographical Society, attempted to obtain government funding for a hydrographic survey of Russia's Arctic waters.[12] But whatever concerns the Soviet state had with the Arctic during these years were connected solely with the exigencies of the Civil War. Lenin signed a number of decrees regarding the North from 1917 through 1919, but these dealt almost exclusively with troop movements, railroad construction, fuel shipments, and similar matters.[13]

By 1920, however, the Bolshevik government was ready to give fuller consideration to Arctic affairs. The most dramatic of the factors that stirred the regime to action in the North was the great famine that struck the Volga basin and Ukraine in 1920 and worsened in 1921–1922. In July 1920, the regime devised an attempt to forestall the crisis by shipping food supplies to the center from the newly conquered zones east of the Urals. Overland transport was deemed to be unacceptably slow, so Lenin allocated 41.3 million rubles to ship the cargo north, along the Ob River, to the Arctic Ocean. Oceangoing vessels then carried the food to Arkhangelsk through the Kara Sea. The Great Siberian Bread Expedition of 1920 proved a success; not a single ship was lost, and almost 11,000 tons of grain reached central Russia. Of course, the famine took place regardless, and compared with the levels of assistance later provided by foreign agencies, especially the International Red Cross and Herbert Hoover's American Relief Administration, the role of the mission in relieving the hunger was minimal. But in the context of developing the North, the Bread Expedition was the direct precursor to the famous Kara Expeditions and can be considered the USSR's first major operation in the Arctic.[14]

Moving into the Arctic

When the Bolshevik regime set its sights on the Arctic in 1920, its short-term goals were relatively straightforward.[15] The state had three immediate concerns in the region. The first involved the basic question of political and administrative authority: how was Moscow to establish "Soviet power" in the North? In the Arctic, military conquest (which was not even complete in some parts of the area until well after the end of the Civil War) did not automatically constitute real territorial control. In fact, from April 1920 to November 1922 most of Russia's Pacific seaboard was not even part of the territory officially claimed by the USSR; instead, it comprised the Far Eastern Republic, a short-lived buffer state created by Moscow to reduce tensions with Japan. The Bolshevik presence was reasonably strong in the major cities along the Trans-Siberian Railway, but to the north of the railroad there was no preexisting institutional framework for the Soviets to co-opt, as was their practice elsewhere in the country. For the time being, Moscow left the administration of Siberia to local soviets, Party cells, and executive committees, but these units were most often tiny and primitive. As a result, actual responsibility for the region fell to the Siberian Revolutionary Committee (*Sibrevkom*); the Siberian Bureau of the Party Central Committee; and the regional executive committee of the Urals, based in Sverdlovsk (currently Yekaterinburg).[16]

The second question related to the native Siberians, or the "small peoples of the North," as they were designated by the regime.[17] In theory, the preservation of the rights of the non-Russian nationalities living within the Soviet Russian Federation was an issue of great importance to the Bolsheviks. In practice, it received little attention, at least in the Arctic. During the early 1920s, two attitudes emerged regarding the "small peoples." The first, held mainly by ethnographers and cultural workers, conceived of the northern tribes as the youngest children in the great Soviet family. This "soft" theory maintained that it was the responsibility of the state to "civilize" the native Siberians—to incorporate them benevolently into modern Soviet society. This became the appointed task of the Committee for Assistance to the Small Peoples of the North (more popularly known as the Committee of the North), established in July 1924.[18] In marked contrast to this view was a second line of thinking that perceived the native Siberians strictly in utilitarian terms: first as economic assets, later as obstacles to industrial and commercial progress in the North. This second outlook was eventually adopted by the regime and thus prevailed over the more accommodating approach.

Moscow's third priority—realizing the untapped economic potential of the Arctic—was by far the most urgent, as well as the most complicated. By necessity, the regime's immediate ambitions were modest. At the outset, the state concentrated primarily on animal industries and foreign trade. Hunting, trapping, and fishing remained a key part of the Siberian economy, even after the Revolution. Much of what little infrastructure the Soviets had in the Arctic wilderness was built on the trading posts and fur-gathering centers (*faktorii*) that had grown out of the old ostrog system. Northern fisheries helped to feed the Soviet population, and, after nations in the West began to resume economic relations with Russia, Siberian furs brought in badly needed manufactured goods and hard currency from abroad. In general, Soviet levels of foreign trade—especially with Britain, Germany, and the Scandinavian countries—were substantial, and a fair amount of that trade took place in the Arctic.[19] One of the Soviet products most in demand on the world market was cheap Siberian timber, and the most efficient way to ship lumber was up the Ob and Yenisei to the Kara Sea. To attract capital and defray the costs of developing the region, Lenin's government granted several mining concessions in the Arctic to Germany; the Soviets also obtained for themselves a similar concession from Norway, allowing them to mine for coal at two sites on the island of Spitsbergen after 1920. Until the end of the decade, foreign commerce in the North was conducted competently under the auspices of the People's Commissariat of Foreign Trade (*Narkomvneshtorg*).

Matters became far more confusing when the Soviets began to shift their focus to long-term, comprehensive work in the Arctic and sub-Arctic. Failing to take into account the inherent complexities involved with operating in the polar regions, Moscow initially treated the development of the North as it would the development of any other part of the USSR. Throughout the early to mid-1920s, various administrations and commissariats were simply detailed to carry out in the Arctic the same duties they performed elsewhere; the Council of People's Commissariats (*Sovnarkom*), the Council of Labor and Defense (STO), and the Supreme Council of the National Economy (VSNKh) coordinated their work, but only loosely. During these years, a bewildering alphabet soup of agencies, committees, and institutes—numbering in the dozens—came to work in the Soviet Arctic.[20] Precisely what they were supposed to do, not to mention how they were to do it, was never made clear, and this cloudiness of purpose led to a good deal of befuddlement and disorganization.

To begin with, practically every commissariat at all connected with economic activities or transport found its way to the North. The People's Commissariats of Food Production (*Narkomprod*), Supply (*Narkomsnab*), Agriculture (*Narkomzem*), and Forest Industries (*Narkomles*) all worked in the region, competing for jurisdiction over the fur, fishing, hunting, and timber industries. Narkomvneshtorg shepherded the growth of foreign trade along the Arctic coast. The People's Commissariat of Water Transport (*Narkomvod*) conducted independent sea and land expeditions in the North and organized the Administration for the Guarantee of Navigational Safety on the Kara Sea and the Mouths of the Siberian Rivers (UBEKO), a safety commission and insurance agency headquartered in Omsk. The People's Commissariat of Ways of Communication assumed similar responsibilities in its efforts to create railroads, air routes, and waterways throughout the region. The People's Commissariat for Internal Trade created its own Arctic division, while the People's Commissariat of Trade and Industry formed a Commission for the Study and Practical Use of the Russian North.

Other economic bodies appeared as well. The State Commission for the Electrification of Russia (GOELRO), one of Lenin's pet projects, formed a Siberian Committee in 1920. Another agency, the Committee of the Northern Sea Route (Komseveroput, or KSMP), destined to become the dominant entity in the Arctic by the end of the 1920s, got its start that same spring. The relative liberality of the New Economic Period, which provided for limited entrepreneurial activity, encouraged the formation of joint-stock companies; several operated in the North, the largest being the Sakhalin Stock Company (ASO) and the Kamchatka Stock Company (AKO). In September 1927, all the gold-mining operations of northeastern Siberia and the Arctic were placed under the control of the All-Union Trust of the Gold Industry (*Soiuzzoloto*).[21]

Closely tied to the matter of economic development was that of scientific research. A more intimate understanding of the Arctic was indispensable if the Soviets were to make any headway there, yet even the most basic information about the region was outdated or lacking altogether. Therefore, the USSR's scientific community was called upon to bolster the state's practical concerns in the North. In 1923, the Academy of Sciences formed a Polar Commission, which remained in operation until 1928. The following year, the Academy created a Yakut Commission, which continued to work until 1931, under the leadership of famed geologist A. E. Fersman. The Soviet Navy's Hydrographic Department lent its efforts to Arctic exploration, and, in March 1921, Lenin himself signed into existence the Marine Scientific-Research Institute (*Plavmornin*), a branch of VSNKh whose purpose was to conduct oceanographic surveys of the polar seas. In 1922, Plavmornin became the proud owner of the *Persei*, Russia's first oceangoing vessel specially fitted out for aquatic research.[22] It was in March 1920, however, that the scientific agency that would eventually overshadow all the others was formed. This was the Northern Scientific-Commercial Expedition (*Sevekspeditsiia*). During the 1920s, Sevekspeditsiia grew steadily stronger; finally, in 1930, it was upgraded to all-union status and became the Arctic Scientific-Research Institute (the Arctic Institute, or VAI), by far the most important body involved with the scientific study of the polar regions.[23]

For the most part, the hustle and bustle generated by this muddle of bureaucracies did little to further the government's ambitions in the North. Few of the commissariats and commissions assigned to work in the Arctic had the training or equipment to function there. Bureaucratic overlap and a mean-spirited sense of competition sapped Soviet efforts in the North of their effectiveness. On the most basic level, financial costs and sheer physical effort prohibited the state from being able to support the unwieldy array of agencies. In short, Moscow had blithely pressed forward into the Arctic, assuming that its normal approach to development would suffice there—only to learn that work in the North was anything but business as usual.

This is not to say that early Soviet efforts in the North were entirely fruitless. If economic and administrative development lurched along fitfully, explorers and scientists made at least some advances toward simple geographic mastery over the region. Nonetheless, the Soviet presence in the Arctic was in sore need of being revamped and streamlined. As centralization became the watchword in the North, three institutions in particular managed to rise above the bureaucratic tangle: the Committee of the North, the Arctic Institute, and Komseveroput. All of them wielded significant authority in the Arctic until the early 1930s, but, of the three, the most powerful was Komseveroput.

The Rise of Komseveroput

The Committee of the Northern Sea Route began its jack-of-all-trades career humbly enough. In April 1920, it was formed by Sibrevkom as a joint-stock company responsible for overseeing shipping along the Northern Sea Route. Three years later, Komseveroput became one of the many trusts operating under VSNKh; at the same time, it was owned in part by Narkomvneshtorg. In June 1928, it was expanded by the STO into a large conglomerate, administered mutually by the Commissariats of Foreign and Internal Trade. Initially, KSMP was run by a five-person committee, one member appointed by each of the following: Sibrevkom, Narkomprod, Narkomvneshtorg, Narkomvod, and VSNKh's Urals-Siberian Committee. Operating from its headquarters in Omsk and Novosibirsk (and later Moscow), Komseveroput grew in size and independence. In 1931, during the First Five-Year Plan, KSMP attained all-union status and a good measure of institutional autonomy.[24]

Much of this had to do with the fact that Komseveroput's bailiwick, the Northern Sea Route, had become central to the state's plans for the future of the Arctic and northern Siberia. When geographers pondered how Siberia as a whole might best be developed, they envisioned a transportational network (*set'*) in the form of a gigantic grid that could be superimposed upon the subcontinent. The north–south lines of the grid—the Ob-Irtysh, Yenisei, Lena, and Indigirka-Kolyma river basins—were already in place. In the south, the rivers were linked west to east by a main line: the Trans-Siberian Railway. All that was needed was another line farther north, to parallel the Trans-Siberian, and the grid would be in place, enabling people and goods to move freely throughout Siberia.[25]

But what should that second line be? This question prompted a series of sharp debates throughout the 1920s. A number of planners proposed the construction of a "Great Northern Railroad," passing through Sverdlovsk, then canting north-ward on its way to the Pacific. Others argued for the creation of artificial water-ways that would lead east from the Urals and cut across the Siberian rivers. Most, however, including Sergei Bernshtein-Kogan, one of the USSR's premier trans-portation experts, advocated the development of the Northern Sea Route. After all, the distance between Leningrad and Vladivostok via the route was only 8,100 miles, as opposed to 14,309 miles via the Panama Canal or 16,844 miles via the Suez Canal. True, the polar seas were dangerous, and shipping costs in the Arctic were precipitous, but railroads and canals, while safer, would be frightfully ex-pensive to build in the North. Moreover, the expense of maintaining them was expected to remain constant or even increase. On the other hand, the costs of op-erating along the Northern Sea Route were projected to decrease, as the Soviets learned to cope with the difficulties of Arctic navigation.[26]

Unsurprisingly, Komseveroput personnel came down unanimously on the side of the Northern Sea Route in this debate, and when the argument was re-solved in favor of the route, KSMP benefited greatly. Ironically, it was this victory that also prepared the way for Komseveroput's ultimate downfall. Although the government's approval of the Northern Sea Route as the principal vehicle for Arctic and sub-Arctic development propelled Komseveroput to dominance in the region, the idea of the "network" filled the regime with unrealistic expectations. The attractiveness of the grid model lay in its simplicity, but the state mistook simplicity in theory for simplicity in practice. As a result, the government's de-mands grew more and more unreasonable, swiftly outstripping Komseveroput's actual capabilities.

All the same, Komseveroput's assumption of a leading role in the North led to some noteworthy achievements during the 1920s. In particular, the rise of KSMP coincided with the advent of three innovations that helped the Soviets make great progress in the Arctic. The first and most straightforward involved the concept of combined efforts. Traditionally, trips to the Arctic had been narrowly defined in function. To eliminate redundancy and cut down on expenses, the Soviets began to plan multipurpose expeditions; this economy of motion went a long way to-ward saving time and resources.

Second was the idea of permanence. Unlike most Arctic explorers, interested only in quick dashes to the pole and back, the Soviets had taken upon themselves the goal of transforming the North into part of their homeland. Comprehensive development called for techniques that would allow the Soviets to remain in the Arctic for long periods of time. As a result, scientists, technicians, and builders, in many cases accompanied by their families, lived and worked in remote corners of the North for months, even years, at a time. It was in this way that the smattering of ports, radio stations, and supply bases sprinkled throughout northern Siberia grew into the transport-communications network that enabled the Soviets to begin their full-scale absorption of the Arctic in the 1930s.

The third change was the most exciting of all: the arrival of the airplane. Pilots of all types had made their bids to conquer the polar skies since 1897, when Swedish balloonist Salomon Andree took to the air in the *Eagle*, crashed on his way to the North Pole, and died. Later, dirigibles found their way to the Arctic; in 1926, South Pole hero Roald Amundsen and American explorer Lincoln Ellsworth flew the airship *Norge* over the North Pole, while Germany's *Graf Zeppelin* visited the Soviet Arctic in 1931. But the future belonged to the airplane. In 1914, the Russians flew airplanes above the Arctic Circle, and it was the *Josephine Ford*, piloted by U.S. naval officer Richard Byrd in May 1926, that was credited as the first aircraft to fly over the North Pole.[27] By the mid-1920s, both land-based and ship-based polar aviation had become feasible, and no nation embraced the possibilities that Arctic flying offered more eagerly than the USSR. The Soviet Union was a charter member of Fridtjof Nansen's International Society for the Study of the Arctic by Means of Airships—Aeroarctic, founded in 1924—and it went on to produce the world's finest corps of polar fliers. The many ways in which aviation could prove useful in the Arctic were obvious. Nothing could beat the airplane as a tool for charting new territory. Pilots scouted ice conditions along the Northern Sea Route, making maritime traffic easier and safer. Aircraft also proved invaluable for supply and communication; leapfrogging through the Arctic with passengers, mail, and provisions, the airplane did more than anything else, with the possible exception of the radio, to bind the growing polar infrastructure together.

With these general changes taking place in the background, Komseveroput began to move into the heart of the Arctic itself. In this, it was greatly assisted by the scientists of the Arctic Institute. The first priority was to chart properly the island groups of the Arctic Ocean, many of which had never been visited before. In 1921, scientists surveyed Novaia Zemlia and the straits of the Kara Sea. Two years later, the Soviets traveled to the Franz Josef archipelago, establishing a Russian "Farthest North." In 1924, an expedition led by geologist Georgy Ushakov landed on Wrangel Island, claiming it as Soviet territory.[28] In 1927, the Soviets paid their first visit to the New Siberian Islands, charting the Laptev Sea along the way. Finally, in 1930, Ushakov completed the circuit by wintering on Severnaia Zemlia.

Komseveroput and VAI also made great progress along the Siberian rivers. Every passing day brought the Ob and Yenisei increasingly under the control of Soviet settlers, timber workers, and bargemen. In 1923, P. G. Milovzorov led the first expedition to sail down the entire length of the Kolyma River. In 1927, he completed the first full navigation of the Lena.

The Soviets enjoyed special success in adapting the airplane to Arctic work.

Polar aviation was by no means cheap or risk free, but the rewards were well worth the danger and financial investment. In spite of accidents and high costs, Soviet pilots pioneered key air routes. In autumn 1924, Boris Chukhnovsky performed the first ice-reconnaissance missions, aiding shipping between the Barents and Kara seas. From 1927 to 1929, *Osoaviakhim*, the USSR's mass civil-defense organization, sponsored a yearly Northeastern Air Expedition, led by G. D. Krasinsky. Major sites joined to the growing Arctic air network included Tobolsk, Krasnoiarsk, Irkutsk, and Yakutsk.

One of the most striking flights—a multinational operation conducted under the auspices of Aeroarctic—came in 1931, after three years of planning. This was the voyage of the German dirigible *Graf Zeppelin*. Carrying forty-six passengers, among them Dr. Hugo Eckener, the expedition leader; American explorer Lincoln Ellsworth; Hungarian journalist and novelist Arthur Koestler, writing as the science correspondent for a German newspaper chain; and four Soviets, including Rudolf Samoilovich, head of the VAI, the airship left the Friedrichshafen dirigible works for Leningrad on 24 July. The *Zeppelin* then traced a circular route through the Soviet Arctic: from Leningrad to Franz Josef Land, then to Severnaia Zemlia, the Taimyr, Dikson Island, Novaia Zemlia, Arkhangelsk, and back to Leningrad. The flight of the *Zeppelin* marked the climax of Aeroarctic's efforts to foster international exploration in the Arctic; it was also one of the high points of Soviet–German cooperation during the interwar period.

If any single indicator serves to demonstrate Komseveroput's growing aptitude in the North, it is the success of the yearly Kara Expeditions. Inspired by the Siberian Bread Expedition of 1920, the Kara Expeditions were begun in 1921 to stimulate foreign trade and provide Soviet seamen with experience in dealing with Arctic conditions. During the 1920s, the USSR traded with a number of countries in the Kara Sea, its main partners being Germany, Norway, and Britain. The expeditions continued into the 1930s, but their heyday lasted from 1921 to 1928, with 1929 and 1930 being important years as well.[29]

The Kara Expeditions united the efforts of Narkomvneshtorg; the All-Russian Cooperative Society (ARCOS), with its offices in London and Berlin; Narkomvod; and the regional executive committees of Siberia, the DVK, the Urals, and Kazakhstan. By the mid-1920s, KSMP took upon itself the role of coordinating the expeditions. Throughout the decade, the expeditions grew in scope, but the basic procedure remained the same. The USSR traded raw materials from the participating regions—primarily timber, wool, cotton, and metal ores—for manufactured goods and industrial equipment from the West. At the beginning of the summer, these materials were gathered at Novosibirsk, Tomsk, Tiumen, Tobolsk, and Krasnoiarsk. From there, barges carried the goods north to the Arctic coast. At the same time, Soviet escorts rendezvoused with foreign ships and guided them through the Kara Sea to the mouths of the Ob and Yenisei. Upon reaching the transfer zones, the foreign ships unloaded their freight, took the Soviet goods on board, and departed. The Soviets loaded the foreign cargo onto their barges and made their way south; the goods were then distributed to their assigned destinations.

The first expedition took place in summer 1921; its leader was Mikhail Nikolaev, head of the Siberian Bread Expedition, with Norwegian Otto Sverdrup, who had accompanied Nansen on the *Fram*, as chief consultant. The expedition ended reasonably well. Not only did it complete the cargo transfer as planned, but it transported almost 10,000 tons of grain from Siberia to Arkhangelsk. Two ships were lost, however, and over the next four years the Soviets struggled to keep the Kara Expeditions operational. In 1922, unseasonably heavy ice stopped all traffic along the Yenisei, and cargo turnover fell short of expected levels by over one-third. The following year proved even worse; diplomatic tension caused by the Ruhr crisis in Germany all but canceled the 1923 expedition. Poor weather hampered the 1924 expedition, and although the 1925 expedition proceeded normally it still failed to match the volume of the 1921 venture. In 1926, however, a turning point was reached. That year, Nikolai Yevgenov took over the leadership of the Kara Expeditions from Nikolaev, who died in 1925. Largely because of Yevgenov, the expeditions of 1926, 1927, and 1928 were great successes: cargo turnover increased each year, and the expeditions themselves became safer and more efficient than ever before.

Table 1.1 shows the uneven progress of the Kara Expeditions in terms of cargo turnover. But the expeditions' successes and failures cannot be measured by numbers alone. Although the volume of shipping was slow to recover after 1921, the actual monetary worth of the cargo increased as more easily transported items replaced cheap, bulky lumber. In addition, the level of Soviet exports rose almost every year. This was especially notable, since import–export deficits were a sad fact of life in Soviet foreign trade. Although the USSR had a positive balance of trade in the Arctic only two times during this period (in 1926 and 1928), it did manage for the most part to increase its export-to-import ratio year by year.

After 1928, the economic importance of the Kara Expeditions began to wane. The Soviets moved on to more easterly sections of the Northern Sea Route, and foreign trade trickled off after 1931, although the 1929 and 1930 expeditions yielded an overwhelmingly positive balance of trade for the USSR. Of the 73,560 tons of cargo moved during the 1929 expedition, 60,060 tons consisted of Soviet exports; in 1930, exports made up 142,000 of 158,000 tons.

In terms of sheer volume, the Kara Expeditions played only a minor role in Soviet foreign trade during the 1920s. But the expeditions were not primarily about economic utility—at least not at the outset. Instead, they were enormously beneficial as training exercises for work in the Arctic. In eight years, the Soviets made sixty-two voyages in the Kara Sea, losing only two ships, both during the first expedition in 1921. Insurance costs plummeted, and the navigational season increased substantially. In 1920, the Soviets could operate no more than forty-eight days in the Arctic; by 1928, they had extended that season to seventy days, and it would grow even longer in years to come.

In 1928, the Soviets had the opportunity to display before the entire world the skills it had gained from the Kara operations. In May of that year, Italian aviator Umberto Nobile attempted to fly the dirigible *Italia* over the North Pole. The airship reached the pole but crashed shortly thereafter. The whereabouts of the crew remained unknown until June, when a Russian radio enthusiast picked up a weak broadcast for help. The USSR took the leading part in the international res-

Table 1.1   Cargo Turnover (in Tons) on the Kara Expeditions, 1921–1928

Year	Exports	Imports	Totals
1921	4,877 (5,362)	8,440 (9,820)	13,317 (15,182)
1922	5,837 (6,413)	7,790 (8,856)	13,627 (15,269)
1923	24	1,076	1,100
1924	4,418 (4,558)	6,528 (7,151)	10,671 (11,709)
1925	5,582 (6,133)	7,602 (8,394)	13,184 (14,527)
1926	10,070	9,090	19,168
1927	11,114	13,314	24,428
1928	17,107	12,271	29,378

Source: RGAE, f. 9570, op. 1, d. 195, ll. 18–20; SoS 1, no. 3 (March 1930): 75. Where the figures are at variance, those in parentheses come from RGAE.

cue mission that followed: two Soviet icebreakers, the *Malygin* and the *Krasin*, reached the stranded crew first, and all survivors were retrieved by mid-July. The *Italia* rescue attracted attention from around the globe, and the Soviets' role in it prefigured the Arctic exploits that would bring them worldwide renown during the 1930s. For the time being, however, the triumph of the USSR was obscured in the eyes of Western onlookers by the death of Roald Amundsen, who perished in an airplane crash while searching for Nobile's men.[30]

By 1928, then, the Soviet Union had made great progress in the Arctic, and much of it was due to the work of Komseveroput. But this achievement can be measured only in the most basic of terms. By the late 1920s, KSMP had secured a rudimentary presence in the North; it had not actually begun to establish control. And although gaining even a simple foothold in the Arctic was, in and of itself, an impressive feat, a foothold did not suffice for the government, which had plans for the rapid transformation of the entire country, the Arctic included. Moscow was interested in results, not rationalizations, and failed to realize—or refused to acknowledge—that the development of the North could not be hurried. Moreover, Komseveroput itself suffered from certain structural shortcomings. For over half a decade, KSMP had been able to disguise its flaws and carry on with its work. After 1928, however, times changed, and all of the agency's imperfections would be thrown into sharp relief during the fever and frenzy of the First Five-Year Plan.

The First Five-Year Plan and the Fall of Komseveroput

Soviet Siberia is not a miracle but the natural product of historical development. Therefore, we cannot simply demand wonders from Soviet Siberia.

Leon Trotsky

In October 1928, the Soviet regime inaugurated the First Five-Year Plan: Stalin's great crusade to industrialize the entire country, all at breakneck speed. The years that followed also included the rapid collectivization of agriculture and the four years of turmoil in the sphere of arts, letters, and professions known as the Cultural Revolution. The period from 1928 to 1932 has been labeled the Great Turn, the Revolution from Above, and the Stalinist Revolution. Whatever the name, it was a time of great change and even greater upheaval throughout the USSR.

The tumult and uproar of the period reached the North as well, and much was expected of the region during the First Five-Year Plan. One of the plan's declared intentions was "to extend the ways of approach to Siberia"; another was to make the North more than "a raw material appendage to Central Russia," by "draw[ing] it into the orbit of socialist construction."[31] At this stage, the development of the Arctic was part of a larger goal: to reshape all of Siberia into the great wellspring of the Soviet economy. As a famous children's book about the five-year plan put it:

> During five years we shall build thousands of new factories. And each factory will turn out thousands of tons of freight. Over a network of railways and waterways this freight will flow in all directions. Hundreds of rivers of freight will flood the entire country like waters in springtime. . . .The most powerful of such rivers will flow from Siberia to Moscow.[32]

The plan set no direct quotas for Komseveroput itself or for the "North" or "Arctic." Instead, the plan assigned output levels for Western Siberia, Eastern Siberia, and the Far East. In all of these regions, the plan called for gigantic increases in sea and river shipping, air traffic, manufacturing, and mining. Although KSMP was initially obliged only to organize the logistic underpinnings of this proposed growth, its duties soon expanded to include actual production and development, and the agency grew accordingly. In March 1929, the gifted and dynamic Boris Lavrov was appointed to lead Komseveroput. Two years later, KSMP became an all-union institution, with a 1932 budget of 8.65 million rubles. Komseveroput now commanded five geographical sectors, six administrative divisions, and twelve departments; it controlled airfields, ports, lumber trusts, state reindeer farms, and factories. By the end of 1931, Komseveroput had a net worth of over 84 million rubles; a year later, that figure rose to almost 93 million.[33] In 1932, the agency had almost 40,000 people on its payroll.[34]

With these gains, however, came unprecedented responsibility. Also, KSMP now had to answer not only for its own work but, indirectly, for the success or failure of the agencies it provided with transport. Despite its new burdens, Komseveroput achieved much during the five-year plan. The gradual growth of the northern infrastructure continued; KSMP's greatest coup in this sphere was the establishment of Igarka, the Yenisei river port that would become the principal processing center for the Siberian timber industry. Komseveroput also logged impressive results in the area of transport and communications. New aerial trunk lines were normalized, including one from Moscow to Novosibirsk, via Sverdlovsk, and another from Irkutsk to Vladivostok, via Khabarovsk. The plan summary likewise praised "the heroic work done by aviators in the opening up of the Arctic" on expeditions to Severnaia Zemlia, Novaia Zemlia, Wrangel Island,

and the Taimyr Peninsula.[35] Sea and river transport in the region improved as well. As the plan summary noted:

> During the first Five-Year Plan, great progress was made in the opening up of river-ways and sea routes in the far North and the Arctic. Tremendous progress has been made in the development of Arctic navigation; during the last year of the Five-Year Plan period, a special expedition demonstrated the possibility of sailing from Arkhangelsk to Vladivostok in one season.[36]

General growth in the North was further indicated by the population boom that took place during the five-year plan. By July 1930, the population of Siberia had grown to such a degree that the region was divided—over 8 million people now lived in Western Siberia, while 1.5 million resided in Eastern Siberia.[37]

Regardless, there were problems and failures in the Arctic, some quite severe. Progress in the North was anything but consistent. Exploration and scientific research, for instance, went well; production and economic work did not. Perhaps the most conspicuous failure involved the collectivization of agriculture, a vital issue for two reasons. First, collectivization was seen as the means by which to rationalize the economy of the native Siberians. By gathering the natives' reindeer into state and collective farms (*sovkhozy* and *kolkhozy*), the state could compel the natives to realign their economy—which also included fishing, hunting, and fur trapping—along Soviet lines. Second, shipping food from the center to support the population in the North was becoming more costly as the number of people living there increased. The state hoped to make the Arctic as self-sufficient as possible by means of collectivization and agricultural experimentation. Properly speaking, responsibility for this effort fell to Narkomzem and the Committee of the North, not just to Komseveroput.

Whoever was accountable, collectivization failed, and miserably. Although certain crops and livestock were capable of surviving Arctic conditions, full-scale farming yielded poor results; by the end of the five-year plan, the government found itself compelled to reduce or even abolish agricultural production quotas in many areas throughout Siberia and the DVK.[38] The Integral Cooperatives, created by the Committee of the North in January 1930 to sovietize the economies of the native Siberians, proved an utter farce. So did KSMP's Motorized Fishing Stations, Industrial Hunting Stations, and Motorized Sea-Hunting Stations, which were pale, unsuccessful imitations of the Machine-Tractor Stations that appeared throughout the rest of the USSR during the collectivization drive. Finally, just as it did elsewhere, collectivization led to the deaths of hundreds of thousands of livestock—in the case of the Arctic, the reindeer upon which so much of the native way of life was based. In 1926, there were approximately 2.2 million domesticated reindeer in the Soviet North. By the end of 1932, that number had fallen to 1.8 million, and by the end of 1933 it fell again, to 1.6 million.[39]

Neither were difficulties absent from transport and communications. Increased tempos often led to increased inefficiency. Mistakes and accidents, especially along the rivers, became endemic; the Soviets had come a long way since 1920, when they had tried to use river barges to navigate the Arctic Ocean (only to watch in amazed despair as they overturned on the high seas), but inexpertise still led to logistical problems and the occasional catastrophe.[40] Incompetence and corruption caused supply shortages, misdirected shipments, and outright theft. It was here that Komseveroput truly began to falter; its real weakness involved the hundreds of minor mishaps and mistimings that plagued its work. A discernible malaise set in, a dry rot that undermined the agency in countless small ways.

But the agency also suffered because of factors beyond its control. First was a major change in the state's priorities. Earlier, the government had emphasized timber, fur, and fisheries as the principal elements of the Arctic economy. Accordingly, KSMP had made significant progress in developing those industries. During the five-year plan, however, the state shifted its interest to heavy industry, especially to the vast mineral reserves of the Arctic and sub-Arctic. Potentially the most lucrative enterprise in the North, the mining industry was also the most complex, and Komseveroput was ill equipped to make a rapid switch to such a difficult undertaking. By the end of 1932, KSMP found that much of its progress over the past half-decade was suddenly unappreciated.

Just as important, the government's overall expectations for the North were simply too high. The Soviets had made a good start in the region, but they had not yet come far enough to be able to "force" or "storm" the Arctic, as their five-year plan slogans urged them to. Moscow chose to ignore this reality and thus doomed KSMP and its efforts to failure.

However, if that failure was due to a classic case of Moscow's asking for too much too soon, it was due also to an inherent flaw in KSMP's design. Komseveroput had been cobbled together in a piecemeal manner over a number of years, and even in its prime its fundamental character was ad hoc and haphazard. The agency was too weak to cope with its unorthodox mission; it possessed great responsibility but not great power. The rigors of the First Five-Year Plan persuaded the state that a new approach to the development of the Arctic was needed, and that new approach was soon in arriving. Komseveroput's disappointing performance made it all the more vulnerable to the massive bureaucratic realignment that took place throughout the Soviet economic-administrative structure as the First Five-Year Plan came to an end. Komseveroput's parent organization, VSNKh, was disbanded in 1932, and KSMP quickly followed. In December 1932, the regime leveled a variety of complaints against KSMP: it was consistently failing to keep records or balance its budgets, graft was prevalent, and, worst of all, production was subpar.[41] That month, Komseveroput's work was brought to a halt. Only a few months later, by the spring of 1933, KSMP was completely dissolved and replaced by a new agency that would eclipse it completely in fame and might: the Main Administration of the Northern Sea Route, better known as Glavsevmorput.

TWO

The Commissariat of Ice
The Rise of Glavsevmorput, 1932–1936

The Arctic and our northern regions contain colossal wealth. We must create a Soviet organization which can, in the shortest period possible, include this wealth in the general resources of our socialist economic structure.

Joseph Stalin

Here is the raw material for a great new empire.

John Littlepage, American engineer
visiting Siberia

On 28 July 1932, a small icebreaker set out from Arkhangelsk, bound for Vladivostok on a voyage that would bring sweeping changes to the Soviet Arctic. The expedition had been planned as part of the USSR's commemoration of the Second International Polar Year, and the ship's mission was to complete the first single-season traversal of the Northeast Passage in history. Two months later, on 1 October, the *Sibiriakov* limped into the Bering Straits, after a wearying journey. Plowing through the ice-choked polar seas, the ship had snapped both of its engine screws and, near the end, was able to move only under the power of a tarpaulin sail jury-rigged by its crew. But move it did, and the voyage proved successful. After clearing the straits, the *Sibiriakov* continued on to Vladivostok, its place in the annals of Arctic exploration secured.[1]

The significance of the *Sibiriakov*'s voyage involved more than a simple mark in the record book. That a ship could cross the Northern Sea Route in the course of one navigational season was the best indication to date that the route could indeed be transformed into the regular, operational sea-lane that the Soviets had labored over a decade to build. The plans of those who saw the Northern Sea Route as the key to unlocking the material potential of Siberia and the Arctic finally seemed within reach.

Certainly the importance of the *Sibiriakov*'s triumph was not lost on the expedition's leader, Professor Otto Yulevich Shmidt, destined to become "the direct and omnipotent ruler" of the Soviet Arctic.[2] Shmidt left for Moscow soon after the *Sibiriakov* lowered anchor in Vladivostok, and he arrived in the capital in mid-December. For five days he conferred with the Council of People's Commissars and, by all accounts, with Stalin himself. Afterward, on 17 December

1932, it was announced that a new organization was to be created for the purpose of exploring and developing the Soviet Arctic: the Main Administration of the Northern Sea Route, more famous as Glavsevmorput, or GUSMP.[3]

Its innocuous title notwithstanding, the new agency was both immense and powerful from the outset and would grow even more so over time. Glavsevmorput received control over all Soviet territory east of the Ural Mountains and north of the 62d parallel, including the island groups of the Arctic Ocean. This territory amounted to 2 million square miles, or roughly one-quarter of the USSR's total area. Glavsevmorput's jurisdiction extended to all spheres—cultural, economic, and administrative—and, with few exceptions, it displaced or subsumed the many agencies that had previously worked in the Arctic. Over the next five and a half years, Glavsevmorput reigned supreme in its Arctic kingdom. A socialist counterpart to the mighty British East India Company, as one reporter put it, GUSMP enjoyed a status equal to that of a subministry, received a princely budget, and became one of the largest agencies working for the Soviet state during the 1930s.[4] Within months, GUSMP's flag—a blue ensign with the hammer and sickle on a red field in the upper left-hand corner and a gold anchor in the middle—became a common sight throughout northern Siberia and the Arctic seas.

At least in the abstract, Glavsevmorput represented one of Moscow's most deliberate attempts at supercentralization. Glavsevmorput was often compared to a state within a state, and Shmidt was fond of boasting that he was in charge of a "multi-People's Commissariat."[5] The reasons for this unusual concentration of power were simple. During the First Five-Year Plan, the government had come to realize that the special conditions of the Arctic called for a special approach to development. If the scores of organizations working in the Arctic before 1932 had not been strong enough to overcome the rigors of the North on their own—and if efforts to coordinate their activities had led only to chaos and redundancy—then a new strategy was needed. Professor Shmidt proposed a solution: the establishment of a single agency dedicated solely to the Arctic, large and strong enough to assume a wide variety of duties and responsibilities.[6]

An unusual agency, Glavsevmorput had an unusual leader as well.[7] Otto Shmidt was a scientist of great versatility and an administrator of remarkable energy. Born in Mogilev in 1891, Shmidt was educated at Kiev University; he excelled at physics and mathematics, studying the latter under the renowned Dmitry Grave. Originally a member of the Menshevik Party, Shmidt joined the Bolsheviks in 1918 and distinguished himself during the Civil War with his work in the People's Commissariats of Finance and Food Production. His efforts caught the eye of Lenin himself, who called Shmidt "our Professor Otto" and described him as "irrepressible." After the war, Shmidt became chairman of the State Publishing House (*Gosizdat*), head of the Central Statistical Administration, and editor-in-chief of the *Great Soviet Encyclopedia*. Until 1930, he also worked in various capacities with the People's Commissariat of Education (*Narkompros*).

Shmidt's first experience with exploration came in 1928, when he was asked to help lead the world's first expedition—a joint Soviet–German venture—to the Pamir glacier.[8] The following summer found him heading a trip to Franz Josef

Land, with the aim of setting up the USSR's first polar station in that area. Also in 1929 Shmidt joined a government commission created to develop new approaches to the Arctic; the commission was chaired by General Sergei Kamenev, whose interest in the North was a long-standing one. In July 1930, Shmidt returned to Franz Josef Land and visited Severnaia Zemlia. That same year he became chief of the Arctic Institute, and it was in this capacity that he arranged his historic voyage in the *Sibiriakov*.

Precisely why Shmidt became involved with Arctic exploration is unclear. Shmidt was chosen for the Pamir expedition partly because he was an avid alpinist (and spoke German fluently), and this hobby may help to explain his growing interest in the North. Shmidt loved the outdoors, and he was a robust man—indeed, at well over 6.5 feet tall, sporting the huge, bushy beard he had cultivated since his university days, he looked the part of the consummate polar explorer. Shmidt was temperamentally suited for exploration as well; even his varied career path reveals a certain wanderlust. Shmidt was a man of multiple talents, unwilling to restrict himself to one endeavor, and polar exploration seemed to offer him the best means by which to engage his capabilities—and ambitions—to the fullest.

Shmidt's assignment to the Arctic, however, may not have been altogether voluntary. Shmidt's personality was a forceful one; although he was widely noted for his charm, he could be inflexibly stern, and he had a wrathful temper when roused. As leader of the 1928 Pamir expedition, Shmidt allegedly gunned down two members for "rebellion" ("iron Bolshevik discipline" in action!) and threatened to shoot anyone who disobeyed him during the *Cheliuskin* adventure of 1934.[9] In combination with his tendency to monopolize any undertaking, such traits could make him vexingly difficult to work with. Shmidt's relationships with his supervisors tended to be fiery ones; during his years at Narkompros, for example, his quarrels with Anatoly Lunacharsky grew violent enough to require Lenin's intervention. Such episodes were not uncommon, and it may be that Shmidt was sent to the Arctic after antagonizing enough of his superiors—or the wrong one. In the end, however, it is impossible to ascertain what combination of compulsion from above and personal inclination led Shmidt to the Arctic.

Whatever the case, it was there that Shmidt gained his greatest fame; he had been well known before, but now his presence in the national media was constant. Shmidt led Glavsevmorput from December 1932 to the spring of 1939. After his years with GUSMP, Shmidt went on to establish scientific institutes, publish journals, continue his work on the *Great Soviet Encyclopedia*, and become the vice-president of the Academy of Sciences. But it was in the Arctic, playing the role of the "Commissar of Ice," as the Soviet press dubbed him, that he reached the pinnacle of his career. When Otto Shmidt joined Glavsevmorput in 1932, his fortunes, like those of his new agency, were on a decided upswing.

The Growing Giant: GUSMP's Central Apparatus, 1933–1935

Glavsevmorput did not simply spring into existence fully formed; almost two and a half years passed before it reached the height of its powers. This time lag was due partly to the unavoidable delays involved with setting up shop in a region like the Soviet Arctic. But it had even more to do with the fact that a host of organizations continued to operate in the North, and all of them were eager to claim any portion of the Arctic pie that they could. Dispute resolution in the region was governed by a bureaucratic version of the law of tooth and nail, by which only the strong survived. For a number of months, then, GUSMP found itself embroiled in an ongoing battle to drive out or absorb the many rivals remaining in its Arctic domain.

Glavsevmorput's first order of business was to finish dismantling the hapless Komseveroput, which lingered on until its formal dissolution by Vyacheslav Molotov, then head of the STO, in March 1933.[10] This was no easy task; a number of other agencies did their best to strip away KSMP's assets for themselves. Komseveroput's Liquidation Committee continued to parcel off its holdings until 14 October 1933; Valerian Kuibyshev, sent by the STO to preside over the breakup, mediated the various altercations that arose.

Several of these struggles ended in short-lived compromises. Narkomles and Narkomvneshtorg retained their footholds in the Arctic, administering the Northern Lumber Trust in tandem with GUSMP. For the time being, the Soviet Fur Trust (*Soiuzpushnina*) won joint custody over two dozen fur-gathering points, and Glavsevmorput was also forced to split the vital icebreaker fleet, which included only nine vessels, with the People's Commissariat of Water Transport.

Some skirmishes GUSMP won outright. The All-Union Arctic Institute, the premier research organization in the North, was given over to it immediately. Glavsevmorput also won all fishing rights off the Chukchi and Kamchatka peninsulas. It kept hold of KSMP's eighteen reindeer state farms, as well as the fish and animal industries of the North. Glavsevmorput even set the powerful People's Commissariat of Heavy Industry back on its heels by seizing partial control over the coal and nickel mines of Norilsk.[11]

For the most part, GUSMP received the bulk of its inheritance from KSMP intact. It absorbed UBEKO, assumed control over all of KSMP's seventeen polar stations, and built six new outposts before the year was out. The entirety of Komseveroput's polar aviation fleet passed to GUSMP. Also by the end of 1933, Glavsevmorput had organized its holdings into three large trusts: the North-Urals Trust, centered in Obdorsk; the Taimyr Trust, in Igarka; and the Yakutsk Combine, in Yakutsk.

Even in this embryonic state, Glavsevmorput was formidable; a few basic statistics serve to demonstrate how powerful it was. At its largest, Komseveroput had employed approximately 40,000 people, including support workers and manual laborers; many of its full-time employees joined GUSMP. Glavsevmorput started off with almost 30,000 workers, *before* the influx from *Komseveroput*, and *excluding* construction and low-level workers; by 1937, its total workforce would grow to almost 200,000 (including support and manual labor).[12] At its peak, KSMP had a budget of 8.65 million rubles; Glavsevmorput began its career with almost 44 million rubles in its coffers.

All the same, Glavsevmorput's control over the territory that nominally belonged to it was incomplete as 1933 came to an end. Therefore, during the course of 1934, GUSMP waged a fierce campaign to eliminate its rivals in the North. Before the year was out, Glavsevmorput proved victorious in almost all its conflicts, and it became the undisputed master of the Arctic — at least for the time being.[13]

The principal actor in this struggle was Sergei Bergavinov, formerly the regional Party secretary of the DVK, now the head of GUSMP's powerful Political Administration (*Politupravlenie*). In an unceasing barrage of letters and telegrams, Bergavinov tirelessly petitioned Sovnarkom and the Party Central Committee for permission to commandeer resources from other agencies working in the Arctic. In doing so, he pursued an effective twofold strategy. First, Bergavinov insisted on a literal interpretation of Glavsevmorput's original charter, which granted it control over "the *entire economy and all enterprises* north of the 62d parallel."[14] Second, he went to great lengths to convince the government that GUSMP would be unable to fulfill the tasks assigned to it unless it received clearance to enlarge itself. In a characteristic letter, written in this case to Lazar Kaganovich, Bergavinov explained that GUSMP had made great progress but could not be expected to move forward without more material support: "we have completed the first stage of our work, but we are now about to undertake much more complex and difficult tasks."[15]

Bergavinov's efforts in badgering the central authorities paid off. On 24 July 1934, Sovnarkom and the Party Central Committee issued a decree that settled almost all jurisdictional questions pertaining to the Arctic in GUSMP's favor.[16] The July Decree was a veritable bonanza. The agency now controlled 18 reindeer state farms, 37 fur-gathering facilities, and 54 polar stations (as well as 120 outposts in the sub-Arctic zone). The July Decree also placed the bulk of the Northern mining industries into GUSMP's hands. These new gains included the flourine mines of Amderma; the salt, oil, and coal deposits of Nordvik (*Nordvikstroi*); the coal mining trust on Spitsbergen (*Arktikugol'*); a share in the coal and polymetal reserves at Norilsk (*Noril'stroi*); and all lead, nickel, copper, and coal mines at or on Vorkuta, Pechora, Anadyr, Sangarsk, Vaigach Island, Novaia Zemlia, and the Taimyr.[17]

Other assets came Glavsevmorput's way, such as tractors, automobiles, and radio transmitters. The Civil Aviation Administration (GUGVF, or *Aeroflot*) surrendered all aircraft in the Arctic and the northern Urals to GUSMP. Likewise, Osoaviakhim was ordered to transfer 715 pilots and technicians to the Arctic, as well as to build an aviation-training school for GUSMP. Finally, Glavsevmorput gained more ships; among them were six whalers (the *Smolny, Lensovet, Lengostorg, Nerpa, Murmanets,* and *Novaia Zemlia*) and four large steamers (the *Makarov, Davydov, Dobrynia Nikitich,* and *Truvor*). Most important, GUSMP, in a great triumph over Narkomvod, succeeded in gaining sole proprietorship of the USSR's collection of icebreakers, the flagships of the Arctic fleet (see Table 2.1). The Narkomvod chief himself, Nikolai Yanson, was transferred to Glavsevmorput, where he became Shmidt's deputy.

Table 2.1   The Soviet Union's Icebreaker Fleet, 1917–1939

Ship	Year Built	Horsepower	Tonnage
Krasin	1917	10,000	8,750
Yermak	1899	9,500	8,250
Lenin	1917	7,980	6,000
Litke	1909	7,900	3,028
Sibiriakov	1909	2,000	2,600
Rusanov	1908	2,200	2,600
Sedov	1909	2,360	3,056
Malygin	1912	2,800	3,200
Sadko	1913	3,500	3,350

Source: F. I. Dirgo, "Stroitel'stvo ledokol'nogo flota," *SA* 1, vol. 2 (September 1935): 8. Technically speaking, only the first four ships are icebreakers (*ledokoly*); the smaller ones are ice-forcing ships (*ledokol'nye korably*). The *Krasin* was originally the *Sviatogor;* the *Lenin,* the *Alexander Nevsky;* the *Litke,* the *Canada;* and the *Malygin,* the *Solovei Budimirovich.*

By 1935, GUSMP was reaching the full height of its powers, and it was safe for Yanson to claim that the agency had become "a self-made People's Commissariat of Transport, Economy, and Culture."[18] Its labor force was growing steadily; by this point, GUSMP employed well over 100,000 people.[19] In July 1935, the Committee of the North was disbanded, and the job of administering the affairs of the native Siberians—as well as the committee's academic bodies, the Institute of the Economy of the North (IES) and the Institute of the Peoples of the North (INS)—passed to GUSMP. In August 1935, GUSMP began to publish its own professional journal, *Soviet Arctic* (*Sovetskaia Arktika*), whose monthly circulation of 10,000 issues was larger than most scientific or economic periodicals of its type. As a further sign of the government's blessings, Shmidt and his deputies each received a personal limousine from the state.[20]

More substantively, Glavsevmorput's budget increased at a phenomenal rate during the Second Five-Year Plan, as shown in Table 2.2.

It was also in 1935 that Glavsevmorput assumed the final form it would take until its downfall in late 1938. Initially, GUSMP had governed its territory by means of its trusts in the northern Urals, the Taimyr, and Yakutsk; shortly thereafter, it had added a fourth to administer Chukotka. After the end of 1934, GUSMP completely rearranged its internal organization, placing its holdings under the authority of seven large territorial administrations (*terupravleniia*). In addition to exercising physical control over its assigned area, each administration was responsible for certain specialized functions. The Leningrad terupravlenie served as Glavsevmorput's general headquarters (GUSMP also maintained an office in Moscow, on Razin Street, near the Kremlin). The Murmansk administration dealt with supply, ship repair, and marine shipbuilding. Arkhangelsk ran the hunting industry; the construction of polar stations; coal-mining concessions on the island of Spitsbergen; and the economies of Kolguev Island, Novaia Zemlia, Vaigach Island, and GUSMP's holdings in the Komi ASSR (including coal bases at Vorkuta). The Ob terupravlenie, based first at Omsk, then Tobolsk, supervised affairs along the Ob-Irtysh river basin. The huge Krasnoiarsk administration, head-

Table 2.2   Reported GUSMP Budgets, 1933–1937 (in millions of rubles)

	Shmidt	RGAE	Politupravlenie	Bergavinov
1933	40	43.6	46	n/d
1934	103	107.5	103	103 (193)
1935	251	262.6	245	251 (411)
1936	451	436.5	431	431 (821)
1937	540	607.6	579	540 (1,400)

Source: O. Iu. Shmidt, "O nashikh dal'neishikh zadachakh," SA 3, vol. 4 (April 1937): 6–21; RGAE, f. 9570, op. 2, d. 94, ll. 300–301; RTsKhIDNI, f. 475, op. 1, d. 21, l. 100. Bergavinov's figures come from RTsKhIDNI, f. 475, op. 1, d. 5, l. 48. They include a sizable ship fund that was added to GUSMP's budget annually.

quartered in Igarka, controlled the Yenisei region, the large Krasnoiarsk Aircraft-Repair Factory (KARZ), and GUSMP's facilities at the Norilsk mining complex. Yakutsk oversaw the Lena basin and the Sangarsk coal mines. Finally, the Far Eastern terupravlenie, located in Vladivostok, administered GUSMP's Pacific fleet and, from afar, the agency's holdings in the Chukotka and Indigirka-Kolyma regions.[21]

At the center, in Glavsevmorput's Leningrad and Moscow offices, the agency was organized according to function.[22] Immediately under Shmidt were two deputies, each chosen by Sovnarkom (in consultation with Shmidt). A small central council assisted Shmidt and his deputies in providing executive direction for the agency. Divisions run directly by this council included the agency's Secretariat, the Cadre Selection Group, the Bureau of Ice Prognostication, the Publications Office, the Cryptography Section, the Inspection Department, and the Material-Technical Supply Office. Certain special bodies, such as the INS, the IES, the Arctic Institute, and the major mining trusts, also reported to the central council. Beyond that, there were twenty departments in GUSMP's executive apparatus: Political Administration, Maritime Transport, River Transport, Polar Aviation, Shipbuilding, Polar Stations/Meteorology, Hydrography/Hydrology, Mining/Geology, Agriculture, Reindeer Industries, Promotion of Native Culture, Fur Industries, Hunting/Fishing, Trade/Industry, Planning/Economic, Finance/Bookkeeping, Mobilization, Labor, Medical, and General Offices.

One of the bodies above deserves special mention: the Political Administration, with Sergei Bergavinov as its head. In essence, the Politupravlenie amounted to a second organizational network running parallel to Glavsevmorput's central apparatus. Its ostensible functions were to promote Party work in the wilderness and to aid GUSMP's far-flung branch offices by facilitating day-to-day administration. Its main purpose, however, was to supervise personnel conduct, often in conjunction with the local organs of the NKVD, the Soviet secret police. In the field, the Political Administration operated eleven political departments (politotdely), one in the headquarters of each terupravlenie, as well as in Dikson, Irkutsk, Tiksi, and Anadyr. The Politupravlenie also maintained Party organizations (partorgy) in all of GUSMP's major facilities: icebreakers, towns and settlements, factories, polar stations, the INS, the IES, the Nikolaev School (the training center for

Arctic pilots provided for GUSMP by Osoaviakhim), and the Arctic Institute. The Politupravlenie grew into one of the most influential components in the GUSMP system, and its chief became a key power broker in the agency.

Glavsevmorput's new structure was approved by the regime in January 1935 and reaffirmed in June 1936.[23] At this point, it had truly become a giant in the Arctic. In a way, however, it can be argued that size and might were as detrimental to GUSMP's fortunes as they were positive. In arrogating so much power to itself, Glavsevmorput took upon itself a huge variety of responsibilities—and ended up biting off more than it could proverbially chew. This quandary was reflected in the agency's constant efforts to define itself. From 1935 onward, there would be hard times as well as triumphs ahead for Glavsevmorput, and the agency's ultimate fate was the result of a combination of many factors: its inherent design, the demands of the government, the individual actions of thousands of people, and random chance. Among the most important ingredients in this mix were the fundamental decisions that GUSMP made about its own future. Looking backward, it is clear that the choices facing the agency were anything but easy.

Science, Economic Development, and the State

Precisely how was Glavsevmorput to pursue its goals in the Arctic? Although it was occupied during its early years with the process of reaching full maturity, GUSMP also found it necessary to consider this matter seriously. Doing so, however, involved far more than simple policymaking. For Glavsevmorput, charting its course of action represented a struggle for its very identity, since the main issue it had to confront was whether it would become primarily a scientific body or primarily an industrial-developmental agency. In principle, these two options were not mutually exclusive. Nonetheless, the circumstances under which GUSMP operated conspired to make them so, and, over time, this caused serious rifts within the agency's apparatus.

Science was obviously a crucial aspect of GUSMP's work. Without continued research, prospects for progress in the Arctic were nil. Some of the most rudimentary questions about the North remained unanswered. How could meteorologists more accurately make judgments about the capricious climatic conditions of the circumpolar latitudes? Where were the richest mineral deposits to be found? What kinds of crops could be grown? How did deep ocean currents affect the pattern of ice formation in the Arctic seas? What could engineers build on the thick layers of permafrost that covered so much of the subcontinent? Even basic geographical facts continued to elude the Soviets. As late as 1939, for example, scientists remained in doubt as to whether two large islands—Sannikov Land and Andreev Land, rumored to lie near the mouth of the Kolyma—existed or not. Both had been the stuff of legend for years; in a famous turn-of-the-century novel, distinguished geologist Vladimir Obruchev created a Jules Verne–style adventure in which Russian explorers actually find Sannikov Land and encounter a hidden world of savages and prehistoric creatures.[24] Eventually, both islands' supposed existence would be disproven. But during the 1930s, it was still the job of the USSR's Arctic experts to put such uncertainties to rest.

To conduct scientific work in the Arctic, Glavsevmorput had a number of tools at its disposal. Six of the agency's subsections were dedicated at least partially to scientific endeavors. Beyond that, GUSMP had under its control the All-Union Arctic Institute, which, over the span of a decade, had transformed itself into the preeminent research organization in the Soviet North. Operating out of its stately headquarters on Fontanka Street, in downtown Leningrad, the VAI maintained a popular museum, published several prominent journals, and dispatched expeditions of all kinds to every corner of the Arctic. Almost 300 scholars and explorers staffed the institute's nine departments (Geology, Hydrology, Biology, Geophysics, Geodetic Research, Laboratories/Workshops, Publishing, Museum, Library). After it was handed over to Glavsevmorput in December 1932, the VAI became one of the agency's most valuable assets.

There were, however, certain problems with the relationship between GUSMP and the institute. To start with, there was a noticeable amount of functional overlap in their work. Second was a clash of basic philosophies. The institute's leaders tended to support the pursuit of both pure and applied science; by contrast, most key members of the GUSMP administration looked askance upon scientific work that had no demonstrable practical application. The most divisive problem of all, however, boiled down to the elementary issue of power. For more than ten years, the Arctic Institute had prided itself on its relative autonomy, and the majority of its personnel regarded its new position under Glavsevmorput as a form of subjugation. The strongest opinions on this matter came, naturally enough, from the institute's chief, Professor Rudolf Samoilovich. Except for a two-year hiatus between 1930 and 1932, Samoilovich had led the Arctic Institute from the time of its creation in 1920. The institute had been formed largely because of his energy and initiative, and, over the years, he had developed a deep sense of attachment to the agency and its employees. Ordinarily, the bald, walrus-mustached Samoilovich was an extremely personable individual who loved nothing so much as spending an evening playing the piano and singing with his family and friends.[25] For Glavsevmorput, however, he had nothing but dislike, and the special target of his resentment was none other than Shmidt. Not only did Samoilovich feel that the GUSMP boss had usurped his authority, but he saw in Shmidt an arrogant maverick, a scientific dilettante who had no real grounding in Arctic science. For as long as the two men worked with each other, their association was a tense and chilly one.

The Arctic Institute's second-in-command, the dour and "super-intellectual" Vladimir Vize, was able to accept the new order of things with more grace.[26] Although Vize was one of Samoilovich's closest friends, he also managed to maintain a rapport with Shmidt; their relationship was formal but respectful. Due in great part to Vize's skills as a liaison, the palpable friction that existed between GUSMP and the institute did not prevent them from carrying out dozens of effective operations in the North. Among the most prominent were Samoilovich's 1934 attempt to drift to the North Pole in the icebreaker *Sedov* and the three high-latitude voyages of the icebreaker *Sadko*, led by Samoilovich and Georgy Ushakov during the summers of 1935, 1936, and 1937.

Despite such successes, trouble remained; the Arctic Institute and the people who worked for it continued to be unhappy about what they perceived as their inferior status. Under Glavsevmorput's wing, the VAI flourished as never before, but its increased prestige and financial well-being had been bought at the price of obedience. Moreover, there was an underlying trend in GUSMP policy that gave rise to even greater distress for the institute: as time passed, scholarly research slipped down the ladder of Glavsevmorput's priorities, losing its place to the rising concerns associated with economic and industrial development.

In a general history of polar exploration, one author claims that Soviet successes in the Arctic were attributable to the fact that the USSR could easily afford to sponsor expensive expeditions there, "the profit motive [being] more or less absent from Marxism."[27] Perhaps this was true in some idealized socialist universe, but not in the world of Stalinist economics, where getting a return on its investments was a matter of the utmost urgency for the state. In the case of the Arctic, there was no mistaking what the regime wanted: a suitable payoff in exchange for the resources it had bestowed upon Glavsevmorput. Therefore, GUSMP did not have the luxury to content itself with scholarly dabbling in the North. Moscow wanted to make the Arctic economically self-sufficient, then to make it turn profits. Above all, this called for development.

The most tangible index of the state's desires here was the Second Five-Year Plan.[28] The State Planning Commission (*Gosplan*) did not set specific quotas for GUSMP, but it did target the Arctic in the area of transport. In January 1932, the Communist Party officially declared its intention to create a nationwide network of river routes and waterways.[29] In keeping with this, the plan shifted the USSR's overall ratio of transport activity somewhat toward seas and rivers and away from railroads; the Arctic could only benefit from this change, since waterways were the only feasible modes of large-scale transportation in the region.[30] The plan also referred to the need for the rapid development of the Northern economy and explicitly called on GUSMP to help make industrial work in regions such as the northern Urals, Eastern Siberia, Yakutia, and the DVK succeed.[31] Accordingly, the state's capital investment in Glavsevmorput grew steadily, rising from 26 million rubles in 1933 to 80 million by 1937.[32]

As a further indication of the Arctic's importance in the USSR's economic aspirations, a number of Glavsevmorput personnel were invited to help shape the Second Five-Year Plan. Among the special scholarly consultants assembled to advise Gosplan was Otto Shmidt. He was joined by other members of GUSMP, including Samoilovich; geologist Alexander Fersman; petrogeologist Ivan Gubkin; the venerable Vladimir Obruchev, who had surveyed the Siberian subcontinent during the days of the tsars; and famed plant geneticist Nikolai Vavilov, who advised GUSMP on matters agricultural.[33] In short, it was obvious that Moscow had its eye on the Arctic and that it was determined to see that its long-term designs were realized.

If the demands of the state were clear, how they were to be met was not. Moscow had placed two great tasks before GUSMP: to achieve physical mastery over the Arctic and, at the same time, to move forward with rapid economic development. In reality, the simultaneous prosecution of both goals was next to impossible, but while Glavsevmorput's leaders perceived this, the Stalinist regime did not. Refusing the state, however, was not an option, and GUSMP was obliged to make a critical decision: would it emphasize exploration and research, or would it push full steam ahead with its economic concerns?

In the process of trying to answer this question, a deep cleavage arose within GUSMP's ranks. Those departments concerned with economic and developmental work argued that GUSMP should concentrate its resources directly on its economic and productive duties. In contrast, the divisions involved with scientific research, exploration, and transport insisted that economic efforts would be a waste of time and money without a better comprehension of the Arctic's geography and climate. Both arguments had merit. It was undeniably rash to dive headlong into intensive economic work in a hostile area. But research expeditions were a serious drain on finances; a single expedition could cost from 80,000 to 650,000 rubles.[34] Worse yet, expeditions could not be hurried, whereas the Second Five-Year Plan left Glavsevmorput in no position to be prodigal with time. For GUSMP to risk the wrath of the authorities by taking a gradual approach to its economic responsibilities was almost as dangerous as rushing in without proper preparation. This dilemma had brought KSMP to its ruin; its successor now faced the same problem.

Who were the major players in the attempts to resolve this issue? Shmidt, of course, along with the various men who served as his deputies: Semyon Ioffe and Georgy Ushakov, then Yanson and marine-transportation expert Eduard Krastin. Members of Glavsevmorput's central council also had a say; among them were Bergavinov; the seven terupravlenie heads; the leaders of GUSMP's various departments; Samoilovich and Vize; Boris Lavrov, the former chief of KSMP, currently director of the IES; Mark Shevelev, in charge of polar aviation; Anatoly Skachko, previously the assistant head of the Committee of the North, now responsible for native affairs; and Sergei Natsarenus, head of the agency's Planning-Economic Department. From 1933 to 1936, the debates raged. Eventually, the proponents of development, including Bergavinov, Yanson, and Natsarenus, gained a slight upper hand (although not all of them came to a happy end before the decade was out). Advocates of the more scientific, deliberative approach found themselves shunted out of the agency's circles of power—or worse. Those who were interested mainly in transport, like Krastin, Lavrov, and Shevelev, tried to stake out an intermediate position but found it unwise to remain neutral; they either chose sides or suffered for not seeking safe haven with one camp or the other.

The most striking sign that the economic-productive strain of thinking was ascendant was that Glavsevmorput began to resort to the most extreme developmental method of all: forced labor. That it did so should come as no surprise. During the 1930s, it was virtually impossible for any major industrial or developmental body in the USSR to avoid being connected in some way to prison-camp labor. As one expert on the subject notes, the GULAG became a great clearinghouse, "a big contractor supplying labor force to enterprises in the administration of other commissariats."[35] In addition, GUSMP operated in an environment that made it difficult to recruit a sufficient labor force, even with the help of financial incentives. A limited body of evidence, gleaned from the papers of the Politupravlenie, proves that the agency indeed made use of convict labor. In 1935, Sovnarkom directed the NKVD to provide GUSMP with 5,000 inmates or, at its discretion, volunteers who had finished their sentences and were willing to work in the Arctic for bonus wages; GUSMP was responsible for supplying and housing this new "personnel."[36] The following year, the NKVD was ordered in a secret circular from the Party Central Committee to transfer 10,000 prisoners to Glavsevmorput's salt mines at Nordvik.[37] Explicit archival references to forced labor are rare, but, almost certainly, those that exist only begin to scratch the surface. Glavsevmorput was in charge of too many sites that became notorious prison camps before the decade was out—Norilsk, Pechora, Vorkuta, Novaia Zemlia—not to have been even more heavily involved in the utilization of forced labor than formal documentation suggests.

Furthermore, at least two of Glavsevmorput's top officials were enthusiastic spokesmen for the policy of putting prisoners to work in the Arctic. The first was Nikolai Yanson. In 1928, Yanson was appointed the People's Commissar of Justice of the RSFSR; in this capacity he became one of the prime movers in introducing forced labor into the Soviet prison system.[38] Later, as head of Narkomvod, Yanson assisted with the construction of the infamous White Sea–Baltic Sea Canal (*Belomor*, or BBK), the first major forced-labor project of the 1930s.[39] The building of Belomor, which killed at least 100,000 prisoners, was closely connected to the regime's overall plans for the Arctic; the 168-mile canal was intended to link the ports of Arkhangelsk and Murmansk to Leningrad and the Gulf of Finland (unfortunately, the utility of the BBK was not nearly as great as its planners had hoped, since only barges were able to travel through the canal after its completion). One of Yanson's like-minded colleagues came to join Glavsevmorput as well. This was Matvei Berman, one of the chief architects of the BBK and, during most of the 1930s, head of the entire GULAG system. The extent of Berman's involvement with Glavsevmorput is unknown; he may have been there to assist in linking Belomor with the Northern Sea Route. Whatever the case, Berman was almost appointed by Sovnarkom in summer 1936 to replace Ushakov as one of Glavsevmorput's deputy heads. Berman, however, was called away to become deputy director of the NKVD, and Shmidt nominated Eduard Krastin in his place. Still, with individuals such as Yanson and Berman in GUSMP's apparatus, it is certain that forced labor played a significant role in the agency's operations.

Where did Otto Shmidt fit into this institutional soul-searching? Confronted with the choice between economics and science, his personal inclinations seem to have been toward the latter. A scholar by training and an outdoorsman by nature, Shmidt was most drawn to hands-on research ventures; his greatest talents lay in designing the grand expeditions that made GUSMP—and him—so famous. Shmidt's emphasis on exploration increased his country's understanding of the North; the publicity he gained was an added bonus. But there was also a downside. In chasing after his adventures, Shmidt neglected many of his administrative duties. Just as important, when it came time to decide whether GUSMP should cast itself as a scientific or a developmental body, Shmidt wavered, and his disregard for—or inability to deal with—the agency's economic responsibilities would lead to dire consequences.

But real blame for Glavsevmorput's dilemma should be assigned to the Stalinist state. During the 1930s, the regime had the opportunity to be a positive force in the settlement and development of the Arctic. When scientific and technological undertakings require national governments to take active roles in helping them come to fruition—the building of a space program, the creation of a defense industry, the construction of dams, railroads, or highway systems—they have a choice in how they will play their parts. The state can facilitate, or it can impede (at times, it is best left out of the picture, according to a humorous—but "not entirely far-fetched"—*New York Times Magazine* piece on privatizing a mission to Mars: "the wilderness has not usually been conquered by bureaucrats").[40] Such was the case with the USSR's campaign in the Arctic. The Kremlin could have supervised GUSMP's efforts with more care. It could have been more forgiving of errors that were unavoidable. Most of all, it could have been more realistic in its expectations. But none of this was in the Stalinist style, and the state crushed Glavsevmorput with pressures, punishments, and deadlines. Eventually, GUSMP became the principal victim of what was a deeply flawed national strategy for development in the North.

On the Periphery: Glavsevmorput in the Field

According to the laws and ordinances of the realm, GUSMP was the viceregal lord of the Soviet Arctic. In actuality, its sway over the territories apportioned to it was less than complete. To tame 2 million square miles of the world's harshest and most hostile land was a daunting prospect: one that would strain the capabilities of any organization. For the Soviets to gain genuine control over the North would require initiative, material investment, hard work, and, most of all, patience. In the meantime, GUSMP would have to make do with a tenuous hold on its domain.

In the field, this was exactly the situation that prevailed. Glavsevmorput's authority over the Arctic most closely resembled a patchwork quilt, and a rather tattered one at that. Glavsevmorput was slowly building a network in the North, steadily improving its ability to bind the scattered reaches of the region more tightly together. But that network was, for the time being, fragile. In other words, the perspective from the periphery was radically dissimilar to that from the center, from GUSMP's sheltered offices in Leningrad and Moscow. And it was precisely out in the periphery—on one of the archipelagos in the polar seas, in a faraway research station, on an icebreaker adrift for months at a time—that the true vastness of GUSMP's task revealed itself. It was also there that the manifold difficulties that Glavsevmorput faced in that task became all too apparent.

"Foreposts of Culture": GUSMP's
Remote Facilities

The skeletal frame into which Glavsevmorput hoped to breathe life consisted of the agency's various remote facilities. Out of its logging camps, mines, cultural bases, reindeer farms, fisheries, and airfields, GUSMP planned to generate a permanent, fully functional presence in the Arctic. Together with the larger ports and railheads in its support zone, these facilities were to become the nodes in GUSMP's ever expanding developmental and transport grid.

Especially important were GUSMP's polar stations, which ranged from small to large and served a variety of purposes: transfer points for lumber and fur, storage depots, centers for ice reconnaissance and weather forecasting, coastal coal bases (extremely important, since icebreakers burned an inordinate amount of fuel), radio beacons, and scientific outposts. In spring 1935, Glavsevmorput had seventy-two polar stations at its disposal; at least nineteen more were to be operational by 1937. From 1933 to 1937, GUSMP spent 22,584,000 rubles on the construction of polar stations; capital investment in them exceeded 159 million rubles.[41] The stations' design and construction also reached a new level of sophistication. The first station to be built by the Soviets was erected in 1923 by Nikolai Matusevich (later vice-president of the Soviet Geographical Society) at Matochkin Shar. From that date to 1928, stations remained poorly equipped, limited in function, and few in number. Over the next five years, more stations, capable of performing complex duties, began to appear. After 1933, GUSMP built new polar stations and renovated and enlarged most of the old ones, with the idea that each should be a major center of activity, able to extend its influence outward over a constantly increasing radius.[42] Eventually, the stations' spheres of influence would intersect, and GUSMP's grid would be fully interactive.

To the government, the Soviet public, and the targets of its recruitment drives, Glavsevmorput conveyed an idealized—one might say fraudulent—image of its field facilities. Thus, polar stations became the "foreposts of Soviet civilization." Staffing them were the USSR's finest and fittest individuals. They came complete with every possible amenity: movie theaters; athletic equipment; libraries stocked with the classics of Marx, Lenin, and Stalin; musical instruments; and other creature comforts. In brief, Arctic settlements were portrayed as state-of-the-art workplaces and perfect living environments for the latter-day pioneers residing in them.

To be fair, Glavsevmorput attempted to live up to its advertising. There were indeed libraries, film collections, and other similar entertainments. In 1935, GUSMP sponsored the first "polar theaters": troupes of actors and musicians who made circuits throughout the Arctic, offering stage productions, opera, and jazz. In 1935–1936, Glavsevmorput claimed to have supplied its polar stations with the following: 430,000 rubles' worth of books; 700 phonographs, along with 21,000 records; 42,000 rubles' worth of toys; 175,000 rubles' worth of bicycles; 550,000 rubles' worth of sports equipment; 800,000 rubles' worth of musical instruments; and, on top of that, ten pianos and enough assorted trumpets and horns to fit out five full brass bands.[43] With respect to more salient matters, GUSMP was, by 1937, spending over 1.5 million rubles on schools for the 2,176 children living in or near polar stations.[44] It also did its best to increase the number of hospitals, doctors, and nurses.[45] Most of all, Glavsevmorput offered financial incentives to sweeten the lot of the average Arctic worker; in 1933, Sovnarkom authorized a 150 percent wage increase for personnel working above the 55th parallel and a 200 percent increase for those whose duties took them above the 60th.[46]

Nevertheless, none of Glavsevmorput's intentions could alter the inescapable fact that the conditions actually found in Soviet polar stations bore no resemblance to the fantastic visions spun out by the agency's propaganda. A casual remark in the memoirs of Ernst Krenkel, one of the USSR's most admired polar heroes, speaks volumes. Discussing his assignment to a Novaia Zemlia station in 1926, Krenkel comments, "no one had any particular desire to go to the Arctic in those years"—an enormous understatement.[47] Even during the 1930s, certainly more than one GUSMP novice, lured to the North by dreams of living under the glow of the aurora borealis and working valorously on the last frontier, experienced shock and disappointment upon arriving in the *real* Arctic. According to reports sent back to headquarters by GUSMP's political inspectors, the state of things in the field was, with few exceptions, lamentable.

Physical conditions alone were more than enough cause for despair. The climate—marked not only by hellishly cold winters but also by humid, sweltering summers made intolerable by gigantic swarms of mosquitos—was only the beginning. As one young bargehand complained after being posted on the Yenisei, life there was "dirty, squalid, and primitive."[48] He was not alone in his sentiments; even in the consistently positive record of American journalist Ruth Gruber's visit to the Arctic, readers can find a number of forcefully voiced complaints about everything from hospitals to public privies.[49] Living quarters often consisted of nothing more than ramshackle heaps, overrun with rats, bedbugs, and lice. After a visit to the logging center of Igarka, one official criticized the town's freezing, overcrowded, and vermin-infested dormitories for visiting aviators; no human being, he concluded, much less a pilot who had hundreds of miles to fly after only a short rest, could possibly get a decent night's sleep in such buildings.[50] Even provisioning oneself could be an exercise in frustration. Getting a sufficient supply of food became a very real problem, and the threat of scurvy was constant in all but the largest settlements. Due to the scarcity of luxury items in the Arctic—or even staple goods, since supply shipments frequently failed to arrive on time or at all—local systems of exchange took on the character of the gold-rush economies of the Klondike and the California hills. According to the special scale of exchange by which Glavsevmorput sold imported commodities, it took 1,300 rubles' worth of furs or other goods to pay for a bar of soap (until 1935, cash purchases were not permissible); a pair of shoes might cost as much as 2,000 rubles.[51] Such prices technically applied to purchases made by native Siberians, but Glavsevmorput employees were sometimes forced to pay them as well.

If material conditions were wretched, a good portion of GUSMP's personnel made little effort to rise above their surroundings. Far from being red-blooded paragons of Bolshevik virtue, many Russians in the Arctic conducted themselves in ways that ranged from slothful to deplorable. One basic problem was that Glavsevmorput suffered from a constant shortage of qualified, educated field workers. The Cadre Selection Group had an especially difficult time filling positions that required high levels of skill: teachers, doctors, agronomists, ship's captains, and veterinarians. Neither was political awareness a strong point; one Party functionary wrote to his Politupravlenie superiors in shock, amazed that many of the workers assigned to him in the Arkhangelsk sector had no idea who national leaders such as Vyacheslav Molotov or Mikhail Kalinin, the USSR's titular head of state, were.[52] The level of ignorance among the rank and file was frightfully high, and many men and women occupied jobs for which they had no credentials or training.

Motivation and morale were typically low as well. To begin with, a number of GUSMP personnel had come to the Far North—or had been sent there—because they were unable to integrate themselves into Soviet society at large. But not just the outcasts and misfits had trouble adjusting to the Arctic; the grim environment engendered a widespread feeling of discouragement and despondency. The perpetual darkness of polar night, when the sun disappeared from the winter sky for months on end, led to mass outbreaks of unbearable depression. The lopsided ratio of men to women lowered spirits significantly (the shortage of females in the northeastern periphery was pronounced enough for *Komsomolskaia pravda* to launch a "Girls, Come to the Far East!" campaign, centered on the comely Valentina Khetagurov, the wife of a DVK army officer, in February 1937).[53] Material deprivation, cramped and unsanitary housing, and sheer boredom also fed the ever widening streak of discontent and sullenness that became a very real—and very malign—presence in GUSMP's remote installations.

For the most part, malcontents chose to express their dissatisfaction by brooding, grumbling, or dragging their feet on the job. But more serious responses were common as well. Many Arctic cadres turned to substance abuse. As a flood of telegrams from local officials attests, Glavsevmorput personnel drank, and heavily.[54] Despite the fact that alcohol was legally available only at special GUSMP stores (for exorbitant prices), alcoholism was everywhere, from Arkhangelsk to Zyrianka, and it became one of the most disruptive forces in the Arctic (narcotics consumption also took place but was much less prevalent).[55] Even in the most propagandized accounts of life in the Arctic, drunkenness makes cameo appearances. Geophysicist Yevgeny Fedorov recounts the story of a co-worker who made it a habit to beg for inordinate quantities of cologne from fellow station members. After a short time, Fedorov and his colleagues discovered that this had nothing to do with vanity; instead, "Ivan" was guzzling the borrowed scent to get drunk.[56] Ernst Krenkel encountered even worse: the doctor attached to his Novaia Zemlia station preferred to administer his drugs to himself rather than to his patients. In the end, the morphine-addicted physician died of an overdose.[57] More typical was the tendency of many polar workers to allow themselves to break down mentally and physically. As one inspector ruefully noted after a tour of Nordvik and Igarka, a large proportion of GUSMP's workforce "let themselves slip into darkness, dreadful filth, and rude savagery."[58] In most cases, the degeneration was relatively minor: a worker might stop shaving and bathing, or he might become surly with his fellow employees. But he could just as easily become insubordinate, neglect his duties altogether, or resort to violence. And it was not unheard of for Glavsevmorput cadres to go insane or commit suicide.

Not surprisingly, all of this—carelessness, lack of training, alcoholism, and laziness—took its toll on GUSMP's work. Accidents and injuries occurred on a regular basis. In 1937 alone, thirty-eight people died in Glavsevmorput's Spitsbergen mines; nine more perished in the first quarter of 1938.[59] From 1934 to 1937,

GUSMP's Polar Aviation Administration logged 655 accidents.[60] River traffic was particularly dangerous. In purely physical terms, shipping freight up and down the Siberian waterways was one of GUSMP's most complicated tasks. Tight spots on the rivers left passing ships little room to maneuver. Worse, the rivers' water levels changed from year to year, and the contours of their banks shifted as well. Only a skilled navigator, in charge of an alert crew, could guarantee a successful voyage. But experienced captains were scarce, and barge sailors were Glavsevmorput's least valued and least dependable personnel—they were also the ones most likely to be on the job after having punished a few bottles of vodka or home-brewed moonshine.

Another facet of Glavsevmorput's poor field performance involved its inefficient supply system. At times, the errors were mind-boggling. Even when ships and airplanes reached their destinations safely, they sometimes brought with them the wrong cargo or none at all. In early 1934, a Tiumen newspaper complained that only 60 percent of all goods shipped on the Ob-Irtysh got to their correct destination.[61] The Northern Urals Fur Center twice received shipments of guns without ammunition.[62] The outpost at Cape Shmidt received enough canned meat and macaroni to last at least four years; on the other hand, a shipment to the Krasnoiarsk district was delayed so long that 3 million rubles' worth of canned fish went rotten before arrival. A station on the Arctic coast received swimsuits instead of desperately needed winter coats, while an 81,000-ruble shipment of snowboots to the Northern Ob actually contained canvas tennis shoes.[63] Finally, in perhaps Glavsevmorput's most ridiculous supply snafu, 10,000 rubles' worth of toothbrushes mysteriously appeared at Chaun Bay, on the Chukchi Peninsula. As the local station head remarked, Chukotka now had enough dental hygiene equipment to keep every mouth in the region clean for over a decade. To his further dismay, the station head also received several crates of silks and cosmetics instead of the nails and windowpanes that he had ordered.[64]

Clearly, all was not well with Glavsevmorput on the periphery. Beyond the incompetence, the flaws, and the internal weaknesses, there were crime and corruption. Profiteering and embezzlement were pervasive. Violence was commonplace, as tempers flared out of control in settings of claustrophobic proximity. Life on GUSMP's Arctic frontier resembled the stories of Joseph Conrad (in which so-called civilization collides with the "wilderness" to such disastrous effect) far more than it did the profusion of glorious images found in the agency's propaganda. And while the disparity did not invalidate the Soviets' genuine accomplishments in the field or preclude the possibility that the USSR could, over time, bring the Arctic under its control, it did not portend well for Glavsevmorput's future.

The Small Peoples: Glavsevmorput and the Native Siberians

In July 1935, Glavsevmorput claimed the Committee of the North as the latest victim in its campaign to expand its jurisdiction. This added yet another obligation to its list of responsibilities: the stewardship of the native Siberians. The "small peoples of the North" consisted of twenty-six ethnic groups, lumped together by Russian authorities according to "tradition, political exigencies, and contemporary linguistic and ethnographic data": the Khanty, Mansi, Chukchi, Koriak, Nenets (Samoyed), Enets, Eskimo, Aleut, Saami (Lapps), Evenk (Tungus), Yukagir, Selkup, Nganasan, Dolgan, Ket, Even, Chuvan, Itelmen, Nivkh (Giliaki), Negidal, Nanai, Ulch, Oroch, Orok, Udege, and Tolafar.[65] Larger groups, such as the Yakut (Sakha), Komi, or Buriat, were not considered part of this category; each was granted its own autonomous region. As late as the 1930s, the small peoples were still primarily nomadic and numbered somewhere between 150,000 and 200,000.[66]

The Committee of the North had been the custodian of the small peoples for over ten years, since the agency's foundation in July 1924. Its head was Pyotr Smidovich, a prominent Old Bolshevik; the committee's board included such notables as Avel Yenukidze, Emelian Yaroslavsky, Nikolai Semashko, Leonid Krasin, and Anatoly Lunacharsky. The participation of such celebrities, however, was strictly ceremonial; in the committee's case, "big names were expected to compensate for the lack of a budget."[67] Even Smidovich's presence was largly symbolic, and day-to-day leadership fell to his assistant, Anatoly Skachko. Another leading figure in the agency was the eminent ethnographer Vladimir Bogoroz-Tan. By the early 1930s, the committee's authority had begun to fade, and its position was made even more precarious by the growth of Glavsevmorput. During 1933 and 1934, GUSMP's Cultural Department, with the help of the Politupravlenie, zeroed in on the vulnerable committee. In October 1934, Bergavinov attempted to bully Smidovich into admitting officially that the committee's existence was superfluous.[68] Smidovich refused, but the government sided with Bergavinov in the end. When Smidovich died in April 1935, the Committee of the North was dissolved in a matter of weeks; all of its duties and assets passed to Glavsevmorput. Skachko joined GUSMP and became the head of its reconstituted Administration for the Promotion of Native Culture.

The state's concerns with the native Siberians had always been dual: political and cultural on one hand, economic on the other. Political work alone was a complex matter. Merely making the small peoples of the North aware of the new Soviet regime, much less deciding how they fit into it, was no easy task. The tiny, wandering tribes were extremely hard to govern. In response, the state ignored the distinguishing characteristics of each tribe and bunched them together indiscriminately. In October 1926, the Committee of the North, with its "Provisional Statute of the Administration of the Native Peoples and Tribes of the Northern Borderlands of the RSFSR," encouraged the native Siberians to form "clan soviets," "regional native congresses," and "regional native executive committees." The small peoples obeyed, but most considered these bodies to be meaningless. Likewise, in 1931–1932, the committee divided the tribal territories into eight "national districts" and eight "regions." The tidy lines looked attractive and reassuring on the map but had little significance in reality.[69]

During its eleven-year career, the Committee of the North directed its main efforts toward "civilizing" the native Siberians. Consciously modeling itself on institutions like the United States' Bureau of Indian Affairs, the Committee of the North saw its principal mission as the protection of the small peoples and the promotion of their welfare.[70] A good part of this work involved overcoming centuries-old stereotypes. For all their rhetoric about the equality of nationalities, the Soviets harbored deep-seated prejudices against the native Siberians. The peoples of the North were universally perceived as the most primitive in the USSR. A widely read children's primer depicted the inhabitants of the Siberian taiga as "people with squinting eyes, clad in strange dress made of animal skins."[71] The natives of Vladimir Obruchev's fictional Sannikov Land—who speak a rudimentary language, worship mastodons and sacred stones, and exhibit every other stock feature of the typical science-fiction tribe of savages—are likened to the Chukchi of northeastern Siberia.[72] Even an old Russian legend that the small peoples were descended from a tribe expelled from the empire of Alexander the Great because of their uncleanliness managed to survive into the twentieth century.[73]

On the whole, the committee's cultural work met with limited success. This was due mainly to the fact that the committee's attitude toward the native Siberians resembled that of a missionary group: replete with noble intentions but condescending as well. To carry out its work, the committee built fourteen cultural bases (kul'tbazy): complex centers offering vocational training, medical services, language instruction, entertainment, and veterinary aid. The committee envisioned the bases as great magnets that would entice the native Siberians to come from hundreds of miles around and learn about the wonders of modern Soviet life. The small peoples, however, content to live their lives as they had for generations, spoiled the committee's grand schemes by opting to visit the kultbazy in underwhelming numbers. To its credit, the committee worked toward what it thought was best for the indigenous peoples of the Arctic. And for over a decade it succeeded in safeguarding the small peoples from less solicitous Soviet interests. But with respect to its professed goals to "enlighten" the natives the committee had to content itself with only meager results.

This is not to say that cultural work failed altogether. Literacy increased, both in Russian and the scripts devised by ethnographers for the languages of the small peoples. The natives also came gradually to adopt modern sanitary methods, technology, and standards of hygiene. Attempts to appeal to the Siberians worked best when they demonstrated clear practicality or were adapted to the indigenous lifestyle. Cultural workers who cured the sick with Soviet medicine, gave natives traps and fishing hooks made of Soviet steel, or showed how Soviet radios and vehicles made hunting easier tended to score successes with the natives. In rewarding the Chukchi who assisted with the rescue of the Cheliuskinites in 1934, the authorities showed genuine insight: instead of showering the tribe with useless honors, they handed over a motorboat and a hundred Winchester rifles.[74] There were also other ways of growing closer to the natives: one committee worker was said to have won the hearts of a Siberian clan by playing tunes on his balalaika.[75] Such successes, however, were exceptions; mutual miscommunication remained the rule.

Another reason for the Committee of the North's downfall had more to do with economic factors. By the end of the 1920s, the Stalinist regime had ceased to be interested in the native Siberians, except insofar as they helped or hindered economic development. The committee had been assigned the duty of rationalizing the small peoples' productive "industries" and integrating them into the Soviet national economy. But the committee made a shambles of economic work, and it was largely because of this that control of the native Siberians was transferred to GUSMP.

In keeping with the times, Glavsevmorput took a much more utilitarian stance toward the small peoples.[76] Not that it discontinued cultural work. Many of the committee's ethnographers joined GUSMP's Administration for the Promotion of Native Culture. Glavsevmorput inherited and maintained the Committee's kultbazy.[77] It also experimented with another idea pioneered by the committee: a smaller, mobile version of the cultural bases, called the "Red Tent" (*Krasnyi chum*). Red Tent volunteers ventured out into the natives' territory, attempting to make contact with them in the field. In theory, this was tactically preferable to waiting passively for the Siberians to come to the bases. But the Red Tents proved just as ineffective as the kultbazy, as demonstrated in a widely quoted remark by a member of the Khanty tribe: "You've come for nothing; we have no use for the Red Tent. Neither our fathers nor our grandfathers knew anything about Red Tents, yet they lived better than we do now."[78]

The Committee of the North felt quite wounded by such sentiments; GUSMP was less distressed by them, mostly because it was steadily losing interest in cultural work. In 1937, Glavsevmorput spent only 292,000 rubles on its kultbazy and Red Tents; it paid lip service to the notion of advancing the cause of the native Siberians but did little to back its words up with actions.[79] Not only were the native Siberians' Latin-based alphabets converted to Cyrillic, but in 1935, GUSMP arranged for the Leningrad Party Publishing House to halt altogether the production of printed material in the languages of the small peoples.[80] In 1936, GUSMP employed only 1,242 natives; a year later, that total barely rose to 1,513.[81] Glavsevmorput made much of the fact that the Eskimo Taian was appointed in October 1938 to be the political administrator of Wrangel Island, but this was a case of blatant tokenism.[82] Even the Institute of the Peoples of the North—which the native Siberians were said to refer to as the "Tent of Miracles"—was staffed almost exclusively by Russians; nearly all of its graduating students were Russian as well.[83]

Regarding the Siberians, Glavsevmorput concentrated on two priorities: eradicating anything about the native way of life that could be seen as threatening to its authority and harnessing the productive capacity of the small peoples. With respect to the former, nothing roused GUSMP's suspicions more than shamanism, the backbone of the native Siberians' religious systems. Even the Committee of the North had disapproved of shamanism, viewing it as an impediment to social progress in the North.[84] But Glavsevmorput's antipathy was not merely a function of the general Marxist line against religion; the agency feared the shamans as a potential source of opposition and resistance. Glavsevmorput also seemed to be afraid of the shamans' influence on the Russians themselves; at least one political inspector reported that local shamans were plying young GUSMP personnel with alcohol and, worse yet, narcotics.[85]

Whatever the case, GUSMP came down as hard as it could on shamanistic practices. Just as Party activists in other parts of the USSR shot guns into the sky or
took worshipers for airplane rides to "prove" that there were no gods or angels in
the heavens, polar explorers and cultural workers campaigned against native religion in the Arctic. In one incident, reminiscent of the ruse used by Mark
Twain's Connecticut Yankee, a cultural worker consulted an almanac to predict
an eclipse of the moon and thus embarrass a Chukchi shaman.[86] Georgy
Ushakov proved exceptionally adept at discrediting the shamans of Wrangel Island. On one occasion, he pretended to be a demon; unsurprisingly, the
shaman's attempts to exorcise him failed. Another time, Ushakov faked his own
death then rose from his "deathbed" and killed a bear, proving that he was
stronger than the grave itself.[87]

Far more important than religious matters was the place of the native Siberians in the economy of the North. After 1935, Glavsevmorput pressed on with its
efforts to organize the natives' reindeer, fur, fishing, and hunting industries. The
most sensitive issue involved the small peoples' reindeer herds. As noted in chapter 1, over 600,000 reindeer died as a result of collectivization between 1927 and
1933. Numbers had recovered somewhat by 1934, increasing to 1.9 million, and
GUSMP's task was to help the small peoples replenish their herds. Glavsevmorput
took over the eighteen reindeer sovkhozy that had been built in 1929. But since
the state farms were the last institutions that the Siberians were inclined to trust
with their reindeer, GUSMP put more emphasis on support centers and aid stations geared to providing veterinary assistance. Twenty-six of these centers were
maintained by the VAI; whether the small peoples took advantage of them is
unclear.[88]

The native Siberians' other "industries" were an exasperation for GUSMP.
When it came to hunting, fishing, and trapping, the small peoples had in their
favor methods honed by centuries of experience, even though they were disad-
vantaged by their low level of technological advancement. The Soviets, however,
considered the natives' economic production to be flawed, because it lacked systematic organization and financial rationality. The Committee of the North had
tried to introduce the small peoples to Soviet methodology by means of the Integral Cooperatives, an exchange system created to unify the natives' economic
activities into a single whole and make them profitable. As Pyotr Smidovich
explained:

> All industries in the North are mutually related to each other. Products of various
> industries are exchanged for other goods needed by natives of one and the same co-
> operative. All this is tied up in a single system; hence the unified network of coop-
> eratives.[89]

In the end, the system of Integral Cooperatives proved unworkable. So when
GUSMP assumed control of the northern territories, it dissolved the cooperatives
and tried a more effective—and more ruthless—tack. Rather than rehabilitating
the economic practices of the small peoples, Glavsevmorput chose to ignore
them, relying on its own fish, fur, and hunting departments. Glavsevmorput's
policy put it in direct competition with the native Siberians for a limited set of re-

sources, and there was no question as to who would win. Better equipped and far more numerous, Soviet hunters, trappers, and fishermen muscled the small peoples out of their traditional modes of subsistence. The agency continued to mouth the standard rhetoric about the amicable relationship between the Russians and the natives, but reality was quite different. In one example, a political worker inspecting the fur centers of the Yamal Peninsula noted that GUSMP blithely ignored its contracts with Nenets and Khanty traders and hunters. Unfortunately for natives throughout the Arctic, this was hardly an isolated instance.[90]

On the whole, the Soviet relationship with the native Siberians worsened over time. As patronizing as it sometimes had been, the Committee of the North had had the welfare of the small peoples at heart. Glavsevmorput, with its vested interest in strengthening the Russian presence in the Arctic, showed little patience toward the natives. And so the Russians kept coming, heedless of the natives or consciously determined to sweep them aside. By 1940, imported cattle outnumbered domestic reindeer in the Arctic. The population of the Russians themselves dwarfed the small peoples' miniscule numbers. In 1926, there were 650,000 Russians in the North; by 1937, that number more than doubled to 1.4 million.[91] As they arrived, the Russians treated the native Siberians in much the same way that colonizers everywhere tend to treat indigenous peoples: they plied them with cheap alcohol, took liberties with the women, disparaged customs and rituals, and interfered with traditional livelihoods. In a contemporary Siberian folktale collected by an ethnographer in the Zhdanikh region, the coming of the Soviets presaged dark times for the local natives: the exile of their shamans, the slaughter of their deer, mass starvation, and even cannibalism.[92] Indeed, as one scholar notes, for all the claims that the USSR made about bringing civilization to the North, the difference between socialist-style "development" and great-power "colonization" was merely a semantic distinction—and a thin one at best.[93]

The Question of Agriculture

In a speech delivered to the Seventeenth Party Congress in February 1934, Stalin himself sent out a warning directed at least partly to the Soviet Arctic:

> It must be remembered that the old division of industrial and agricultural regions has outlived itself. Each region must establish within itself its own agricultural base so as to have its own vegetables, potatoes, butter, milk, and, to a certain degree, its own grain and meat. It must do this if it does not wish to find itself in a difficult situation.[94]

The message was clear: areas like the North needed to start relying more on themselves for their food supplies. Thus, agricultural production became one of Glavsevmorput's most important priorities—or at least one of its greatest anxieties.

Concerns about agriculture were motivated by the fact that shipping foodstuffs to the Arctic was horribly expensive, especially with the Russian population there growing steadily. To reduce costs, the regime wanted the Arctic to become as self-sufficient as possible. This was not as quixotic as one might initially suppose. The North was divisible into three agronomic zones; only in the northernmost, where crops and livestock could not survive without special facilities, was full-scale agricultural production too difficult to contemplate. The middle zone lay just above the Arctic Circle, and, with care, it was possible to grow potatoes and certain green vegetables in the open. The lowest zone was able to sustain a surprising variety of plant life. Shmidt agreed with Stalin that the Arctic territories should learn how to feed themselves (what choice was there?), and GUSMP, with help from the Lenin Academy of Agricultural Sciences, rushed to comply with the agricultural policies handed down by the regime.[95]

Having inherited forty-one state farms and six collective farms from Narkomzem, GUSMP's Department of Agricultural Economy experimented with various crops and animals, trying to discover which were suitable for cultivation or husbandry in the Arctic. Eventually, Glavsevmorput found a number of breeds of cattle, poultry, swine, beets, turnips, potatoes, and even grains that could withstand the harsh conditions of the North. But despite wildly inflated claims, the agency's agricultural successes were modest.[96] As one of GUSMP's more sober experts noted, animal husbandry in the Arctic was "negligible," while most vegetable growth was produced by amateur farmers and gardeners.[97] In 1937, Nikolai Yanson was forced to admit that, since 1933, the agency had sown no more than 3,242 acres throughout its entire territory. Furthermore, the grand total of cattle and pigs living on GUSMP's farms came to 2,469 and 2,802, respectively.[98]

As scanty as such results might seem, especially when GUSMP was spending over 7 million rubles annually on agriculture by 1937, the gains were quite noteworthy when viewed in their context. There were obvious problems, of course, and progress was painfully slow. In 1933–1934, by special decree, Sovnarkom and the Party Central Committee lowered (and, in some cases, canceled altogether) agricultural production norms in Eastern Siberia and the DVK; to make up for the resulting shortfall, Western Siberia was called upon to meet higher quotas than originally planned.[99] All the same, to make the ice-blasted, frost-laden soil of the Arctic support any kind of agricultural base was an admirable achievement—even if Glavsevmorput never got the chance to follow through on it.

Transport: A Balance Sheet

As always, the success or failure of any venture in the Arctic, be it seal hunting, the construction of an elementary school, or mining for graphite, depended on transport. Accordingly, Glavsevmorput's chances of completing the myriad of tasks alloted to it rested on its ability to move in the Arctic and, more specifically, to live up to its less-than-rousing official motto: "to transform the Northern Sea Route into a normal and operational waterway!" From 1933 to the end of 1936, GUSMP made headway in building and articulating its transportational network; Table 2.3 shows how the agency enjoyed a steady rate of growth in this area. Nei-

Table 2.3   Air, Sea, and River Traffic in GUSMP Territory, 1933–1936

	Air Traffic (hours)	Sea Cargo (tons)	River Cargo (tons)
1933	512	136,100	57,300
1934	8,900	156,300	84,800
1935	n/d	230,000	125,000
1936	10,900	271,100	160,000

Source: N. M. Ianson, "Plan raboty Glavsevmorputi v 1937 godu," SA 3, vol. 2 (February 1937): 14–23; RT-skhIDNI, f. 475, op. 1, d. 10, ll. 241–245.

ther did GUSMP skimp where transport was concerned. Table 2.4 illustrates the growing level of its capital investment in transport-related activities. Glavsevmorput placed its greatest emphasis on marine transport, focusing above all else on the Northern Sea Route. In 1934, the icebreaker *Litke* traveled through the Route from Vladivostok to Murmansk without incident, repeating in reverse the triumph of the *Sibiriakov* two years earlier. In 1935, four vessels (the *Vanzetti*, *Iskra*, *Anadyr*, and *Stalingrad*), none of them specially equipped for polar voyaging, traversed the entire route, under icebreaker escort. In 1936, the number of ships navigating the whole route rose to fourteen.

On paper, there was also progress on the rivers. In 1936, GUSMP claimed to have significantly extended the navigable lengths of each of the major Siberian arteries: according to agency statistics, 3,371 miles of the Yenisei were open to traffic (up from 1,992 miles in 1935); 2,419 miles of the Lena (up from 1,309 miles); and 1,627 miles of the Ob-Irtysh (no change).[100] And, as noted in Table 2.3, the level of freight moving on the rivers went up as well.

The most dramatic advances came in the young field of aviation. Efforts to incorporate the airplane into Soviet polar work had paid off, and Glavsevmorput took as much advantage of its pilots and aircraft as it could. By 1936, GUSMP had 125 airplanes stabled full-time in the Arctic, up from only six in 1932.[101] Moscow and Leningrad were already connected with Arkhangelsk, Murmansk, Irkutsk, Vladivostok, Khabarovsk, Yakutsk, and Kamchatka. By 1937, Glavsevmorput intended to have in place additional routes that would link these points with others

Table 2.4   Capital Investment in Glavsevmorput Transport (in millions of rubles)

	Transport Proper	Hydrography	Polar/Radio Stations	Air Service
1933	6.00	0.151	3.62	3.00
1934	11.10	0.599	4.94	5.34
1935	56.87	1.88	4.32	8.47
1936	85.70	1.90	5.40	14.30

Source: G. Gurari, "Nashe kapital'noe stroitel'stvo," SA 2, vol. 1 (January 1936): 109.

Table 2.5   The Progress of Glavsevmorput Aviation Activities, by Function, 1932–1936

	1932	1933	1934	1935	1936
Flying time (hours)	570	1,413	2,766	8,954	20,118
Distance flown (miles)	56,100	138,656	271,480	858,436	2,017,183
Mail carried (pounds)	17	785	6,065	22,367	67,921
Passengers carried	123	374	645	2,811	5,423
Freight carried (pounds)	1,512	8,877	16,690	57,007	90,732
Scientific work (hours)	n/d	134	101	1,488	2,253
Ice patrol (hours)	n/d	171	247	587	1,442

Source: A. Iu. Libman, "Samolet na sluzhbe Severnogo Morskogo Puti," SA 3, vol. 2 (February 1937): 44.

along the entire Arctic coastline, as well as the Siberian rivers.[102] The volume of polar aviation increased as well (see Table 2.5).

In January 1936, Otto Shmidt declared that Glavsevmorput was ready to move on to a new stage in developing the Arctic.[103] This was no mere propaganda claim. On all fronts—the sea, rivers, and skies—the agency could point to a variety of improvements and innovations. As an attractive backdrop to its day-to-day work, GUSMP also had its glamorous exploits, the high-publicity expeditions that made its name a household word. By this point, the Soviet North was even home to the world's first polar railroad project. In 1935, engineers began to lay track for the first railway in history intended for use above the Arctic Circle: the Dudinka-Norilsk line, designed to link the mining complex of Norilsk with the mouth of the Yenisei. The first leg of the railroad—constructed, tragically, by means of forced labor—was open for use by May 1937; the entire route was completed from 1940 to 1942.[104]

Still, Shmidt's remarks were somewhat premature. Much of Glavsevmorput's success with the Northern Sea Route was due as much to luck as it was to the agency's hard work or skill. Certainly the route was not yet as docile or reliable as Shmidt claimed it to be; ample proof of this would come in 1937, when the route gave GUSMP some very hard times indeed. River transport was riddled with problems; one official remarked that difficulties on the rivers were "our agency's greatest handicap," and Shmidt himself admitted that river activity was "lagging."[105] Even the Polar Aviation Administration had its own troubles. Flying in the Arctic was dangerous business, and if Glavsevmorput's pilots were conquering the polar skies, it was at the cost of many accidents and much material damage. Worse than this was the fact that the quality of GUSMP's work could not be measured in numbers alone. It did little good for a ship or airplane to travel hundreds of miles, braving glacial floes or polar storms, only to arrive with its cargo missing, spoiled, or misdirected. And yet shortcomings like these plagued Glavsevmorput's work constantly; if the agency was to bring about genuine success in the Arctic, it badly needed to eliminate such problems. Shmidt was by no means unaware of these deficiencies, and he promised that they would be overcome before the end of the Second Five-Year Plan.[106]

Within two years, it had become clear that Shmidt was unable to make good on his pledge. This was partially because Glavsevmorput had overreached itself; in expanding its power, it had also given itself too heavy a load to bear. In addition, Shmidt's preoccupation with GUSMP's great heroics of 1937 diverted his attention away from the everyday workings of his agency, just as it entered the worst crisis of its history. Most of all, the state simply asked for too much from Glavsevmorput. Moscow envisioned a great tide sweeping inexorably across the North; by contrast, GUSMP was only able to wash over the region in a gentle wave. One evaluation of the Stalinist economy refers to Soviet transport work as a "triumph with reservations," and this serves as a fair description of Glavsevmorput's efforts as well.[107] On the whole, the agency was moving in the right direction, and, as the next chapter shows, it was involved in a number of record-breaking feats considered in their day to be without compare. But it could not live up to the burdens imposed upon it by the regime. Moscow wanted a perfect record in the Arctic, and it wanted increased tempos. The drumbeats of its commands came faster and faster, until GUSMP finally stumbled. Long-term progress the Arctic giant might have been able to deliver. Perfection and speed it could not, and in the end, this was its undoing.

Figure 1. The seven "hero-pilots" after the *Cheliuskin* rescue. V. S. Molokov (*top*);
M. T. Slepnev, M. V. Vodopianov, N. P. Kamanin (*middle*); S. A. Levanevsky, A. V.
Liapidevsky, I. V. Doronin (*bottom*). From E. T. Krenkel', *RAEM Is My Call-Sign*
(Moscow: Progress, 1972), appendix.

Друж. шарж Бор. ПРОРОКОВА

Figure 2. *Ded-Moroz* Shmidt: Otto Shmidt as Grandfather Frost. From *Komsomol'skaia pravda*, 30 December 1935.

WELL, LOOK WHO IS HERE!

Figure 3. "Well, Look Who Is Here!" America's anxiety about Soviet successes in the Arctic. From *Polar Times* (5 October 1937): 6.

В новогоднюю ночь на станции „Северный полюс"

Figure 4. New Year's Eve at the North Pole Station. From *Izvestiia*, 1 January 1938.

Figure 5. "Stalin and the Arctic": publicity poster for the USSR's Pavilion of the Arctic at the 1939 World's Fair. From *Soviet Aviation* (Moscow and Leningrad: State Art Publishers, 1939).

Figure 6. "The Stalin Airway": M. M. Gromov, A. B. Yumashev, and S. A. Danilin. From *Soviet Aviation* (Moscow and Leningrad: State Art Publishers, 1939).

Figure 7. "On the Roof of the World": sketch of Otto Shmidt by Fedor Reshetnikov. From *Otto Iul'evich Shmidt: Zhizn' i deiatel'nost'* (Moscow: Nauka, 1959), 343.

Figure 8. "Entourage": sketch of Otto Shmidt by Fedor Reshetnikov (modeled after Valentin Serov's portrait *Peter the Great*). From *Otto Iul'evich Shmidt: Zhizn' i deiatel'nost'* (Moscow: Nauka, 1959), 349.

Figure 9. "The Son Greets His Father": V. P. Chkalov embracing Stalin at Moscow's Central Aerodrome (also pictured: Lazar Kaganovich, Sergo Ordzhonikidze, G. F. Baidukov). From *Pravda*, 11 August 1936.

Figure 10. "The Kiss": Otto Shmidt embracing Stalin on Red Square. From *Pravda*, 26 June 1937.

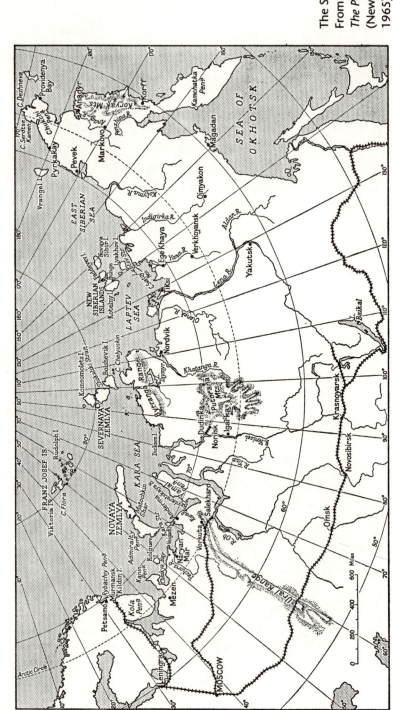

The Soviet Arctic. From P. D. Baird, *The Polar World* (New York: Wiley, 1965), 212.

THREE

Days of Glory
The Major Expeditions, 1932–1939

The Arctic flights are known to everybody. These high points speak for a whole mountain chain of achievements.

—Leon Trotsky

One envies a country that has such heroes; one envies heroes who have such a country.

—*Pravda* headline celebrating the *Cheliuskin* rescues

During the 1930s, there were, in effect, two Arctics that existed in the USSR. The first was the Arctic described in the previous chapters: the Arctic of blunders, crime, and substandard living conditions. This was the grim Arctic of prison-camp labor. It was a rough-hewn region in which the Soviets could—and did—inch forward, but only by means of trial, error, and painstaking effort. It was also a behind-the-scenes Arctic that remained very much hidden from the Soviet public.

The second Arctic, by contrast, was never absent from public view. This was the heroic Arctic, infused with glory, and it was paraded endlessly before the Soviet citizenry in every conceivable way. Through a process discussed at length in chapters 4 and 5, this public image of the Soviet Arctic became a bold, larger-than-life epic. And, of course, this Arctic—the one intended for popular consumption—was simply too good to be true.

All the same, the Soviets did not create a Potemkin village out of the Arctic—at least not completely. The actual substance of this mythic Arctic was drawn from real-life events, in the form of half a dozen major polar expeditions that took place between 1932 and 1939. The images and details of these high-profile exploits were woven together into an almost seamless narrative that depicted the USSR's campaign in the Arctic as a grand adventure with a suitably (and predictably) inspirational ending. Obviously, there were discrepancies and fabrications. But the expeditions themselves did take place, and they were impressive accomplishments. And to this day, they still remain prominent moments in the overall history of the Soviet Union.

The *Sibiriakov* Voyage (1932)

In 1932, the USSR joined the rest of the world in celebrating the Second International Polar Year. To mark the occasion, the Soviets planned an extensive battery of expeditions, but the climax was to be a special tour de force: the world's first single-season crossing of the Northeast Passage. Only three mariners—Nordenskjöld, Vilkitsky, and Amundsen—had ever piloted ships through the passage, and none had been able to do so without spending at least one winter locked in the Arctic ice. If the Soviets could complete a voyage through the passage in one season, not only would it be a historical first, it also would signal that the USSR was ready to move on with its efforts to make the Northeast Passage into a commercially viable seaway.

Otto Shmidt and Vladimir Vize began to plan a traversal of Russia's northern coast as early as 1930. In 1932, Shmidt received governmental approval for his proposal and permission to use the ice-forcing ship *Sibiriakov*. The ship was placed under the command of Vladimir Voronin, the skilled Arctic captain who had taken Shmidt to Franz Josef Land and Severnaia Zemlia in 1929 and 1930. Carrying almost fifty people, along with enough food for at least a year and a half, the *Sibiriakov* set sail from Arkhangelsk on 28 July 1932, starting a three-and-a-half-month journey that would change the face of Soviet polar exploration for years to come.[1]

At first, the *Sibiriakov* enjoyed optimal sailing conditions. The weather was good, and the ship reached its first destination, Dikson Island, quickly and easily. From Dikson, the *Sibiriakov* went on to Severnaia Zemlia, where it relieved the four station members who had been living there since 1930. The base was led by Georgy Ushakov and Nikolai Urvantsev; known widely as the Castor and Pollux of the Arctic, the two geologists were indefatigable veterans of the North, each with several two- and three-winter marathon expeditions under his belt. The Severnaia Zemlia team joined the *Sibiriakov*, while their replacements went ashore. Afterward, the ship went on to the mouth of the Lena, entering the docks of Tiksi Bay on 30 August.

It was after crossing into the East Siberian Sea that the *Sibiriakov* first encountered trouble. The weather grew colder, storms appeared more frequently, and, worst of all, the ice grew thicker. By the first week of September, explosives were needed to move forward. When the ship got stuck—as it did with increasing regularity—the crew would drill holes into the ice and fill them with ammonal. Scampering back to safety (and hoping that they had not placed the charges too close to the ship's hull), the crew would detonate the charges and try to move on.

Stopping to blast pathways through the ice slowed the *Sibiriakov* down, but the ship was still able to continue. On 10 September, however, disaster struck. After a crunching noise audible to everyone on board, the ship came to a dead halt. Upon investigation, it was found that half the blades on the ship's propellor had been sheared off by underwater ice. There were spare blades on board, but the propellor screw needed to be above the waterline in order for the blades to be replaced. After mulling over the problem, Shmidt and Voronin hit upon a solution. Shmidt ordered every ounce of the ship's coal supply to be shifted as far forward as possible, in order to weigh down the boat's bow. After an exhausting day of shoveling coal, the crew was overjoyed to see the ship's stern finally rise above the water's surface. Following a quick repair job, the *Sibiriakov* was back on its way.

But not for long. Just days later, only a hundred miles from the Bering Straits, gears grinded, metal shrieked, and the ship's engine came to a stop for a second time. The damage now was even more severe: the entire propellor shaft—a steel rod seventeen inches thick—had snapped off completely after colliding with a large floe beneath the surface. The engine was totally useless, and it appeared that the *Sibiriakov*'s voyage had come to a premature end.

Luckily, a large supply of thick, heavy black tarpaulin had been stowed on board—large enough, in fact, to fashion an effective, if somewhat crude, sail. When the makeshift mast was set in place, the *Sibiriakov* looked like a slightly delapidated pirate schooner from days long past, but it could at least move. At the less than dizzying speed of nine miles a day, the *Sibiriakov* successfully crawled the rest of its way through the East Siberian and Chukchi seas. On 1 October, the weary ship drifted into the Bering Straits, fulfilling its task and guaranteeing its place in the record books.

Its journey through the passage completed, the *Sibiriakov* could now accept assistance without compromising the integrity of its mission. Once into the straits, the crippled vessel arranged to be towed to Petropavlovsk-na-Kamchatke for resupplying, then to Yokohama for repairs. The ship reached Japan on 11 November; the expedition members spent a few days in Tokyo as guests of the Japanese government, then boarded a steamer for Vladivostok. From there, the crew of the *Sibiriakov* traded their ship's berths for the comparative luxury of the Trans-Siberian Railway; they arrived in Moscow weeks later and entered the capital as heroes. If the voyage of the *Sibiriakov* was at an end, however, the chain of events it had set into motion had only begun. Not only did the mission give birth to Glavsevmorput and change irrevocably how the Soviets conducted affairs in the North, but, just as important, it inspired the many polar exploits that would follow before the decade was out.

The *Cheliuskin* Epic (1933–1934)

Emboldened by the success of the *Sibiriakov* voyage, Shmidt decided to attempt a second traversal of the Northeast Passage the following year. In doing so, Shmidt hoped to put to rest lingering doubts about the efficacy of the Northern Sea Route as a navigational artery. Weather conditions in 1932 had been unusually favorable, and there were skeptics who suggested that the *Sibiriakov*'s success was a fluke, nothing more. In addition, Shmidt, mindful of how the *Sibiriakov* mission had started something of an Arctic craze in the USSR, intended to use this second expedition as a means of enhancing his reputation, as well as that of his new agency. And so, in July 1933, Shmidt, along with 111 crew members and passengers, set sail for Vladivostok in the *Cheliuskin*, in what would become at once the most harrowing and the most triumphant of the USSR's ventures into the Arctic.[2]

Everything about the *Cheliuskin* voyage was bigger and better than the *Sibiri-akov's*. The vessel had 112 people on board: 53 crew members, led by Captain Voronin; 29 scientific personnel; 18 explorers bound for the polar station on Wrangel Island; and a construction brigade of 12. The ship's complement included 10 women and 1 girl, and it would grow to 113 in August, when a daughter was born to one of the scientists on the way to Wrangel. This second child was named Karina, in honor of her birthplace, the Kara Sea, and she became an unofficial mascot for the so-called Cheliuskinites (*Cheliuskintsy*). The airplane attached to the ship was a Sh-2, the most advanced amphibious aircraft in the USSR; it was piloted by Mikhail Babushkin, one of the country's most experienced Arctic fliers. The *Cheliuskin* carried 3,500 tons of coal and an 18-month inventory of supplies that amounted to 850 tons.

The only questionable aspect of the mission was the ship itself. To this day, it remains a mystery as to why the *Cheliuskin* was chosen for the voyage. The *Cheliuskin* (originally the *Lena*) was not an icebreaker or part of Glavsevmorput's fleet. Newly built for the Soviet government by the Danish firm Burmeister, the *Cheliuskin* had nothing to recommend it for Arctic navigation. Its hull was sparsely ribbed and far too thin, its bow wide and squarish. When Captain Voronin inspected the boat upon its arrival in the Leningrad shipyards, he made no secret of his disappointment and, at first, refused categorically to have anything to do with the voyage. Only because of his friendship with Shmidt did he allow himself to be persuaded to help lead the expedition. One of Voronin's conditions for accepting command of the *Cheliuskin* was that an extra layer of plating be added to the hull. The alteration was made, but it was hardly enough to compensate for the ship's shortcomings.

Why, then, was the *Cheliuskin* chosen as the most important element of an expedition in which so much was at stake? There has never been a satisfactory answer. Ernst Krenkel, the ship's radioman, states in his memoirs that the *Cheliuskin* was simply the largest vessel that could be spared from its economic duties in 1933, and there is other evidence, most notably GUSMP's perpetual shortage of ships, to support this assertion.[3] However, both before and after the voyage, Shmidt declared that he and the Soviet authorities had purposely chosen to use an ordinary ship for the mission, on the grounds that the voyage would be more meaningful if a normal vessel proved able to sail freely through the Northern Sea Route.[4] If Krenkel is correct, then Shmidt was forced by circumstance or government dictate to make use of a ship he was unhappy with—and was making a virtue out of necessity in his remarks.[5] If, on the other hand, Shmidt was sincere about using a boat meant only for warm-water travel deliberately to test the Soviets' skill in negotiating the route, then he—or somebody—was taking a frightful risk, all for the sake of increasing the demonstrative value of the voyage. The former scenario seems more plausible, but either way the *Cheliuskin* mission, by virtue of the ship's many obvious flaws, was a gamble and one in which over 100 men, women, and children nearly lost their lives.

Whatever the case, the *Cheliuskin* left Leningrad on 12 July amid great fanfare. Almost immediately, however, trouble with the throttle forced the ship to make a short stop in Copenhagen, site of its manufacture, to have its engine rehauled.

Next, the *Cheliuskin* steamed through the North Sea, rounded the northern tip of Scandinavia, and sailed into the port of Murmansk for a short rest. Then, very gingerly, the ship began its trek into the Arctic Ocean. Its first encounter with the Kara pack ice was not encouraging; some of the plating in the bow was damaged. Babushkin's Sh-2, which was supposed to help with ice reconnaissance, spent more time under repair than in the skies. Still, the *Cheliuskin* pushed on, trusting to the fact that icebreaker assistance had been promised in the event of trouble. After leaving Murmansk, the ship headed for Novaia Zemlia. On 1 September, the ship crested the Taimyr, sailing past Cape Cheliuskin, the northernmost point on the Eurasian continent. Crossing the Laptev Sea proved relatively easy, but there was now worrisome news about what lay ahead. Bad weather was brewing in the East Siberian and Chukchi seas, and the *Cheliuskin* could expect extremely adverse ice conditions. To make things worse, two of the three icebreakers upon which Shmidt was counting if things went wrong, the *Lenin* and the *Krasin*, had been deactivated for repairs; the third, the *Litke*, was operational, but barely.

As expected, the *Cheliuskin* was pummeled by heavy ice in the East Siberian Sea, where 90 percent of the water's surface was covered by drifting floes. Here, the ship's progress slowed considerably, since Voronin was forced to be, in his own words, "dainty" with the ice. Had the *Cheliuskin* been a proper icebreaker, Voronin could have attacked the ice aggressively, counting on momentum and the hull's strength to cut through the frozen crust. Instead, he had to pick his way through the ice with extreme care. The situation grew more dire in the Chukchi Sea, as the autumn weather grew colder. The ship was burning through its coal supply too quickly, so to conserve fuel, the temperature in the ship's cabins was kept below 50 degrees Fahrenheit; as leader, Shmidt set an example by keeping his berth coldest of all. Concerned about the reserves of food and potable water, Shmidt decided to set eight of the Cheliuskinites—individuals who were ill or whose functions were redundant—ashore at Wellen. Shortly afterward, Shmidt's fears were confirmed; in mid-October, off Cape Serdtse-Kamen, only a little more than 100 miles from the Bering Straits, the ship became locked in the tight embrace of the drifting ice. The floes were carrying the *Cheliuskin* eastward, toward the straits, but the ship itself was out of control, and there was no way of knowing whether the ice would continue flowing in the right direction.

For the next two and a half weeks, the Cheliuskinites were tantalized by the hope that prevailing currents might take them to the east, then to the south—and gradually to safety. On 4 November, the *Cheliuskin* actually drifted into the Pacific Ocean (technically fulfilling its mission of negotiating the route before the year was up, although this was hardly the matter foremost in anyone's mind). But then the ship's luck ran out, and the tide, quite literally, turned. By the second week of November, the *Cheliuskin* was drifting backward, to the northwest. On the 14th, Shmidt and Voronin radioed the *Litke* for help. Unfortunately, the *Litke*'s engines were operating at half capacity, and it had to halt 35 miles short of the *Cheliuskin*'s position. The expedition leaders toyed with the idea of ferrying passengers by sled to the *Litke*, but after a few impromptu experiments, which involved attempts to haul brick-laden sleds across the broken floes, they opted to stay with their ship. On 17 November, Shmidt and Voronin made the painful decision to allow the *Litke* to go back to safe harbor. The icebreaker bade farewell to the *Cheliuskin* on the 19th, heading for port to avoid becoming trapped itself.

Over the course of the next three months, the *Cheliuskin* was on its own, as the ice took it on an erratic journey through the Chukchi Sea. And the situation grew even worse. In February 1934, the Cheliuskinites faced the most dreadful catastrophe imaginable: confined for weeks on end in its icy straitjacket, the ship's hull began to weaken perceptibly. Although there was no telling exactly when, it was clear that the sides of the boat would soon buckle completely. Voronin placed the ship's crew on alert, and Shmidt ordered that every piece of equipment on board be prepared for rapid evacuation. The precautions paid off. On 13 February, the ice tore a huge gash in the engine room's forward hold. With its hull punctured, the *Cheliuskin* began to sink.

The Cheliuskinites had just over two hours to get off the ship and remove the gear they needed to survive in the polar wilderness. Every member of the crew rushed to unload tents, blankets, food, heating equipment, construction materials, radios, and everything else they could get their hands on before the vessel went down. Unfortunately, one Cheliuskinite was unable to make his escape in the last moments. Ship's quartermaster Boris Mogilevsky, who had stayed on board until the end, stumbled over a loose barrel as he dashed toward the exit. He hit his head against a beam, knocking himself into a daze, and before anyone could take action to help him, the *Cheliuskin's* stern suddenly heaved into the air. Seconds later, the ship slid out of sight, leaving only a patch of greenish, oily water yawning open, almost tauntingly, in the middle of the ice.

The sinking of the *Cheliuskin* left 104 people, including a young girl and a baby, stranded in a desolate wilderness. The situation, however, was not hopeless: the Cheliuskinites had the food, clothing, and shelter necessary to survive, at least for the moment. In a matter of hours, the castaways assembled a cluster of tents and barracks they named "Camp Shmidt" after their leader. The camp was not excessively far from the Russian coastline; the ship had gone down at a point 155 miles from North Cape (later renamed Cape Shmidt in honor of the event) and 144 miles from Wellen. Most important, the Cheliuskinites had salvaged all the radio equipment they needed to stay in constant contact with the mainland. Still, their predicament was hardly an enviable one. It was the dead of winter, the camp's food supply was anything but bountiful, and the constant shifting of the pack ice made for the very real possibility that crevasses might swallow up the camp altogether.

Upon receiving news of the disaster, the central authorities formed a special body to plan a response. This was the Extraordinary Government Commission for the Assistance of the Cheliuskinites, led by Valerian Kuibyshev, deputy head of Sovnarkom. Kuibyshev was joined by S. S. Ioffe, deputy head of Glavsevmorput; Nikolai Yanson, still at Narkomvod; Sergei Kamenev; and Iosif Unshlikht, head of the Soviet Air Fleet. Georgy Ushakov flew to the Arctic coast to coordinate the rescue locally with the aid of North Cape station head G. G. Petrov.[6]

How were the Cheliuskinites to be saved? No obvious solution presented itself. The government detailed the *Krasin*, *Lenin*, and *Litke* to sail to Camp Shmidt, but there was little hope that any of them would be able to break through before late spring. Could parties on dogsleds or foot reach the castaways? Possibly, but the commission discarded the idea of surface travel as too risky. The only option remaining was to extract the Cheliuskinites by air. Unfortunately, only four aircraft were stationed on the Chukchi Peninsula. In addition, the February weather was less than ideal for Arctic flying, and it was impossible to guess whether aircraft would be able to land on the treacherous surface of the oceanic ice floes. But the commission was left with no choice, so it activated as many pilots as it could to fly to the castaways' outpost and attempt to land there.

During the following weeks, over a dozen aviators made sortie after sortie into the Arctic skies, trying to reach Camp Shmidt. At the same time, the entire country watched and waited with breathless anticipation for daily updates on the rescue efforts and the condition of the Cheliuskinites themselves. The international community also looked on with sympathy. In particular, the United States expressed its condolences and offered to send out rescue missions to supplement the Soviets' efforts. The USSR declined the favor. Officially, Stalin declared it a matter of honor that Soviet pilots should rescue Soviet explorers, but there was an unstated reason as well. The Kremlin was afraid that American pilots might stumble across yet another stranded ship: the *Dzhurma*, a Dalstroi prison steamer bound for Magadan. Allegedly, the *Dzhurma* had 12,000 convicts packed into its holds when it became trapped in the ice less than 200 miles from Camp Shmidt. If the rumors are true, the ship's fate was a gruesome one: all the prisoners were said to have died of hypothermia or starvation, and every member of the crew supposedly went irretrievably insane.[7] The grislier aspects of the tale aside, the Soviets had plenty of reason to fear international embarrassment if American pilots started soaring over the Chukchi Sea while there was a prison vessel wintering in the area.

However, the USSR did accept the further offer of the United States to allow Soviet pilots to fly search missions from Alaska. Mavriki Slepnev and Sigismund Levanevsky were sent to Fairbanks, via Western Europe and the continental United States (it was a sad comment on the state of Soviet transport, of course, that it was faster for the two pilots to travel halfway around the globe than to cross their own country). In Alaska, Slepnev and Levanevsky leased two Consolidated Fleetsters and began to search for Camp Shmidt from the east. The rest of the Soviet rescue group flew from Russia's north coast, using Vankarem and Wellen as their bases. For almost a month, the pilots braved the Arctic winter, trying to force their way through blizzards and fogbanks to Camp Shmidt, but to no avail.

In the meantime, Camp Shmidt became a busy community. The castaways' most important task, aside from keeping themselves fed, clothed, and housed, was to construct a makeshift airfield to accommodate the pilots coming to rescue them. The twelve-man construction crew, along with as many members of the camp as could be spared, labored to smooth out a solid sheet of ice 150 yards wide and 600 yards long. Reserve landing strips had to be built as well, in case the ice shifted and caused cracks in the main field (by April, a total of thirteen airfields were carved out of the snow). Scientific personnel continued with their own work, partially for the sake of the research itself but primarily to assist the pilots on the mainland with meteorological and locational data.

Accounts of everyday life at Camp Shmidt are uniformly positive. Nowhere will one find an instance of shirking or selfishness, a case of grumbling or complaint, or a quiver of fear or anxiety—not even a sniffly nose. The Cheliuskinites deserve credit for the courage and stamina they displayed while stranded on the ice, but the officially sanctioned images of their experience are clearly glamorized (for reasons discussed in chapters 4 and 5). Morale at Camp Shmidt was portrayed as invariably high. The mood was said to have been improved by the presence of a large number of Communist Party members, led by Ivan Baevsky, Ilya Kopusov, and Alexei Bobrov. After a full day of hard work, with perhaps a sports event thrown in for good measure, the Cheliuskinites entertained themselves in a variety of ways. There were domino games in one tent; another, home to the camp's gramophone, might be wafting out the strains of a Tchaikovsky symphony or a Josephine Baker tune. Denizens of Camp Shmidt could also attend the Party cell's nightly lectures, which covered a range of scintillating topics, from economic geography and German poetry to the resolutions of the Seventeenth Party Congress. They could help put together the camp newspaper, *We Will Not Surrender!*[8] Or they could enjoy readings from one of the four books that had been saved: Longfellow's *Hiawatha*, Knut Hamsun's *Pan*; the third volume of Mikhail Sholokhov's *Quiet Flows the Don*; and, best of all, an anthology of poetry by Pushkin.

The boundless attractions of the Camp Shmidt experience notwithstanding, the Cheliuskinites still had to attend to the business of getting rescued. March brought with it mixed blessings. The arrival of spring meant that pilots would have an easier time reaching Camp Shmidt. On the other hand, by softening the surface of the pack ice, higher temperatures might compromise the integrity of the landing strips that the Cheliuskinites had built. Also, since warmer weather led to increased ice movement, the camp ran the very real risk of being completely destroyed by rifts and crevasses. With these dangers in mind, the Cheliuskinites stepped up their plans for evacuation. Shmidt had already drawn up an airlift list, detailing in what order each member of the expedition was to be flown out of the camp. First came the two children; next, much to their indignation, were the female Cheliuskinites, who protested in vain that their gender should have no correlation to their placement on the list.[9] After that, Shmidt based his assignments on the age, health, and job of each expedition member. As leader of the party, Shmidt put himself at the bottom of the list, as evacuee 104.

The airlifts finally got underway during the first week of March. After twenty-eight failed attempts to reach the castaways' camp, Alexander Liapidevsky finally touched down on Camp Shmidt's primitive airfield; it was 5 March. Following a brief celebration, the women and children piled into Liapidevsky's ANT-4. A few tense moments came next, as everyone watched to see if the aircraft, encumbered by its human cargo, would be able to take off from the ice. There was a loud cheer as the plane rose into the air, then the pilot and his passengers were off to Vankarem. And so Liapidevsky became the first of the seven hero-pilots associated with the *Cheliuskin* rescue. He also became known as "the ladies' man," not only because he had rescued all twelve of the female Cheliuskinites but because the comely, unmarried pilot reportedly received "letters by the basketful" from young women for years afterward.[10]

Although Liapidevsky never returned to Camp Shmidt—on his next flight out, he crash-landed near the coast and spent several weeks in a Chukchi village—he had proven that the Cheliuskinites could be saved by airplane. Over the next weeks, the evacuation proceeded apace. Five other pilots began to land at Camp Shmidt—Mikhail Vodopianov; Ivan Doronin; Nikolai Kamanin; Mavriki Slepnev, who thrilled the camp by arriving from Alaska with a cargo of chocolate and American beer; and Vasily Molokov, who earned the nickname "air-trolley" by carrying out thirty-nine of the Cheliuskinites, more than anyone else. One other pilot almost reached the Cheliuskinites: Sigismund Levanevsky, who crashed on his way from Alaska before actually getting to the camp but went on to play a support role during the rest of the operation.

While the Cheliuskinites waited for more airplanes to arrive, two crises arose. First, warmer weather was causing the ice floe that housed Camp Shmidt to disintegrate, so the pilots redoubled their efforts to reach the camp. Second, Shmidt fell victim to a serious medical ailment; during the first week of April, his lungs became severely inflamed, and he began to run a fever of 103 degrees. Although Shmidt insisted on remaining until the end, regardless of his illness, the Cheliuskinites' Party cell voted that he be airlifted to Alaska for emergency treatment. The government concurred; the following day, the Extraordinary Commission ordered Shmidt by radio to leave "with an undisturbed conscience" and to allow himself to be flown out at the earliest possible opportunity. On 11 April, Slepnev took off for Nome from the camp; Shmidt, reluctantly bumped up to 76 on the evacuation list, was aboard. Taking his place as expedition leader was Bobrov, the Party cell leader.

Besides Shmidt, fifty-six Cheliuskinites were evacuated on the 11th and the 12th. By the evening of 12 April, only six of the castaways remained, and they began preparations to shut down Camp Shmidt. The next afternoon, on 13 April, Molokov, Vodopianov, and Kamanin all managed to reach the camp. Before the day was out, all 104 of the castaways had been brought back to safety; not a single life had been lost since Mogilevsky's death in February. The "*Cheliuskin* epic" (*epopeia*), as it had become known, was finally at an end.

The festivities, however, had only just begun; the frenzy of publicity that followed the rescue was nothing short of amazing. After recouping for a short time at Vankarem, the Cheliuskinites, along with the pilots who had saved them, journeyed south to Vladivostok. From there, the new heroes boarded the Trans-Siberian Railway and embarked on a month-and-a-half-long trip to Moscow, stopping to make appearances in dozens of cities along the way. Meanwhile, Shmidt, with Ushakov as his traveling companion, toured the United States after recovering from his surgery. He spoke to the American public on the CBS and NBC radio networks, met New York City mayor Fiorello LaGuardia, and visited with American polar explorer Adolphus Greely. Shmidt was feted at the New York Museum of Natural History and the National Geographic Society; he was also inducted by naturalist Roy Chapman Andrews as a member of the New York Explorers' Club. Before leaving the country, Shmidt even lunched with President Franklin Delano Roosevelt.[11] He set sail for Europe aboard the *Majestic*, then journeyed through the Continent, making appearances in Paris, Prague, and Warsaw. Shmidt returned to the USSR in early June, just in time to greet his fellow Cheliuskinites as they arrived in Moscow. On 10 June, the heroes' train rolled into Belorussky Station; after a triumphant parade down Gorky Street, the Cheliuskinites and pilots were received by Stalin himself in a gala celebration on Red Square and in the Kremlin.

Every member of the expedition received either the Order of the Red Banner or the Red Star, and Shmidt was given the Order of Lenin as well. For the pilots, something even more special was called for. On 17 April 1934, a new medal was struck in honor of the pilots' singular achievement: the Order of the Hero of the Soviet Union, soon to become the most coveted award in the USSR.[12] Liapidevsky was the first to have the prize bestowed upon him; Molokov, Kamanin, Doronin, Slepnev, Vodopianov, and even the unfortunate Levanevsky came next, rounding out the first seven in what would become a long list of the heroes held in the highest esteem by the Soviet nation (see Figure 1). Throughout the rest of the 1930s, the "*Cheliuskin* epic" would be showcased as one of the proudest and most compelling episodes of the decade. And if the voyage of the *Sibiriakov* had brought the Soviet Arctic to the attention of the public, the events surrounding the *Cheliuskin* catapulted it to worldwide fame.

Chkalov, Gromov, and Levanevsky:
The Arctic Flights (1936–1937)

If there was a single venue in which technological development, visions of modernity, and the public imagination can be said to have fully converged during the first half of the twentieth century, it would be in the skies. The classic "golden age" of aviation began with the Wright Brothers' 1903 flights at Kitty Hawk and was still going strong on the eve of World War II. Air races, crossings of the English Channel, dogfights, barnstorming, flights across the Atlantic, and circumnavigations of the globe: all of these worked their magic on the thoughts and emotions of millions for almost four decades. It was small wonder that aviation became a cultural leitmotif of such magnitude in modern, industrialized countries like America and the nations of Europe. Aviation was associated with a broad spectrum of powerful issues: age-old dreams of flight, economic development, national pride, scientific attainment, religious and philosophical musings about the transcendent nature of the heavens, the specter of military destruction, and more.[13]

Much the same happened in the Soviet Union during the 1930s. Indeed, it would be difficult to find anything, excepting the image of Stalin himself, that was more prominent as a cultural symbol in the USSR than aviation.[14] "Airmindedness" became the order of the day. Between 1933 and 1938, the USSR broke no fewer than sixty-two worldwide flying records and made much of the fact.[15] Aviation Day, celebrated yearly on 18 August, became one of the key holidays in the Stalinist calendar. Osoaviakhim, the Defense Society for Assistance to the Aviation and Chemical Industries, became the largest mass organization in the USSR, claiming a membership of over three million.[16] A vast hierarchy of air-related sports—beginning with model building, advancing to parachuting, gliding, and ballooning, and graduating to airplane flying—sprang up in clubs and recreation centers throughout the country. Each major newspaper and periodical sponsored an airplane in the famous "Agitational Escadrille," the flagship of which was the *Maxim Gorky*, the world's largest aircraft.[17] Stalin's personal interest in aviation is well documented; he deliberately sought to cast himself in the public light not only as the "Father of Pilots" but also as the "Father of the Aviation Industry," since "Stalinist aviation" had come to represent the apex of Soviet technological progress.

As the *Cheliuskin* adventure so strikingly demonstrated, aviation became a vital part of the Soviet presence in the North. As far as the public was concerned, aviation was perhaps *the* central aspect of polar exploration and development in the USSR. This intimate connection between aviation—the bellwether of the new era—and polar exploration played a primary role in enhancing the symbolic strength of the Arctic as an element of Stalinist popular culture. This interchange was most apparent in the USSR's next series of premier polar exploits: the Arctic flights of 1936 and 1937.

The name most closely associated with these flights is undisputably that of Valery Pavlovich Chkalov, dubbed by the Soviet press as "the Greatest Pilot of Our Time."[18] The USSR's answer to Charles Lindbergh, Chkalov is still remembered as one of the most beloved aviators in Russian history. He was born in 1904, in the Volga town of Vasilevo (now Chkalovsk). Chkalov was drawn to flying at an early age; at fifteen, he volunteered during the Civil War as an airplane mechanic. Before he was seventeen, he had qualified as a pilot. Chkalov then went on to become a cadet at the Serpukhovsk Aviation School, where he trained under Mikhail Gromov. In 1923, the rising young flier won first prize in the all-union fighter-pilot competition.

Chkalov was a brilliant instinctual flier, preferring to rely on hunches and reflex rather than standard methodology or flying instruments. He was also a daredevil who disdained authority. As a cadet pilot, Chkalov gained a reputation as one of the most undisciplined aviators in the country. He repeatedly flew out of his school's training zone without permission and performed outrageous stunts. In what became his most famous breach of regulations (later immortalized in Mikhail Kalatozov's 1941 film *Valery Chkalov*), the brash young pilot looped and weaved over the city of Leningrad, then swooped under one of the low bridges spanning the Neva River.[19] Chkalov paid for his unauthorized misadventures. He spent many of his cadet days in the garrison guardhouse; more serious, he was condemned to a year in the stockade after nearly causing a fatal collision in 1929. Chkalov was released after serving only nineteen days of this sentence, but he was also discharged from the air force and sent home to the Volga.

In 1930, Chkalov was reinstated and served the air force as a test pilot. In 1933, he resigned from the military but continued to test new aircraft, placing his skills at the disposal of aeronautical designer Nikolai Polikarpov. Chkalov worked at the Polikarpov laboratories for over half a decade, until his death in December 1938.

By the mid-1930s, Chkalov was caught up in the aviation craze of the day: long-distance flying. Of the many ways in which a pilot's or aircraft's capabilities could be pushed to the limit—ceiling, maneuverability, cargo capacity, speed— endurance was paramount during these years. The goals of the many visionaries who hoped to revolutionize transport and communications with the airplane ne- cessitated that aircraft be able to travel over great distances. Other considerations were also important: during the interwar period, the doctrine of strategic bomb- ing—originated and expanded by Giulio Douhet, Hugh Trenchard, and Billy Mitchell—became the dominant concept among theorists of military aviation. Proponents of strategic bombing argued that "air power" would be the key to the wars of the future, and the widespread currency of their ideas led to a broad con- sensus that an airplane's most desirable attribute (aside from its capacity to carry ordnance) was its range—its ability to cover and affect as much territory as pos- sible. The result was to make distance-flying records the most sought-after hon- ors in the world aviation community. This was the case in the USSR, as else- where; of the three elements of the nation's aviation motto—"faster, higher, and farther"—"farther" became the most important. Soviet pilots strove as earnestly as their counterparts in America and Europe to capture distance records for their country, and this was how Chkalov, who had no institutional connection with polar aviation or exploration, came to have his name linked forever with the Arctic.

In July 1936, Chkalov rocketed to worldwide fame. With Georgy Baidukov as co-pilot and Alexander Beliakov as navigator, Chkalov flew almost the entire width of the USSR without stopping. Traveling through the Arctic, from Moscow to Udd (now Chkalov) Island, off the coast of Kamchatka, Chkalov and his crew covered over 5,600 miles in 56 hours. No one before had ever spanned such a dis- tance in an uninterrupted flight, and only the fact that the USSR had not yet be- come a member of the International Aviation Federation (FAI) kept Chkalov from officially claiming the golden prize of the aeronautical world: the long-distance record. Encouraged by Chkalov's success, the Soviets joined the FAI before the month was out. Moreover, official or unofficial, the Udd Island flight made Chkalov a force to be reckoned with in international aviation circles. It also put him among the front runners in the race to fulfill a mission that had become a special priority for the USSR: the quest to combine a world-record endurance flight with a journey over the North Pole.

Glavsevmorput had already attempted one such transpolar flight the previous year. In July 1935, Sigismund Levanevsky, one of the *Cheliuskin* hero-pilots, took off from Moscow, hoping to fly over the pole and go on to Los Angeles. Shortly after his departure, however, his engine developed an oil leak, and he was forced to turn back. The failure left the field open for others to join the race, and over the next two years the star pilots of the Soviet aviation community competed fiercely to become the first to fly to North America over the roof of the world. Spectators expected Levanevsky to prevail; he was among GUSMP's top pilots and, by all indications, a favorite of Stalin himself.[20] Indeed, in February 1937 Levanevsky got the green light from the Kremlin to attempt a second transpolar flight.

But this by no means guaranteed that Levanevsky would be the first to fly over the pole. In the eighteen months between July 1935 and February 1937, competition among the USSR's best distance fliers became extremely heated, and Levanevsky fell behind. To begin with, Baidukov and Beliakov, who had been Levanevsky's co-pilot and navigator in 1935, deserted him for Chkalov. Chkalov also had success on his side: after summer 1936, he was a national hero and an unofficial world-record holder. By comparison, Levanevsky hardly inspired confidence; his crash on the way to Camp Shmidt in 1934 and his 1935 attempt to reach the United States had been terrible embarrassments. The government intended to make the first transpolar flight of 1937 into a media festival, and it had no desire to let a pilot with a history of bad luck spoil its plans. Early in 1937, the Kremlin decided that there would be three flights over the pole that summer; it tapped two additional pilots, Chkalov and Mikhail Gromov, to fly to America via the Arctic—and Chkalov was to be the first.

On 18 June 1937, Chkalov, Baidukov, and Beliakov boarded the Tupolev ANT-25 they had flown to Udd Island. The route they were to fly had been christened the "Stalin Route" (*Stalinskii Marshrut*); those same words were boldly emblazoned on the aircraft itself. Taking off from the Frunze Central Aerodrome in Moscow, Chkalov and his crew soared into the summer skies. Sixty-three hours and 5,288 miles later, they touched down in Vancouver, Washington, having crossed over the North Pole. The three men had set an official world record and opened up a new air route between Russia and North America.

Chkalov and his companions also became instant celebrities the world over. The international press went into an uproar for weeks after the flight. For the next month, Chkalov, Baidukov, and Beliakov toured California, Washington, D.C., and New York City. They returned to Moscow at the end of July, and the reception that greeted them upon their homecoming was spectacular. Chkalov had become far and away the most popular pilot in the USSR, with both public acclaim and governmental cachet in his favor.

But the Arctic extravaganza had just begun. For one thing, Chkalov's flight came on the heels of Glavsevmorput's crowning achievement: the landing of Soviet aircraft at the North Pole in May and the establishment of the world's first outpost there. And the triumphs continued. On 12 July, Mikhail Gromov, with co-pilot Andrei Yumashev and navigator Sergei Danilin, launched a second transpolar flight (see Figure 6) . Gromov, a flight instructor during the early 1920s (with Chkalov as one of his students), occupied a lofty position in the ranks of Soviet aviators. From 1925 to 1929, he took part in several of the USSR's international air expeditions, in which large aircraft, such as the famous *Wings of the Soviets* and *Land of the Soviets*, toured the cities of Europe, Asia, and America. For a short time, Gromov also served as head pilot of the *Maxim Gorky*, the pride of the Soviet air fleet; luckily, he moved on to other duties before the airplane's catastrophic collision in 1935.

Gromov's Arctic flight proved a complete success. After leaving Moscow in their ANT-25 and following the same trail over the pole that Chkalov had blazed a month earlier, Gromov and his crew landed in San Jacinto, California. Their flight path—the "Stalin Airway" (*Stalinskaia Trassa*)—spanned a distance of 6,305 miles, more than enough to gain the USSR another world record.[21] Like Chkalov and his crew, Gromov, Yumashev, and Danilin became media darlings, both in the USSR and the West (a favorite moment for the American press came when Gromov and child actress Shirley Temple traded autographs in Hollywood). Still, even though Gromov surpassed Chkalov's record, he never overtook Chkalov's fame. Chkalov had been the first over the pole; moreover, he was a man of enormous charisma, who easily eclipsed not just Gromov but every other Soviet pilot in public appeal.

Unfortunately, the string of successes abruptly snapped in August. That month, it was Levanevsky's turn to fly across the pole to America. After having watched Chkalov and Gromov heap glory upon themselves, Levanevsky was champing at the bit to step into the limelight himself. Characterized by contemporaries as "tightly buttoned-up," Levanevsky was dogged by a perpetual sense of insecurity.[22] A former flight instructor for Osoaviakhim and one of GUSMP's best Arctic fliers, Levanevsky possessed every qualification necessary to prosper as a pilot of national reputation. Yet his record was blemished—and he was desperate to set things right with his transpolar flight. In August, everything seemed to be in his favor. His flight was not the season's first, but it would be the longest; the "Stalin Path" (*Stalinskii Put'*) led from Moscow to southern California and would take him far enough to break the record set by Gromov in July. Levanevsky's flight was also scheduled just prior to Aviation Day, and it was to be the pièce de résistance in a summer that had already thrilled the Soviet public with a flood of heroics. In the end, however, things went awry for the ill-starred pilot.

On 12 August, Levanevsky and his crew—V. I. Levchenko, N. G. Kastanaev, N. Y. Galkovsky, N. N. Godovikov, and G. T. Pobezhimov—gathered at the Frunze Central Aerodrome to make the final preparations for their flight. After his unhappy experience with the ANT-25 in 1935, Levanevsky chose to make his flight in the larger four-engine ANT-6.[23] Later that day, the airplane careened down the landing strip and into the air, bound for the North Pole and, beyond that, California. It never arrived. Somewhere near the pole, Levanevsky and his crew lost radio contact with the ground and vanished. Despite a search effort that lasted for eight months and involved pilots from the USSR, the United States, and Canada, no trace of Levanevsky, his crew, or their aircraft was ever found.

The disappearance of Levanevsky shocked the Soviet public and sent tremors through Glavsevmorput and the USSR's aviation community. As chapter 6 describes in more detail, the fallout from the Levanevsky case was severe, and it heavily affected GUSMP's fortunes. The effect of Levanevsky's death on the nation's morale was substantial as well; in the long run, it can be seen as the first of a series of setbacks that would soon dim the luster of polar aviation and exploration in the eye of the general populace. For the time being, however, even Levanevsky's doomed flight was not enough to darken the horizon in the North. The triumphs of Chkalov and Gromov continued to resound, and the excitement generated by the simultaneous success of Glavsevmorput's new North Pole station was still running high. Uncontestably, 1937 remained the capstone year for the Soviets in the Arctic.

"The Pole Is Ours!": SP-1 and the North Pole Landing (1937–1938)

As late as the 1930s, not a single explorer had visited the North Pole since Robert Peary made his claim to have done so in 1909. A few aviators—Byrd, Ellsworth, Amundsen, and Nobile—had flown over the pole, but nobody had reached the top of the world for well over two decades. This was not for lack of desire; in particular, Norway's Fridtjof Nansen, hero of the *Fram* drift and founder of the Aeroarctic society, had never abandoned his dream of traveling to the pole. But Nansen died in 1930, his lifelong ambition unfulfilled.

The troublesome thing about venturing to the North Pole was that, with the glory of being the first removed, there was little intrinsic value in getting there—certainly not enough to offset the tremendous effort and financial costs involved. Anyone putting together an expedition to the pole would have to make it special to make it at all worthwhile. It was precisely this that Otto Shmidt determined to do during the 1930s. Shmidt planned to combine a journey to the North Pole with two bold strokes that would make his expedition unique. First, he proposed to make the trip by air and, in the process, land aircraft at the pole for the first time in history. Second, he intended to use the expedition as an opportunity to establish the world's first research base there. According to Shmidt's scheme, a small group of scientists would remain at the pole for a number of months. Over time, the station would gradually drift southward into the Atlantic, where its personnel would be extracted by Soviet ships.

Shmidt most likely began to work out the details of the "North Pole-1" Expedition (*Severnyi polius-1*, or SP-1) in 1934 or 1935. Although the idea seems to have been in his mind even earlier, the aerial rescue of the Cheliuskinites in 1934 showed him how effective the airplane could be in the Arctic. Shmidt drew up his plans with the help of Vladimir Vize, whom he also picked to head the company of researchers who would stay behind with the SP-1 outpost. Helping Shmidt design the flight itself was hero-pilot Mikhail Vodopianov. Early in 1936, Shmidt presented his suggestion to the regime. The Kremlin placed its stamp of approval on the proposal, and the great drive to conquer the Arctic skies—and the North Pole itself—was under way.

The scope of the SP-1 project required an expedition team of forty-four people, thirty-five of whom would be slated to travel all the way to the North Pole. Shmidt himself was the overall leader. Key personnel included the GUSMP pilots who would fly the expedition members and their equipment to the pole: Vodopianov, the squad's commander; *Cheliuskin* pilot Vasily Molokov; Anatoly Alexeev; and Ilya Mazuruk.[24] Other important figures included Mark Shevelev, the project's deputy head; Ivan Spirin, on loan from the air force as chief navigator; Boris Dzerdzeevsky, the senior meteorologist; and Pyotr Golovin, the reconnaissance pilot. Representing the media were *Pravda* journalist Lazar Brontman and *Izvestiia* correspondent Ezra Vilensky.[25]

The leading roles, however, belonged to the four men chosen to remain at the North Pole for almost nine months: Ernst Krenkel, Pyotr Shirshov, Yevgeny Fedorov, and Ivan Papanin, who was selected as the group's head after Vize's health became questionable. Known collectively as the "Papaninites" (*Papanintsy*), the four men were destined to become national heroes. Krenkel, born in 1903, came from a family of Baltic Germans in Bialystok; he was the expedition's radioman. Krenkel began his Arctic career in 1924, as the radio technician for the polar station on Novaia Zemlia. He returned to Novaia Zemlia in 1926 and participated in Shmidt's 1929 trip to Franz Josef Land; that year, Krenkel set a record for the world's farthest-reaching radio transmission by contacting Admiral Richard Byrd's "Little America" base at the South Pole. In 1931, Krenkel was one of the four Soviet passengers on the *Graf Zeppelin*'s trip to the Arctic; in 1932 and 1934, he gained countrywide fame as the radioman of the *Sibiriakov* and the *Cheliuskin*. Krenkel developed a close working relationship with Shmidt, to whom he was extremely devoted, and it was no surprise that he was chosen as the SP-1's radio engineer.[26]

Like Krenkel, thirty-two-year-old Shirshov of Dniepropetrovsk had been on the *Sibiriakov* and *Cheliuskin* voyages; he was the expedition's hydrologist and biologist. Since he also doubled as the Papaninites' doctor, Shirshov received a crash course in field medicine before departure; he reportedly enjoyed unsettling his companions with morbid comments about how he hoped to get a chance to use the skills he had learned in his seminars on emergency amputation (or how he had spent more time flirting with his pretty blonde instructress than studying the finer points of suturing). The third member of the party was the youngest: Fedorov, the station's twenty-seven-year-old geophysicist and meteorologist.[27]

The leader of the four-man group, Ivan Papanin, was one of the most colorful characters in an agency that prided itself on its colorful reputation.[28] By the end of the decade, the short, plump, bristle-mustached Ukrainian had become more famous than any other individual in GUSMP, barring only Shmidt. Born in Sevastopol in 1894, Papanin became a seaman in the tsarist navy's Black Sea fleet. When the Civil War broke out, he deserted, joining a Red partisan unit. Afterward, Papanin served in the People's Commissariat of Communications. In 1931, he came to work in the North and, eventually, for Glavsevmorput, where he gained a reputation for his leadership skills and boisterous, picaresque humor. He rose quickly through GUSMP's ranks, and when Shmidt left the agency in spring 1939, it was Papanin who took his place as chief.

Throughout 1936, the members of the SP-1 team made their various preparations. In March, Vodopianov, along with V. M. Makhotkin, flew north to scout out a base for the final approach to the pole; they decided on Rudolf Island, only 540 miles away. Papanin led a voyage to Rudolf in the *Rusanov* and the *Herzen* to oversee the construction of the way station. In October, Papanin returned to the mainland for the outfitting of the expedition, a massive task that required meticulous planning. The Papaninites would be at their post for three-quarters of a year, yet the sum total of their food, gear, and construction materials could weigh no more than 10.5 tons. Despite some painful choices about what to bring, the Papaninites' storeroom soon looked like "a cross between a department store and a military camp," bursting with mittens, high-powered rifles, sleeping bags, skis, and assorted gadgets.[29] The greatest marvel was the famous black tent that the Papaninites would inhabit during their months on the ice. Twelve and a half feet long, 6.5 feet high, and 9 feet wide, the tent was a product of masterful engineering. Its skin, meant to provide both warmth and waterproofing, consisted of three separate layers: tarpaulin, rubberized cloth, and silk that had been sewn especially for the mission by a group of elderly nuns. Supported by an aluminum frame, the tent weighed only 80 pounds. By the end of January 1937, the equipment for the expedition had been chosen, tested, and packed for transit.

On 13 February 1937, Shmidt and Papanin conferred with Stalin. Also present were Molotov, head of Sovnarkom; Kliment Voroshilov, Commissar of Defense; "Sergo" Ordzhonikidze, Commissar of Heavy Industry; Nikolai Yezhov, head of the NKVD; Lazar Kaganovich; and Anastas Mikoyan. The Kremlin leaders were satisfied with Shmidt's plans and gave final approval to the SP-1 operation. All that was needed now was suitable weather.

On 22 March, the SP-1 expedition left Moscow on its long journey to the North Pole.[30] Six aircraft—four converted Tupolev TB-3 bombers, painted bright orange to stand out against the snow, accompanied by two reconnaissance planes—winged their way toward the Arctic coast. On 29 March, the party put in at Naryan Mar, at the mouth of the Pechora. On 12 April, the airplanes took off for Matochkin Shar, then for Rudolf Island. The party spent the next month at Rudolf, waiting to make the final jump to the pole. It was a restless time. The members of the expedition gathered their strength. They played sports and card games. Mostly they waited, hoping for the weather to improve. Every morning, the expedition's "weather wizard," Boris Dzerdzeevsky, would emerge from his tent after having pored over his meteorological findings and announce with a despondent face that he could not possibly authorize any flying that day.

On 5 May, the weather cleared enough for Golovin to fly a reconnaissance sortie over the pole. Although cloud cover was too thick for optimum visibility, Golovin was able to determine that ice conditions in the Pole's locale were favorable enough for a landing in the near future. Tossing a can of oil overboard as a small token (to help lubricate the rusty axis of the world), Golovin's crew returned to Rudolf to deliver the good news.

But the inclement weather returned; not until sixteen days later did the skies lighten. It was 21 May 1937, and Shmidt decided to mobilize his team into action. Only one airplane was to take off that day: Vodopianov's N-170, the expedition's flagship. Shmidt, the four Papaninites, and the other personnel assigned to the first flight clambered aboard. A short time later, the N-170 reached the pole. Vodopianov made a few passes, looking for a place to land, and descended. He touched down, skidded for a moment as the skis fitted to the landing gear made contact with the ice, then brought the plane to a safe halt. The SP-1 expedition had succeeded in the first part of its mission—the USSR was now the first nation ever to land aircraft at the North Pole.

The passengers of the N-170 allowed themselves a few moments to celebrate, then Shmidt put everybody to work. Krenkel set up his transmitter and sent messages to Rudolf, ordering the three remaining Tupolevs to follow the next day as they could, and then to Moscow, informing the government of the landing. Shmidt and Papanin oversaw the unloading of the equipment. Everyone labored to put a makeshift camp together as quickly as possible. By evening, all that remained was for the rest of the aircraft to arrive. After dinner, Shmidt and *Pravda* reporter Lazar Brontman relaxed over the first game of chess to be played on the roof of the world.

Over the next five days, the rest of the aircraft arrived from Rudolf. On the 26th, Mazuruk's plane, the last to reach the pole, straggled in after a brief emergency landing. By 28 May, the Papaninites' main living quarters had been erected and the team's scientific apparatus unlimbered. When the first week of June ended, it was time for everybody — with the exception of Papanin and his men — to depart.

On 6 June, the entire party staged an elaborate ceremony to commemorate the official opening of the SP-1 station, as well as to bid farewell to the pole and those who were staying there. The flags of the USSR and Glavsevmorput, along with a banner bearing the image of Stalin, were hoisted over the spot marking the pole and saluted with a rifle volley.[31] Shmidt and Papanin each delivered an address, and the meeting closed with a rousing chorus of the "Internationale." Shmidt, the pilots, and the support personnel said their goodbyes to the Papaninites, presenting them with gifts of "contraband": items that the pilots had refused to permit the four men to bring with them on the airplanes, such as playing cards, an extra primus stove, even a gramophone. Soon after, the airplanes were roaring their way through the air back to Moscow. Papanin, Krenkel, Shirshov, and Fedorov were now alone, left to their own devices on the crest of the globe.

While the Papaninites acclimated themselves to their solitude, Shmidt's party came thundering into Moscow on 25 June. A crowd of thousands greeted the conquerors of the North Pole at the Central Aerodrome, and even more turned out to cheer them as they made their grand processional through the city. The fact that Chkalov had completed his transpolar flight only days before added fuel to the fire, and Moscow was in a mood to celebrate. When Shmidt and his companions arrived at the Kremlin, they were opulently hosted by Stalin and the government's highest dignitaries. For his efforts in planning and participating in the SP-1 mission, Shmidt was made a Hero of the Soviet Union. Seven others became Heroes of the Soviet Union; everyone else on the mission received the Red Banner, the Red Star, or the Order of Lenin.[32]

The Papaninites themselves had much to do as they began their life at the pole. Krenkel maintained a constant vigil by the radio, sending updates to the government, broadcasting addresses to the Soviet public, and communicating with ham-radio enthusiasts all around the world. Also, when Chkalov and Gromov overflew the pole, Krenkel relayed navigational information to them. Fedorov had a variety of geophysical and meteorological observations to record. Shirshov labored to collect data about the polar seas, and his research placed burdens on the entire group. Each member of the camp took turns at lowering and raising the 3,000-foot cable that carried Shirshov's nets and buckets down into the ocean deeps. This was a boring, bone-wearying task, and each of the Papaninites dreaded his daily shift at it. Even worse, Shirshov quickly discovered that the spirits he had brought to preserve specimens had somehow evaporated during the trip to the pole, so Papanin called upon his men to make a supreme sacrifice. Heartbroken, they unpacked their single cask of Armenian brandy; from it, Shirshov proceeded to distill the spirits necessary to carry on with his work. The rest of the party was left to reflect on the doleful fact that scholarship sometimes imposes harsh demands upon those who serve it.

Over time, life at the pole became a matter of routine. Aside from his specialized duties, each member of the party helped with the mundane but arduous activities involved with keeping the camp functional: hunting, cooking, rebuilding the foundations of the tent as the ice shifted, keeping a sharp eye out for separations in the floe itself. To rouse himself for the hard work that lay ahead each morning, Krenkel took to suspending a small bite of chocolate just out of reach, giving himself extra incentive to leave the warmth of his sleeping bag. Still, there were relaxations. In the "evenings" (the time of day being relative, due to the peculiarities of polar day and night), the Papaninites would gather by the radio for news or listen to the gramophone. They played cards and chess, and sometimes Krenkel, who had much of the Pushkin canon committed to memory, would recite poetry. There were holidays and special occasions. Krenkel, Fedorov, and Shirshov also amused themselves with the camp's mascot, a Siberian husky named Happy (*Veselyi*). Unfortunately, Papanin's relationship with the dog, whom he considered an ill-tempered beast (who stole food when nobody was looking), was less than friendly. Papanin's dislike for Happy was so strong that, when the SP-1 party returned to the mainland, he tried to give the dog away to the Moscow Zoo. By that time, however, Happy had become almost as popular as the human occupants of the SP-1 station, and a great outcry ensued when the public got wind of Papanin's intentions. In the end, Papanin presented Happy to Stalin as a gift (how Stalin felt about his new pet—or, for his part, Happy about Stalin—is unknown).[33]

By the end of 1937, the SP-1 station was no longer at the North Pole or, for that matter, in the Arctic Ocean at all. The ice floe upon which the outpost had been built was floating steadily south. The Papaninites' mission was scheduled to come to its completion in the middle of February 1938, but there were several concerns about the final phases. The station had drifted to the eastern coast of Greenland, much farther to the west than Glavsevmorput had expected. In addition, the icy foundation of the camp was shrinking at a distressingly rapid rate as it got farther away from the polar seas. Both factors greatly complicated Shmidt's plans to retrieve Papanin and his companions in early 1938.

Indeed, the extraction proved a difficult operation. Shmidt requisitioned the icebreaker *Yermak* as his command center; two steamers, three submarines, and a dirigible accompanied it. The submarines played no real role in the rescue; the dirigible came to a tragic end, killing all thirteen people aboard as it crashed into a low mountain on the Arctic coast. Luckily, the ships fared better. By the second week of February, the steamers—the *Taimyr* and *Murman*—competing for the honor of getting to the camp first, had churned through the stormy waves of the Greenland Sea and were nearing the Papaninites' station.

On 19 February 1938, the *Taimyr* and *Murman* reached the Papaninites and took them aboard. Since neither ship could claim victory in the informal race to the floe, each crew tried to outdo the other in its efforts to persuade the Papaninites to come aboard, shouting out cheerfully that there were cases of beer waiting in the hold or that the other ship's bunks had bedbugs. By this point, however, the situation of the exhausted heroes was urgent enough that they would have gladly hitched a ride on a passing garbage scow: their ice floe, once "the most heavily publicized hunk of ice in the world," according to an American journalist, had dwindled to a frozen sheet measuring only thirty by fifty yards.[34] Krenkel and Papanin boarded the *Murman*, while Shirshov and Fedorov, with the dog, made things fair all around by sailing with the *Taimyr*.

And so the journey of the SP-1 outpost, which had drifted over 1,500 miles in 275 days, came to a close. The *Taimyr*, *Murman*, and *Yermak* conveyed Shmidt and the Papaninites to Leningrad. From there, the heroes took a train to Moscow, arriving in triumph at Oktiabrsky Station. As usual, the Papaninites were honored with a ticker-tape parade through Moscow and, following that, the requisite celebratory spree at the Kremlin, with Stalin presiding. The USSR's greatest accomplishment in the Arctic—a masterful victory over the North Pole—had finally been brought to a triumphant conclusion. The return of the Papaninites also brought an end to what would be Glavsevmorput's finest moment—and, as it turned out, the last good moment that the agency was destined to have.

The Passing of an Era

As events transpired, the USSR was never again able to equal what had been done in the Arctic during 1937 and the half-decade preceding it. In the realm of polar exploration, the months that stretched between mid-1932 and early 1938 had been a glorious time. During these years, even second-tier expeditions—such as Vodopianov's flight from Moscow to North Cape in 1935, the high-latitude drifts of the *Sadko* from 1935 to 1937, or Molokov's two-month, 15,000-mile aerial journey along the entire Northern Sea Route in the summer of 1936—were infused with an aura of heroism and adventure. At least in terms of public perception, those six years were truly a golden age in the Arctic.

All this changed in 1938, when the grandeur of polar heroics began to die away. In fact, the first signs of the oncoming decline were already apparent in late 1937. Not only did the disappearance of Levanevsky in August detract from the brilliant achievements of the summer, but the egregious failures involved with the rescue mission made things worse. The search for Levanevsky lasted until March 1938, cost millions of rubles, found nothing, and resulted only in several accidents, including the death of longtime Arctic pilot Mikhail Babushkin.

Glavsevmorput found 1938 even more frustrating. On top of the hangover caused by the Levanevsky fiasco, the agency was forced to deal with several major transport disasters (discussed at length in chapter 6). Shmidt's plans to establish a second base at the North Pole, the SP-2, with Aref Mineev as its head, were postponed indefinitely.[35] Much to the disappointment of Chkalov, the government remained mute regarding his request to attempt a flight around the world. The Soviets even had their long-distance flying record nullified; in November 1938, an English bomber crew led by Richard Kellett shattered Gromov's record by flying 7,158 miles from Egypt to Australia.[36] The USSR enjoyed only one major aviation success that year: the flight of the *Rodina*. In September, three female military pilots, Valentina Grizodubova, Polina Osipenko, and Marina Raskova, flew an ANT-37 from Moscow to the Khabarovsk region, setting a record for women's long-distance aviation.[37] But the *Rodina* flight was not primarily an Arctic exploit; besides, it was only one small island of encouragement in a sea of setbacks.

As bad as 1938 had been, nothing could prepare the country for what came at the end of the year: on 15 December, while testing a new fighter, the Polikarpov I-180, Valery Chkalov crashed to the airfield and perished in flames.[38] As discussed in chapter 6, the possibility exists that Chkalov was killed on Stalin's orders, although such speculation remains unverifiable. Whatever the case, the death of the "Greatest Pilot of Our Time" was devastating. The government gave Chkalov a stately funeral and buried him in the Kremlin wall with highest honors. But no amount of pomp and circumstance could soften the damage, and it seemed that nothing could be done to revive the flagging fortunes of the Soviets in the North.

Exploits in the Arctic sputtered to a halt in 1939, starting with a humiliating farce in the spring. In April, pilot Vladimir Kokkinaki resolved to restore the pride of Soviet aviation by flying through the Arctic from Moscow to New York City, for the opening of the "Land of Tomorrow" World's Fair. Not only would he regain the long-distance flying record for the USSR, but he would do so in the splashiest manner possible.

Tall and handsome, a professional-quality boxer and weight lifter, Kokkinaki was a distinguished pilot. A specialist in altitude flying, he had earned the USSR's first official aviation record in July 1936, and he still held that record in 1939. Along with Alexander Briandinsky, Kokkinaki had tried his hand at long-distance aviation in June 1938, flying from Moscow to Vladivostok in fewer than twenty-four hours. His Arctic flight, however, was doomed to ludicrous failure; his supreme arrogance during the weeks before the flight—even to the point of discarding his airplane's life raft ("We intend to fly to America, not paddle there!")— only made the outcome more poignant. After crossing the Atlantic, Kokkinaki and Mikhail Gordienko, his new co-pilot, encountered a series of small cyclones and crash-landed in the Canadian countryside. Neither was seriously injured, but Kokkinaki's pride was severely bruised as he arrived at the fair as a passenger in a cargo plane leased on credit by the Soviet Embassy.[39]

A more undignified—and unfitting—conclusion to the history of Soviet accomplishment in the North is scarcely imaginable. Events like Kokkinaki's debacle were draining the vitality from the Arctic, and the big moments—the major feats that had sustained momentum and interest in the region—were no longer forthcoming. The only successful polar adventures that followed the retrieval of the Papaninites were the drift of the icebreaker *Sedov*, which lasted from late 1937 to January 1940, and the 1941 landing at the "Pole of Relative Inaccessibility."[40]

But the "saga" of the *Sedov* was contrived, while capturing the Pole of Inaccessibility proved less than enthralling to the public.

In short, the days of glory in the Soviet Arctic were fading away. But the root cause was deeper—and far less dramatic—than the failures of 1938 and 1939. A number of sea changes were taking place in the USSR, and the circumstances that had brought about the popularity of the Arctic no longer existed. Quite simply, polar exploits were losing their relevance. All fads come to an end, and, with the passage of time, the USSR's Arctic craze was dying a natural death. More important, the threat of war was looming larger with every month; Soviet troops had already clashed with German and Italian forces in Spain and the Japanese in Manchuria, and the Munich Conference had sounded the death knell for collective security.[41] There was little room for adventures in the Arctic as the USSR made its mental and emotional preparations for continental conflict.

And so the heyday of the Soviet Arctic came to an end—but not before it had become firmly embedded in the national consciousness. Not without reason had the heroism and drama of polar exploits thrilled and gripped audiences throughout the USSR. Arctic heroics fit in perfectly with the ideology of the Stalinist regime, and, during the 1930s, they became a vital part of that ideology. Events like the *Sibiriakov* voyage, the *Cheliuskin* epic, the flights of Chkalov and Gromov, and the SP-1 expedition did more than bring fame to Glavsevmorput and a few individuals. As the next two chapters demonstrate, they also played an instrumental part in the development of a national worldview—a modern myth—in Stalin's Soviet Union.

FOUR

From Victory to Victory
The Myth of the Arctic in Soviet Culture

Let him, who would see the genius of humanity in its most noble struggle against superstition and darkness, peruse the history of Arctic travels. There, in the North, are all secrets laid bare.

—Fridtjof Nansen

In the darkness of the polar night, the sun of human intellect now shines brightly.

—Maxim Gorky

As the energy and exhilaration generated throughout the USSR by the adventures described in chapter 3 flared into a nationwide passion, the Arctic and its heroes began to figure prominently in the Soviet public sphere. From late 1932 to early 1939, polar explorers and Arctic pilots appeared regularly in the pages of *Pravda* and *Izvestiia*; became the subjects of innumerable books, films, and radio broadcasts; and inspired a multitude of poems, plays, and other artistic works. They held public office, packed lecture halls, and had their feats celebrated with lavish state rituals. Every sort of cultural ephemera—posters, currency, street names, postage stamps, and school textbooks—bore their images. In short, the Arctic came to occupy a preeminent position in the grand pageant of high-Stalinist propaganda and popular culture for almost a decade, as the Soviets, to borrow a favorite phrase from the press, moved "from victory to victory" in the North.

In doing so, the Arctic took on a character that was decidedly mythic. Not only does the term "Arctic myth" serve as a convenient shorthand for the vast cultural output connected with the USSR's polar exploits, but it hints at something deeper as well. During the 1930s, the Arctic became a key component of the modern mythology that would underpin Soviet culture and society for decades: the cultural ethos of socialist realism, the privileged—even exclusive—framework for public expression in the USSR. Socialist realism grew from a literary movement into a comprehensive worldview that was as readily applicable to reality as to the realm of arts and letters; it became a system of texts, images, and values with which one could perceive and understand the world around oneself.

At the heart of socialist realism was a synergistic relationship between fact and fantasy. In the USSR, especially during the 1930s and 1940s, the artistic conventions of socialist realism shaped the way in which the media covered real-life events. In turn, those events provided the world of art and literature with raw material and inspiration. As Katerina Clark notes in *The Soviet Novel*: "At this time, as at no other, the boundaries between fiction and fact became blurred. In all areas of public life . . . the difference between . . . theater and political event, between literary plot and factual reporting, all became somewhat hazy."[1]

What this symbiosis fed on best was heroism; bold deeds and epic achievements became the cornerstones of Soviet culture during the 1930s. These heroics—both actual and fictional—were meant to represent giant steps forward in the USSR's great march toward the shining dreamland of the socialist tomorrow. Simply stated, socialist realism, while purporting to depict reality, was really about portraying what *should be* in the language of what *actually was*. It was utopia on the most monumental scale imaginable.

It is no coincidence, then, that the study of Soviet culture has long benefited from the examination of the mythic elements involved with socialist-realist discourse.[2] This is because myth in its totality embraces "classificatory schema, assumptions about how things are, cosmologies, world views, ethical systems, legal codes, definitions of governmental units and social groups, ideologies, religious doctrines, rituals, and rules of etiquette."[3] Myths help people "to conceive strategies for placing themselves in the world and grasping events around themselves"; they act as a prism through which one can interpret one's personal and public universe.[4]

The modern myth of socialist realism did this for the citizens of the USSR—or at least was designed to do so. During the 1930s, the accomplishments of the nation's polar explorers and Arctic pilots fit perfectly into the rubric of socialist realism, and the Arctic myth spun out of them became an important, even central, part of the overall socialist-realist worldview. Therefore, unraveling and analyzing the set of tropes and themes bound up in the Arctic myth is an extremely useful way to examine the larger iconography of socialist realism itself. It also enables a better understanding of three broad aspects of the Soviet worldview as it was during the period of high Stalinism: public visions of nature, perceptions of the USSR and its place in the world, and attitudes regarding the individual and his or her relationship to the state.

Outlooks toward Nature: The Arctic as Adversary

From the beginning, Soviet visions of nature were informed by deeply Promethean sensibilities. As the nineteenth century drew to a close, the importation of Marxist ideology—with its high regard for technology and progress—injected a strong measure of antipathy into Russian attitudes toward the environment. During the 1890s, Georgy Plekhanov, the founder of Russian Marxism, inverted Frederick Jackson Turner's famous "frontier hypothesis" to conclude that Russia had been doomed by the forces of nature to a perpetual state of stagnation.[5] In the introduction to his sweeping history of the Russian Revolution, Leon Trotsky restated Plekhanov's argument verbatim: "The population of Russia's gigantic and austere plain, open to eastern winds and Asiatic migrations, was condemned by Nature itself to a long backwardness."[6] And, during the early years of the Soviet regime, the Bolshevik elite, concerned above all with making Russia part of the modern industrial world, came to believe that the advancement of their nation depended on the subjugation of the elements.[7] Of course, Soviet sentiments toward the environment were not wholly negative; poets like Sergei Yesenin and Boris Pasternak lyricized endlessly about the charms of the Russian countryside, while Lenin himself preached the virtues of clean mountain air and long hikes in the forest.[8] Still, a widespread sense existed that nature was a malevolent force: an opponent to be grappled with and overcome.

Soviet hostility toward the natural world reached its peak from 1928 to 1932, during the First Five-Year Plan. Since many of the plan's hallmark projects — taming powerful rivers with hydroelectric dams, linking remote territories with great railways, or carving gigantic mines out of the wilderness — involved head-to-head confrontation with the forces of nature, the "struggle with the elements" (*bor'ba so stikhiei*) became one of the primary cultural leitmotifs in the USSR. During the First Five-Year Plan, the arts, the economy, and the state all joined together to spearhead the country's struggle against the environment.[9] Unyielding antagonism toward nature became the watchword of the day — and it was sharp enough to leave an imprint that lasted long after the five-year plan came to an end. Although Soviet culture came to regard the elements with notably less rancor after 1932, this did not mean that it viewed them with great cordiality. It was against this background that Soviet perceptions of the Arctic were formed.

The Arctic and the "Struggle with the Elements"

As the Soviets strove to become conquerors of their own country, no force of nature posed a greater challenge to them than the Arctic. The Arctic provided the ultimate battleground for the war against the environment. It also became the ultimate enemy, personified by Stalinist discourse as a tangible, anthropomorphic opponent. If the "struggle with the elements" was an integral theme in Soviet culture during the 1930s, that struggle found its highest expression above the Arctic Circle.[10]

Thus, the metaphor of mutual aggression permeates the language used publicly to describe the Arctic. The Soviet media portrayed the exploration of the North as a great military campaign. Glavsevmorput became an "army of polar explorers" (*armiia poliarnikov*). Newspapers and propaganda films spoke of the "Arctic front" and celebrated every attack (*ataka*) and assault (*nastuplenie*); they urged the country on to the final conquest (*zavoevanie*) of the Arctic. On the face of it, this was nothing unusual; Soviet public vocabulary was typically rife with generous helpings of military imagery. But the martial lexicon suited the Arctic particularly well — at any rate, better than it did the "cabbage-harvesting front" or the "socialist offensive against the boll weevil." When a nationwide radio broadcast asserted that "today the Arctic's real master — the great Soviet people — comes to it in force," the words conveyed a feeling of genuine conflict.[11]

At times, the dimensions of the struggle approached the hyperbolic, as triumphs in the Arctic were translated into victories of almost cosmic significance. A headline celebrating the SP-1 expedition boasted that "we have conquered time and space!"[12] When the last of the Cheliuskinites were rescued, *Izvestiia* trumpeted that "technology has conquered nature, man has conquered death."[13] In another case, the citizens of one Arctic community explained to a visiting Englishman why they operated on Moscow, not local, time:

> "Never mind the sun, comrade. If we took any notice of him, we should not be living here at all. We cannot accept all the moods of the Arctic. After all, it's we who are the bosses here."
>
> So that was the law in Igarka! Men decided to live here and they are bending Nature to their command. They do not even abide by the mills of time![14]

Such language reinforced the sense that the heroes who fought the Arctic were the vanguard in their country's struggle against the elements.

Two powerful symbols set Arctic imagery apart from that normally used to describe the conflict with the environment. The first was the polar bear, which, in a real sense, embodied the Arctic itself: the word denoting the region comes from the Greek *arktikós*, meaning "great bear." The polar bear—invariably referred to as the "lord of the Arctic" (*khoziain Arktiki*)—appears in descriptions of virtually every journey to the Russian North. Most frequently, explorers are pictured as triumphant over the bear; by emphasizing their subjugation of the Arctic "lord," the Soviets demonstrated that they were, by extension, the new rulers of the North. In Marfa Kriukova's poem, "Tale of the Pole," the bears submit to the Russians immediately: "The polar bears came to them as helpers, the polar bears bowed low before them."[15] In photographs and films, the bear often appears as a lifeless creature lying at the feet of a hunter or as a trophy, stuffed or skinned. Another common image, that of a pet bear cub in chains, enjoyed more visual appeal but broadcast the message that the mighty monarch of the North was nothing more than a fuzzy, harmless toy. A more understated motif involved the placement of Soviet aircraft, the most potent symbol of the country's technological prowess, above a group of polar bears, who stare quizzically up at the sky as if they were confused primitives.[16]

The North Pole itself served as a second major symbol. Throughout history, compelling metaphoric associations have metamorphosed the pole from a simple geographic designation into one of Western civilization's most enduring archetypes. Although exotic or remote locales—the Indies, the source of the Nile, the Himalayan peaks—are commonly invested with an aura of unattainability, the North Pole remained the epitome of inaccessibility in the public mind. In addition, the pole represented the literal and figurative top of the world: mastery over it amounted to mastery over the highest of high grounds, strategic or sacred.[17] Drawing closer to the pole also involved the uncovering of the earth's final, most jealously guarded secret: the last blank space on the map. All of these attributes combined to make the North Pole into an icy, faraway stronghold: "the polar citadel."[18] The North Pole became a great fortress; the state-sponsored "folklore" of the 1930s often rendered it as the castle of the evil "Tsar of the

North" guarded by his "whirlwind-ministers" and their chairman, "Red-Nose Frost."[19] Upon the success of the polar landing in 1937, the newspapers blared, "the Arctic and the North Pole have been conquered by us!" as if the pole had indeed been a fortress under siege.[20] This image provided an unmistakable link between the Arctic and the words of Stalin himself: "There are no fortresses which the Bolsheviks cannot capture." The continuous exhortations to "storm the Arctic" (*shturmovat' Arktiku*) constantly echoed Stalin's famous slogan; the USSR's multiple victories over the pole throughout the decade represented its quintessential fulfillment.

For its part, the Arctic proved a worthy opponent, consciously fighting to resist humanity's efforts to tame it. The Arctic staged offensives of its own, as seen during the *Cheliuskin* adventure. The entire affair was a Robinson Crusoe story writ large: a perfect setting for the struggle with nature. The Arctic ice put the crew in constant danger. It trapped the *Cheliuskin*, drove it off course, and destroyed its hull. After the survivors abandoned ship and set up their makeshift outpost, the shifting of the ice threatened to open up rifts and swallow the camp. Small wonder that Ernst Krenkel attributes deliberate malice to the Arctic in his memoirs:

> Scarcely had we chipped away and removed a perceptible amount of ice than more ice would swim up from the depths and fill the cut we had made. Silently the ice blocked the space which had been freed around the ship. There was something frightening and oppressive to the spirit in this silent, implacable onslaught.[21]

The ship's geodesist kept a close watch on the spreading cracks in the ice, recording "how the ice attacked and how we defended ourselves."[22] Other missions evoked the same kind of language. Journalist Max Zinger refers to an "uprising of the ice" during an expedition on the Lena River, while one icebreaker captain— Konstantin Badigin of the *Sedov*—talks about his ship's "duel with the ice."[23]

The Arctic attacked in other ways as well. If the ice constituted one of the greatest dangers to life and limb, its psychic counterpart was undoubtedly the long polar night. Explorers could stand bitter temperatures, physical hardships, and the vast distances separating them from their homes, but the perpetual darkness of the winter months greatly debilitated them.[24] The approach of polar night often appears as a major moment in memoirs and diaries. Badigin voices his concern as the crew of the *Sedov* faces a second polar night: "A joyless sky hangs over the ocean. Can our nerves stand another winter on the ice?"[25] Stationed on Severnaia Zemlia and apprehensive of the coming darkness, Georgy Ushakov muses:

> I know of no month more gloomy in the deep Arctic than September, when polar night begins to arrive. In many areas of our homeland, September is often wonderful. People call it "Indian summer" or "golden autumn." But here, at eighty-nine degrees north, it is not golden, and it is not merely autumn.[26]

Symbolically, the approach of polar night highlights other negative events. In describing the death of a member of his Wrangel expedition, Ushakov instantly creates an atmosphere of depression by mentioning that polar night is near.[27] By building up the dreadfulness of the impending polar night, Vodopianov augments the sense of urgency and drama surrounding the 1937 attempt to locate

Levanevsky's lost crew: "The polar day drew to its end. The cruel Arctic began to greet us with cyclones, blizzards, and impenetrable clouds."[28]

Physically and psychologically, then, it was an epic conflict: the might of Soviet technology and heroism ranged against the worst that the forces of nature had to offer. The war in the Arctic stirred the blood and fired the imagination. Over time, however, the Arctic myth evolved beyond simple confrontation. After the early 1930s, the USSR's modern myth started to expand the ways in which the natural world was perceived—and came to rely less on the "struggle against the elements" as a lens through which to view nature.

New Visions of the Arctic

As the white heat of the First Five-Year Plan began to die down, a more accommodating stance toward nature began to emerge. The tendency for a society to put itself on more positive terms with nature when what architect and social critic Lewis Mumford calls its "organic-mechanic polarity" is out of equilibrium is relatively common.[29] And, in the USSR, the advent of socialist realism brought about what one author refers to as a "machine-garden backlash."[30]

This realignment should not be exaggerated; the USSR hardly experienced a pastoral revival during the 1930s. Still, animosity toward nature became much less uncompromising. The influence of certain Western writers—Mark Twain, Jules Verne, H. G. Wells, and, most of all, Jack London—proved to be significant here. Immensely popular in Russia for years, this group of authors had an enormous impact on the development of socialist realism and, as a result, helped to shape how the Russians looked at the elements.[31] Although their outlook was distinctly progress oriented, London and the rest portrayed nature in nuanced and textured ways: not just as a cruel and capricious antagonist but also as a force that could at times be beautiful, even kind.

In the event, friendlier descriptions of the Arctic began to appear more often as the high-Stalinist period began. Visitors paid tribute to the region's natural wonders. Ushakov rejoices in the breathtaking spectacle of the aurora borealis, nicknaming it "the smile of the Arctic."[32] Anna Sushkina, a scientist aboard the *Cheliuskin*, conjures a rapturous vision as she prepares to be evacuated from Camp Shmidt:

> That sunny day, the wild beauty of the primeval chaos about us looked especially brilliant . . . thick ancient floes in emerald blocks; icy grottoes and caves burning with a deep sapphire blue; and the crystals of snow glittering like dazzling diamonds. There were hardly any of the dull grey and white tones in which the Arctic is usually painted.[33]

Max Zinger refers to the Yenisei River as "a handsome fellow," while Shmidt, the staunchest of the Arctic's foes, admits to an audience of schoolchildren that, although the Arctic is a "harsh land," the "beauty of its nature is extraordinary."[34]

Affection found its way into the myth along with admiration. One journalist humorously calls the Arctic "our cold little grandmother."[35] The final chapter of a famous children's book about the *Cheliuskin* bids "farewell to the angry but beloved North," while Molokov, in his own book about the *Cheliuskin* rescue, declares simply that "I love the North!"[36] A front-page cartoon in *Izvestiia* depicted the Papaninites celebrating a festive New Year's Eve at the SP-1 station, with seals, walruses, polar bears, and other denizens of the Arctic as their guests (see Figure 4).[37] Finally, during a 1936 interview in London, Shmidt adopted the slogan of fellow explorer Vilhjalmur Stefansson—"the Friendly Arctic"—declaring that "we are truly making friends with the polar world. We are bringing it to life, and life to it."[38]

Fundamentally, the Soviets' relationship with the Arctic became more mature as their rhetoric began to allow for a certain degree of intimacy with the environment. There were, however, limits. The Arctic became an esteemed enemy, worthy of respect and even fondness.[39] But it remained an enemy nonetheless. Shmidt's words upon the completion of the SP-1 mission provide a perfect summation of the socialist-realist stance toward nature. Preparing to fly back to Moscow from the pole, Shmidt proclaimed to the assembled expedition members: "Today we bid farewell to the Pole—a warm farewell, for the North Pole has proved for us not terrible, but hospitable and friendly, as if it had been waiting for ages to greet the Soviets, its true masters."[40] Later, after returning to the capital, Shmidt went on to say:

> Nature subordinates herself to man when he knows how to arm himself for a fight and when he does not come out alone, but in a large group supported by the warm love of millions of citizens. And in this case, nature had to yield and sign an honorable treaty of peace with man.[41]

So, during the 1930s, the USSR reached a rapprochement of sorts with the elements. That rapprochement, however, was an extremely guarded one—and dictated exclusively on Soviet terms.

The Arctic as Psychological Landscape

Traveling through the Alaskan wilderness, naturalist Barry Lopez observed of the Arctic that it was a "country of the mind."[42] Echoing the same thought, folklorist Jack Zipes says of the fairy tale's enchanted forest that it is more than a wilderness: it "possesses the power to change lives and alter destinies. . . . It is there that [people] lose and find themselves."[43] Consciously or not, the Soviets made of the Arctic an enchanted forest of their own. The process by which they did so was a simple one. Travelers, explorers, and settlers typically configure the new lands they encounter in terms of the preconceptions they bring with them from their own world. At the same time, the psychological tension of facing the unfamiliar forces visitors to reexamine themselves and their worldviews.

In keeping with this, men and women writing about the Soviet Arctic at times acknowledged that it was a metaphysical landscape, a wilderness in which one could travel psychically as well as physically. The effects of polar night on the explorer's mental state have already been mentioned. And, as VAI chief Rudolf

Samoilovich told an American reporter, only half-jokingly, "the Arctic does strange things to men."[44] Most frequently, the Arctic enticed and beguiled. Soviets living and working in the North describe this phenomenon with great consistency. Taking his cue from Jack London's masterpiece, *The Call of the Wild*, Vodopianov writes that "the North calls" to him: "all a pilot needs is one flight to the Polar regions and he's hooked." He will be "pulled there by an irresistible strength," and the "fever of the North" will burn in his veins.[45] Papanin remarks that "the grim North, the endless icy waste, has bewitched me."[46] Levanevsky heard the call as well; he refers to the Arctic as "my element," which "has long had a hold on me."[47]

Journeys into the Arctic could also bring about moments of profound crisis and insight. Being alone or lost in the endless desolation of the North is the ultimate in bleakness: it juxtaposes the individual with absolute nothingness and compels him to confront himself and his place in the universe. Robert Service lightheartedly hints at this in his comic poem about the Klondike, "The Shooting of Dan McGrew": "Were you ever out in the Great Alone, when the moon was awful clear/And the icy mountains hemmed you in with a silence you could almost *hear*?"[48] Compare this with the epiphany Ernst Krenkel undergoes during an evening stroll, shortly after receiving his first posting in the North. Unable to find words adequate to express himself, Krenkel borrows an excerpt from "The White Silence," a Jack London story:

> I was surrounded by silence. To call it dead silence would be putting it mildly. Nature has many tricks wherewith she convinces man of his finity—the ceaseless flow of the tides, the fury of the storm, the shock of the earthquake, the long roll of heaven's artillery—but the most tremendous, the most stupefying of all, is the passive phase of the White Silence. All movement ceases, the sky clears, the heavens are as brass; the slightest whisper seems sacrilege, and man becomes timid, affrighted at the sound of his own voice. Sole speck of life journeying across the ghostly wastes of a dead world, he trembles at his audacity, realizes that his is a maggot's life, nothing more. Strange thoughts arise unsummoned, and the mystery of all things strives for utterance. And fear comes over him.[49]

There was an ambivalence within the Arctic myth regarding the transformative power of the elements over humankind. On one hand, the Soviets accepted that nature could be a testing ground, a crucible in which their national character was molded and altered. Karl Marx himself had written that "in changing nature, man changes himself."[50] Gathering material during World War II for the second volume of *The Two Captains*, Veniamin Kaverin spelled this idea out just as clearly: "The hero of *The Two Captains* gets his tempering by struggling against Nature. He is typical of all polar explorers. The North gave my hero his strength, and it is back into the North that he is returning it all."[51] For the most part, however, the Soviets—at least those involved with designing the Arctic myth—were uncomfortable with the notion that the forces of nature might have a meaningful internal influence on *homo Sovieticus*. If the elements could affect the men and women of the USSR desirably, they could do so in unwanted ways as well. And if the Soviets allowed for the possibility that the latter could happen, they sabotaged the entire discursive scaffolding they had constructed to prove that they were firmly and unshakably in control over the natural world. In essence, the Soviets were happier showing how their actions affected the environment rather than vice versa. Still, it was impossible to prevent at least a few examples of the psychological effects of nature from creeping into the Arctic myth.

Cosmographies: Perceptions of the USSR and the World

As one historian of exploration notes, terra incognita invariably acts as "a mirror for the habitual."[52] Speaking specifically of the Arctic, another author comments that "we turn these exhilirating and terrifying new places into geography by extending the boundaries of our old places in an effort . . . to make the foreign comprehensible."[53] Similarly, the language used in the USSR to describe the North reveals as much about attitudes toward the Soviet Union itself as it does about the polar world. The Arctic myth touched upon the way the Soviets perceived their nation's future, past, and present. In effect, the Arctic itself became a looking glass, helping the Soviets to create images for themselves out of those they used to depict the northern periphery.

Looking to the Future

More than once, Fridtjof Nansen called the Russian North "the land of tomorrow," and the Soviets eagerly took his words to heart. Accordingly, the vast polar expanses served as the perfect blank slate—a discursive tabula rasa—on which the Soviets could inscribe their visions of the USSR as they hoped it would be in the future. The socialist-realist myth made out of the Arctic a land of gleaming new cities and settlements, sparkling under the glow of the northern lights, untainted by any vestige of the old, corrupt tsarist order. Steel and concrete began to rise rapidly from the ice and snow in what the press called "a region born of the five-year plan."[54]

One of the brightest jewels in this Arctic crown was the young city of Igarka, which became a favorite emblem of the USSR's expansion into the polar wilderness. In 1938, the regular media attention was amplified by the publication of a popular book entitled *We Are from Igarka*.[55] Edited by Maxim Gorky until his death in 1936, then by children's writer Samuil Marshak, the volume consisted of a collection of letters written by the boys and girls of the town. The portrait that the children paint is uniformly robust and exuberant. As grim as its physical surroundings might be, Igarka lacks for nothing. It has a growing, happy population, an attentive city government, and excellent hospitals and schools.[56] More important, Igarka radiates the camaraderie and vibrancy that can be gained only by *building* civilization rather than merely enjoying its benefits. As the children themselves write, "Soviet power has made the North unrecognizable. . . . Igarka is not only a town or a port. It is a forepost of culture."[57] The press concluded much the same: *Pravda* made "the good life in Igarka" into a synecdoche of the "good life" that the whole country should be striving for—Soviet socialism at its best and bravest.[58]

Portraits of Glavsevmorput's major expeditions conveyed the same message. In the press, the *Sibiriakov* became a "floating republic."[59] The *Cheliuskin* experience gave the media even more opportunity to emphasize this theme. The painstakingly crafted depiction of the Cheliuskinites' two months on the ice presented Camp Shmidt as a microcosmic USSR in the wilderness—the "perfect bolshevik collective" sustained by the "iron discipline" and "nurturing goodwill" of Otto Shmidt.[60] The castaways did not merely huddle on the ice or wait passively for rescue but carried on with their scientific work and devoted their energies to maintaining the camp. The Party members "published" their handwritten wall newspaper. The Cheliuskinites celebrated Red Army Day (23 February) and other major events in conjunction with the rest of their country. The stranded Soviets played volleyball and soccer during the day, then gathered in the evenings for songs and poetry. Shmidt himself entertained his fellow Cheliuskinites with a series of dazzling lectures, his encyclopedic knowledge allowing him to speak freely and authoritatively about topics ranging from Freudian psychoanalysis, Russian monasticism, and theoretical biology to Norse mythology and the anatomy of the penguin. On one occasion, Shmidt refused to answer a radio call from the mainland because he was in the midst of explaining the intricacies of dialectical materialism to an enraptured audience.

Of course, this picture was obviously painted in overly bright colors. Even if Shmidt's lectures were as enthusiastically attended as the stories make them out to be, for example, one can be forgiven for suspecting that this was due more to the opportunity to share body heat in a crowded tent than to Shmidt's gifts as a public speaker. Also, little was said about certain breaches of discipline: the hoarding of food or the threat of the construction workers bound for Wrangel to abandon camp and walk back to the mainland on their own (only after Shmidt promised to execute anyone who left did they agree to stay). Nor was there any hint of the boredom and despair that the Cheliuskinites certainly felt during their ordeal on the ice. But official accounts of life at Camp Shmidt were not about capturing reality. They were about proving that the Soviets could impose communist-style social organization anywhere they chose, no matter how adverse the conditions.

The Arctic also played a role in charting the mythical landscape of an idealized USSR. According to the cultural geography mapped out by socialist realism, Moscow was the *axis mundi*—the physical and spiritual center around which the Soviet universe turned. At the very center was the Kremlin, the holy of holies in which Stalin, the great father of nations, sat enthroned in glory. In his sanctuary, Stalin remained hidden from ordinary eyes, but his love and concern extended from the Kremlin to every man, woman, and child in the *Rodina*, the socialist motherland.

The Arctic stood out in complete contrast to Moscow. It was as far from the capital as one could get: the "essential elsewhere" in the Soviets' "mythical wilderness."[61] Untamed and unknown, the Arctic was the ultimate frontier, the very end of the world; it was there that the civilizing influence of Moscow could be expected to be at its lowest. And yet that influence made itself felt. Levanevsky refers to Moscow as a "powerful magnet" that guides his flying in the trackless wastes of the Arctic.[62] The explorers themselves brought Moscow with them to the wilderness. They conscientiously observed every holiday in the Soviet calendar, from New Year's Day and May Day to Stalinist Constitution Day, with as much pomp and ritual as surroundings permitted. The miracle of radio enabled them to follow soccer championships, elections to the Supreme Soviet, and show trials almost as if they were home on the mainland. Standards of cleanliness and hygiene were scrupulously maintained; when members of the SP-1 expedition placed a sign reading "Wipe Your Feet!" at the North Pole, it was only partially in jest.[63] This also explains why Soviet explorers were depicted as clean shaven; a smooth face demonstrated that no citizen of the USSR would even think of allowing the rigors of the wilderness to overcome the code of cultured behavior (*kul'turnost'*) to which every Soviet man and woman was supposed to adhere. In one famous instance, Vasily Molokov refused to allow any man with an unshaven face aboard his aircraft during the SP-1 mission (an exception was made for Otto Shmidt, since, as Molokov explained, "the whole world knows and loves his beard").[64] The underlying subtext was to show how the USSR was able to establish order in the midst of chaos.[65]

Upon returning from their exploits, polar heroes were typically invited to the Kremlin, often to an audience with Stalin himself, along with the nation's leading officials: the archangels perched at the right hand of the Great Leader. These visits took on the flavor of a religious pilgrimage, bringing the hero into the presence of the living embodiment of Soviet power. Thus did the journey of the polar hero turn full circle: from Moscow to the Arctic, then back from the most remote wilderness to the center of the world. In the process, Moscow's place of primacy was reaffirmed. This was the message of a playful poem by Viktor Gusev, "The Cheliuskinites Are Coming."[66] Gusev's verses tell how the various cities of Russia compete among themselves for the attentions of the Cheliuskinites after their rescue. Each city tries to convince the new heroes to visit and bide a while. Vladivostok curses like a sailor when the Cheliuskinites leave it behind, Viatka calls to them in the wooden voice of the forest, Tashkent extends its invitation in the seductive whisper of the East, and so on, until a cacophony of pleas and entreaties breaks out. Suddenly, the voice of Moscow, quiet but firm, cuts through the din and silences the quarrel. The capital asserts the privilege of rank to whisk the Cheliuskinites back to Moscow with lightning speed; when they arrive, they are enveloped in the nurturing embrace of their homeland. Gusev's poem, like so much else in the Arctic myth, was a clear reflection of the Soviets' great cosmographic goal in the North: to link the antipodes to Moscow, binding up everything in between into a unified whole. This was the intention boldly stated by Mikhail Vodopianov in his renowned essay "A New Year's Dream": "the world will revolve upon a Bolshevik axis."[67]

Reexamining the Past

Arctic imagery helped the Soviets to orient themselves in terms of their past, as well as their future. As part of the Stalinist regime's ongoing campaign of legitimation, the USSR's exploits in the Arctic were meant to demonstrate the superiority of the communist regime over the old imperial order. Mikhail Koltsov, one of *Pravda*'s top reporters, made this idea the central thrust of an essay entitled "The Discovered Motherland." Koltsov argued that old Russia's literary greats—Pushkin, Gogol, Dostoevsky, and Tolstoy—had never been able to feel true pride in their backward and oppressive nation. By contrast, exploits such as the *Cheliuskin* rescue made Soviet Russia a land of which writers like Koltsov could be proud.[68]

Likewise, Arctic heroes seized every opportunity to criticize the old regime. Shmidt noted that "the tsarist government had no idea what to do with the Arctic."[69] In a book for children, Papanin wrote that prerevolutionary explorers received little, if any, support from their government: "[They] perished in the North because no one gave them assistance. With us, it is another matter. The whole country helps us, even Comrade Stalin himself helps us."[70] Time and again, explorers and pilots contrasted Soviet initiative in the Arctic with what they denounced as inaction and shortsightedness on the part of the tsars.

Arctic heroes also recounted how they experienced misery and injustice as young men before the October Revolution. Liapidevsky's family lived under the thumb of a wealthy kulak.[71] Mazuruk describes long hours of toil in the smithy of his impoverished father.[72] Stationed in Sevastopol as a young seaman in the imperial fleet, Papanin was greeted everywhere in restaurants and parks by signs reading "Sailors and Dogs Not Allowed."[73] Molokov reminisces with exceptional bitterness about the economic degradation that he and his family suffered under the old order. He goes on to accuse the tsarist regime of having deprived him of his childhood, then lauds the Soviet government for having provided him with the possibility of self-advancement: "Before October I could neither read nor write. And I want to note straight away that only Soviet power has given me any chances in life at all, and that my life is divided into only two periods: before the Revolution and after it."[74] Fiction painted much the same picture; in *The Two Captains* Kaverin portrays the tsarist regime as horrifically callous. When a polar explorer goes missing, not only does the government refuse the family's request to send out a search mission but the Minister of Marine himself pettily minces that "it is indeed a pity that your Captain Tatarinov has not returned. I should have had him prosecuted for negligence in the handling of government property!"[75]

Despite this condemnation, the Arctic myth did not reject Russia's past altogether. The ideology of the USSR was syncretic, making selective use of history to construct a worldview for the present. One of the preoccupations of Soviet culture during the period of high Stalinism was the search for a great tradition. To this end, the Soviets resurrected certain prerevolutionary figures as suitable symbols of modernity, progress, and genius. During the 1930s, the Arctic myth incorporated many of these individuals into its cast of characters.

Among them were the aerial heroes from the early days of Russia's Age of Flight. During the first two decades of the twentieth century, aviation captivated the imaginations of thousands of Russians; the barnstorming of turn-of-the-century fliers like Mikhail Yefimov and Sergei Utochkin influenced an entire generation of Soviet pilots—polar aviators among them—as children.[76] Engineers such as Alexei Mozhaisky and Nikolai Zhukovsky also became part of the Arctic myth as charter members in a pantheon of designers and scientists that would eventually be used to demonstrate the inexorable progression of Soviet aeronautical achievement from the earliest biplanes to Sputnik. Several Arctic pilots began their careers under Zhukovsky or at least in the Central Aero-Hydrodynamic Institute (TSAGI) he founded in Moscow.

Other figures from Russian history populated the Arctic myth as well.[77] Yermak, the Cossack conquerer of Siberia, was cast as a sixteenth-century precursor of the USSR's northern heroes. Also present was Admiral Stepan Makarov, who lobbied for the acquisition of an icebreaker fleet before his death in the Russo-Japanese War. Another motif of Arctic "right-mindedness" was chemist Dmitry Mendeleev, who forcefully argued for the development of the Northern Sea Route. The myth also featured Mikhail Lomonosov, Russia's eighteenth-century scientist, poet, and renaissance man. Lomonosov's origins were especially appropriate: born to a poor family in Kholmogory, on the White Sea coast, the story of how he traveled by foot from the North to Moscow to seek his education is one of Russia's most appealing (if somewhat mythical) success stories. He distinguished himself with his intellectual versatility; this associated him in the public mind with Otto Shmidt's reputed breadth of knowledge. Most significant was Lomonosov's interest in Arctic exploration, as shown in the following poem, written in honor of Bering's Great Northern Expedition:

In vain does stern Nature
Hide from us the entrance
To the shores of the evening in the East.
I see with wise eyes:
A Russian Columbus speeding between the ice floes—
Defying the mystery of the ages.[78]

Finally, the Soviets held certain prerevolutionary explorers, particularly those from the late imperial era, in high esteem. Not all were suitable for inclusion into the Arctic myth: Baron Ernst Toll was rejected because of his noble origins, Alexander Kolchak for his role as a leader of White forces during the Russian Civil War. However, Georgy Sedov, Vladimir Rusanov, and Georgy Brusilov held a special place in the hearts of Soviet polar explorers. Several of the scientists who became famous during the 1930s, including Samoilovich and Vize, trained under these men before the Bolshevik Revolution. Their ideological credentials were also in order; the Soviets even claimed Rusanov as an early communist. Most important, Sedov, Rusanov, and Brusilov formed a trinity of sympathetic martyrs. Without help from their homeland, they had gone bravely into the Arctic and died there. The Arctic myth made their failures a testament to the flaws of the old tsarist order. Their Soviet successors held their names in almost religious reverence, both as a reproach to the selfish cowardice of the imperial state and as an inspiration to all Soviet citizens.

Charting the Present

Symbols drawn from the Arctic myth also helped to situate the USSR in the turbulent 1930s. This was especially the case with the Soviet Union's presentation of itself to the rest of the world. Deliberately or not, the Soviets defined their country in two different ways. On one hand, the USSR projected an image of itself as a friendly, peace-loving nation. On the other, it portrayed itself as a mighty military power, ready to defend its borders with overwhelming force. The Arctic myth played an important part in erecting both parts of this foreign-policy facade.

As part of its efforts to build up the peaceful aspect of its outward demeanor, the USSR demonstrated its national prowess by highlighting civilian, rather than military, exploits. This was typical of the times. When Mussolini built *autostradi* throughout Italy, when the Nazis turned the Berlin Olympics of 1936 into an overblown paean to themselves, when the United States constructed engineering marvels like the Hoover Dam and the Empire State Building, it was as much a statement to the rest of the world as it was anything else. During the 1930s, the USSR took similar pride in pointing out to the foreign community its world-class accomplishments in a variety of fields: sports (although the USSR did not participate in international competition until after World War II), music, chess, the ballet. And, of course, aviation.

Exploits in the Arctic were thus used to boost the USSR's prestige in international circles. On the whole, they met with success. The foreign press brought "Russia's polar empire" to the attention of the Western public, noting with admiration that "new cities have sprung up where a few years ago there were only scrawny settlements or frozen wastes."[79] As the *Cheliuskin* adventure reached its thrilling conclusion, British playwright George Bernard Shaw exulted, "What a country you have! You have turned a tragedy into a national triumph!"[80]

The Soviets took care to stress friendship and cooperation in their rhetoric. The USSR, unsettled by the emergence of Adolf Hitler, sought to end its diplomatic isolation by joining the League of Nations in 1934, signing treaties of mutual defense with France and Czechoslovakia in 1935, and sending Maxim Litvinov, the affable Commissar of Foreign Affairs, to spread the gospel of collective security. All of this was reflected in the Arctic myth, which depicted the North as a great leveler of national differences. Vodopianov, normally the fiercest of Soviet patriots, good-naturedly referred to the polar regions as an "international hotel."[81] From 1934 through 1937, the August celebrations of Aviation Day—which showcased Arctic flying as the pinnacle of achievement in the air—adopted the slogan "Wings of Peace."

Interestingly enough, much of the myth's good spirits were directed toward the United States. America, by virtue of its presence in Alaska, was one of the USSR's closest neighbors in the Arctic. In addition, the Soviets felt a measure of grudging respect for America's economic and industrial capabilities.[82] Russians and Americans regularly lent each other assistance in the North. In 1933, Levanevsky saved James Mattern when he crash-landed near the Anadyr River trying to break Wiley Post's around-the-world record.[83] When Levanevsky vanished in 1937, Mattern tried to repay his debt by leading the American and Canadian pilots who took part in the search effort. In 1934, the USSR awarded the Order of Lenin to American mechanics Clyde Armistead and William Lavory, who provided ground support in Alaska for Levanevsky and Slepnev during the *Cheliuskin* rescue. In 1937, Gromov struck up a close acquaintance with American World War I ace Eddie Rickenbacker and had the chance to repay Rickenbacker's hospitality in 1943, when the U.S. pilot accompanied a diplomatic mission to Moscow.[84]

Much was also made about the warm welcomes that Russia's Arctic heroes received in America. Shmidt's tour through the United States in 1934, which came only months after FDR's diplomatic recognition of the USSR, was seen by the Soviets as a great step in improving relations between the two nations (seven years later, when the Soviets were at war with Nazi Germany, the regime chose Shmidt to address the United States by radio in an attempt to persuade the Americans to aid Russia against Hitler).[85] The crews of Chkalov and Gromov were greeted by huge crowds as they traveled through the States after their transpolar flights. There was even talk about using the flights as an opportunity to develop the transpolar route into a regular commercial flight path.[86] Finally, in a somewhat eccentric episode, Glavsevmorput gave its approval to an odd request from America: John Horward, a Boston lawyer with a yen for bear hunting, wrote the USSR for permission to travel on a Soviet icebreaker in hopes of hunting polar bears. Glavsevmorput officials informed him that they would be only too pleased to allow him on one of their ships, so long as the extended duration of the voyage and the lack of creature comforts did not bother him. In the end, Mr. Horward chose to track down his bears in Canada instead.[87]

It was impossible, however, for the Arctic myth to maintain consistently this sense of goodwill. The Arctic had always been an arena for intense international competition, and, although polar exploration and aviation were essentially civilian endeavors, they emanated a tough, quasi-military aura that easily gave rise to confrontational language. If the Arctic myth was about convincing countries like France and England that the USSR was an ally worth having, it was also about trying to persuade nations like Nazi Germany and Japan that it was an enemy to be feared. And so there was an aggressive streak to the myth as well as a friendly one. After the rescue of the Cheliuskinites, for example, an open letter from the workers of the Red Putilovets Factory, one of the country's largest armaments plants, appeared in *Pravda*. The authors boldly declaimed that the Soviets' victory in their "cruel and pitiless war with the elements of the Arctic" should be seen by fascists everywhere as a sign of how the USSR would perform in a real war against its enemies.[88]

A competitive tone emerged even in connection with the countries that the Arctic myth held in reasonably high regard. Again, the case of the United States is illustrative. Americans were much less excited about the USSR's polar exploits than the Soviet media claimed; the public was interested more in aviation than the Land of Soviets itself. The American military establishment expressed open hostility to the idea of Soviet pilots flying into U.S. airspace. Major General Oscar Rickover, head of the Army Air Corps, was reluctant to grant Chkalov and Gromov permission to fly to the West Coast but did so under orders from the federal government. He did, however, stand firm on one demand: that the visiting aviators be denied entry into military installations during their trips through the States.[89] Later in 1937, America's "Lone Eagle," Charles Lindbergh, began a verbal shooting war with the USSR when he allowed his views about Soviet aviation to be leaked to the press in England. In August, Lindbergh attended Moscow's Aviation Day ceremonies. Earlier, Lindbergh had publicly praised Soviet pilots, especially Chkalov and Gromov, as individuals, but he had no liking for the Stalinist regime. The holiday proceedings failed to impress him, and he later said so to friends in Britain. As such comments will, Lindbergh's remarks found their way into the London newspapers. In response, the Soviet aviation community regularly issued bitter denunciations of Lindbergh well into 1938.[90]

Even when American admiration was genuine, it was often mixed with unease. Historian Kendall Bailes postulates that, during the 1930s, the two future superpowers were engaged in a technological competition that would eventually expand into the postwar space race and arms race.[91] As this "tech race" escalated, Americans could not help but view Soviet accomplishments, those in the Arctic included, with some distress. Everything seemed to be going the USSR's way. In 1934, as GUSMP aviators flew through polar storms to rescue the Cheliuskinites, air-mail pilots in America were falling victim to accidents almost every week, in ordinary weather (this crisis was serious enough to warrant the formation of a special presidential committee that included Charles Lindbergh and Orville Wright).[92] The next year, Wiley Post, along with America's most beloved humorist, Will Rogers, died in a plane crash in Alaska. In summer 1937, the flights of Chkalov and Gromov stood out in painful contrast to the disappearance of Amelia Earhart over the Pacific.[93] By 1939, when the USSR held a comfortable lead in aviation world records, fewer than three years after joining the FAI, Soviet fliers appeared dauntingly impressive.[94]

It was no wonder that Americans sometimes felt defensive. Journalist Ruth Gruber describes her sense of embarrassment as an Arctic settlement's American-made generator fails to work (a rush of relieved pride follows when the *Amerikanskii motor* finally starts).[95] A cartoon showing Santa Claus watching a Russian bear salute a Soviet flag at the North Pole, under the caption "Well, Look Who Is Here," betrays a very real American anxiety concerning Soviet encroachments on the top of the world, both real and symbolic (see Figure 3).[96] And when Soviet aircraft touched down at the pole in 1937, most people in the United States probably agreed in their hearts with Matthew Henson—the African-American explorer who accompanied Peary to the pole in 1909—when he grumbled that "It was a damn sight harder the way we did it!"[97]

The insecurity, however, was mutual. The Soviets had their own setbacks to contend with: the crash of the *Maxim Gorky*, the failure of Levanevsky's flight, the death of Chkalov. A mutual inferiority complex lay at the core of the U.S.–USSR "tech race," and the Soviets reflexively compensated for their own failings by using the Arctic myth to criticize the Americans and reinforce popu-

lar clichés about them. The Soviet press accused America's methods of exploration of being haphazard and exploitative, in contrast to the "collective spirit,
planning, and persistence" of Soviet explorers.[98] America itself was riddled with
crass commercialism; a popular anecdote about Chkalov illustrated the difference between good communist values and American greed. At a news briefing in
London, an American reporter asked Chkalov if he was rich. Chkalov answered:

> "Yes, I am very rich!"
> "How many millions do you have?" the foreigner asked.
> "One hundred and seventy million!" Chkalov answered mischievously, a sly
> look on his face.
> "One hundred and seventy million what? Rubles? Dollars?"
> "One hundred and seventy million people!" Chkalov laughed. "All of them
> work on my behalf, and I work for them as well."[99]

The Arctic myth also belittled American achievements in the North. If the Soviets praised Mattern for his help during the search for Levanevsky, they also
ridiculed his fears about "the mountains of ice!" and the "madness!" of flying
during polar night.[100] They also complained about the fact that Mattern's corpo-
rate sponsor, the Republic Oil Company, billed the USSR for services provided.[101] When Slepnev flew from Alaska to Camp Shmidt, he broke the wheel
strut of the Fleetster rented to him by the Americans. A film clip portraying the
incident crows, "American airplanes are not accustomed to our icy landing
field!"[102] The Soviets also disparaged Robert Peary's 1909 expedition to the North
Pole as unscientific and sport oriented. When the Soviets landed at the pole in
1937, their attacks increased. Initially, the USSR—not without grounds—dis-
puted that Peary had even reached the pole and asserted that Shmidt's party was
the first to reach the top of the world. The Soviets quickly abandoned this claim
but continued to criticize Peary.[103]

Needling the Americans, however, was small change compared with what the
Soviets hoped to do with the more aggressive aspects of the Arctic myth: to in-
timidate immediate enemies like Germany and Japan. But the Soviets met with
little success here. The vaguely militaristic undertones of Arctic aviation, for instance, were too subtle to concern Hitler or his *Luftwaffe*. And, by 1938 and 1939,
polar exploration was losing its power to impress, even in the USSR. The Soviets
were preparing for war in earnest, and the media began to rechannel national
pride in the direction of martial pursuits. As a common epithet for Soviet pilots,
the warlike "hawk" (*iastreb*) began to take its place alongside the more regal "falcon" (*sokol*), which had been in vogue throughout most of the 1930s. In the same
vein, the aviation slogan that had spurred Arctic fliers onward to the pole—
"faster, higher, and farther!"—was giving way to calls for pilots to "shoot straighter!"
and "maneuver well!"[104]

The heroes of the Arctic tried to adapt to the changing times by lacing their
rhetoric with a more militant tone. At the Eighteenth Party Congress in March
1939, Papanin attempted to claim military relevance for the Arctic by thundering
before his audience that there would be "no more Tsushimas."[105] Kokkinaki,
with talk about "terrible clouds of war" and "crushing our enemies," tried his

hand at the new style as well.[106] Baidukov went even farther with his short story "Fantasy of a Future War," in which he depicts a Ukrainian bomber crew in the North Pacific heroically choosing to destroy an enemy cruiser (presumably Japanese) kamikaze-style, after being fatally disabled by anti-aircraft fire.[107] But efforts to keep up failed. Likewise, Gromov's insistence in 1939 that "the world's aviation records shall be ours!" and Vodopianov's hope that the Soviets would soon fly over the South Pole were increasingly out of step with the public spirit.[108] As the USSR geared up for war, the Arctic myth began to fade away, its symbolic power depleted in an age that had dramatically different concerns.

A Nation of Heroes: The Individual and the State

The most clearly expressed message encoded in the socialist-realist worldview involved the relationship between the individual and the Soviet state. The cornerstone of high-Stalinist culture was the positive hero, the shining example of all that was good, proper, and virtuous. This heroic "paradigm of the New Soviet Man"—both real-life and fictional—was displayed before the people of the USSR as a behavioral and attitudinal model for all to emulate.[109] According to the modern myth of socialist realism, to be a good citizen was to be as much like the positive hero as possible—indeed, the USSR as a whole was to become a nation of heroes.

Ironically, the hero had recently gone through rough times in the USSR. For the most part, the cultural ethos of the First Five-Year Plan period minimized—even eliminated—the role of the hero. In the hero's place, five-year plan culture substituted technology, slavishly idealizing the machine. In novels and films, tractors and blast furnaces were treated more heroically than the humans who operated them; in the aesthetic sense, Soviet society became a mighty machine in which the individual was reduced to a tiny, insignificant cog.[110]

All this changed after 1932, when the great shift to socialist realism began. This was only natural: machines made boring heroes. Socialist-realist culture did not reject technology, but it did emphasize the role of humanity as its creator and master. During the 1930s, the hero reemerged, stronger than ever before—once again, giants walked the earth in the USSR. And, of course, polar explorers and Arctic pilots were paramount among them.

Defining the Hero

Although the positive hero was a uniquely Soviet cultural creation, he (and she) possessed a mixed pedigree. Ostensibly, socialist realism was about providing Russian communism with a literary and artistic dimension. But, as one cultural historian notes, it was "a tortuous compromise between the art of old masters, folk culture, ideology, and some elements of popular commercial art."[111] Far from being purely a creature of Marxism, then, the positive hero was an eclectic amalgam. Included in socialist realism's literary foundation was a select group of the best-loved Russian poets and novelists, ranging from Pushkin to Gorky. As noted above, socialist realism borrowed extensively from certain European and American authors (and other artists as well; in March 1933, the editor of *Izvestiia* told the Union of Soviet Artists that "socialist realism is Rubens and Rembrandt put to serve the working class"[112]). Hegelian thought and German romanticism found their way into the new movement, as did Nietzschean philosophy.

Socialist realism drew upon sources that were even older. It co-opted tropes from the saint's life (*zhitie*), which allowed it wider access to the populace at large, including people living in remote or rural locales. In addition, the zhitie's themes of asceticism, devotion to a higher ideal, and martyrdom served communist ideology well.[113] Even more prominent was the revival of folklore.[114] The new folklore gave extra color to the positive hero and especially suited the Soviets' adventures in the Arctic. Polar explorers were identified with the *bogatyr*, the heroic warrior-giant of antiquity. Otto Shmidt made a particularly good bogatyr— with his great height and the most famous set of whiskers in the USSR, he fit the part as no one else could. Shmidt's appearance also invited comparisons with other figures from the past, most notably Grandfather Frost (*Ded Moroz*), the Russian Father Christmas (see Figure 2).[115] Arctic pilots, like all Soviet pilots of the 1930s, became "falcons" (sokoly): "proud" (*gordye*), "bold" (*smelye*), and "bright" (*iasnye*). The falcon was the royal bird of grand prince Vladimir, the "Bright Sun," who ruled ancient Kiev in the old tales and epics. Stalin became a modern Vladimir—the "Red Sun" (*krasnoe solnyshko*)—and, from his royal court in the Kremlin, he dispatched his bogatyri and his falcons to the top of the world for the greater glory of the Soviet homeland.

Finally, it should be noted that, although socialist-realist heroes could be of either gender and any nationality, the principal polar heroes were, without exception, male and Russian—or at least from the European parts of the USSR. With regard to gender, the Arctic myth exhibited the same patronizing hypocrisy that socialist-realist ideology did in general. When females appeared, it was to draw attention to the USSR's professed commitment to women's equality. The media highlighted "women of the Arctic," such as the female Cheliuskinites or Valeria Ostroumova, the political director of Igarka. Katya Tatarinova, heroine of *The Two Captains*, is fully emancipated, as seen when her husband informs her that they are both going on a mission to search for her long-lost father:

> "I'll be the fifth. You're the sixth. I suggested you as the daughter."
>
> "Oh, you did? I thought I was entitled to join the expedition not merely as the daughter of Captain Tatarinov. Is that what you wrote—'profession: daughter'?"
>
> "I don't see that it matters," Sanya muttered. "Otherwise it would look like I was trying to get my wife in."
>
> "I did not ask you to 'get me in,' Sanya. Daughter, wife! I'm also a senior geologist, Sanya, and I asked the Chief of GUSMP to include me as a geologist, not as your wife!"[116]

Valentina Grizodubova, head pilot of the *Rodina* flight, boasted that only in the USSR were women truly free: "Could I, as a woman, possibly have become such a pilot in a capitalist country, or in the fascist states, where they do not love humanity?"[117]

Stalinist feminism, however, was mostly sham. Against their wishes, the female Cheliuskinites were the first to be evacuated from Camp Shmidt. The public image of the *Rodina* pilots was derived as much from their roles as wives and mothers as their bravery or skill as aviators. Most of all, the presence of women in the Arctic myth was simply minimal. In the USSR, as in Europe and America, pursuits such as aviation and exploration remained preserves dominated almost wholly by males.[118] As a result, women remained junior partners—at best—in the socialist-realist fellowship of heroes.

The same dynamic applies to the issue of ethnicity. Socialist realism spoke at length about self-determination and equality for the USSR's 100-plus nationalities, but very few of the country's Arctic celebrities were of non-European stock. Instead, they were Slavs, Russianized Germans, Jews, Balts, or Finns. The absence of native Siberians from the ranks of polar heroes is particularly noteworthy—although not surprising. The Siberians appeared frequently in the Arctic myth, but their place there was defined by the words of Stalin himself: "the October Revolution, having broken the old chains of the forgotten peoples of the North, has given them new life."[119] Typically, the myth assigned to the natives the role of simple, loyal folk whose purpose was to provide exotic color and to play supporting roles—Gunga Dins of the North, so to speak. Heroism was reserved for the Russians and their European cousins.

The positive hero, then, was a curious being: shaped by gender and ethnic bias, cloaked in Marxist trappings, a mix of ancient and modern, Russian and foreign. This leads to the question of what made the socialist-realist hero *heroic*. The defining characteristic of the positive hero involved the combination of a certain heroic spark with maturity and moral uprightness. In this, socialist realism was not unlike other conceptions of heroism found in the wider Western tradition: Stoicism, chivalry, the "muscular Christianity" of the Victorian era. The common factor uniting these ideals is that they require the hero to be not merely heroic but *virtuously* so. In this conceptual framework, the socialist-realist hero, at least with a few external trimmings removed, could easily step out of the pages of *Tom Brown's Schooldays* or the official Boy Scout Handbook.

The heroic spark consists of a nebulous blend of courage, willpower, skill, and luck. It enables the hero to take superhuman risks, overcome insurmountable obstacles, and accomplish unimaginable deeds. Without it, the hero simply cannot be a hero. But the heroic spark is not sufficient for true heroism. Uncontrolled, heroic energies can evolve into classic daemonic forces: hubris (the downfall of the warrior Ajax), impetuosity (the recklessness of Icarus), or mad rage (the all-consuming wrath of Achilles).[120] To reach full potential, the virtuous hero must attain the self-discipline necessary to temper the raw power within himself or herself. This calls for a profound internal transformation, during which the hero integrates the various elements of his or her personality—and becomes a hero in the real sense of the word. In this, socialist realism's heroic model resembles that of the *bildungsroman*, the romantic era's novel of self-discovery and personal growth. It also descends partially, by way of Gorky, from the "heroic morality" of Nietzsche's so-called superman.

This common myth can be framed in a Marxist context; Katerina Clark does so in *The Soviet Novel*. Clark equates the qualities outlined above with the dialectic terms "spontaneity" (*stikhiinost'*) and "consciousness" (*soznatel'nost'*), most often used to depict the working class on its path to political self-awakening.[121] Just as "spontaneity" applies to the working class in its raw, untutored state—possessed of great, elemental power but unable to use it to its full capacity—it describes the heroic spark.[122] The term "consciousness," which refers to the working class after it has achieved an awareness of its real might, symbolizes maturity and self-discipline. The positive hero represents the dialectical synthesis of spontaneity and consciousness. Without stikhiinost, there is no strength. But without soznatelnost, that strength is undeveloped and wasted.

To a degree, this formulation is artificial. As Clark herself mentions, no Soviet writer knowingly uses these terms to describe a protagonist.[123] In addition, stikhiinost and soznatelnost can be seen simply as restatements of what Nietzsche called the "Dionysian" and the "Apollonian." Without the chaotic and ecstatic spirit of Dionysius, a society is passionless and uncreative. But without the controlled and contemplative refinement reflected in the figure of Apollo, passion and creativity can be meaningless, even dangerous.[124] Still, Clark's terminology provides a good abbreviation of ideas that are complex and cumbersome. More important, it underscores a crucial point about the deeper meaning of the socialist-realist hero: the personal development of the hero as he or she resolves spontaneity with consciousness is intended to mirror the development of socialist society at large. In other words, socialist realism compresses the blueprint for the evolution of Soviet society into the adventures of a single figure—real or fictional.

This dynamic was faithfully replicated in the Arctic myth, and polar celebrities were portrayed as paragons of heroic synthesis. All of them brim with generous helpings of spontaneity; they exude bravery, confidence, and unswerving persistence. Just before attempting to break the world altitude record, Kokkinaki coolly remarks that "I consider the record to be in my pocket."[125] Krenkel's outburst at an ambassadorial luncheon, where he blurted to Western reporters that "the North Pole belongs to those who fly there and stay there the most often!" may have bruised the niceties of diplomatic protocol—but it provided singular proof that the bold spirit of a Soviet hero was not to be trifled with.[126]

Even the scholars were fearless. The socialist-realist ethos repudiated the "armchair scientist," who never ventured forth from the laboratory, or whose work had no practical value. The villain of *The Two Captains* is "simply a type of pseudo-scientist who had built his career only on books."[127] Stalin himself spurned such "scholars": "Science deprived of any connection with practicality or field experience—we ask you, what kind of science do you call that?"[128] But Arctic scientists were a different breed: daring and active. One individual used commonly in the Arctic myth as a foil to demonstrate how bold most GUSMP scientists were was Dzerdzeevsky, the SP-1 meteorologist. Every account of the expedition recounts how, at Rudolf Island, the group's frustration mounted as Dzerdzeevsky repeatedly denied permission for the pilots to take off for the pole, plaintively muttering every morning that "I don't recommend flying today." Finally, Vodopianov, bristling to make the final flight, lost his patience and shouted, "Boris Lvovich, enough of you! We leave tomorrow, no matter what you say!" And, indeed, the SP-1 pilots flew the very next day.[129]

No individual embodied spontaneity more conspicuously than Chkalov, whose bravery was legendary. In mythic terms, his boisterousness is seen as an asset; his antics as a young aviator are forgiven—or at least winked at fondly. His fearlessness is demonstrated in countless ways. When Chkalov is asked by journalists why he prefers the single-engine ANT-25 to the ANT-6 (supposedly safer because it had four motors), his blithe response typifies heroic spontaneity: "Why bother with four engines? That's just four times the risk of engine failure!"[130] Chkalov is also powerful; he is praised for his ability to sweep aside petty limitations and ordinary conventions, and his intrepid spirit is described in the following passage: "Limited and malicious people tried to force Chkalov into the dead-end of old norms, of limits to the possible, of regulations. Nevertheless, he—true Soviet man that he was!—shattered all of these impediments with one bogatyr-like thrust of his shoulder."[131] In the socialist-realist universe, nothing can withstand the single-minded tenacity of stikhiinost, which allows heroes like Chkalov to achieve what ordinary humans can only dream of.

All the same, stikhiinost remains incomplete until it is joined with its counterpart, soznatelnost. Bold the Arctic heroes might be, but they combined courage with iron self-control. Vasily Molokov, or "Uncle Vasya," became a living icon of soznatelnost; he was described invariably as "an exceptionally modest man."[132] His humility and maturity were said to have come from his peasant mother, who, in a letter to *Pravda*, tells how she had always taught her son to renounce vanity and pride.[133] Molokov learned his mother's lesson well. He rescued more Cheliuskinites than any other pilot but shrugged off all praise, insisting that "I have fulfilled my duty, nothing more." Although heroically courageous, Molokov eschewed careless adventuring in favor of training and foresight: "People say that Soviet pilots gamble with death. But if we play a game with death, it is based on carefully calculated odds. We study our own strength and that of the Arctic—and only then do we fly."[134]

At the pinnacle of the Arctic myth, Otto Shmidt exemplified the perfect unity of spontaneity and consciousness. As one contemporary said of him, "[Shmidt] had only to enter a room for everyone immediately to feel that this man knew everything, understood everything, and could do everything."[135] The superlative fulfillment of virtuous heroism, he joined bravery and determination with erudition, cool-headedness, and selfless dedication to the Soviet cause. Shmidt's own words voice the proper socialist-realist attitude toward heroism: "We do not chase after records (although we break not a few upon the way). We do not look for adventures (although we experience them with every step). Our goal is to study the North for the good of the entire USSR."[136]

Even the firebrands displayed consciousness. The flamboyant Vodopianov is described as "daring, yet cautious."[137] Chkalov, criticized as "insanely brave" in his youth, has soznatelnost to spare as an adult.[138] In one famous anecdote, Chkalov shares his maturity with a small boy caught fighting with a little girl. After breaking up the melee and giving the boy a good dressing-down, Chkalov asks him:

> "What do you plan to be when you grow up?"
> "A border guard!" The boy replied.
> "A border guard?" mocked Chkalov. "Do you really think that our great Soviet nation would entrust its borders to an undisciplined little anarchist like you?"

Chkalov later sends the boy a note telling him to "study well and stop fighting with your playmates."[139] According to the story, the youth saved the note and eventually became a gold-medal student. The point here was critical: a troublemaker himself as a young man, Chkalov, in becoming a hero, had gained not only wisdom but also the capacity to transmit that wisdom to others. The synthesis—the cycle of spontaneity and consciousness—was therefore complete.

Rites of Passage

Having determined what *makes* the positive hero heroic, it remains to be seen how the hero *becomes* heroic. In the realm of Soviet fiction, the hero's personal transformation proceeds along the lines of a rigid formula that one scholar terms the "master plot."[140] This template contains a prescribed sequence of conventional situations that can, given socialist realism's mythic character, be interpreted as rites of passage. In media treatments of real-life heroics, the master plot was, by necessity, more flexible—although it still included stock episodes. By the same token, the Arctic myth contained its own set of ritual moments.

The first rite of passage involved the greenhorn's first encounter with extreme cold. The Russians prided themselves (and still do!) on their ability to live and work in subzero temperatures. To mix a metaphor, then, the neophyte's initial experience with the bone-chilling cold of the Arctic is a trial by fire.[141] Traditionally, those sailing on the polar seas for the first time underwent an "Arctic baptism," in which a bucket of icy water was upended over their heads.[142] Frivolous as they might seem, such ceremonies were symbolically important. Not only did they demonstrate the readiness of newcomers to carry on the struggle against the elements in the Arctic, but they touched on an even larger issue. Most of the pre-revolutionary Bolshevik elite, including Lenin, had been banished to the North at least once by tsarist authorities. Stalin himself suffered exile above the Arctic Circle, and he frequently reminisced about how he had overcome the polar wilderness and escaped from it. Stalin's time in the Arctic became an important part of his public image, and polar heroes often wrote about their own first exposure to Arctic conditions in connection with Stalin's past, using their personal achievement to magnify the greater glory of their Leader.[143]

The polar bear had ritual significance as well. The symbolic associations attached to the bear have been discussed above, and the Arctic myth reinforced them by making encounters with the bear noteworthy moments. Simply seeing such a striking animal for the first time, especially in the wild, is an unforgettable experience. Even more so is one's first bear hunt—always a standard rite of passage, fraught with challenge and excitement. On occasion, the ritual becomes inverted: the explorer, alone and unarmed, stumbles upon the bear and becomes the hunted himself (certainly a memorable way to be introduced to the North!).[144] Whatever the case, meeting the polar bear leads the hero to a closer acquaintance with the Arctic environment as a whole.

A more substantive turn of events came when the Arctic hero joined the Communist Party. Practically speaking, entering the Party ranks placed one among the nation's social and political elite; figuratively, it signaled an individual's willingness to assume an extra share in the task of building socialism and, conversely, official recognition of his or her worthiness to do so. Most of the major polar celebrities became members of the Party; for younger heroes, doing so went hand-in-glove with the attainment of heroic consciousness. This connection was made most explicitly in official accounts of the *Cheliuskin* epic.[145] The heads of the expedition's Party cell describe how dozens of the Cheliuskinites flooded them with applications for membership during the cross-country journey that followed their rescue. Although the setting—a stuffy, overcrowded train compartment—was informal, the occasion was a serious one, with the air of a new believer being welcomed into the religious fold. The petitioner began by stating how the Party's inspirational conduct at Camp Shmidt had stirred within him a greater sense of maturity and a corresponding desire to serve his country more actively. The ship's physicist, for example, "came to see more clearly that it is in a collective that people *grow up*. He compared the part played by the Party cell to that played in the human organism by the heart." Next came a period of intense soul-searching—the Marxian version of a priestly confession—during which the applicant assessed his flaws and strengths. Shirshov (expelled from the *Komsomol* in 1930) had to grapple with "a false conception of pride, plus a petty-bourgeois anarchistic individualism." Krenkel was asked if he would be able to conform to Party discipline ("You're an individualist, you know!"). In the end, the activist judged the hero fit to become a Communist. The whole ceremony was punctuated by stalwart embraces and manly tears of pride and joy; Levanevsky was said to have "blushed like a child." Such emotional responses were perfectly appropriate; having completed this particular rite of passage, the Arctic hero gained a heightened sense of communion with his people and his homeland.

Other rites of passages involved *kairotic*, or life-changing, encounters. A number of such meetings lay on the road to Arctic adventures. The interview during which a polar hero receives his first assignment to the North is generally described as a key moment. Further encounters provide opportunities for patronage or promotion. Most crucial, however, is the hero's encounter with the individual who will become his teacher. In the Arctic, such figures included ship captains, senior scientists, Party activists, polar-station heads, and so on. A common mentor among scientists was Rudolf Samoilovich. Otto Shmidt, however, was chief among the teacher figures in the Arctic myth. As the following excerpt shows, encounters with him were often marked as powerful rites of passage:

Every man meets a great number of people in the course of his life. Some are quickly forgotten, others pass without a trace. But some meetings remain in one's memory for many years—sometimes one's whole life. Among the latter I count my meetings with Otto Yulevich.[146]

Shmidt's role as a teacher figured most prominently in his friendship with Mikhail Vodopianov. The fiery, impulsive pilot met Shmidt briefly during the *Cheliuskin* rescue, but their first important encounter took place after the publication of Vodopianov's play *A Pilot's Dream*, which outlined a plan to land aircraft at the North Pole. As the myth has it, Shmidt read the play and summoned the young aviator to him one evening. When Vodopianov arrived, Shmidt laid out an incredible proposal:

> "Listen, Mikhail Vasilevich, do you truly dream of flying to the North Pole?" Shmidt asked.
> "Yes!" I replied.
> "That is precisely why I have called you here: to be a dreamer," said Otto Yulevich, smiling warmly. "Let us work to fulfill our common dream together."[147]

Out of this meeting, it was said, the SP-1 project was born. Although this was untrue, Vodopianov mentioned repeatedly that the encounter changed his life forever. His acquaintance with Shmidt deepened, and he began to gain wisdom and maturity as a result. Nor was Vodopianov alone in perceiving Shmidt as a mentor; as head of Glavsevmorput, the shaggy-bearded adventurer played a similar role for all Soviet polar heroes—at least according to the Arctic myth.

The Great Family: Stalin as Father

As an added dimension to the hero–mentor relationship, nearly all the Arctic myth's teacher figures were father figures as well. Shmidt repeatedly refers to Glavsevmorput as "my great family."[148] In turn, a host of Arctic heroes name him as a "polar godfather."[149] Such language squared seamlessly with the socialist-realist vision of the Soviet state itself. In contrast to the ideal of fraternal equality generally associated with the culture of the 1920s, a rigid patriarchalism emerged during the 1930s (although the USSR continued to profess itself the most egalitarian country in the world).[150] The socialist-realist myth pictured Soviet society as a "great family," in which a hierarchy of father figures led the Soviet people, the *narod*. At the apex of this pyramid stood the towering presence of Stalin, the "Father of Nations."

During the period of high Stalinism, polar heroes were among the favorite sons in this great family. Stalin himself, with his limitless soznatelnost, imparted wisdom and consciousness to all of them. The Leader's unparalleled genius and force of character molded them as personalities. Not only as teacher but also as father, Stalin guided every one of his hero-children as they developed into true Soviet men and women.

The Arctic myth transferred the splendor of the polar heroes' exploits directly to their figurative father. Stalin's name and image were interwoven into the narrative history of every heroic episode that took place in the North. In Perets Markish's poem "The Stalin Route," it is Stalin's brilliance that inspires Chkalov and his crew:

"By Your hand will be traced
The swift path above the wintry peaks!
At the behest of our Leader, with the support of our people,
We will blaze a path from Pole to Pole."

During their flight, the aviators, surrounded by the bleakness of the polar landscape, invoke the name of Stalin, almost as if in prayer:

Their lips quietly whispered:
"Leader and Friend, guide us from afar!
Against these storms and winds,
Above these deserts of eternal ice!"[151]

This theme was repeated endlessly. Films and newspapers showed Stalin as the driving force behind the *Cheliuskin* rescue. Memoirs routinely referred to him as the mastermind of the SP-1 expedition. He was said to have plotted the aerial pathways—the "Stalin Route" and "Stalin Airway"—that Chkalov and Gromov followed over the pole from Moscow to America. Even the idea for the establishment of Glavsevmorput was attributed to Stalin. This all-pervasive presence in the Arctic myth was rhetorically connected to wider questions of authority. Papanin, for instance, speaking before the Eighteenth Party Congress, likened the USSR to a mighty icebreaker, with Stalin as its sturdy, steel-willed captain.[152]

To complete this process of symbolic displacement, Stalin was shown in constant proximity to the explorers and aviators who labored on his behalf. The moments in which Stalin and his heroes came together were exceptionally important. For the Arctic hero, an encounter with Stalin was a watershed in his career. It was a supreme rite of passage that eclipsed all others and elevated the hero into the rolls of the country's elect: the so-called best people of the USSR. As the journal *Tvorchestvo* so fulsomely put it, "to see Stalin, to shake his hand, is the supreme reward for the crème de la crème of the people of the Soviet country."[153] Meeting Stalin was also a numinous experience: being in the Leader's presence provided the hero a tactile link with the sacred, with the essence of Soviet nationhood itself, encased in flesh and blood. Moreover, such encounters symbolized the perfect joining of the Soviet family circle, in which father and child were united as one.

These encounters are steeped heavily in the air of ritual.[154] Prior to actual contact with Stalin, the hero experiences unbearable apprehension but also delightful anticipation; in Papanin's words, "my hands and knees were shaking with excitement, but my heart was overflowing with joy."[155] When Stalin appears, he is simultaneously dazzling and down to earth. To describe the Leader's overpowering presence, Valentina Grizodubova quotes the first lines of a Georgian song: "When you see the sun in the heavens/You cease to notice the stars."[156] Despite this, Stalin is never distant or remote. Instead, he is warm and attentive, modest and informal; he is, after all, the hero's spiritual father. Whether he or she stands with Stalin on Lenin's tomb, stargazes with him in a Kremlin courtyard, or plays billiards with him at a country retreat, the hero is instantly reminded of this unbreakable bond of kinship.

In the Arctic myth, the patriarchal theme is articulated most fully in the relationship between Stalin and Chkalov. All aviators were dear to Stalin during the 1930s. But of these many surrogate children, Chkalov was portrayed as the best loved: the eldest son in the great Soviet family. The relationship proceeded metaphorically from cradle to grave. Chkalov was one of Stalin's falcons; like other Soviet pilots, he was a "fledgling" (*pitomets*), reared with great care by the Leader himself. As Chkalov grew, Stalin bestowed fatherly wisdom upon him, tempering his recklessness and watching over him with great solicitude. Stalin strove to teach him how best to control his heroic spark: safety, planning, and, above all, discipline were the Leader's chief priorities. For example, when Chkalov, seized with the desire to fly to the North Pole, came to the Kremlin in 1936 to have his proposal approved, Stalin counseled him and ordered him to be more cautious. As Chkalov himself writes:

> As is well known, we wanted to fly immediately to the pole. Joseph Vissarionovich listened to us in silence, then began to criticize our plan. He spoke almost in a whisper, but his words were firm and decisive. "Why the North Pole? You pilots act as if risk means nothing. Your bravery is commendable, but why such risk without reason? You need to practice first!"[157]

And so, on Stalin's recommendation, Chkalov flew to Udd Island instead. In another well-known vignette, Stalin, out of parental concern, publicly chided Chkalov at a Moscow airfield upon discovering that he often flew without a parachute:

> "Valery Pavlovich, why do you refuse to use your parachute?"
> "The material components of the airplanes I fly are expensive, Comrade Stalin. I am entrusted with costly experimental aircraft, and I do not wish to squander them by abandoning them. We are trained to save the airplane and ourselves at the same time. Parachutes may be wonderful things, but I prefer to go without them."
> "Valery Pavlovich, your life is more important to me, to the Soviet people, than any machine, no matter how costly. You must absolutely carry a parachute, and you must make use of it if there is need!"[158]

Chkalov returned Stalin's affection with a filial love that was made apparent to the entire nation. A famous photograph shows Chkalov locked in a powerful embrace with Stalin, poised to kiss him on the cheek, after his return from the flight to Udd Island (see Figure 9).[159] Chkalov also summed up his relationship with the Leader in an essay entitled "Our Father" (*Nash otets*), first printed in *Izvestiia*. Speaking for all Soviet aviators, Chkalov declared, "he is our father. He teaches us and rears us. We are as dear to his heart as his own children. We Soviet pilots all feel his loving, attentive, fatherly eyes upon us. He is our father."[160]

Stalin stood by his sons even in death. After Chkalov's fatal crash in 1938, Stalin planned for him a funeral worthy of the highest dignitary.[161] Chkalov's body lay in state as thousands of mourners streamed into the Hall of Columns to pay their respects. Afterward, Molotov, Andreev, Voroshilov, Kaganovich, Beria, and Stalin himself served as the fallen hero's pallbearers. They deposited Chkalov's remains in the Kremlin wall, in the distinguished company of the USSR's most hallowed individuals.

If Stalin was the father of Arctic heroes, the narod, the Soviet nation, was their extended family. This was a vital rhetorical point, for it was the means by which the socialist-realist myth connected Stalin and the polar celebrities with the population as a whole. The Arctic myth depicted the narod as animating and sustaining all of the USSR's efforts in the North. The success of the *Cheliuskin* rescue was the "victory of the country's single will."[162] Telegrams from the Papaninites stressed repeatedly that the concern and encouragement of the Soviet people was a palpable force aiding them in their efforts. As one broadcast stated, "we are far from home, far from our fellow countrymen and friends. But no distance can truly separate us from the Soviet Union, from the Bolshevik Party, or from the love and warmth of the people of our country."[163]

The myth's point was clear: the narod was an indispensable factor in the USSR's successes. To begin with, this reflected the premium that communist ideology placed on teamwork and collective effort. Also, by providing such an intimate link between the narod and the heroes of the Soviet Union—Arctic or otherwise—the socialist-realist myth symbolically displaced heroic glory yet again, but in the opposite direction: toward the common man and woman. In "March of the Happy Fellows," the signature song for one of the decade's most popular musical comedies, poet-songwriter Vasily Lebedev-Kumach conveyed this message explicitly:

> We will achieve, grasp, and discover it all,
> The cold North Pole and the blue vault of heaven!
> When our country commands that we become heroes,
> Then anyone among us can become a hero.[164]

The socialist-realist worldview diffused heroic status among the Soviet people, who were thus united, high and low, in what the media called the "Stalinist tribe" (*Stalinskoe plemia*), the most advanced and progressive genus of humanity on earth.[165] Polar heroes were inseparable from their fellow countrymen, since, according to the Arctic myth, every Soviet citizen was joined together by the responsibility of making exploits in the North succeed. Hence, every Soviet citizen shared in the rewards as well.

Living the Great Dream

As noted earlier, the deeper meaning of socialist realism as a modern myth was to depict what should be in the language of what actually was. There was no other way to reconcile the manifold hardships and anxieties of the 1930s—the material shortages, the threat of global war, the Great Purges—with Stalin's dictum that, in the USSR, "life has become happier, life has become more joyous."[166] Not surprisingly, this disparity led to an inherent internal contradiction: a "modal schizophrenia" that made socialist realism into what one scholar calls "the impossible aesthetic."[167]

At the heart of this impossible aesthetic was a great dream, *the* great dream. And its fundamental message was that every man, woman, and child in the Soviet Union could become—indeed, must become—a hero. Building socialism was the greatest adventure in the history of humanity, and it required the utmost from every person in the USSR. The heroism celebrated publicly in the press and on Red Square was only the most visible manifestation of the everyday heroism that was called for in the factory, on the collective farm, or in the classroom.

It was in this way that Arctic heroics helped to shape the myth of socialist realism. Polar exploits were consistently and explicitly linked with the great dream. A radio broadcast declared that "our northern heroes, under the leadership of Comrade Stalin, the great genius and greatest leader of humankind, have transformed the dream of socialism into reality."[168] When the hero of Vodopianov's popular play *A Pilot's Dream* is warned by a friend that his plan to fly to the North Pole will be ridiculed by the authorities, he replies without hesitation:

> Laugh at me? I am certain that they will help me. After all, I live in the USSR! This project will be supported by the whole country, by everyone in our great nation. There are many dreamers like me among us, many of them. And because they live in the Soviet Union, they are realistic dreamers.[169]

The great dream was ubiquitous. The Stalinist regime purported to offer the highest of adventures to its people; they needed only the imagination, the energy, and the desire to embrace it. As Otto Shmidt wrote in *Pravda*, "life in our country flies faster than a dream. It is joyous to live and work in a country where bold dreams receive such realistic support. Here in the Land of Soviets, and only here, are the great and small dreams of humanity fulfilled."[170] With these words, Shmidt communicated the basic point of the entire body of high-Stalinist culture. Through its portrayal of polar heroics, the socialist-realist myth attempted to demonstrate to all that, just as the Arctic could be conquered only by the Soviet Union, only in the USSR could the collective and individual aspirations of humanity be realized.

FIVE

Between Rhetoric and Reality
Manufacturing the Arctic Myth

A ruler should show himself a lover of talent, and honor those who excel in any endeavor . . . . Furthermore, he should keep the people entertained with feasts and spectacles.

—Niccolò Machiavelli

ANDREA: As it is said, "Unhappy is the land that breeds no heroes."

GALILEO: No, Andrea: "Unhappy is the land that *needs* such heroes."

—Bertolt Brecht

On the evening of 21 May 1937, a play opened at the Variety Theater in Moscow. The offering that night was Mikhail Vodopianov's *A Pilot's Dream* (*Mechta pilota*), a melodrama depicting a squadron of Soviet pilots landing at the North Pole. The remarkable thing about *A Pilot's Dream* has nothing to do with its literary qualities (which are meager) but rather the timing of the play's premiere. When the curtain went up, the author of the play had actually arrived at the pole only hours beforehand, having piloted the lead aircraft of the SP-1 expedition to the top of the world. In other words, the opening of the play was deliberately staged to coincide with the real-life fulfillment of the fantasy portrayed on stage.

The story behind *A Pilot's Dream* is only one of countless illustrations that demonstrate how the socialist-realist worldview was manipulated in Stalinist Russia. Like most myths, the Arctic culture of the 1930s contained a measure of both fact and fancy. At its core was a series of events that actually took place and a group of individuals who made them happen. But the ways in which those events and individuals were presented to the Soviet public were often distorted or misleading. As a result, the Arctic myth occupied a shadowy borderland, one located somewhere between rhetoric and reality.

Nonetheless, the Arctic myth—however unsavory the political motivations that prompted it—was extraordinarily rich in texture and color, and it came to play much more of a role in the lives of Soviet citizens than most propaganda campaigns did. The purpose of this chapter is to ask how the Arctic myth was created and received. The first section deals with the Arctic myth as an instrument of the state; the second addresses the role of the media in giving shape to it. The

chapter then turns to the public's different responses to the Arctic myth; it con-
cludes with a brief discussion of the effects and limitations of Soviet propaganda.

Engineering Human Souls: The Arctic Myth as State Policy

One of the most famous remarks attributed to Stalin is the assertion that writers—and, by extension, other artists—are "the engineers of human souls." Even
though the comment is likely apocryphal, there is no denying that Stalin acted
in accordance with it. As it did with the production of socialist-realist culture
in general, the regime maintained a close connection with the Arctic myth.
At times, Stalin and his closest associates involved themselves directly with its
fashioning.

The Management of Culture: Stalin and the Arctic

It was in summer 1928 that the Soviets first realized how immense the publicity
value of the Arctic could be. In May, Umberto Nobile's dirigible *Italia* went
down over the Arctic Ocean, and, as described in chapter 1, the Soviet Union
played the starring role in the multinational expedition to save the survivors. The
response in the USSR to the *Italia* rescue was overwhelming. Between 200,000
and 300,000 people gathered in Leningrad to greet the icebreaker *Krasin* as it returned to port.[1] Book-length retellings of the adventure became great hits with
Soviet readers. For the next four years, expeditions such as the flight of the *Zeppelin* and the voyages of the *Sedov* began to receive greater media attention.
Then, in 1932, the *Sibiriakov's* traversal of the Northern Sea Route transformed
the Arctic trend into a national mania. And the state proved more than eager to
take advantage of the public's enthusiasm for things polar.

On the whole, the ways in which the regime managed culture were obvious.
Stalin's personal interest in cultural affairs is well known; at least in theory, everything in the public sphere—novels and newspaper headlines, poems and paintings, movies and symphonies—was subject to his review and approval.[2] Where
Stalin did not take a direct hand, he had at his disposal an elaborate apparatus to
guarantee that cultural production conformed to his wishes. Facilities such as
publishing houses, film studios, theaters, radio stations, and the presses were
owned by the regime. After the early 1930s, professional associations, the most
prominent of which was the Union of Soviet Writers, carefully monitored the
domain of arts and letters. Added to this was the sheer coercive power of the state.
Small wonder, then, that the crafters of the socialist-realist myth took care to tai-
lor it to Stalin's newest slogans and the latest Party pronouncements.

Such was the case with the myth of the Arctic. Exploits in the North captured
Stalin's interest because of their effectiveness in enhancing his public image, his
concern with which was perpetual and all consuming. In *The First Circle*,

Alexander Solzhenitsyn shows how Stalin's monumental vanity affected the production of Soviet culture:

> On the ottoman reclined the man whose likeness had been sculpted in stone; painted in oil; . . . carved from ivory, . . . and pictured in the sky by squadrons of planes. . . .
>
> This man's name . . . had been given to a multitude of . . . cities, . . . universities, . . . mountain ranges, canals, factories, mines, . . . farms, battleships, . . . fishing boats . . . and a group of Moscow journalists had proposed that it be given also to the Volga and the moon.[3]

The Arctic myth joined this list as one of the many means by which Stalin saturated the public sphere with his name and image (see Figure 5). When Stalin appeared on Red Square to salute the Cheliuskinites, or on the front page of *Pravda*, embracing figures like Chkalov or Shmidt, he absorbed much of their glory.[4] The same was true of a publicity photograph for the Supreme Soviet elections of 1937. In the foreground, Shmidt is casting a ballot; looming over him is a gigantic banner with Stalin's face on it, staring out into the eyes of the viewer.[5]

If the messages and motives behind the Arctic myth are clear, the actual decision-making process of the regime is less so. That Stalin and his Politburo were actively involved in the manufacture of the myth is evident; the specifics of *how* are harder to pin down. Protocols of Politburo sessions from the 1930s reveal that popular-culture items were considered at the highest levels of leadership; the acquisition of Charlie Chaplin films and arrangements for cross-country bicycle races were discussed in the same forum as matters of national security and political economy.[6] The Politburo turned its attention to the Arctic as well. Unfortunately, the archival sources available at the present time reveal only *which* topics the Politburo discussed, not *what* was actually said about them. The Politburo deliberated at length about how to celebrate the polar exploits of the 1930s.[7] How were these questions decided? On this, the protocols are silent. All that can be said for certain is that Stalin and the leading lights of his government were heavily involved with planning, designing, and promoting the Arctic myth.

Masking Reality? Case Studies in Deception

In his account of how America's first astronauts were transformed into national icons, Tom Wolfe describes how the Mercury pilots, most of whom were headstrong, hard-drinking womanizers, were presented to the American public as a "goddamned amazing picture of the Perfect Pilot, wrapped up in a cocoon of Home & Hearth and God & Flag!"[8] All propaganda campaigns touch up reality to some extent or another: some whitewash here, a facelift there. In the case of Stalinist popular culture, however, the degree of distortion was quite high, and the question of how consciously the state used the Arctic myth to mask reality is one worth asking.

The minor ways in which the Arctic myth was deceptive were countless; even the simplest of lies contributed to a larger culture of untruth. In one example, the diminutive Stalin is shown to be taller than Otto Shmidt as they embrace on Lenin's Mausoleum—even though Shmidt was well over 6.5 feet tall (see Figure 10).[9] Public mention was almost never made of setbacks or accidents. The myth remained silent on the general squalor of life in the Arctic, breaches of discipline, and the GULAG. Even the heroes were often less than heroic.

One of the most striking cases of how the state used the Arctic myth to perpetuate untruth involves the children of Igarka. As discussed earlier, 1938 saw the appearance of the well-publicized *We Are from Igarka*, an anthology of letters written by the town's schoolchildren. Released on the tenth anniversary of Igarka's founding, the volume cataloged the various delights of pioneer life there. Arctic heroes appear throughout the book: the Cheliuskinites visit, Vodopianov and Molokov take the local boys and girls for airplane rides. Shmidt himself delivers a lecture at one of the city's schools, and the children interact with him in an easy, comradely way ("'Why is your beard so long, Otto Yulevich?' Our guest began to laugh. 'My beard is long not because I am old, but because I use it to keep me warm when I am in the North'").[10]

However, the happy, homey tone that echoes through the book hides the grim reality behind its creation. In actuality, almost all of the 2,500 children who lived in Igarka were the children of kulaks and other "enemies of the people" forcibly exiled to the Yenisei backwater.[11] As a recent documentary film—*And the Past Seems But a Dream*—reveals, writing the letters that were eventually published was not the children's idea.[12] Instead, one of the city's schoolteachers (remembered fondly by the people interviewed in the film) encouraged the children to put their impressions about Igarka down on paper, then told them to write Maxim Gorky about their project. Gorky saw in this simple classroom activity the potential for a public-relations coup and responded immediately. He suggested an outline, told the children to write "as though you were telling the conditions of your life to someone close to you—for instance, to your friend Comrade Stalin," and asked them to send him a manuscript as quickly as possible.[13]

Not surprisingly, *We Are from Igarka* made no mention of the children's background, although the comment of one girl—that she found her new home "unpleasant" when she first arrived—takes on a new dimension when the entire story is known.[14] Gorky and Samuil Marshak, his co-editor, were certainly aware that the children were disenfranchised exiles. Before 1938, at least two Western journalists visited Igarka, and even they, with their travels closely supervised, discovered the kulak population there. Harry Smolka found that the town's children were quite open about their social standing; as one girl commented:

> Naturally [my parents] are unhappy because everything was taken away from them. I remember we had a fine house, and I also liked our old village better than Igarka at first. But now I understand that we had no right to own all that, and I am very glad that I can be a member of the Pioneers. The teacher at school talked very frankly to all of us and said Stalin had told the Communists that the children of the former capitalist classes must not suffer for the sins of their parents. My elder sister is even going to marry a Party member. We shall all be completely absorbed into the new society and all have reason to be grateful, because our life will be much happier and more cultured than that of our parents.[15]

While Smolka questioned his interviewee's sincerity, Ruth Gruber proved more naive about the exiles' plight. After speaking with an elderly woman sent to Igarka as a kulak, Gruber dismissed her griping as an older person's unwillingness to come to terms with a new order ("Was it possible that she had been banished here on no grounds at all? That seemed hardly likely").[16] Nevertheless, Gruber, like Smolka, was aware that a good number of people were living in Igarka against their will—and it was impossible that anyone involved in publishing We Are from Igarka would not have known it as well.

Gorky also played a role in a more notorious popular-culture deception connected, if only tangentially, to the Arctic myth: the enormous propaganda campaign surrounding the completion of the Belomor Canal in August 1933. As the USSR's first large-scale construction project built primarily by means of prison labor, the entire enterprise was overseen by Genrikh Yagoda, head of the secret police. But there was nothing secret about the use of forced labor—quite the contrary. Far from hiding the fact that inmates were at work on the BBK, the Soviet government eagerly publicized what it claimed were the rehabilitative effects of convict labor; Molotov was heard to boast that "many an unemployed worker of the capitalist countries will envy the living and working conditions of the prisoners in our northern camps."[17] To spread Belomor's fame even further, the regime commissioned thirty-seven authors to tell the world about it. Headed by Gorky, this army of writers included Vsevolod Ivanov, Valentin Kataev, Alexei Tolstoy, and humorist Mikhail Zoshchenko; their efforts culminated in the publication of The Stalin White Sea–Baltic Sea Canal.[18]

The Stalin Canal painted a wonderful picture of prisoners rebuilding their lives under the beneficent guidance of the Stalinist state. What it failed to note was that the treatment of the laborers was so horrendous that over 100,000 of the 300,000 inmates are reputed to have died.[19] Were Gorky and his colleagues aware of the terrible conditions and widespread abuses? Although no concrete evidence exists, it would strain the limits of credulity to suppose they were not, and Gorky's reputation has suffered as a result; for Gorky's willingness to lend his name to the Belomor project, Solzhenitsyn has poured venom on him as "a slobbering prattler, an apologist for executioners."[20] Meanwhile, The Stalin Canal was withdrawn from circulation and dragged off the bookshelves in 1937. Not only had Yagoda been denounced and executed as an enemy of the people, but, by this point, the Soviet regime had grown much more reticent about its labor-camp system.

What of the frequent claim that the Arctic myth was nothing more than a means of drawing public attention away from the unpleasant realities of life in the USSR? A number of scholars have concluded that polar exploits were merely a "heroic diversion," elaborately timed to distract the public from the terror and hardships of the 1930s.[21] The most strongly stated of these arguments comes from Anton Antonov-Ovseenko, son of Old Bolshevik Vladimir Antonov-Ovseenko, who was purged by Stalin in the terror. Antonov-Ovseenko attributes deliberate, almost superhuman, malice to Stalin in the staging of the Cheliuskin expedition. Emphasizing the fact that the Cheliuskin was unsuitable for Arctic navigation, Antonov-Ovseenko advances the idea that, in order to score publicity points, the government intentionally designed the ship's voyage to fail:

This expedition was known to be impossible. The vessel was old and didn't have much power; it could do nothing in heavy ice. But if the *Cheliuskin* hadn't been trapped by giant ice floes, there would have been no one for Stalin's falcons to save heroically. And there would have been one less pretext for nationwide rejoicing.[22]

Even as conspiracy theories go, this is implausible. True, taking a ship like the *Cheliuskin* into the Arctic Ocean was ill advised. However, it was a choice that can be put down to poor judgment, not to some malevolent master plan. Not that Stalin was one to have shrunk from such calculated manipulation, if such an idea—and a way to make it work—had occurred to him. But it was impossible that Stalin or anyone else could plan both the ship's accident and the aerial rescue that followed with anything like the precision necessary to ensure that such an intricate and difficult operation would succeed.

Perhaps the best commentary on the matter comes from Kendall Bailes, who argues that, although "one can be excused for interpreting . . . these spectaculars . . . as a means of diverting attention from the abuses of the regime . . . it would be folly to assert that [their] sole purpose . . . was to divert attention from the purges."[23] One might also recall that, far from being silent about the great purges, the regime made every effort to keep its war against "enemies of the people" as public as possible. Of course, it would be a mistake to argue that the state was not manipulative in the way it used the Arctic myth or that socialist realism did not seek to conceal the more unpleasant features of the Soviet experience. But the way in which this was done appears not to have been as consistent as is commonly assumed.

Carnivals and Jubilees: Large-Scale Manifestations of the Myth

The deliberate shaping of culture by the state was most obvious in large-scale cultural phenomena: the lavish public spectacles designed to commemorate significant moments or achievements. The sheer effort and expense behind the planning of a museum, an exhibition, or a holiday parade automatically reveals the hand of the state, since only the government possessed the resources and authority to support such enterprises.

When Arctic heroes returned from their exploits, they followed a choreographed pattern. They made their way to Moscow by air or train, stopping in towns and cities along the way. Not only did this maximize the exposure of the heroes to the population at large, but it gave Moscow sufficient time to prepare its own celebration. Upon reaching the capital, the heroes were met by thousands of people, then conveyed to the Kremlin down Gorky Street, where a ticker-tape parade awaited and huge crowds thronged the avenue. A procession on Red Square followed, and, inside the Kremlin itself, the heroes were received by other heroes and the highest leaders of the land. The state played a paramount role in this process, not least by the visible presence of figures such as Kalinin, Ordzhonikidze, Kaganovich, Molotov, Voroshilov, and Stalin in the parades and receptions. Bodies that aided Glavsevmorput in staging Arctic celebrations included the Moscow Central Committee, led by Alexander Shcherbakov, and the city council. At times, GUSMP reported directly to the Kremlin.[24]

Elaborate measures were sometimes taken to conform to the state's sense of theater, as after the rescue of the Cheliuskinites. Although the last of the Cheliuskinites were airlifted before mid-April, their return to Moscow was postponed until June. To begin with, many members of the expedition required a period of recuperation (it would hardly have done for the USSR's best and bravest to straggle up the steps of Lenin's tomb, frostbitten and gaunt with hunger). More important, however, was that Otto Shmidt was recovering from the lung surgery he had undergone in Nome and, along with that, enjoying his grand tour of the United States. It was impossible to celebrate the heroes' safe return while their leader was sightseeing at the Empire State Building and sipping cocktails with the president. Thus, the odyssey of the weary explorers was prolonged for over two months to satisfy the state's sense of ceremonial propriety.[25]

Glavsevmorput and the state also built special exhibitions and museums dedicated to the North. Under the curatorship of Ivan Suslov, the VAI established an impressive Arctic Museum—which still functions today—in Leningrad. In Moscow, two exhibits stood out far above the rest. The first was the "Soviet Arctic" pavilion, at the All-Union Agricultural-Economic Exhibition (VSKhV), precursor to the more famous Exhibition of the Achievements of the People's Economy (VDNKh). With the words of Sergei Kirov—"there is no land that Soviet power cannot transform for the good of mankind"—as its slogan, the pavilion brought the excitement of "Socialist Herding of Reindeer" and "Soviet Industrial Development of the North" to the capital. Designed by A. A. Abakumov of GUSMP's Propaganda-Agitation Department, the pavilion featured mockups of two icebreakers and a life-sized model of the renowned SP-1 tent. The expense was considerable—GUSMP spent 147,000 rubles to maintain the pavilion in 1935, then 180,000 rubles in 1936—but the outlay was seen as a worthwhile investment.[26]

Even more popular was GUSMP's "Development of the Arctic" (*Osvoenie Arktiki*) exhibition, located in Gorky Park.[27] The exhibition opened in August 1935, under the direction of N. K. Levitsky. Despite the fact that "Development of the Arctic" opened late in the summer, it drew almost 51,000 visitors and proved a great success. The exhibit's budget for 1936 was substantially increased—from 180,000 rubles to 259,000—and Levitsky turned the "Development of the Arctic" into a multimedia attraction. In 1935, the exhibit had consisted mainly of photographs and paintings; in following seasons, it included rousing music and documentary films. There were stuffed polar bears, panoramas of Tiksi Bay and Dikson Island, and a Red Tent replica. Visitors could participate in special events, such as occasional quiz games ("What Do You Know about the Arctic?") and the "Holiday of Plenty," a salute to the fishing and hunting industries of the North. They could gaze on the actual tent that the Papaninites had lived in at the Pole, as well as the *Stalin Route*, the ANT-25 that Chkalov had flown to America. The polar heroes themselves made frequent appearances; on New Year's Eve in 1936, Otto Shmidt was master of ceremonies at the exhibition's fireworks display.

In conjunction with the Moscow City Council and the city's park commission, GUSMP spent a good amount of money on Osvoenie Arktiki: by 1938 the yearly cost of the exhibit had escalated to more than half a million rubles. But popular response made up for the cost. In 1936, almost 400,000 people visited the exhibition. Figures for attendance in 1937 are unavailable, but taking into consideration the propaganda blitz prompted by the SP-1 expedition and the flights of Chkalov and Gromov, it is probably safe to assume that the park met its target figure of 500,000 visitors. The number of entrants tapered off to 261,245 in 1938. Paralleling the decline of the Arctic's position in Stalinist popular culture by the end of the decade, the number fell to 106,900 in 1939.

The Stalinist regime also put the Arctic myth on the world stage, particularly at the New York World's Fair. Organized around the central theme of the "Land of Tomorrow," the 1939 World's Fair was the interwar period's single most elaborate tribute to technological progress and modernity. The USSR was not about to let itself be outdone in such a milieu, and Stalin earmarked the equivalent of $4 million—the largest amount devoted to the fair by any national government—to prepare the Soviet exhibit.[28]

The Russian Arctic figured prominently in New York. In addition to its own Main Pavilion, the USSR maintained a Soviet Pavilion of the Arctic. Heading south from the Main Pavilion on Congress Street, a visitor would have to walk only a few seconds for the Arctic Pavilion—an imposing three-tier ziggurat—to come into view. In front of the pavilion sat Chkalov's aircraft, the *Stalin Route*. The pavilion's interior contained illuminated maps of the 1937 transpolar flights, a large graphic depicting the drift of the SP-1 outpost, and the actual SP-1 tent itself (on loan, like the *Stalin Route*, from the Osvoenie Arktiki exhibit). General consensus had it that the USSR's show at the "Land of Tomorrow" was impressive (if a little overdone, in the opinion of some)—and much of the credit belongs to the grand display at the Arctic Pavilion.[29]

Nevertheless, pageants and tableaus went only so far in promoting the Arctic myth, whether at home or outside the country. On their own, festivals and spectacles are not sufficient to maintain a real connection between the institutions sponsoring them and the individuals targeted by them. They may inspire, they may inculcate awe and respect, but they are so macroscopic in scale that their symbolic power is diffused.[30] Jubilees and carnivals put polar exploits in the foreground of the public sphere and made them shine there. But for the Arctic myth to become a sustainable part of the socialist-realist worldview, something more was necessary: it needed to become polished and better articulated. For this, the Soviet state turned to the media.

Crafting the Myth: The Media and the Arctic

After returning home from several years of employment in the USSR, American engineer John Littlepage made the following comment about Soviet propaganda:

> It is difficult for an outsider to imagine what the propaganda machine in Russia can do when it is turned loose on a single subject. American advertising men or press

agents must turn green with envy at the thought of it. When the Bolsheviks give orders for universal promotion . . . the country simply hears of nothing else for days or even weeks on end.[31]

It was to this mass-media complex that the Stalinist regime assigned the task of shaping the specifics of the Arctic myth into a coherent set of images and ideas. Without a doubt, this "propaganda machine" was solidly under the control of the government. In his bitter indictment of Stalinist cultural policy, concert violinist Yuri Yelagin, who fled the USSR after World War II, states that "in Soviet films everything is a figment of the imagination . . . [and] beginning with the Thirties all books written by Soviet writers are dishonest in varying degrees."[32] On the other hand, the Soviet media should not be seen merely as passive or ineffectual. It contained individuals of all types, engaged in work of all kinds, and the state had neither the time nor the resources to supervise it completely. In addition, if the state wanted socialist-realist culture to be at all appealing—and it did—it could not entirely eliminate talent and creativity. This meant that opportunities for self-expression—however limited—never disappeared completely. Each individual involved in crafting the Arctic myth left a unique and sometimes lasting imprint on the official rubric.

The Arctic in the Press

Of the media harnessed by the state in manufacturing the Arctic myth, the one with the most conspicuous role was the press. In a way, it was the press that prompted the myth's creation. According to Ivan Gronsky, one of *Izvestiia*'s chief editors, it was due almost completely to the unauthorized actions of his newspaper that the USSR took part in the *Italia* rescue of 1928. After the dirigible's crash-landing, Gronsky ran a front-page story in *Izvestiia* about plans for an international rescue effort. He also mentioned that the *Malygin* and *Krasin*, currently in dry dock, would soon leave Leningrad to help save the stranded aviators. Unbeknownst to Gronsky, however, Stalin had just decided to keep the USSR out of the rescue mission. The operation would be costly, and, besides, why should the Land of Soviets risk two of its precious icebreakers to lend a hand to Italy, birthplace of fascism? Unfortunately, *Izvestiia* had neatly committed the Soviets to doing exactly that. Reportedly, Stalin was furious at having his hand forced. Luckily for Gronsky, the *Italia* mission proved a brilliant success. And, of course, it opened the authorities' eyes to the propaganda possibilities of the Arctic.[33]

On the whole, the press served as a pliant tool of the regime. From 1932 through 1939, the number of newspapers in the USSR hovered between 7,356 and 10,668, with a total circulation of 34.7–38 million. During the same period, 2,000-plus magazines and journals published between 202.4 million and 340.2 million issues annually.[34] Taken in combination with the USSR's massive book-publishing industry, the press was a powerful mechanism in the dissemination— not to mention shaping—of information.

The press paraded the Arctic myth before the Soviet public in grand style. When the premier polar exploits took place, headlines and articles about them drowned out almost everything else in leading periodicals like *Pravda* and *Izvestiia*. Fed by stringers and wire reports, local papers from Baku to the Bering Straits took their cues from the center. All the major publishing houses turned out titles on the Arctic by the hundreds. Journalists, scholars, and professional authors wrote biographies, expedition histories, and propaganda pieces; the polar heroes themselves contributed to this body of literature by producing a sizable corpus of memoirs.

Poems, essays, and vignettes devoted to the Arctic abounded in newspapers, literary journals, and special anthologies. A list of the literary figures who lent their efforts to the Arctic myth reads like a veritable *Who's Who* of the Union of Soviet Writers: Gorky, Marshak, Alexander Fadeev, Konstantin Fedin, Lev Kassil, Viktor Gusev, Nikolai Aseev, Valentin Kataev, Demian Bedny, Alexander Tvardovsky, Vasily Lebedev-Kumach, Konstantin Simonov, Perets Markish, and the list goes on. Poets Ilya Selvinsky (famous as an early leader of the constructivist movement) and Sergei Semenov took part in the *Sibiriakov* and *Cheliuskin* expeditions; later, Selvinsky drew upon his experiences to create two monstrously long poem cycles—*Cheliuskiniana* and the three-part *Arktika*—as well as a theatrical comedy, *Umka the Polar Bear*.

Furthermore, a small cluster of journalists accompanied the major Arctic expeditions. Aside from the memoirs of the heroes themselves, it was the work of these reporters that provided the public with the most intimate accounts of the USSR's polar adventures. They included *Izvestiia's* Boris Gromov, who traveled on the *Cheliuskin*; Ezra Vilensky, *Izvestiia's* correspondent for the SP-1 expedition; and Lazar Brontman, who journeyed to the pole for *Pravda*. Also noteworthy were Lev Khvat, who covered the flights of Chkalov, Kokkinaki, and the *Rodina* pilots; and Max Zinger, *Pravda's* full-time special correspondent for the North.

As with any mass-produced popular-culture phenomenon, the press's treatment of the Arctic myth varied in quality. In terms of artistic merit, the myth ranged from saccharine and didactic to exciting and inspirational. Physically, the production value of books and other materials connected with polar exploits was uneven; although much was packaged poorly, the print industry could also rise to the occasion and produce far better. A prime example is the official history of the *Cheliuskin* epic—*The Voyage of the* Cheliuskin, *Diaries of the Cheliuskinites*, and *How We Saved the Cheliuskinites*—the three-volume *Trekhtomnik*.[35] The brainstorm of Shmidt and his political officers, this collection was transfigured from a rough, humble set of diary entries and photographs into a lavish showpiece. The Politburo sponsored and funded the publication of the three books, and the results were spectacular.[36] For those accustomed to the general shoddiness of the majority of books published in the USSR during the 1930s, the *Trekhtomnik* stands out like a Gutenberg Bible in the middle of a rummage sale. All three volumes literally burst with fabulously reproduced photographs and full-color sketches. Party slogans appear in red-letter print on expensive tissue-thin paper; the words of Stalin are embossed in gold leaf. As the unusual craftsmanship of the *Trekhtomnik* demonstrates, when the press put its mind to it, it could make the vision of the state a vivid and captivating one.

The Fictional Arctic

The Arctic myth became fictionalized as well as publicized. After all, *Literaturnaia gazeta* had proclaimed that polar exploits such as the *Cheliuskin* epic were "living example[s] of the sort of socialist realism that our literature is striving to attain."[37] And so Arctic adventures gave rise to a socialist-realist subgenre in its own right: the "ice romance," a perfect vehicle for excitement and adventure.

A miscellany of authors wrote short stories or novels set in the Arctic.[38] Some were explorers by profession—Konstantin Badigin tried his hand at writing, and Mikhail Vodopianov dabbled in fiction as well.[39] Vodopianov's voluminous literary career is discussed in a later section, but it should be mentioned here that his play *A Pilot's Dream* had a significant impact on the Arctic myth. Popular in both the tsarist and Soviet eras was geologist and science-fiction author Vladimir Obruchev, whose two major works, the novels *Plutoniia* and *Sannikov Land*, enjoyed a great following.[40] The former, written in 1915, portrays an underground odyssey to the earth's core. The second describes a scientific team's efforts to locate the mysterious Sannikov Land, reputed for centuries to lie somewhere in the Arctic Ocean. Of course, the Russians find the island, along with friendly natives, a lost graveyard of woolly mammoths, and evil cave-dwelling savages. Obruchev evidently had plans to continue writing about the Arctic. In the 1940s, he outlined plots for two novels: *The Conquest of the Tundra*, about pilots pioneering air routes along the Yenisei, and *The Extinguished Sun*, the story of a new ice age in the Russian North.[41] Neither was ever completed, but Obruchev did leave behind another work connected to the Arctic: "An Incident at Neskuchny Garden." This whimsical tale recounts the events that transpire after the body of a woolly mammoth, preserved in the ice of Wrangel Island, is brought back to Moscow. By melting the ice, experts at the Paleontological Institute revivify the mammoth. The creature escapes, then goes strolling around the city, where it proceeds to cause no small amount of mayhem. Although the mammoth's jaunt drives the institute's director (not to mention the Moscow traffic police) to distraction, the animal is befriended by a group of Young Pioneers and, in the end, finds a happy home in the Moscow Zoo. Published in 1940, "Incident" became an instant favorite with Soviet readers.[42]

Even more dedicated to the Arctic was Max Zinger, who, of all the journalists covering the Arctic, logged the most travel time there. Zinger's lifelong acquaintance with the Arctic gave weight to his writing; as Pyotr Smidovich, chairman of the Committee of the North, said in a testimonial, only "one glance" was needed to tell that "his work was not written in the quiet of an office or a study."[43] The most unforgettable aspect of Zinger's stories is his use of animal characters: a wolf who befriends a doctor stationed at a lonely outpost; a walrus who fights a polar bear to the death; and a rooster who serves as the "living alarm clock" aboard an Arctic vessel. His most popular work was the story of Vaska, the "winter cat." There was, in fact, a real Vaska, who became a mascot for several ships, including the *Litke*. The twist was that Vaska brought bad luck, not good: any ship with the cat on board invariably spent the winter stranded in the ice. Sailors felt that it would be worse luck to do away with Vaska (a hilarious episode depicts a group of seamen trying to send him by mail to Moscow but failing due to paperwork), so the ships of the fleet simply traded him back and forth, sharing the bad luck as equitably as possible.[44]

By far the most renowned work of fiction associated with the Soviet Arctic is Veniamin Kaverin's *The Two Captains*.[45] Written in 1937 and reworked over the next nine years, the novel is a remarkable contribution to the Arctic myth. By any standards, Kaverin was a writer of considerable talents. In his youth, he belonged to the famous "Serapion Brothers," the small literary circle whose members learned their craft under the tutelage of Yevgeny Zamiatin. Kaverin repeatedly ran afoul of the official cultural establishment, and *The Two Captains* represents his attempt to reenter the literary mainstream.[46] He could hardly have picked a more effective way to do so. The book sold (and continues to sell) millions of copies; in 1955, it was made into a popular film by Lenfilm Studios.

The Two Captains tells the story of Sanya Grigorev, who grows up in a small village on the northern coast. Throughout his childhood, Sanya is intrigued by a sheaf of papers in his family's possession. Found drifting on the seashore, the weatherbeaten documents seem to be part of the log of a polar expedition, but no one in the village is able to determine what they truly are—and the mystery contained within them is never far from Sanya's mind.

After the Revolution, Sanya runs away from his village and finds himself in Petrograd (later Leningrad); he spends his teenage years there, in a school for orphans. At first he is a quick-tempered, unmanageable child, but he comes under the influence of the schoolteacher Ivan Korablev, who teaches him self-discipline. Sanya begins to do well at school and resolves to pursue the best and boldest of all professions: he decides to become a pilot.

While in Leningrad, Sanya also makes the acquaintance of the woman he will eventually marry: Katya Tatarinova, a bold-spirited, intelligent girl from a once-proud family. Katya is the daughter of Ivan Tatarinov, a polar explorer who has been missing since 1911, after a failed expedition to the North Pole. Tatarinov's untimely death, seemingly caused by incompetence, has made him a laughing-stock in scientific circles, and the family fortunes have suffered. The Tatarinovs' affairs are run by Ivan's cousin, Nikolai Antonovich, a vain, shallow man who emerges as the story's chief villain. Over time, it becomes clear that the papers that have obsessed Sanya all his life come from Captain Tatarinov's travel diaries; they also indicate that all is not as it seems with the official story of his death. Sanya and Katya pledge to each other that they will unravel the enigma surrounding Tatarinov's last expedition. They also begin to fall in love.

After graduating from school, Sanya trains as a pilot. With his interest in the Arctic deepening—and since all the "first-rate" fliers are working there—Sanya applies for duty in the North. One of his instructors is "Pilot C., a man the whole country knows and loves" (an obvious fictionalization of Chkalov). Sanya becomes a pilot for Glavsevmorput; he meets "Professor V." (Vize) and "the Chief" (Shmidt) and convinces them to stage an expedition to investigate Captain Tatarinov's disappearance. Unfortunately, GUSMP's pressing economic concerns come first, and the mission is canceled. By now, Sanya and Katya have married. Nikolai Tatarinov has become a famous Arctic scholar, making a name for himself by disparaging the legacy of his long-dead cousin. Sanya sees service in the Spanish Civil War, fighting for the Loyalists, then comes back home to fly transport missions in the North.

Then comes World War II, and Sanya sees combat on the Northern front. As the novel climaxes, Sanya's plane crash-lands on the Arctic coast. In one of destiny's great turns, the site of the wreck is the final resting place of Captain Tatarinov. At the makeshift grave, Sanya discovers Tatarinov's journal, which reveals the truth behind the mystery that has puzzled Sanya and Katya all their lives. Tatarinov's expedition failed due to deliberate sabotage: the ship's stores were tampered with by none other than Nikolai Antonovich, who doomed Tatarinov and his men to die because he was jealous of his reputation and in love with his wife. Sanya returns to Leningrad and denounces Nikolai Antonovich as a treacherous murderer. The memory of Captain Tatarinov is vindicated, and the action of the book comes to a happy close.

The Two Captains proved immensely popular. It was immediately compared by reviewers to *David Copperfield*, and Kaverin acknowledged his debt to Dickens in several interviews.[47] Despite its deus-ex-machina plot devices, the novel also rang true with authenticity: Kaverin did extensive research and spent time on the Northern front as a wartime correspondent for *Izvestiia*. All in all, *The Two Captains* was cast from a unique mold, and it became one of the most compelling portraits of the Arctic that the Soviet public was privileged to see.

Sight, Sound, and the Arctic

Images speak to a viewer in a direct, emotive way that words cannot. It was only natural, then, that the Arctic myth contained a wealth of images, all of which gave it an added dimension of appeal and, in every sense of the word, visibility. A key source of those images was the work of the photographers who accompanied polar expeditions and voyages. As with the journalists who specialized in writing about the Arctic, this was a select group. The veteran among them was Pyotr Novitsky, noted for shooting the first Soviet documentary film in 1918; in 1933 he was invited by Shmidt to be the photographer for the *Cheliuskin* expedition. Also important was *Izvestiia* photographer Dmitry Debabov, a close friend of filmmaking great Sergei Eisenstein. Debabov traveled to the North many times, capturing the heart of the Arctic on celluloid and plastic. When his photograph *Polar Night*, featuring the profile of a white wolf howling at the full moon, was displayed at the New York World's Fair, it caught the eye of Franklin Roosevelt, who purchased it for his private study. Yakov Khalip traveled to the North Pole with the SP-1 expedition, and his work in documenting the mission was popularly and critically acclaimed. Khalip also gave the four Papaninites a course in elementary photography, so they could make their own record of their months on the ice.[48]

Just as important in framing public perceptions of the Arctic was the medium of film. Movies were a serious matter in the USSR. Lenin had declared, "of all the arts, for us the most important is cinema"; Stalin echoed him by stating that "cinema is the greatest means of mass agitation."[49] By 1940, over 31,000 cinema facilities were open in the USSR, up from 17,000 in 1927. The number of movie tickets sold annually increased threefold between 1928 and 1940, from 300 million to 900 million.[50] The effect of all this can be summed up in the observation of one scholar: "everybody saw everything."[51] Film was one of the principal means of entertainment and information dispersal in the Soviet Union, and it became very much a part of the Arctic myth. During the *Italia* rescue in 1928, the *Krasin* and *Malygin* both took cameras on board; the result was the documentary *Exploit on the Ice.*[52] Afterward, it became standard practice to bring film crews along on expeditions to the North.

It would be difficult to overestimate the importance of the footage taken of the polar expeditions by directors and cameramen like Vladimir Shneiderov, V. D. Kuper, Mark Troianovsky, and Arkady Shafran. The films provided clips for the newsreels that millions of citizens saw throughout the country. In expanding the visual dimension of the Arctic myth, stills taken from the films complemented the pictures taken by photographers. And, of course, in their complete form, they were full-length adventures with the power to sweep audiences into a different world.

Neither was there any shortage of fictional films. In general, science, exploration, and aviation provided the basic premise for a high proportion of the 308 features distributed in the USSR during the era of high Stalinism.[53] Among the most popular was the dramatized biography *Valery Chkalov*, based on a screenplay by Baidukov and directed in 1941 by Mikhail Kalatozov, later famous for *The Cranes Are Flying* and *Moscow Does Not Believe in Tears.* The biggest exploration blockbuster of the decade, however, was *The Seven Bold Ones* (*Semero smelykh*), directed in 1936 by Sergei Gerasimov, whose work includes adaptations of such socialist-realist classics as *Young Guard* and *Quiet Flows the Don.* The *Seven Bold Ones* was a saga in every sense of the word; to make it as convincing as possible, Gerasimov hired Mikhail Yermolaev, a seasoned Arctic explorer, as a creative consultant.[54]

The Seven Bold Ones depicts a group of Komsomol members who travel to the Arctic on a geological expedition. The party consists of Ilya Letnikov, the team's geologist and leader; Zhenya Okhrimenko, the doctor (and the only woman on the expedition); Osya Korfunkel, the meteorologist; Sasha Rybnikov, the motorist; Kurt Shefer, the radio operator; Bogun, a Chukchi pilot; and Petya Molibog, the cook. The action gets under full swing when Ilya and Osya leave the station to conduct a mineral survey, despite the threat of bad weather. In the meantime, a group of Chukchi from a nearby settlement come to the encampment, asking for help; the chairman of their village council is seriously ill and needs emergency surgery. With Bogun, Zhenya flies to the settlement, arriving just in time to save the life of the Chukchi leader.

By now, the weather has grown fearsome, and Bogun and Zhenya are forced to make their way back on foot. When they return, they find that Ilya and Osya have not come back from their survey. The remaining team members venture into the blizzard to look for their missing companions but find nothing. Luckily, the neighboring Chukchi, in gratitude for Zhenya's kind help (and in a show of good Soviet ethnic solidarity), join the search and locate the two men. Although he is badly frostbitten, Ilya is alive, but Osya dies just as help arrives.

Undaunted by Osya's tragedy or the harsh winter, Ilya's group completes its mission by uncovering a rich vein of tin ore. In the spring, a ship comes to relieve the seven bold ones. However, Ilya and Zhenya, who have become romantically attached, choose to remain at their Arctic outpost for another year, dedicating themselves to their Party and socialist motherland. Fond farewells all around. With adventure, romance, a mighty struggle against the elements, and patriotism all wrapped up into two hours, *The Seven Bold Ones* took Soviet theaters by storm.

Arctic imagery was also found in the plastic arts. Vera Mukhina, who gained international fame with her gigantic sculpture *Worker and Collective Farm Girl*—which became a signature emblem of the Soviet regime after its appearance at the Paris International Exhibition of 1937—produced a series of busts depicting pilots of the 1930s, Kokkinaki among them. In 1938, Natalia Danko of Leningrad's Lomonosov Porcelain Factory, along with other artists, turned out a number of vases and figurines inspired by the SP-1 expedition.[55] Even more noteworthy were painting (for example, Mikhail Nesterov's full-length portrait of Otto Shmidt—surrounded in his study by books and maps—made a handsome addition to the Arctic myth), posters, and cartoons. Poster art was still a useful propaganda instrument during the 1930s, and polar heroes appeared in a number of placards and murals.[56] Cartoons gave the public an intimate and humorous perspective on the Arctic myth. By far the most unique vision of the Arctic to come out of the cartooning art was that of Fedor Reshetnikov, who accompanied the *Sibiriakov* and *Cheliuskin* expeditions. Reshetnikov's application to travel with the *Sibiriakov* was originally turned down, but when he presented himself at GUSMP headquarters, Shmidt was so taken by the young artist's infectious energy that he relented and took him on board. Reshetnikov eventually became a prominent member of the Moscow Academy of Art, but he is perhaps best remembered for the sketches he drew to depict the *Cheliuskin* adventure. The high-spirited Reshetnikov conveyed the experience of the Cheliuskinites with puckish, eccentric humor and a sense for the poignant. His cartoons picture Shmidt scaling the side of the globe or marching through the icy wilderness, with polar bears striking up a brass band (see Figures 7 and 8). They depict Liapidevsky's airplane as a kindergarten, with diapers hanging from clotheslines and even a cow or two to provide milk for the youngest Cheliuskinites. Molokov's plane is an "air-trolley," with dozens of people packed in the seats and dangling from the fuselage. The castaways are shown playing dominoes or listening to Shmidt's lectures. All of the drawings tickle the funnybone—and, in the long run, Reshetnikov's work became one of the most endearing collection of images to appear in the Arctic myth.[57]

A note should be made about radio and music as well. Along with cinema, radio was the state's most effective means of communicating with the Soviet public. Thanks to the great effort made during the 1920s to fulfill Lenin's dream of electrifying as much of the country as possible ("Communism equals Soviet government plus the electrification of the whole country"), the USSR had a respectable radio network in place by the 1930s. In 1933, there were sixty radio stations operating in the Soviet Union, wired to 1.3 million registered speakers and receivers. By 1940, the total had climbed to ninety stations and almost 7 million speakers and receivers.[58] Not only was news about polar exploits broadcast constantly over the airwaves, but special radio programs were devoted to the Arctic as well.[59]

Music is a difficult medium to pin down, since it involved a certain amount of cross-production, in conjunction with movies, plays, and poetry. Yet it is clear that a good deal of music was created as part of the Arctic myth. Upon leaving the "Development of the Arctic" pavilion in Gorky Park, composer Daniil Pokrass wrote the following comment in the guestbook: "This exhibit has inspired me greatly with ideas for my own creative work."[60] Whether or not Pokrass ever followed through on his impulse is unclear, but a number of other musicians celebrated the Arctic in their work, including Nikolai Kruchinin, founder of the Ethnographic Ensemble of Old Gypsy Music; Dmitry Kabalevsky; Leonid Bakalov; I. M. Abramovich; and Alexander Anoshchenko.[61]

The Arctic and the New Folklore

One of the staples of high-Stalinist culture was the celebration of Russian folk art. Condemned as a relic of the past during the years of the Cultural Revolution, folk culture—dance troupes, peasant choruses, balalaika orchestras, and cottage crafts—flourished after 1932.[62] At the First Congress of the Union of Soviet Writers, Maxim Gorky proclaimed that "the beginning of our art is in folklore."[63] Even Stalin spoke out, encouraging the Red Army Chorus to "supplement your repertoires with folk songs; use them as much as possible."[64]

There was nothing unusual about this; in Europe and America folkloric research has been tied to the creation of ethnic identity since the romantic era. The appropriation of folk imagery has also played a role in legitimating governments everywhere, from Nazi Germany, where "Teutonic archaicisms" helped to prop up Hitler's regime, to the democracies of the West.[65] After all, as one scholar of the USSR's Lenin cult notes, "all folklore is fundamentally connected with power."[66] Folklore in Stalinist Russia was no exception, and the regime thoroughly incorporated it into the country's official culture. First, the mass media began to use folk motifs to describe figures and events of the present day. Aircraft were "steel firebirds"; icebreakers and battleships moved across the seas by means of "silver sails." The subway system under construction in Moscow was an "underground kingdom"; in the hands of Lenin, Marx's *Communist Manifesto* became a "wizardly book."

The Soviets also manufactured entirely new works of folklore. All the traditional folk genres were resurrected: the folk or fairy tale (*skazka*), the epic (*bylina*), the extended poem (*starina*, rechristened the *novina* to reflect its newness), the lament (*plach*), and the short, light peasant verse (*chastushka*). The morphology of the old forms—the language, devices, and tropes—was replicated faithfully. The subject matter, however, was radically different. The bulk of this new folklore was created by a distinct group of artists and performers; chief among them were M. R. Golubkova, G. I. Sorokovikov ("Magai"), A. M. Pashkova, E. S. Zhuravleva, Ivan Kovalev, and, especially, Marfa Kriukova, the first lady of the novina.

Arctic exploits, replete with high drama and mythic overtones, easily found a place in the new folklore. All the artists listed above produced works devoted to Soviet achievements in the North. Pashkova compares the Papaninites to ancient bogatyri, such as Sviatogor, Dobrynia Nikitich, and Diuk Stepanich, rejoicing that the Land of Soviets has new heroes to carry on the bold traditions of the past.[67] Golubkova celebrates the might of Soviet technology in "A City Has Sprung Up amidst the Tundra," which describes the construction of Naryan Mar amid the bleak Pechora wilderness.[68] Chkalov's death prompted a flood of laments.[69] In Pashkova's "The Winds Obeyed Him," the waters of Lake Onega are troubled, the earth trembles, and the sky weeps in sorrow; the narrator urges Stalin to place Chkalov's body in a coffin of crystal.[70] Zhuravleva declares that she will petition Stalin to allow her to travel far and wide, in order that she might find "living water" to bring Chkalov back to life.[71]

Some of the new folktales were especially fanciful. Kovalev's "The Prophetic Ring" transforms the SP-1 expedition into an epic fantasy, beginning with the theft of an enchanted ring by a rapacious pike from a widow fishing in a river. This is a tragic loss; the widow's grandmother had entrusted her with the ring, charging her to give it to the leader of Russia when the country finally becomes free. Over time, she hears that the evil Tsar of the Sea, who lives at the top of the world, is in possession of the ring. She seeks out the help of a bearded explorer named "Searcher" (Iskatel'), who is, of course, Otto Shmidt. Searcher vows to recover the ring and sets out with his friends "Watergrabber" (Vodokhvat) and "Radiolistener" (Radioslukh)—Vodopianov and Krenkel. The three heroes defeat the Tsar of the Sea, raise a Soviet flag at the top of the world, and recover the ring. When the widow presents the Leader of Nations (Stalin) with the ring, it begins to shine, revealing for the Russian people all the precious metals concealed beneath the earth's surface—a metaphor for GUSMP's role in locating the vast mineral wealth contained in the Arctic.[72]

Just as colorful are the Arctic tales of Marfa Kriukova. Kriukova, born in the northern town of Zolotitsa, on the White Sea coast, was the acknowledged queen of the new folklore. The daughter of an accomplished storyteller, Kriukova had been singing byliny for over four decades before she began to create Soviet-style *noviny* (a term she herself coined). Her "Not Alone Is the Glorious Hero in the Soviet Land" is a tribute to the Papaninites.[73] "Beard-to-the-Knees and the Bright Falcons" is a retelling of the *Cheliuskin* voyage, starring the wise and fearless bogatyr Beard-to-the-Knees (*Pokolen-boroda*, an obvious nickname for Shmidt).[74] Her most famous Arctic novina is "Tale of the Pole," a rendition of the North Pole landing. Stalin, the "great chieftain," orders his explorers to the top of the world to learn how to control the weather: "Reconnoiter and inquire wherefore the morning sun arises, wherefore the blustery winds blow . . . when and whence the gentle rains do fall, and when the cruel drought does occur." The journey will be arduous; as the tale warns, many have tried to conquer the northern lands, but all have failed. Nonetheless, the bold Soviets, led by Ivan Longbeard (a composite figure of Shmidt and Papanin), reach the top of the world, where they build a tower of ice to look down upon the storms below. They place a red banner on the axis of the earth and study the movement of the planet about it by diving beneath the sea's surface. Ivan Longbeard has huge walls of ice constructed, by which his "wondrous knights" can control the climate: "now is the weather made for our homeland by Soviet heroes!" Not only does this hint specifically at the scientific purpose of the SP-1 mission—meteorological and oceanic research—but it also reinforces the general themes of technological progress and the struggle against the elements.[75]

Even more than noviny, two other genres were lauded as natural products of the USSR's folk voice. First was the art allegedly created by ethnic minorities. In the case of the Arctic, native Siberians were said to have engraved walrus tusks and whalebones with designs depicting the *Cheliuskin* adventure and the SP-1 mission. Hundreds of their songs and tales supposedly praised the glory of Stalin, "Great Friend to the Peoples of the World!" Such items did exist, but how genuine the sentiments behind them were is open to question.[76]

Equally important were the chastushki: short peasant verses sung in a distinctively dissonant tone and often improvised. During the 1930s, literally tens of thousands of new chastushki—extolling the virtues of political leaders, rejoicing at the arrival of tractors at the local collective farm, and expressing admiration for the glories of modern Soviet life—were collected and published. Hundreds, including the following, celebrated the heroes of the Arctic:

I will hug Baidukov,
I will kiss Chkalov.
Around Beliakov
I will tie a crimson ribbon.

A bird flies above our kolkhoz.
With steel wings,
Three heroes fly to the North.
Fair weather to you, friends!

Last night I had a dream,
A pleasant dream indeed.
Molokov fell in love with me,
And called me to be with him on Dikson Island.

When I finish school, brothers,
I have a plan prepared:
I will sail on an icebreaker
Across our Arctic Ocean.[77]

As charming and amusing as Soviet folk culture could sometimes be, it was hardly authentic. For one thing, much of it was fabricated in accordance to state directives. Folkworks were generally presented as having been collected by professional ethnographers, and they often included detailed documentation. But ethnography as an academic field came under strict governmental control during the 1930s, so such "proof" can hardly be taken at face value. Just as important was a more abstract issue: the new Soviet folklore fell into the category of what distinguished folklorist Richard Dorson calls "fakelore"—mass culture that uses folk stylization and is produced to make a profit or to pursue a political agenda. Far from being a spontaneous expression of popular sentiment, Soviet folklore was shaped in many ways by the regime. Golubkova, for example, was coached by an ethnographer in the pay of the state. Folklorist Viktorin Popov supervised Marfa Kriukova constantly; he made her read the works of Lenin and Stalin, edited her poems for content, and suggested ideas to her. He also labored endlessly to eliminate Kriukova's White Sea accent (*not* a practice recommended by most ethnographers in preserving the integrity of their informants' cultural creations!).[78] Even low-profile or anonymous folk pieces such as chastushki betrayed a certain level of artificiality. Composed as classroom assignments, as entries in folk competitions, or as ways of impressing local officials with one's loyalty, such items might, in certain cases, show creativity or sincerity as well. But they could hardly be classified as "pure" folklore.

Why folklore? What reasons did the state have for investing such time and effort into creating, or at least controlling, such an elaborately contrived body of "art"? The answer had to do with the commonly held notion that folklore represents the pristine, undistilled expression of the popular will. Whether or not the regime subscribed to this belief, it promoted it, and heavily. In this way, folklore was the ultimate legitimating device. What better way to prove that the state had mass support than to display a vast outpouring of artistic creations that welled forth from the very hearts of the people? And in cases where the creations were genuine, so much the better. Folkloric imagery also served a wider purpose: by combining folklore with its cult of technology and utopian vision, socialist realism created a syncretic totality depicting Russia's past, present, and future as a unified whole.

Individual Agendas: The Heroes as Mythmakers

It was good to be a Soviet hero during the 1930s. For the "Best People of the USSR"—Stakhanovite workers, prize-winning pig breeders, world-class violinists, and so forth—a bounty of rewards awaited. Along with national prestige and heightened social status, tangible benefits came with heroic status: household appliances, monetary awards, automobiles, and other perquisites. Arctic heroes received their fair share of the booty. After their transpolar flight, Chkalov, Baidukov, and Beliakov each received a cash bonus of 30,000 rubles.[79] Every participant in the SP-1 expedition received similar awards: most members were given 5, 10, or 15,000 rubles, while ten (including Shmidt, Papanin, and Vodopianov) topped the list at 25,000 rubles.[80] Ordinarily, Arctic pilots made 3,000 rubles a month (approximately seven times the pay of a university professor, or four times the salary of an experienced engineer), plus premiums.[81]

With so much at stake, GUSMP took the Arctic myth very seriously. Ever anxious to present the agency in the best light possible, the Politupravlenie created a Propaganda-Agitation Department, which operated GUSMP's printing house, handled news releases, organized public-relations events, and ran the exhibits at

Gorky Park and VSKhV. The department also monitored media coverage of the agency's activities and, on occasion, tried to influence it. In one instance, the department took issue with *Izvestiia's* treatment of the SP-1 expedition; in another, a cinema consultant for GUSMP complained to Sergei Gerasimov that newsreels needed to portray the agency "more heroically."[82]

The heroes themselves joined in manufacturing the Arctic myth. To start, they were swarmed with constant requests to give interviews, deliver lectures, and write newspaper articles and biographical essays (for those who lacked the inclination or talent to provide the public with accounts of their adventures, there were ghostwriters and literary "assistants"). Almost all of the heroes were eager to make sure they had at least some control over how they appeared in the public sphere. And so they became involved with the construction of the mythic environment in which they existed. Some contributed to it or helped design it. Others manipulated it to their own advantage and, on more than one occasion, thoroughly violated its heroic ideals. Virtually all of them wanted something for themselves out of it. Examples of how this dynamic played itself out are legion; the two best illustrations are those of Otto Shmidt and Mikhail Vodopianov.

Chief among the polar heroes in rank and fame, Shmidt dominated the Arctic myth in more ways than one. He served as an example of the ideal union of stikhiinost and soznatelnost. Next to Stalin, he was the chief father figure in the Arctic myth. During every New Year's celebration from the end of 1935 to 1938, he became Grandfather Frost for the entire nation, visiting classrooms and hospitals, posing for photographs, and endearing himself to millions.[83] Finally, Shmidt was consistently depicted as being in close proximity to Stalin himself.

If Shmidt played the leading role in the pantheon of Soviet polar heroes, he was also best equipped to manipulate the Arctic myth. In doing so, his chief concern was with power: power to keep his expeditions funded, power to keep his agency intact when it began to falter, even the power to keep himself alive and free at the height of the great purges. Perhaps more than anyone else, Shmidt realized what kind of strength celebrity status had to offer. When he began his Arctic career, he exercised his flair for show business by inviting members of the media to accompany him on expeditions and voyages. As Krenkel commented, "since coming to the North, I had seen a great many [journalists], and not by chance. For when the government had commissioned Otto Shmidt with the important business of Arctic exploration, this wise man had immediately understood the necessity of making friends with the press."[84] When asked why he routinely reserved such a large amount of expedition space for reporters and cameramen, Shmidt replied:

> Our Northern expeditions are the affair of the entire country. The country follows their progress with the utmost of attention. The country wants to know—and rightly so—how we work, what obstacles we meet, and how we overcome them. This connection between our expeditions and the people on the mainland is an eternal source of energy and strength.[85]

It was a useful source of fame as well. Shmidt's real intention was to keep GUSMP and its exploits, not to mention himself, as squarely in the public eye as possible.

Not only did Shmidt encourage the production of Arctic culture, he became a part of its manufacture. At his disposal was a combination of positions in the Soviet bureaucracy and a vast array of personal ties in the USSR's world of arts and letters. Shmidt had been a mid-level functionary in the Soviet elite since the days of the Civil War, and his position as GUSMP head was roughly equivalent to that of a deputy People's Commissar. He held a number of cultural posts throughout his career, while he and his wife, Vera Ivanovna, belonged to Moscow's most celebrated intellectual circles.[86] In addition to his years with the *Great Soviet Encyclopedia* and Narkompros, Shmidt worked on a government commission dealing with cinema affairs, headed the State Publishing House, and served on the boards of several prestigious theaters in the capital (among them the Chamber and Vakhtangov). Shortly after returning from the United States in 1934, he was invited to deliver an address at the First Congress of the Union of Soviet Writers.[87]

With his network of cultural connections, Shmidt influenced the shaping of the Arctic myth. Most of the writers and journalists who accompanied expeditions to the North were handpicked by Shmidt, making him, in mass-media terminology, a "gatekeeper." Furthermore, a number of those individuals became dependent on Shmidt as a patron; poets Ilya Selvinsky and Sergei Semenov, both members of the *Cheliuskin* expedition, wrote him several times to plead for money or introductions to "the right people."[88] In addition, many of the hundreds of books, songs, and plays dealing with Arctic exploits were submitted to Shmidt for comment and evaluation. Sofia Mogilevskaia asked Shmidt to review early versions of her popular book on the *Cheliuskin*.[89] Nikolai Aseev, Alexander Fadeev, Samuil Marshak, and former Commissar of Health Nikolai Semashko (now director of the Children's Publishing House) all petitioned Shmidt to look over drafts, include certain authors on expeditions, or transfer GUSMP personnel with literary promise to Leningrad or Moscow, where they could more easily write.[90] Even the Arctic epics of Marfa Kriukova were forwarded to Shmidt before release.[91]

The result was to allow Shmidt to make himself into a popular-culture icon of unrivaled stature. And, in the long run, his efforts paid off. When GUSMP began to suffer setbacks after its brilliant summer in 1937, Shmidt, as the agency's head, bore the responsibility. The crises could not have come at a worse time. Not only had the purges visited mass arrests and investigations upon Glavsevmorput, but Shmidt was faced with the beginnings of an internal power struggle, staged by Ivan Papanin. By whatever logic applied to the terror, Shmidt should have been a frightfully conspicuous target. But instead of falling victim to the purges, Shmidt managed not only to survive but to do so without overly severe consequences. Although GUSMP was stripped of most of its power in August 1938, Shmidt suffered no apparent harm. In March 1939, he relinquished the leadership of Glavsevmorput to Papanin, then went on to become vice-president of the Academy of Sciences until 1942. He worked actively in the fields of mathematics and planetary studies until his death in 1956.

Was Shmidt saved by his prominence as a national hero? Regardless of whether Shmidt gave up his GUSMP post voluntarily or was forced out, the fact that he avoided arrest or death is remarkable. While fame ordinarily conferred little or no protection against the NKVD, the *type* of Shmidt's fame may have been extraordinary enough to make his case special. The major Arctic heroes, Shmidt above all, seem to have possessed a certain superstar quality that made them genuinely popular as well as famous—and that popularity may have made the difference. To purge a Bukharin or a Tukhachevsky was to eliminate a figure who was well known, perhaps even respected, but not necessarily well liked. To purge a hero who was truly beloved by most of the entire nation and who had been built up as an embodiment of Soviet virtue would have been to rip the heart out of the very ideals upon which Stalinist culture itself was based. Did the regime choose to leave Shmidt in peace to avoid doing irreparable damage to the socialist-realist worldview it had labored to create? The answer is unclear. Either way, Shmidt's fame was hardly a liability in his efforts to come through the difficult years of 1937 and 1938 unscathed. And, by means of the Arctic myth, he had generated that fame largely through his own efforts.

Mikhail Vodopianov also took his public image into his own hands. Although Vodopianov enjoyed a close relationship with Shmidt, who took the young pilot under his wing as a protégé, his background, personality, and approach to the Arctic myth were the diametric opposite of Shmidt's. Before the October Revolution, Shmidt had received a first-rate education; he was cultured, fluent in several languages, and able to maneuver himself into the Soviet elite quickly and easily. By contrast, Vodopianov had been an illiterate shepherd before 1917. After fighting for the Red Army during the Civil War, Vodopianov became a mechanic, then a pilot. During the 1920s, he received a transfer to Eastern Siberia. In the early 1930s, he took part in several Arctic endurance flights, but it was in 1934, when he became one of the first Heroes of the Soviet Union for his role in the *Cheliuskin* rescue, that he achieved nationwide renown.

Vodopianov's attitude toward his newfound fame was anything but sophisticated; his main imperative was to improve his material and social position. Ironically, considering that he had not learned to read or write until the age of twenty, Vodopianov chose the field of letters in which to make his mark. The choice proved successful, and before his death in 1980, the self-made aviator became the most artistically prolific of the Arctic heroes, bar none. Vodopianov told (and retold) the story of his adventures and rags-to-riches advancement; he also tried his hand at fiction. The work that launched his literary career was A *Pilot's Dream*, an imaginary account of an air expedition to the North Pole, starring the semiautobiographical pilot Misha Nameless (*Bezfamil'nyi*). Vodopianov wrote A *Pilot's Dream* in 1935; the following year, the manuscript caught the attention of *Komsomolskaia pravda* editor Mikhail Rozenfeld, who arranged to have it published in play and novel form.[92] As described in the introduction to this chapter, the play opened in May 1937.

At the time, popular wisdom had it that A *Pilot's Dream* was the inspiration for Shmidt's SP-1 expedition. This was not true, but the play did have one lasting effect: it exposed Vodopianov to the literary bug, and the play's success only confirmed him in the belief that writing was the key to his future. Although Vodopianov had literary ambition in abundance, however, he had no artistic agenda to advance. His work fell solidly into the category of pulp fiction: his plots were simplistic, his characters taken directly from the socialist-realist stockpile of positive heroes, his worldview thoroughly Soviet.

Again, Vodopianov's principal concern was personal advancement. Although his patriotism was genuine, he lusted after the lifestyle that fame had to offer and believed wholeheartedly that his heroic endeavors entitled him to it. Unfortunately, the more famous Vodopianov became, the more his personal conduct began to diverge from the heroic ideal set forth in the Arctic myth. For one thing, it took only a short time for his literary pretensions to become an annoyance. Convinced that he deserved to be made a member of the Union of Soviet Writers (despite his need for a writing coach), Vodopianov determined to prove his worth as an author by spending more time writing, to the point of disregarding his duties as a Glavsevmorput pilot. No matter how exasperated his superiors became—and the Politupravlenie took the matter to the highest level, complaining to Georgy Malenkov that "all our efforts to make Comrade Vodopianov see reason with regard to his 'literary' activities have come to nothing"—he kept on writing.[93] Even Shmidt grew weary of his comrade's artistic exercises. When foreign reporters asked him in 1938 if Vodopianov's latest project, a novel about Antarctic exploration, had any bearing on Glavsevmorput's future plans, Shmidt dismissed Vodopianov's writings with a discernable note of peevishness.[94]

To make things worse, Vodopianov's free-wheeling lifestyle caused the authorities no small amount of consternation. Glavsevmorput found the boisterous pilot's liking for copious amounts of alcohol disturbing and felt it necessary to reprimand him more than once about his "unbecoming" conduct concerning young women. The burly Vodopianov also had a distressing tendency to start brawls in public; one of his most embarrassing moments came in December 1939, when he began a drunken fistfight with fellow *Cheliuskin* pilot Mavriki Slepnev at a New Year's Eve party at the Central House of Cultural Workers.[95]

Vodopianov's rivalry with Slepnev illustrates the atmosphere of intense competition among the polar heroes. In contrast to the image of mutual effort and comradely support put forward by the Arctic myth, the heroes' community became a wasps' nest of betrayal and swollen egos. Vodopianov's and Slepnev's mutual dislike manifested itself in ways far more serious than fisticuffs. For months, Vodopianov filed bitter accusations against Slepnev, apparently trying to get him demoted or arrested. Vodopianov charged Slepnev with using the *Cheliuskin* mission solely as a means of gaining glory. His "proof" consisted of the fact that Slepnev made only one flight to Camp Shmidt, where he rescued two people: "just enough to collect his Hero of the Soviet Union award, and no more." Instead of returning to the Cheliuskinites' camp, Slepnev volunteered to fly Shmidt to Alaska for medical treatment, showing an "unhealthy desire to travel to America." Vodopianov also hinted that Slepnev had cozied up too closely to Charles Lindbergh when the American pilot visited Moscow. Finally, he pointed (rather hypocritically) to Slepnev's "debauched" lifestyle as inappropriate for a Hero of the Soviet Union.[96] The authorities duly noted Vodopianov's accusations but never acted on them, and Slepnev went on to become head of GUSMP's Polar Aviation Administration.

Despite all of his antics, Vodopianov succeeded in his fundamental goal; aside from the occasional dressing-down, he experienced almost no bumps in his path to prosperity. After the peak of his fame passed, Vodopianov served with moderate distinction in World War II, training pilots, then went back to his writing. For the rest of his days, he lived a life of comfort and prestige. Heroism—and the Arctic myth—had been very good to him.

Unsurprisingly, Shmidt was not alone in his manipulation of the Arctic myth, and Vodopianov's hijinks were by no means isolated. A broad spectrum of responses to the mythmaking process existed among the Arctic heroes. A few individuals refrained from misusing their celebrity status. Chkalov and Gromov seem to have been circumspect in their character and conduct. Molokov was said to have been as humble in real life as in the Arctic myth, and GUSMP officials constantly exhorted other pilots (especially Vodopianov) to behave more like him. Krenkel may have been more brash than Molokov but was almost as scrupulous in his behavior.

One figure who carved out a unique image in the myth was Ivan Papanin. Described by reporter Ruth Gruber as a "clowning Napoleon," Papanin hardly fit the heroic mold, so he defined himself in contrast to it by lampooning heroic conventions in an earthy, self-deprecating manner. In one instance, Papanin toyed with the bogatyr metaphor by assigning a specific folkloric identity to each of the four SP-1 scientists: Shirshov became Alyosha Popovich, Fedorov was Solovei Razboinik, while the mighty Ilya Muromets was an obvious choice for the tall, rugged Krenkel. When he came to himself, Papanin joked that he was chubby enough to assume the role of both Ruslan and his sweetheart Liudmila.[97] And only Papanin could reduce a roomful of reporters to helpless laughter by inspecting the SP-1 equipment and demonstrating in graphic detail the structural difficulties the initial underwear design posed when it came to relieving oneself in the snow ("it is clear that the ladies who sewed these have never had to do their business in the middle of a blizzard!").[98] In essence, Papanin became a jester, transforming his own personal quality of irreverence into a great joke and somehow making it an acceptable part of the Arctic myth.

Success, however, went a long way toward spoiling many of the Arctic heroes, who misbehaved, grandstanded, and shamelessly abused their good fortune to line their pockets or bolster their career prospects. A number of Arctic celebrities indulged in extravagant profiteering, especially on the lecture circuit, which was highly, even illegally, lucrative. In one instance, Krenkel was horrified when the sponsors of one engagement offered him 450 rubles to speak, when, according to the official payscale for public lectures, Heroes of the Soviet Union were entitled to receive only 250 rubles per address. Krenkel's indignant refusal to accept such a large sum amazed the sponsors, who informed him that other Arctic heroes (particularly Slepnev) had been demanding rates in excess of 500 rubles.[99] Similarly, some Arctic heroes used their fame to jockey for promotions, and a few became petty tyrants of the worst type. In the most notorious case, Ilya Mazuruk used his status as an SP-1 pilot to become the head of the Civil Aviation Administration (Aeroflot). Almost immediately upon arrival, Mazuruk began to browbeat his employees mercilessly, harassing them with such ominous remarks as, "I will have you shot," or, "how would you like me to acquaint you with Yezhov?"[100]

The dilemma of the unheroic hero, of course, is by no means confined to the Soviet experience. In a waggish short story entitled "The Greatest Man in the World," American humorist James Thurber begins by informing his readers that

> ever since Kitty Hawk, America had been blindly constructing the elaborate petard by which, sooner or later, it must be hoist. It was inevitable that some day there would come roaring out of the skies a national hero of insufficient intelligence, background, and character successfully to endure the mounting orgies of glory prepared for aviators who stayed up for a long time or flew a great distance.[101]

The story goes on to recount the tribulations of the government and press as they cope with the behavior of the man who becomes America's newest aviation hero: Jack Smurch, a garage mechanic who manages to fly nonstop around the world. Smurch, a distinguished alumnus of his hometown reform school, swills home-brewed gin and smugly informs reporters that "youse guys can tell the cock-eyed world dat I put one over on Lindbergh, see?" In short, Smurch's unsuitability as a national hero was "the most desperate crisis the United States of America had faced since the sinking of the *Lusitania.*" Fortunately for the entire country, the secretary to the mayor of New York City disposes of the problem by deftly maneuvering the surly pilot out of a nine-story window.

No doubt the architects of the Arctic myth (and the other heroic myths of Stalinist Russia) longed on occasion to solve similar problems in a similarly neat fashion—for there were many more Smurches than Lindberghs in the circle of Soviet heroes. By the time the Arctic myth reached the public, the polar heroes were already essentialized and packaged as hagiographic figures, reduced to a set of standard Soviet virtues and one or two individualizing attributes. But in real life they were flesh-and-blood human beings who refused to allow themselves passively to be absorbed into the Arctic myth without their needs and desires being met. Therefore, they became factors in the actual creation of the myth, not just emblems within it. Most of the Arctic heroes simply demanded that they be permitted to benefit from their mythic status; a few, such as Vodopianov and Shmidt, took a hand in manufacturing the myth themselves. Whatever the case, all of them left their own imprint on the worldview that their exploits helped to define.

Consuming the Myth: The Public Responds

Upon Chkalov's death, poet Alexander Tvardovsky wrote the following eulogy of the fallen pilot: "We loved him so much that he seemed to belong to each of our lives, as if each of us had been his personal friend, as if each of us had drunk with him, eaten with him, and flown with him."[102] Was this really the case? How did the Soviet people react to the Arctic heroes? And specifically with what about them did the public identify?

These are not easy questions. Measuring public response in any society is difficult. In countries like the USSR, it is even harder, since most of the sources that scholars typically use in doing so—letters, newspaper editorials, or journals—are, for obvious reasons, suspect. Accurate demographic information from the 1930s is almost completely lacking, and piecing together the prevailing attitudes of a large, heterogeneous society that had limited opportunities for self-expression and left behind no coherent record of what it thought or felt is a trying exercise.[103]

Still, it seems clear that, by and large, Arctic heroes enjoyed a tremendous amount of genuine appeal during the 1930s. Even afterward, when they and their deeds no longer occupied center stage, they continued to be popular. It is important to note, however, that the fact that the Arctic heroes, along with their exploits, were well liked, even beloved, does not automatically imply that the messages encoded within the Arctic myth were equally so. This portion of the chapter will proceed to examine the ways in which the public understood and consumed the Arctic culture of the 1930s.

The Appeal of the Arctic

By all indications, ordinary Soviet citizens—at least those from Russia and the European portions of the country—found Arctic heroes to be admirable and the Arctic myth to be more exciting than most Stalinist propaganda efforts. This should come as no surprise: the conquest of the poles was one of the hallmark enterprises of the modern age, and millions of people worldwide thrilled to polar exploits for more than a century. It was only natural that the Russians, whose affairs had always been closely linked to the Arctic, should be enthusiastic about their polar heroes.

Polar exploits seem to have proven especially popular with children and adolescents. Instinctively drawn to drama and color, young people made a perfect audience for the Arctic myth. The Children's Publishing House (Detizdat) and Young Guard (Molodaia gvardiia) took the lead in producing books about the Arctic for children and teenage readers; many were written by polar heroes (or their ghostwriters). Such works deliberately attempted to inculcate good Soviet values; they urged their readers to study hard and to become virtuous citizens. Arctic heroes spoke to children over the radio, posed with them in photographs, and visited them in the classroom. On one occasion, Shmidt spoke to a group of Young Pioneers, proclaiming that,"yours is a happy generation, fortunate that it will be able to give itself entirely to the service of its Motherland."[104] The media linked Arctic celebrities to children time and again. Memoirs teem with stories about how the words and deeds of polar heroes inspired and motivated young people. When Chkalov perished, he was said to have gone to his death with a sheaf of kindergarteners' letters in his jacket pocket, over his heart.[105] One propaganda booklet boasted that "each child dreams of becoming another Chkalov."[106]

Was this true? After his visit to the Soviet Arctic, journalist Harry Smolka seemed to think so, commenting that "a Russian schoolboy will dream of [polar celebrities] as a French child dreams of Napoleon or an Australian boy of Bradman."[107] Smolka related a famous story about how a group of students had been discovered plotting to kidnap Molokov and make him the honorary chair of their Pioneer cell.[108] Many accounts depict children playing at being Cheliuskinites or Papaninites, the way American children play cops and robbers and cowboys and Indians.[109] Throughout 1938, the children's magazine *Murzilka* received a cascade of mail from boys and girls expressing their excitement about the SP-1 expedition.[110] *Izvestiia's* semiregular cartoon feature, "Of What Our Children Dream," depicted polar exploration as the career to which most Soviet youth aspired.[111] In a quasi-autobiographical account of childhood in the countryside, one author describes how, as teenagers, he and his friends embraced the Cheliuskinites as heroes:

> We heard about the Cheliuskinites and their rescuers . . . and shouted until we were hoarse and the last of the Cheliuskinites was taken from the ice and brought back to the mainland. Our joy was so great that we . . . did not feel fatigue, and asked the brigade leader to leave us out in the field for the night.[112]

It is safe to suppose that young people in the USSR—who were most susceptible to the bright and flashy aspects of high-Stalinist culture—enjoyed at least some aspects of the Arctic myth. On the other hand, children and teenagers were more likely to miss the myth's deeper meanings than older audiences.

Adult responses to Arctic culture tended to be more complicated. For the most part, the myth was received well. To begin with, polar exploits were entertaining and diverting. In fact, this quality alone accounted for much of the myth's success in reaching the everyday lives of Soviet individuals. The citizenry's apparent liking for Arctic adventures was caused in part by the simple fact that there were few things in Soviet society to like. The 1930s were characterized not only by hardship and oppression but also by extreme boredom. Film scholars, for instance, are in general agreement that the popularity of the Soviet cinema during these years was due to a serious dearth of venues for entertainment, such as cafés, bars, or dance halls: "People, especially the young, went to the cinema, not so much to see a particular film, but because there was literally nothing else to do."[113] On his visit to the USSR in 1935, American literary critic Edmund Wilson remarked on the "paleness and sadness" of Gorky Park, with its "slow quiet crowds" and "no gaiety."[114] Against such a drab backdrop, polar heroics could not help but be a welcome diversion.

Just as important, in an environment where, as musician Yuri Yelagin describes, "overnight the idols of yesterday were stamped as Fascists, Trotskyists, spies . . . and enemies of the people," finding public figures to admire and emulate was somewhat risky for most Soviet citizens. If "the average person looked in bewilderment and horror at the list of generals, writers, members of the government, Marxist philosophers, engineers, and scientists who had disappeared in Yezhov's meat grinder," in whom and about what could that average person feel at least some measure of pride, either for the purpose of presenting a suitably loyal public facade, or out of the natural human desire to feel proud about *something*? Yelagin's answer is simple: "In the entire country, only fliers, musicians, and chess players seemed to have their feet on solid ground; a person could associate with them without fear of being accused of harboring subversive views"—

and therefore "the Soviet masses shifted their adoration to the representatives of these three professions."[115]

On the other hand, the Arctic myth by no means generated a uniformly positive response. Some reactions were neutral or noncommital; to gauge how many is impossible. Others reacted to the myth unfavorably, in some cases because they identified it with the less attractive aspects of Stalinist rule. Rather than detracting from the importance of the myth, however, even negative reactions signal that it took hold—or at least struck a nerve—in the Soviet popular imagination. In objecting to Arctic symbols, in poking fun at them, even in distorting them unintentionally, Soviet citizens injected a measure of symbolic inversion— of the sort found in Bakhtin's treatment of the carnivalesque—into the discourse of the state.[116] In small ways, they subverted official ideology. Still, the Arctic myth seems to have won support, and a good deal of it. That the myth was ubiquitous is self-evident. That it was popular is likely, although less certain. Whether support of the myth equaled support of the Stalinist order is very much an open question.

Vox Populi: Positive Feedback

The most visible expression of public opinion regarding the Arctic myth consists of the thousands of letters printed in the central press and cited in books and memoirs. Such materials, however, are not completely reliable; letters were routinely screened and altered, assuming that they were not completely contrived. In addition, letter writing was not always voluntary: it was frequently a classroom assignment or a work-related exercise, prompted by one's labor union or Party cell. Even letters that convey the genuine attitudes of the author may not be written by people with widely representative opinions.

Still, such material cannot be rejected out of hand. Exaggeration and miscontextualization, rather than complete untruth, are the trademarks of effective propaganda campaigns; even tainted expressions of public sentiment most likely represent an attempt to amplify and broadcast feelings that really existed. And people did write. Authors like Kaverin, Zinger, and Obruchev received vast amounts of fan mail. Periodicals claimed to be swamped with letters from the public; the day before the Cheliuskinites returned to Moscow, *Pravda* printed a front-page letter from "the Workers, Engineers, and Staff of the Red Putilovets Factory." The authors gushed that

> our country is the pearl of the earth and the hope of all humankind. Your exploits, comrades, have illuminated the countenance of our entire nation. You have set a wondrous example of heroism and patriotism for the whole country. We are thankful to you from our very souls.[117]

The rest of the issue was festooned with mail—supposedly from people of all walks of life—containing exclamations such as "we never doubted!" and "I am proud that my native land is the USSR!" One letter even invited the Cheliuskinites to the October Revolution Collective Farm for tea and *bliny*.[118] When

Shmidt's expedition landed at the pole and Chkalov and Gromov made their transpolar flights, letters bearing titles such as "To the Victory" or "The Soviet People Are Enraptured by the Courage and Bravery of Their Heroes!" appeared in the flagship papers.[119]

Additional reactions were printed elsewhere. The newspaper *Stalinets* published a letter entitled "Be Thus—Like a Hero-Pilot," purportedly written by one Kuznetsov, a locomotive fireman, to his son Vanya. Vanya is about to begin his career as a naval pilot, and Kuznetsov urges him to conduct himself as the *Cheliuskin* pilots do, ending his letter with the proud statement that "I tell myself always to act as a rock-hard Bolshevik, like Shmidt. And I have written my son, saying, 'Vanya, be a brave and honorable pilot, like our heroes Molokov and Kamanin.'"[120] Comments in the guestbook at the Osvoenie Arktiki exhibition revealed similar sentiments: "All that I have read about in the papers has come alive for me!" or "I am transported! This exhibition depicts wonderfully the achievements of our Stalinist epoch!"[121] In his memoirs, Krenkel mentions a radiogram sent to the Papaninites by two brothers, Kolya and Seryozha Bibin. The two boys, inspired by the SP-1 mission, declare their intention to become explorers when they grow up. They also include a special request, cast in the form of a poem:

> We wish to go to the pole,
> Where the cold and frost reign,
> And we wish to see
> The axis of the Earth.
> But by the time that we have grown,
> All the poles will be discovered.
> By the time ten years have passed,
> Not a "white spot" will remain.
> We will agree to wait—but
> We insist on one condition:
> Please leave for me and Seryozha
> Just one "white spot" on the map![122]

A last anecdote concerns an unlucky victim of excessive enthusiasm about the Arctic: a hapless young girl whose parents made her a "living monument" to the North by saddling her with the name Lagshmivara, after Camp Shmidt (LAGer'-SHMIdta-V-ARktike-A).[123]

An interesting set of positive responses to the Arctic myth can be found in the recollections of various celebrities and literary figures. Cosmonaut German Titov, the second man in space, notes in his autobiography how he was impressed by polar exploits (and *The Two Captains*) as a boy.[124] Poet Marina Tsvetaeva delighted in the thrill of the *Cheliuskin* adventure, as shown in the exuberant last stanza of her verse about the event:

> Today—long live
> The Soviet Union!
> With every muscle
> I support you—
> And take pride in you:
> For the Cheliuskinites are Russian![125]

Perhaps the most engaging literary portrait of a reaction to the Arctic myth comes from Lidia Chukovskaia, daughter of Kornei Chukovsky, the USSR's most beloved children's author. In Chukovskaia's novel *Sofia Petrovna* (hardly a pro-Stalin work), both the title character, a young typist, and her best friend, Natasha, are profoundly affected by the *Cheliuskin* saga. Sofia clips pictures of the Cheliuskinites from the newspapers and caches them away in a box full of childhood treasures. Natasha's feelings are even more intense:

> And how she worried when the ice crushed the *Cheliuskin*! She was never far from a radio. Out of the newspapers she cut photographs of Captain Voronin, Camp Shmidt, and, later on, the pilots. When the news about the first Cheliuskinites to be rescued was announced, she began to cry tears of happiness, right there at her typewriter.[126]

Whether the reactions of Sofia and Natasha reflect the feelings that Chukovskaia herself had about the *Cheliuskin* is unknown, but they are almost certainly drawn from some real-life experience in her youth.

Even more solid as an index of public opinion about the Arctic is the torrent of letters sent by Soviet citizens to Glavsevmorput or the heroes themselves. Unsolicited, unaltered, and rarely made public, these letters tend, with very few exceptions, to be positive and enthusiastic. One event that prompted a huge wave of mail was the *Cheliuskin* crisis.[127] Most writers simply expressed their sympathy and support, but a number demonstrated extraordinary levels of excitement and concern. Many people wrote to recommend ideas or offer assistance. A Leningrad rail worker was so moved by the drama that he begged Glavsevmorput to "please let me help in the rescue!" Others offered elaborate plans, often inspired by the memoirs of Nansen and Peary. Perhaps the most unusual letter came from Yuri Lapitsky, a Minsk agronomist. Lapitsky proposed a "straightforward and infallible plan" to save the stranded explorers: he suggested that the rescuers simply walk from the Chukchi coast to Camp Shmidt over the frozen ocean. To avoid losing its way, the search party would set up a signal marker after each kilometer and take readings every twenty-two kilometers. Each time the party halted to get its bearings, it would also build a "modest" supply base, equipped with sleeping bags, food, and huts for shelter.[128] Precisely how this "medium-sized" party was supposed to navigate by dead reckoning through the storms of an Arctic winter, much less haul with it supplies sufficient to provision a small army, all over uneven terrain, were issues that the earnest young agronomist failed to address. The folly of his scheme aside, however, Lapitsky's letter reveals an avid preoccupation with the Arctic, if not a terribly impressive understanding of it.

As the most overpowering presence in the Arctic myth, Otto Shmidt naturally attracted a great deal of attention. Ruth Gruber discovered the extent of Shmidt's appeal when she shared quarters with a young Soviet woman in a Sverdlovsk dormitory. The girl reacted to Gruber, an obvious foreigner, with great suspicion—until shown a letter of conduct written by Shmidt:

> I showed her Shmidt's letter of recommendation. The young woman acted as if she had seen the Holy Grail. I had a letter from Otto Yulevich. I was sacrosanct.

"But did you meet him personally?" she asked a little breathlessly.

"Yes."

"Is he really as handsome as his picture?"

"More so." She was my good friend now.[129]

In keeping with this, Shmidt received literally thousands of letters, which tend to follow one of several patterns.[130] The author is typically between grade-school age and the mid-twenties. A sizable portion of the letters come in large packets sent by entire classrooms, a sign that writing to Professor Shmidt was a common schooltime activity. The majority of correspondents, however, appear to have written on their own initiative. The younger the writer, the more he or she is simply thrilled with the glamor of addressing such a famous celebrity; a few even refer to Shmidt as Grandfather Frost. Older writers are often interested in becoming polar scientists or explorers; many include résumés and credentials with their letters. Both boys and girls express a strong interest in working in the Arctic; a number of the girls appear to be equally interested in Shmidt romantically. The following excerpt leaves no doubt that the tall, heroic Commissar of Ice set a number of hearts aflutter: "Dearest Professor Shmidt! How I wish I could be older and know as much as you! I would ask you to take me away with you on a new expedition. . . . Please send me a letter or picture in reply. I will keep it under my pillow and remember you in my dreams.[131]

Shmidt referred often and fondly to his young correspondents, remarking in one interview that "I cannot help but be touched every time I receive a letter that goes something like this: 'Comrade Shmidt, please take me to work in the Arctic. To serve in the Arctic has been my lifelong dream—and I am already nineteen years old!'"[132] Shmidt seems to have answered as many letters as he could personally. His usual reply included a tactful apology that GUSMP had more than enough explorers at the moment. He encouraged those who wrote him to study diligently. And, for those young people who seemed truly interested in the Arctic, he suggested that they write GUSMP's Politupravlenie for more information or that they become pen pals with personnel stationed in the agency's remote outposts.

Dissenting Voices: Negative
Responses to the Myth

Other reactions to the Arctic myth are harder to trace. Since people seldom take the trouble to record how they do *not* care about something, neutral responses are almost completely absent. But although it was dangerous to air them, negative responses were not uncommon. As shown in chapter 6, many GUSMP employees had a jaded view of their agency's exploits, and some made no secret of it. On occasion, the general public felt the same way. One of the most caustic criticisms directed toward polar heroics comes from the journal of Andrei Arzhilovsky, a well-educated and extremely sharp-witted peasant who eventually perished in the purges of 1937 (the excerpts that follow were underlined by NKVD investigators and used against him in his "trial"). In reaction to the SP-1 expedition, Arzhilovsky writes that "our pilots have landed at the North Pole, and now we are making a great show of our pride. They'll slide around on the ice up there, pocket their extra travel money, run up an incredible expense account and fly on home, where the fools will shower them with flowers. . . . What is there to gain from sliding around on the thick polar ice? If you ask me, not a thing." When Chkalov and Gromov fly to America across the pole, Arzhilovsky rails about the fact that Arctic heroes receive extravagant prizes while ordinary people like himself struggle to keep themselves fed: "No wonder those pilots work so hard: they don't care about conquering the North Pole, they just want to get something to eat. In addition to their regular salary with all those extra zeroes, they get a bonus of 25,000 rubles. They can make it through a whole year without hunger!"[133] How many others despised polar heroes as thoroughly as Arzhilovsky did is impossible to tell, but the unfortunate peasant was surely not alone in his desire to peel back the layers of deception and hypocrisy that candy-coated socialist-realist culture.

Damning comments about the Arctic myth also came from the literary intelligentsia. In an eerie passage from her diary, Anna Akhmatova recounts a conversation she had with fellow poet Osip Mandelstam, two years before he was arrested and taken to the GULAG. During their meeting, Mandelstam told Akhmatova of an "attack of frenzy" he suffered one night in the city of Voronezh. During the seizure, Mandelstam fell under the delusion that Akhmatova had been executed by the secret police, and he found himself wandering aimlessly, searching for her corpse. He came across an arch erected in honor of the Cheliuskinites; under the influence of his temporary madness, it struck him that the arch had actually been built to celebrate Akhmatova's death.[134] Such a disturbing image signals a strong subconscious identification of the Arctic myth with the most terrifying aspects of Stalinism. Years afterward, Mandelstam's widow Nadezhda described the *Cheliuskin* epic as one of "the relics of Stalin's empire."[135]

When a new generation of writers came of age, a number of them treated the Arctic myth in a more comic vein. After Stalin's death, many authors satirized the socialist-realist worldview that they had been exposed to constantly during their youth, and polar celebrities did not escape the ridicule. For example, Private Ivan Chonkin, Vladimir Voinovich's lovable, dim-witted hero, has a serious problem in *Pretender to the Throne*. Not only is he being court-martialed, but he finds it impossible to stay awake, since the prosecutor insists on droning endlessly about the innumerable achievements of the Stalinist state before getting on with the case. High on the list of items putting poor Chonkin to sleep are Ivan Papanin and Polina Osipenko.[136] In Fazil Iskander's *Sandro of Chegem*, an Abkhazian village completely mangles the meaning of the Arctic myth; the most popular song in the settlement is about the *Cheliuskin*, but it is a lament entitled "Death of the Cheliuskinites" (a piquant comment on the Arctic myth's ineffectiveness in reaching the USSR's non-European ethnicities meaningfully).[137] *The Burn*, by Vassily Aksyonov, sends up Stalin's Arctic heroes in the zaniest fashion of all. One of the novel's minor characters, "Airplane Airplanovich Chkalov," is a helicopter pilot and accused felon, charged with pelting the psychiatric personnel of the Second Five-Year Plan Sanatorium with pastries.[138]

Among the most interesting examples of unfavorable feedback to the Arctic myth are jokes and anecdotes that made light of polar exploits. Of these, the best documented concern the *Cheliuskin* voyage. In 1935, a fourth-grade student in Leningrad was caught spreading this morbid couplet: "They've killed Kirov, they've sunk the *Cheliuskin*,/Maybe they'll kill Stalin, too."[139] Even more famous was an anonymous ditty known as "Song of the *Cheliuskin*," one version of which went as follows:

> Greetings, Levanevsky, greetings, Liapidevsky,
> Greetings, Camp Shmidt, and farewell!
> How did this affair happen?
> The *Cheliuskin* sank.
> Perhaps they were drinking vodka?
> They took off from Leningrad and got their just rewards.
>
> What was so bad for them on the ice?
> What did they lack?
> They had cheese, butter, preserves, and sausage.
> What was there to stop them from calling
> Vankarem and sending to the Central Committee for more?
> Shmidt sat on his ice-floe, safe as in his feather-bed.
> If not for Mishka, Mishka Vodopianov,
> You would never have seen your native Moscow again.
>
> You wouldn't have heard all the greetings,
> You wouldn't have gotten all the gifts.
> And now the heroes live quite well—
> A little money in their pockets, their faces on the big screen.[140]

"Song of the *Cheliuskin*" traveled widely (according to some reports, people had to pay up to a ruble to hear the song). The variant above was collected by GUSMP authorities in Arkhangelsk, but the song is thought to have originated in Leningrad, where it was first encountered by NKVD officers investigating rumors in the wake of the Kirov assassination in December 1934. Other renderings of the song surfaced throughout the country, with minor alterations in the text.

Unsurprisingly, such humor was seen by the authorities as politically danger-ous. It should be noted, however, that doggerel like "Song of the *Cheliuskin*" did not necessarily amount to opposition to the regime or even dislike for the Arctic myth (although in some cases it did). People tell jokes about every topic—and for every reason—imaginable, and it is perfectly plausible to suppose that Soviet cit-izens made off-color quips about polar exploits as much to vent cynicism, to cope with frustration, or simply to get a laugh, as to make a political point. Many may have grown tired of the overly ponderous nature of socialist-realist propaganda. In 1938, a remarkably brave (or foolish) Leningrad Communist wrote to Andrei Zhdanov to complain that "everything is Stalin, Stalin, Stalin." Among the "hun-dred examples" of how "Comrade Stalin's name has been very much abused," the author listed such icons of the Arctic myth as "Stalin's Route" and "Stalin's Pole." He then went on to make a sarcastic but shrewd point about the overexpo-sure of high-Stalinist symbology: "this sacred and beloved name may make so much noise in people's heads, that it may possibly have the opposite effect that it is supposed to."[141] With this, he no doubt put his finger on one of the reasons that unflattering anecdotes about the Arctic myth began to emerge. It is a failing of dictatorships, however, that they take themselves too seriously, and, out of insecurity and paranoia, the Stalinist leadership was unable to accept any critical representation of it or the things it held sacred. So the NKVD did its best to collect political jokes and stories (and, as the old adage goes, the people who told them) and keep them under wraps—regardless of what their tellers actually intended by them. And no exception was made for expressions of negative sentiment about the Arctic myth.

Propaganda: Effects and Limitations

In his classic treatise on modern means of mass persuasion, Jacques Ellul argues that propaganda is

> a matter of reaching and encircling the whole man. We are here in the presence of an organized myth that tries to take hold of the entire person. This myth becomes so powerful that it invades every area of consciousness, leaving no faculty or motivation intact. It has such motive force that, once accepted, it controls the whole of the individual, who becomes immune to any other influence.[142]

In a similar manner, Antonio Gramsci describes how hegemonic discourse—with propaganda as its carrier—compels a downtrodden population to accept its plight: "their understanding of the world leads them to collaborate in their own oppression."[143] How valid is this grim, Orwellian view of propaganda? Was the socialist-realist worldview—and the Arctic myth with it—a sinister tool of the state? Did it enthrall the Soviet populace, inculcating within it a blind, subservient obedience? Did it indeed "reach and encircle the whole man"?

The evidence given above indicates that it did not. Soviet propaganda, which was produced by many individuals and institutions, did not speak merely with a single voice. More important, the Soviet citizen was capable of reading culture in a number of ways. Instead of subscribing to the official, privileged reading offered by the state, people developed alternative, even oppositional, readings of their own. In other words, Soviet citizens were not helpless victims of their government's propaganda efforts, for there are definite limits to what propaganda and mass media can do. The process of transmitting even the most basic message through the media is a complicated process. The sender must create the message, which must be encoded, then pipelined through the medium. The message must get to the audience by means of the appropriate receiver, then be decoded by the target. With every step that stands between the sender and the audience, the more potential there is for the message to be comprehended by the audience in a way not necessarily intended by the sender.

All of this helps to explain why the classic "magic bullet" theory, which postulates that media messages can be tailored to have predictable effects on all members of an entire population or specific demographic, has been discredited time and again.[144] With respect to the USSR, the Harvard Interview Project of the late 1940s showed that the individual response of the Soviet citizen to his or her country's media messages was far more complex than complete acceptance or outright negation: men and women in the Soviet Union sifted through the media for nuggets of truth, shadows of verity. As one interviewee remarked, "I taught myself to translate the lies of the press into my own language of relative truth."[145] Despite arguments to the contrary, Soviet propaganda was not an easy matter of programmatic compulsion.

In time, each Soviet individual learned his or her own "language of relative truth," making Ellul's nightmare vision of propaganda's iron grip on hearts and minds much less viable. Even so, propaganda is not without its effects. Ellul makes an astute point regarding long-term exposure to even the most unbelievable or ludicrous propaganda: "When one reads [something so egregious] once, one smiles. If one reads it a thousand times, and no longer reads anything else, one must undergo a change."[146] This was the fundamental strength of the Stalinist regime in crafting the socialist-realist worldview: its ability to manipulate the symbolic environment. The state might not be able to control how people reacted to state-sponsored myths and symbols, but it could control what was available to react to. This in itself had its own effect: as one historian notes, "the Soviet people ultimately came not so much to believe the Bolsheviks' worldview as to take it for granted."[147]

This represented a victory of sorts for the state, but not a complete one. With respect to polar exploration, it can be said that the Soviet public appreciated the Arctic and its heroes. Did it appreciate, or even grasp, the set of messages and values encoded within the Arctic myth? In some cases, yes. In others, no. Either way, people were still able to enjoy the heroics, without necessarily caring about or being conscious of the "moral" tagged on to them by the state and the media. In the end, the Soviet public can be said to have taken great pleasure in its country's triumphs in the Arctic and to have felt much affection for its polar heroes — but also to have had a fairly wide range of options when it came to equating those feelings with what the Arctic myth had been created to bring about: admiration for the Stalinist regime.

SIX

Polestar Descending
Glavsevmorput in Decline, 1936–1939

But it stank, too, even way up north, beneath
the Arctic storms, at the polar stations so beloved in the legends of the thirties.

—Alexander Solzhenitsyn

In July 1937, in the wake of his successful expedition to the North
Pole, Otto Shmidt gave a public address at Moscow's Regional
Council of Professional Labor Unions. Afterward, Shmidt was asked by a reporter
why Levanevsky had not yet made a transpolar flight to America. After all, both
Chkalov and Gromov had done so. Why not a Glavsevmorput pilot? Shmidt answered by repeating the question: "Why, indeed, has Levanevsky not flown this
year?" He paused, allowing a grin to appear on his face: "Remember, my com-
rades, the year is not yet out." In other words, bigger and better things were yet to
come from GUSMP.[1]

If Shmidt had been able to see only a short distance into the future, his remarks undoubtedly would have been less sanguine. By the last quarter of 1937,
Glavsevmorput would be in free fall, heading for disaster. Levanevsky's death in
August was only the beginning. The number of accidents in the air and at sea was
steadily increasing. Economic yields were flagging. Construction slowed. Transport and communications became sluggish. In short, GUSMP was having difficulty
making anything in the Arctic work at all, much less with the efficiency and ra-
pidity demanded by the Kremlin.

To a degree, Glavsevmorput's woes were part of the overall economic slump
that the USSR experienced between 1936 and 1940.[2] But more immediate factors
were also at work. As discussed below, GUSMP lost the use of the better portion of
its fleet in autumn 1937. To make things worse, the great purges hit GUSMP hard
in 1937–1938. Finally, it was at this time that Glavsevmorput gained a dangerous
rival: Dalstroi, the secret police's Main Administration for Construction in the
Far North, which began to challenge GUSMP for supremacy in the Arctic.

All of this was enough to bring Glavsevmorput to its knees. By autumn 1938,
GUSMP had been downgraded and stripped of all its economic and administrative
functions. In spring 1939, the once-proud "Commissariat of Ice" lost its leader as
well. Shmidt stepped down as GUSMP chief, leaving behind Ivan Papanin as his
replacement. And with Glavsevmorput thus unseated from its position of glory, a
truly memorable era in the history of Arctic exploration came to an end.

This chapter's purpose is to trace the course of GUSMP's downfall. It will begin with the various crises that the agency contended with from 1936 onward. Second, it will discuss the impact of the purges on the struggling agency. Third, the chapter will conclude with Glavsevmorput's demotion and Dalstroi's assumption of its place in the North.

Glavsevmorput in Crisis

In newspapers and on the silver screen, GUSMP made exploration and development look easy. In reality, the agency was scrambling to make its proverbial ends meet—especially in 1936 and 1937, the final years of the Second Five-Year Plan. There were economic quotas to be filled everywhere: lumberyards, mines, reindeer farms, whaling ships. But, just as it was reaching its crowning glory in the public sphere, GUSMP faced the prospect of failing at its mundane, practical work in the Arctic.

As described in chapter 2, one of the things obstructing Glavsevmorput was the deep rift separating the personnel who thought the agency should emphasize economic production from those who felt its primary missions were research and transport. As a result of the split, neither aspect of GUSMP's work went particularly well between 1936 and 1938. In terms of production, Glavsevmorput was starting to fall short of its yearly goals. In 1936, its fisheries caught only 92 percent of their quota. The fur trade generated 11.9 million rubles in 1936, a 3-million-ruble increase from the year before, but still inadequate. The reindeer population grew by 25,637 in 1936, but even more of an increase had been expected.[3] At this point, Glavsevmorput's economic situation was far from optimal. Still, it was not hopeless. The agency was behind in production but not yet dangerously so—it had even turned out 153 percent of its coal-mining quota. As 1937 approached, a chance remained that, if all went well, GUSMP would be able to marshal its efforts and fulfill the Second Five-Year Plan. But things would have to go very well indeed.

In the fields of science and transport, Glavsevmorput's situation was ambiguous. On one hand, research proved extremely fruitful. In many ways, transport work also went well. Insurance rates for shipping in the polar seas dropped steadily. The Soviets had tripled the Arctic navigational season from one month to three (sometimes even four).[4] In 1936, GUSMP's shipping volume rose to 135 million ton-kilometers, up from 93 million in 1935.[5] Fourteen ships sailed the entire length of the Northern Sea Route, and marine cargo turnover came to 271,000 tons. Cargo turnover along the Siberian rivers amounted to 160,000 tons. Also in 1936, Glavsevmorput pilots logged 10,900 flight hours.[6] However, GUSMP's balance sheet was not entirely healthy. For a start, the numbers that Glavsevmorput registered in 1936 were too low: the agency's plans had called for 285,000 tons of cargo to be shipped by sea and 181,000 tons to be moved along the rivers; pilots were to fly 20,000 hours.[7] As a result, 1937 found GUSMP already behind in its efforts, and the new year promised to be even more strenuous, with increases across the board: 351,800 tons in marine cargo, 240,000 tons in river turnover, and 22,000 flight hours.[8]

Table 6.1   Proposed Additions to the Glavsevmorput Icebreaker Fleet

Ship	Horsepower	Tonnage
Stalin	10,000	10,000
Molotov	10,000	10,000
Kaganovich	10,000	10,000
Shmidt (Mikoyan)	10,000	10,000
Levanevsky	2,400	3,500
Dezhnev	2,400	3,500

Source: RGAE, f. 9570, op. 2, d. 86, ll. 11–12; V. I. Voronin, "Znachenie ledokolov v poliarnykh plavaniiakh," in *Za osvoenie Arktiki*, 89–102. After Shmidt's resignation from GUSMP, the name of the fourth icebreaker was changed to *Mikoyan*.

Another fundamental problem was GUSMP's perennial need for more ships, especially icebreakers and ice-forcing vessels. Ordinary ships the government could provide relatively easily, by leasing them through Narkomvod. Icebreakers, however, took an inordinate amount of time and money to build. Glavsevmorput controlled the USSR's nine-vessel icebreaker fleet (Table 2.2). But nine ships were not enough, and all of them were aging rapidly; the newest had been built in 1917. All during the Second Five-Year Plan, Shmidt and his deputies begged Stalin for more icebreakers. The government promised to build six new ships—four icebreakers and two ice forcers (Table 6.1)—and have them ready by summer 1937. As it turned out, not one of them was seaworthy until January 1939, when the *Stalin* entered into service. The rest became operational in 1940 and 1941—far too late to ease GUSMP's Second Five-Year Plan worries. The four icebreakers cost 20,500,000 rubles each, and the two ice forcers cost 8,500,000 rubles apiece, bringing the grand total to 99 million rubles—a hefty investment by any standards.

Glavsevmorput also faced a more deep-seated predicament: it was pushing itself too hard and too fast in its attempt to keep up with the pace demanded by Gosplan and the regime. In 1937, GUSMP was on the verge of finishing the Second Five-Year Plan unsatisfactorily, and it was clear that the Third Five-Year Plan's quotas for 1938–1942 would be even more staggering. The level of marine cargo, for example, was projected to rise from 351,800 tons in 1937 (an amount that GUSMP was unsure of reaching in the first place) to a formidable 758,000 tons by 1942.[9] With this kind of pressure from above, Glavsevmorput sought to quicken the speed of its operations as much as possible. Unfortunately, haste caused GUSMP as many problems as it solved: increases in cargo turnover and flight times were accompanied by a corresponding rise in logistical errors. As described in chapter 2, the mixups and snafus that took place in the Arctic ranged from annoying to uproarious, but all were potentially dangerous in their consequences. And they became far more frequent as Glavsevmorput tried to move forward with ever greater celerity.

Even more serious were the accidents resulting from GUSMP's heightened tempos. In 1936–1937, Glavsevmorput sustained losses of over 27 million rubles from accidents just on the rivers alone.[10] Polar aviation was even more dangerous. For

Table 6.2   Aviation-Related Accidents and Incidents in the Arctic

Year	Catastrophes and Accidents	Other Incidents
1934	8	75
1935	9	94
1936	14	122
1937	21	312
1938 (first quarter)	11	112

Source: RTSKhIDNI, f. 475, op. 1, d. 5, ll. 25–27; d. 15, ll. 22–30. "Catastrophe" refers to incidents in which lives were lost, while "accident" indicates that injury and/or loss of aircraft took place. The second column includes forced landings, breakdowns, and mechanical failures.

a start, GUSMP had no cold-weather training facilities for its novice pilots and me-chanics; its training center, the Nikolaev School, was located in the sunny prairies of Ukraine. Combined with the inherent risks involved with flying in the North and GUSMP's growing tendency to press for more flight hours, this unpre-paredness made polar aviation increasingly unsafe. Table 6.2 demonstrates how the number of mishaps in the air rose from 1934 through the first quarter of 1938.

As if all this were not enough, nature itself took a hand in making Glavsev-morput's tasks truly insurmountable. After spring 1937, weather in the Arctic re-gions became unusually cold. Since GUSMP's navigational season peaked in late summer and early autumn, the climatic conditions could not help but prove detrimental to the agency's work on the rivers and at sea. Worst of all was the heavy oceanic pack ice, which formed much earlier than normal. The great freeze transformed 1937 from Glavsevmorput's year of triumph to its year of disaster. Literally everything that the agency was involved with, from the small-est scientific expedition to the largest mining enterprise, was disrupted by the weather.

Most devastating of all was the fact that, by the end of the autumn, twenty-six of GUSMP's ships had become trapped in the pack ice—including eight of its in-dispensable icebreakers. The freeze thoroughly paralyzed Glavsevmorput, just as it was racing to overcome the shortfalls of 1936 and make 1937 its most productive year ever. Moreover, the loss of the icebreakers meant that almost all traffic along the Northern Sea Route would be shut down until the trapped ships could be freed. This effectively immobilized almost eighty additional craft, or approxi-mately half of GUSMP's entire fleet. It was up to the one mobile icebreaker, the venerable *Yermak*, to make its long, slow way through the Arctic Ocean and res-cue the stranded vessels. The *Yermak* first liberated some of the other icebreakers, which then helped it to save the remainder of the ships. But the job remained unfinished until January 1940, when the icebreaker *Sedov*, the last of the unlucky twenty-six, returned to port.

Those two and a half years proved fatal to Glavsevmorput. The agency spent the last quarter of 1937 and the better part of 1938 trying to free up as many of its ships as possible. In the meantime, its administrative and productive operations, all of which depended on steady and reliable shipping for their lifeblood, atrophied. Not until the beginning of 1939 could GUSMP be said to have regrouped. By then, of course, it was too late. The failures of 1937 left GUSMP abysmally short of the targets set by the Second Five-Year Plan and got it off to a less than ideal start for the third. Even in the most favorable of circumstances, the consequences of such a horrible and conspicuous failure would have been frightful. But 1937 was hardly the best of times, and what followed for Glavsevmorput was fearsome indeed. The agency's misfortunes, natural and otherwise, struck just as the great purges reached their zenith. The terror would undoubtedly have come to GUSMP, no matter what. But Glavsevmorput had made itself tremendously vulnerable to criticism and investigation at the worst possible moment—so when the purges did fall on GUSMP, they fell with sledgehammer force.

Glavsevmorput and the Great Purges

No amount of distance from the center could make Glavsevmorput immune from the great purges—after all, one of the major effects of the terror was to erase regionalism and bring peripheral areas more closely under control.[11] To the extent that the purges followed a discernible pattern, it was mirrored in the Arctic, and before the end of 1938 GUSMP was engulfed top to bottom in the firestorm.[12] No data indicate explicitly how many people in the agency were fired, sentenced to the GULAG, or executed, although any reasonable estimate would run well into the thousands. Luckily, however, it is possible to get an idea of how the purges affected GUSMP as a whole. The papers of the Politupravlenie contain a fascinating—if at times incomplete—record of denunciations, case histories, and correspondence with the NKVD and the highest levels of leadership. With the help of such documents, a clear picture of how the purges ran their course in the North begins to emerge.

An Agency Beset

Following the assassination of Sergei Kirov in December 1934—the event considered by consensus to have set the terror into motion—GUSMP personnel underwent the same series of preliminary purges (*chistki*) that the whole nation experienced. These were not blood purges; in 1935–1936 they consisted of verification campaigns (*proverki*) and document exchanges (*obmeny*), whose official purpose was to cull out individuals who had taken jobs without possessing proper qualifications, joined the Party under false pretenses, or lied about their personal backgrounds. There were exceptions, but being "purged" at this point generally meant losing one's job or Party membership rather than one's freedom or life.

In August 1936, however, with the opening of the famous Moscow show trials, the purges evolved quickly into a full-blown terror campaign. As Procurator-General Andrei Vyshinsky "proved" Old Bolsheviks Grigory Zinoviev and Lev Kamenev guilty of forming a "Trotskyite bloc" and conspiring to kill Kirov, the scope and brutality of the investigations widened alarmingly. The media worked nonstop to whip the Soviet public into a frenzy of apocalyptic hysteria: saboteurs and spies were said to be everywhere—in one's workplace, one's neighborhood, even one's family—and every good citizen of the USSR was obliged to safeguard the Motherland against these "enemies of the people" (*vraga naroda*). Two more show trials followed: the January 1937 "Trial of the Seventeen" and the March 1938 "Trial of the Right Deviationists," in which Nikolai Bukharin, once acclaimed as "the darling of the Party," was sentenced to death. The Red Army lost almost 40 percent of its officer corps in a savage purge. From September 1936 to the end of 1938, Nikolai Yezhov—the pathologically murderous NKVD head who lent his name to the purges' crescendo (*Yezhovshchina*)—extended the effects of the terror to every level of Soviet society. Not until early 1939, when Yezhov, like his predecessor, Genrikh Yagoda, was arrested and shot, did Stalin draw the purges to a close.

In Glavsevmorput's case, the initial chistki were carried out by the Political Administration, which reviewed the files of thousands of employees. In 1935–1936, the Politupravlenie transferred or demoted people as it saw fit. More important, it gathered a wealth of freshly updated information about the majority of people working for GUSMP—just as the purges were beginning to take on a more dire character. This spelled little good for anybody but least of all for Glavsevmorput's leaders and senior scientific cohorts. Despite Stalin's oft-repeated assertion that "sins of the fathers should not be visited upon their children," merely fitting any of the socioeconomic profiles that were considered "class-alien" could lead to prosecution. And the single group within GUSMP most likely to have a checkered pedigree was the agency's leadership, along with those scientists old enough to have received their education before the October Revolution. Most of Glavsevmorput's scholars came from families that had been well-to-do before 1917. Many had been schooled at Russia's and Europe's finest universities. Some spoke foreign languages (most often German), traveled abroad, and maintained close relationships with foreign scientists. A good number were of German extraction or Jewish, which placed them in an unofficially (even semiofficially) undesirable category. The end result was to make many of GUSMP's most learned and valuable personnel into prime targets for the terror.

At large, Glavsevmorput responded to the purges in the same way that most institutions and workplaces did: it started to break down into an array of smaller camps. Each corresponded more or less with one of the agency's geographic or functional units, each tried to accumulate its own power base, each operated according to a system of patronage, protection, and, of course, betrayal. Although backbiting and infighting were almost as prevalent within departments as they were between them, section heads typically attempted to guard their jurisdictions and personnel to the best of their abilities. Especially in the center, key figures in the Glavsevmorput apparatus gathered large followings about themselves. This quasi-feudal arrangement made certain individuals quite powerful, but it also involved substantial risks. Since guilt by association played such a large role in the purges, every act of intervention or protection represented not only the sacrifice of political capital but the very real chance of self-implication. It is no surprise, then, that department chiefs and terupravlenie heads were purged with increasing regularity.

Another interesting aspect of the purges is that they provided an arena in which certain antipathies within Glavsevmorput's ranks were acted out. A definite social conflict was at work here. Roughly, two types of people were employed by GUSMP. First, there were highly educated personnel, most of whom were well placed in the agency's hierarchy. Most had gained their credentials before or not long after the Revolution, and their relationship with the new Soviet order was sometimes quite cool. On the other hand, GUSMP's ranks swelled with uneducated laborers, Party activists, Komsomol youth, and junior scientists who had received their education courtesy of the Communist regime; they tended to be younger and more zealous in their admiration for the Stalinist government. On the whole, these two groups were inherently suspicious of each other; as the purges ran their course the rift between them grew wider. And, in many cases, the latter used every advantage bestowed upon them by their more acceptable social origins in order to supplant the former.[13]

One last general point remains. The acute stress and tension caused by the purges exacerbated Glavsevmorput's normal problems and difficulties. The agency's task—to transform 2 million square miles of the bleakest territory on earth into a land of plenty—was an enterprise of Herculean proportions, one in which the risk of failure was quite high, even in the best of conditions. So, just as GUSMP's errors and blunders brought down the fury of the purges, the actual impact of the terror—in removing qualified personnel from their posts, elevating inexperienced cadres to positions of responsibility, and spreading confusion and crippling fear through the ranks—further hamstrung Glavsevmorput's performance.

The reason for this was clear—the spirit of the times translated every misstep into a potential crime against the state. Every mistake, no matter how inadvertent, might be an act of sabotage. Every negative comment, no matter how inconsequential, might be an act of treason. Accusations and recriminations came naturally and freely, and GUSMP cracked under the watchful eye of the secret police. Glavsevmorput personnel entered into a frenzy of denunciation—to save themselves from blame, to advance their own positions, to settle personal scores, or to protect an agency that some believed was genuinely in danger from harmful influences. As the purges raged on, GUSMP became a vast hunting ground in which each individual was, potentially, both hunter and hunted.

Crimes on the Periphery

To catalog completely how the great purges played themselves out in the Arctic is unfeasible: thousands of crimes were investigated, prosecuted, and punished. What follows is a sampling of case histories. Beginning with fairly minor offenses, this selection works its way up to the most important crimes that were said to have taken place in GUSMP's territory.

Some of the most common offenses involved crimes of sentiment. These could include idle gossip, political ignorance, or any active articulation of political unorthodoxy. The most trivial indiscretion, so long as it could be construed as hostile in any way toward state authority, was liable to prosecution under the RSFSR Criminal Code. Article 58, Section 10, outlawed "propaganda or agitation containing an appeal for the overthrow, subversion, or weakening of Soviet power" and called for a ten-year minimum sentence.[14]

Such "crimes" were common within the ranks of Glavsevmorput. Wherever the Politupravlenie or the NKVD's local organs cared to listen, they heard what could be interpreted as "anti-Soviet agitation." Passing through Nordvik, a Political Administration officer concluded from the loose talk he heard there that it was "a breeding ground for Trotskyism."[15] A GUSMP pilot in Khabarovsk was severely reprimanded for telling an unflattering joke about the crash of the *Maxim Gorky*.[16] The irreverent "Song of the *Cheliuskin*" (reproduced in chapter 5) seemed to appear everywhere. The Politupravlenie worried about potential disloyalty at the Nikolaev Aviation School; as one inspector wrote after a visit there, "here on the peaceful bank of the Bug River, we have many enemies in our midst."[17]

If any specific crime of sentiment was guaranteed to attract the attention of the authorities, it was to criticize Stalin. This kind of *lèse-majesté* was perceived as ipso facto proof of treason, but it seems to have been anything but rare. The head of the Khatanga Lumber Trust was sent to the local NKVD for "a consultation" after being heard to say, "although Stalin is very clever, he is evil. Soon he will have shot all of the Old Bolsheviks."[18] In Eastern Siberia, a pilot was said to have voiced the following: "Why is it that we hear nothing about Lenin nowadays? All they talk about is Stalin. After all, it was Zinoviev who was Lenin's best student."[19] Whether people actually made such remarks, whether they were attributed to them by ill-meaning acquaintances, or whether they were trumped up by the NKVD remains unclear. Whatever the case, the Politupravlenie worried incessantly about the mood of cadres working in the North. Political Administration officials constantly suggested that levies of Party members and Komsomol youth be sent to the Arctic, not merely to increase the labor force and inculcate proper "Stakhanovite" working habits but to help GUSMP enforce political orthodoxy in the wilderness.

Tangible crimes of action were also commonplace. Most of the offenses typically associated with frontier life—drunkenness, graft, abuse of the native population, even assault and murder—abounded, flooding the desks of Politupravlenie officials and regional NKVD investigators with new cases. For the most part, crimes of this sort were lacking in political content. But in the climate created by the purges, nothing was as simple as it might seem, and ordinary misdemeanors and felonies were typically interpreted as having deeper, more nefarious significance.

In the USSR during the 1930s, "deeper significance" meant sabotage, espionage, and wrecking (*vreditel'stvo*). Glavsevmorput's work, of course, was inherently difficult and dangerous, and many things, from the nonsensical to the lethal, were bound to go wrong. But since every miscalculation or minor error could be considered evidence of wrecking, it was impossible to dismiss such accidents as random mishaps. Furthermore, as GUSMP's fortunes declined, particularly after the transport debacle of 1937, the search for scapegoats intensified. And when they were found, it was not for incompetence, poor performance, or bad luck that they were called to account. It was as enemies of the people that they were cast—hideous "mad dogs" and "black-hearted monsters"—and they paid for their supposed crimes dearly.

The pages of GUSMP's professional journal gave the impression that the agency was literally honeycombed with spies, wreckers, and Trotskyites. Espionage and sabotage were the easiest answers for those seeking to explain Glavsevmorput's woes and misfortunes. As the lead article of *Sovetskaia Arktika* declared in June 1938: "Were there really no signals warning us of the serious shortcomings in our agency's work? Without a doubt, there were signals—the anti-Soviet activities of the many wreckers in the ranks of GUSMP!"[20] Never mind the brutal climate, the equipment shortages, the perpetual human-power problems, and the fact that mass arrests were steadily depleting Glavsevmorput of its most skilled personnel. As the agency became increasingly predisposed to hunt down and unmask enemies of the people, those enemies, unsurprisingly, became easier to find.

So-called wreckers were exposed at all levels of the agency. Richard Pikel, invited to Spitsbergen to write a children's book about GUSMP's Arktikugol coal-mining complex, was arrested for espionage and tried in August 1936 as one of the sixteen victims of the Zinoviev-Kamenev show trial. Later, Arktikugol's head, Mikhail Plisetsky, was fired and accused of wrecking, in part because he had allowed the pernicious Pikel to snoop around.[21] In 1937, a doctor working at Nordvikstroi was denounced as a wrecker by a young hydrologist because he was "overly interested" in the mining operations.[22]

Field expeditions were especially fertile breeding grounds for criminal accusations. To begin with, there was a good chance that one or more members of an expedition might actually be trying to evade justice. The probability that many individuals volunteered for duty in the North to put as much distance as possible between them and the purges in the center is accepted widely—albeit informally—by Russian scholars. The case of Nikolai Krashenninikov, a GUSMP physician posted at Wellen, indicates that this did indeed take place. The NKVD —which, in the end, apprehended the doctor—informed Glavsevmorput that Krashenninikov's willingness to work on the northeastern coast had been motivated by his efforts to escape charges already brought against him.[23]

More often, expeditions contained within themselves seeds of dissension that frequently led to accusations and denunciations. There were, for instance, built-in conflicts between the leaders and the led. Coupled with preexisting tensions between Glavsevmorput's older and younger cadres was the fact that expedition leaders and station heads generally enjoyed a number of privileges that rank-and-file personnel did not: higher pay, larger rations, greater access to medical supplies, and the right to be accompanied by one's spouse. Such inequities could be expected to cause resentment in any environment; in the Arctic, they proved particularly divisive.

A typical example involves the fate of GUSMP's three-man station on Domashny Island. Domashny's young meteorologist, one Gorvachenko, began to harass the station head, senior geologist Alexander Babich. The situation grew unbearable, and Babich radioed Glavsevmorput headquarters, requesting Gorvachenko's removal. Instead, the entire group was recalled, and it was Babich who suffered punishment, after Gorvachenko denounced him as a German spy. Gorvachenko's Komsomol membership served him well during the investigation; the authorities chose to believe his version of events and made him the Domashny station head. Babich, with no Party affiliation, was sent to the camps as a spy and a wrecker.[24]

In 1936, a GUSMP survey seeking out coal deposits on Dikson Island experienced a multitude of conflicts. The mission collapsed completely, with the junior members turning on their leaders and branding them as enemies of the people. The expedition chief was Grigory Kurbanovsky, condemned by his underlings as a self-important, quarrelsome buffoon. Unsurprisingly, Kurbanovsky was significantly older and better educated than his accusers. Another target of rage was Kurbanovsky's wife, Marina Rupasova. Included on the expedition as the team's nurse and cook, Rupasova was, in the words of one member, "neither one nor the other." That Rupasova's presence proved so incendiary comes as no surprise. On small missions, the presence of female explorers frequently sparked sexual tensions and jealous rages.[25] Although some women fared well on remote expeditions — including the wives of Papanin, Fedorov, and Mineev — Rupasova was not so lucky. Hideously unpopular with her fellow surveyors, she was roundly disparaged as a "mean-spirited troublemaker," a "shrew," and a "bitch."

Not only were Kurbanovsky and Rupasova convicted of wrecking, but their arrests dragged even more people into the web of implication. In connection with the Dikson case, two senior officials in GUSMP's central apparatus were confirmed as wreckers: Ivan Ananev, head of the Mining-Geological Administration, and A. V. Ostaltsev, head of the Cadres Selection Group. Both had fallen under suspicion earlier; that they had handpicked the members of the Dikson expedition was seen as further evidence of their crimes. Conversely, the fact that two such highly placed saboteurs had planned the survey and chosen the leaders was used as proof of Kurbanovsky's and Rupasova's guilt: a textbook example of the NKVD's adept use of circular reasoning.[26]

The conviction of I. M. Popovian illustrates how ordinary Glavsevmorput workers learned to use the vocabulary of the Stalinist legal system to achieve what they wanted. In 1937, Popovian, the chief physician for the Barentsburg coal-mining complex on Spitsbergen, was sentenced to hard labor for the crimes of wrecking and spying for Germany. In reality, his only offense seems to have been that he was a poor doctor. In 1935–1936, the Politupravlenie received a number of reports concerning Popovian's medical abilities and, particularly, his skills as a gynecologist. The most distressing of the letters came from a woman who had been told by Popovian that she would die in three days unless she agreed to have her right ovary removed. But he had misdiagnosed the woman's ailment, and the operation was completely unnecessary. On top of that, Popovian botched the procedure, leaving the patient a "sexual invalid," whose husband then divorced her. Furthermore, a glance at Popovian's overall record shows that he was an equal-opportunity provider of substandard care: the doctor at the nearby Grumant mine testified that Popovian had "mangled" no fewer than nine women and eleven men while at Spitsbergen.[27]

As mentioned in chapter 2, primitive medical services were an occupational hazard in the Arctic; stationed at Novaia Zemlia, for instance, Ernst Krenkel and his companions were cursed with the presence of "Dr. F.," whom they called "death's assistant."[28] The problem was serious, but with such a shortage of competent medical staff in the North, there was little to be done. So the Political Administration ignored Popovian's case for months—as long as the letters they received dealt exclusively with his performance as a doctor.

Things changed quickly, however, when reports about Popovian began to include spicier accusations. A wave of letters in late 1936 and 1937 arrived at GUSMP headquarters, informing the Politupravlenie that the doctor was engaged in every kind of counterrevolutionary activity imaginable. According to one miner, "Popovian has transformed his hospital—which is hardly worthy of the name—into a center for agitation and propaganda against the Communist Party and our mining complex's social organizations." Moreover, Popovian and his wife, Zabudina, had turned the Barentsburg pharmacy into a private drugstore, charging exorbitant prices for medical supplies. Popovian was a vile drunk, and, even worse, he had begun to surround himself with "known Trotskyites." To add to his crimes, Popovian had also turned spy. When a German-speaking scientist came to visit Barentsburg, one young woman noted that Popovian became altogether too friendly with him: "Doctor Popovian met with him very intimately, behind the closed doors of his office. Their conversation took place in English, but also in German. And it was always very, very quiet." What the enterprising eavesdropper failed to recognize was that the visitor was not German but Norwegian. In fact, he was the highly respected Otto Sverdrup, who had sailed with Nansen on the *Fram* and advised the USSR during the first Kara Expedition in 1921.[29]

Essentially, the luckless doctor fell victim to a tactic that came to be used widely in the USSR during the Purge years. Soviet citizens soon learned how to adopt the language of denunciation and investigation for their own ends. In this case, the angry miners of Spitsbergen recognized that, while their medical concerns might go unheeded indefinitely, they were likely to be heard if they used the discourse of the terror. The tactic worked: Barentsburg got its new doctor, even if an innocent person went to the GULAG in the process.

On occasion, the Arctic was the scene of the most outrageous crimes. Disgruntled with their wages and rations, workers near Obdorsk were said to have gone on a "terrorist spree," attacking the local sawmill and flooding it.[30] The yearly Deer Festival at GUSMP's Amderma station was ruined in 1936 when a carpenter killed a Party member in a drunken frenzy.[31] In September 1937, a dramatic uprising broke out near Zhdanikh, near the mouth of the Khatanga River. When Politupravlenie workers and the Krasnoiarsk branch of the NKVD went to investigate rumors about the event, they uncovered a hotbed of counterrevolutionary activity. The disturbances reputedly had to be suppressed by squads of Komsomol toughs and local Communists, and, when the investigations began afterward, they revealed a vehement—almost crazed—antipathy toward the Soviet regime. According to Politupravlenie files, a mechanic at the local cultural base declared that "Comrade Stalin should have been killed a long time ago." A member of a GUSMP construction brigade denounced the Leader even more passionately: "Why was Zinoviev shot? Why did people die in such massive quantities in Ukraine during the famine of 1933? Do you know that even as we speak, they are shooting thousands more people? And who is to blame for all of this? Stalin!" As they continue, transcripts of the interrogations convey a growing sense of hysteria, even a detachment from reality. One worker, accused of being part of a band of Zinovievites and Trotskyites, coldly replied, "Yes. And I am not alone. You will kill me, but others will kill you." At the height of the actual uprising, the deputy director of the regional reindeer farm was said to have proclaimed proudly that "Soviet power no longer exists. Comrade Stalin has been arrested. Comrade Voroshilov has been executed. Comrade Kaganovich has left the country. All of the Communists have left Khatanga. We are representatives of the new authority." One of the "Khatanga conspirators" succinctly summed up the defiant posture of the rebels by flatly stating that Stalin was "the son of Satan himself."[32]

By far the most notorious crime said to have taken place in the Soviet Arctic was the *Semenchukovshchina*, a murder case that was tried in Moscow by the Supreme Court of the RSFSR in May 1936. Two men stood trial during the six-day proceedings: Konstantin Semenchuk, head of Glavsevmorput's Wrangel station, and Stepan Startsev, the station's senior dogsled driver. Both were charged with a variety of crimes, the most important of which were banditism, oppression of Wrangel's native population, and premeditated murder. The prosecuting attorney in the case was Andrei Vyshinsky, who only three months later would achieve international fame as the chief prosecutor in the Zinoviev-Kamenev trial. In fact, it was the Semenchuk case that made Vyshinsky a nationally recognizable public figure. As a preview of the show trials, the Semenchukovshchina was an important moment in the legal history of the times—and a critical episode for GUSMP.[33]

According to the prosecution, the facts of the case were as follows. In 1934, Semenchuk became head of the Wrangel station, following in the footsteps of two of the agency's leading lights: Georgy Ushakov, who had formally claimed Wrangel as Soviet territory in 1924, and Aref Mineev, the island's second chief. Both Ushakov and Mineev testified at the trial, and Vyshinsky used their success at transforming Wrangel into "a forepost of Soviet culture and civilization" as a foil with which to blacken Semenchuk's name. The prosecution argued that Semenchuk had failed absolutely at developing the island's economy. Every index of production pointed to his ineptitude and sloth: the number of dogs bred on the island fell, fewer fish were caught, the seal harvest declined. At the least, Semenchuk was unfit for his position.

But Semenchuk was guilty of more than incompetence; deliberate malice lay at the heart of Wrangel's misfortunes. The first inkling that wrongdoing was involved came in August 1935, when Taian, the leader of the Eskimos living on the island, wrote an impassioned letter to GUSMP headquarters. Taian told a blood-curdling tale of systematic abuse, starvation, and violence. Semenchuk's chief accomplices were his wife, Nadezhda; his co-defendant, Startsev; and the station's biologist, Ivan Vakulenko, who committed suicide for unexplained reasons in March 1935. Not only did the four shamefully neglect their duties, Taian wrote, but they oppressed the Eskimos. Semenchuk refused to give the natives any fuel. Even worse, in exchange for the fish, fur, and meat they brought into the station, Semenchuk gave them only one can of preserves per family, per month; during the winter season the Eskimos were forced to subsist on a diet of walrus skin and blubber. As a direct result of Semenchuk's cruelty, at least a dozen Eskimos were said to have perished of cold or hunger during the winter of 1934–1935.

Semenchuk compounded his crimes after encountering resistance from his subordinates. Although several individuals tried to smuggle food and firewood to the Eskimos, only two dared to stand up to Semenchuk openly: Nikolai Vulfson, the station's doctor, and his wife, Gita Feldman. On 27 December 1934, Vulfson was murdered, apparently by Startsev (according to Vyshinsky, Startsev killed Vulfson on direct orders from Semenchuk, but there were also rumors that Startsev had fallen in love with Feldman and killed Vulfson out of jealousy).[34] Semenchuk and Startsev were imprisoned at the North Cape station; in November 1935, Otto Shmidt issued a decree condemning Semenchuk. Shortly thereafter, the two men were brought to Moscow to undergo trial. They were defended by star attorneys Nikolai Kommodov and Sergei Kaznacheev and, interestingly enough, were not forced to confess their crimes, as defendants in the show trials yet to come would be. Still, blasted by Vyshinsky during the trial as "human waste," both were found guilty, sentenced to death, and shot.

As dramatic as the Semenchuk case was, why did the authorities focus such public attention on it? And what greater significance did it hold for Glavsevmorput? One purpose of the trial was to provide the Stalinist regime with a great symbolic demonstration of its declared commitment to protect the non-Russian peoples of the USSR. Time and again, Vyshinsky emphasized this theme. Semenchuk was accused of setting up his own personal "satrapy," in which the defenseless Eskimos suffered under "predatory" and "colonial" economic conditions. His predecessors, Ushakov and Mineev, were said to have "instilled in our Northern friends love and trust for their Soviet brothers." Semenchuk had broken that trust; speaking as a witness for the state, Ushakov stated that the worst of Semenchuk's crimes had been "the conscious desire to compromise Soviet nationality policy." A second reason for the Semenchukovshchina's prominence was to show that the Stalinist legal system was omnipresent. The long arm of Soviet law extended to even the farthest reaches of the nation; whether in Moscow or in the loneliest, most desolate wilderness, the organs of justice would detect every crime and punish every criminal.

In large part, that message was aimed at Glavsevmorput. On the face of it, the agency came off quite well during the trial. Vyshinsky went to great lengths in praising GUSMP's achievements. Shmidt and the agency's leadership were publicly absolved of guilt in the matter; GUSMP's error in selecting Semenchuk to head the Wrangel station was put down to its preoccupation with the *Cheliuskin* rescue. And so all was well—at least seemingly. In reality, any involvement with such an affair was a liability, and no amount of praise or prestige could erase the blot it placed on Glavsevmorput's record. With the benefit of hindsight, the Semenchuk trial can be seen as a harbinger of the purges that would soon descend upon GUSMP—perhaps even the dress rehearsal for those purges.[35]

No discussion of crime in the Arctic would be complete without an account of the case of the Wrangel mammoth. In October 1937, Otto Shmidt and Vladimir Komarov, president of the Academy of Sciences of the USSR, each received an urgent telegram from G. G. Petrov, Semenchuk's replacement as head of Glav-sevmorput's Wrangel station. The wire contained exciting news: Petrov and his men had found the fully intact skeleton of a woolly mammoth, preserved in perfect condition. At the time, this was a find of major scientific significance, and word of the Wrangel mammoth kicked up a sizable stir among scholarly circles in Moscow. By November, the Academy's Paleontological Institute and Zoological Museum were embroiled in a heated debate over who had the most legitimate claim to the new prize.

Caught up in the enthusiasm, Glavsevmorput and the Academy began to mount a recovery expedition. The timing, however, was less than convenient: Petrov's discovery came on the heels of the great freeze that had trapped GUSMP's twenty-six ships, and any expedition to Wrangel would be troublesome and expensive. Nonetheless, GUSMP was prepared to spare no effort in bringing back the mammoth for the glory of Soviet science—all on the word of Petrov and I. V. Shuvalov, his Party organizer.

What Komarov and Shmidt failed to take into account was that neither Petrov nor Shuvalov had any training in zoology or paleontology. So, when the recovery team arrived at Wrangel in early 1938, it found—much to everyone's dismay—that the much-vaunted mammoth skeleton was nothing more than the remains of a perfectly ordinary whale that had washed up on the beach. Under other circumstances, the incident might have been written off as a waste of time and energy. It might even have been seen as humorous—indeed, it was this event that later prompted Vladimir Obruchev to pen the short story "An Incident at Neskuchny Garden."[36]

At the time, however, the authorities were not inclined to see the "Wrangel Mammoth Affair" as a laughing matter. In the course of the investigation, which was completed in August 1938, the NKVD unearthed "evidence" that "proved" Petrov to be "psychologically abnormal," temperamentally "mercenary," and an alcoholic (how he managed to conceal such glaring personal flaws while assembling an impeccable service record—he had played an instrumental role in coordinating the *Cheliuskin* rescue from North Cape—was left unexplained). For his part, Shuvalov was labeled the "lackey" of Sergei Bergavinov, who, by this time, had been dismissed as the head of the Politupravlenie and executed. In the end, both Petrov and Shuvalov were shot as wreckers, all for an innocent, if regrettable, mistake. The case of the Wrangel mammoth became the most extravagant example of how, in the Arctic and elsewhere, the great purges could transform a logistical vexation into a criminal case—with the most fatal of consequences.[37]

The Central Apparatus under Attack

It took little time for the cycle of denunciation, investigation, and arrest to spiral inward toward Glavsevmorput's central apparatus. Boris Lavrov, former chief of Komseveroput, builder of Igarka, and head of the IES, was arrested and shot.[38] Nikolai Yevgenov, veteran of the Kara Expeditions and deputy head of GUSMP's Hydrographical Administration, was arrested, as was Mikhail Yermolaev, who had helped Sergei Gerasimov to film *The Seven Bold Ones*.[39] Excoriated in a Politupravlenie report entitled "The Figaro of Glavsevmorput," Sergei Natsarenus, head of the Political-Economic Administration, vanished.[40] G. D. Krasinsky, who, in the service of Osoaviakhim and GUSMP, had opened up much of northeastern Siberia to air traffic, was taken into custody after Shmidt's denunciation of him as "a cunning Menshevik." Krasinsky was fortunate: after two years of imprisonment, he was freed and reinstated to his GUSMP post.[41] Similarly, geologists Georgy Ushakov and Nikolai Urvantsev survived their arrests to work in the Arctic once again. The former was sent to the camps shortly after losing his post as Glavsevmorput's deputy head; Urvantsev followed soon after. Both were rehabilitated and released after World War II.

Some individuals remained untouched, even though entire cases were prepared against them. Geologist Sergei Obruchev had in his file a report that he had "conspired" with Rudolf Samoilovich to review each other's books favorably and pocket the profits.[42] After Samoilovich's arrest in 1937, such a charge was potentially deadly, but Obruchev was never brought up on it (although he was fired from the Arctic Institute in summer 1938). Likewise, the Politupravlenie had an accusation of "arrogant slander" readied against Nikolai Zubov, one of Glavsevmorput's most respected oceanographers. During a fit of jealous pique in 1935, Zubov had carped unhappily about Shmidt's growing fame: "As the academic secretary for Soviet participation in the Second International Polar Year, I established more polar stations and did much more in the North than Shmidt. But now I am just a little man, and Shmidt is a big man."[43] For such a remark, Zubov could have been disposed of effortlessly. But, for whatever reason, the incriminating evidence was never used against him.

As the terror worked its way up Glavsevmorput's ranks, it began to reach even the heroes of the Arctic myth — at least those in the lower echelons. A March 1938 document lists 299 GUSMP personnel who had received high honors in the previous four years; of the awardees, 11 had been arrested, 24 had been fired or demoted, and 7 had died.[44] There were enough celebrities in the Arctic pantheon that being a hero of middling fame helped little in shielding oneself from the purges. Pavel Khmyznikov, the *Cheliuskin's* hydrographer, was arrested, supposedly for having concealed his past as a White officer during the Civil War.[45] For almost two years, Ilya Baevsky, Ivan Kopusov, and Alexei Bobrov, the leaders of the *Cheliuskin's* Party cell, fought prosecution but fell in the end. All three had gained a substantial measure of nationwide fame in the wake of the *Cheliuskin* rescue, and Shmidt himself tried to clear their names. Still, none of this proved any use against the charges they faced: Trotskyism, counterrevolutionary tendencies, and — perhaps not far off the mark — neglecting their duties and becoming "Cheliuskinites by profession." All three were arrested and exiled to the GULAG.[46]

In the same way, Glavsevmorput pilot V. M. Makhotkin, who had accompanied Vodopianov on several long-distance flights (and was even singled out by Vyshinsky for praise in uncovering a band of conspirators on Franz Josef Land), disappeared into the GULAG.[47] In late 1938, polar aviator V. I. Galyshev perished in a purge that claimed seventy-four lives in Yakutia.[48] Fabii Farikh, an Arctic flier of moderate renown, was taken to task by the Politupravlenie for a public address he gave in autumn 1938. The dressing-down was prompted by an angry letter sent to *Komsomolskaia pravda* by a young pedagogical student. Not only did Farikh begin his lecture half an hour late, the student indignantly wrote, but he also made "offensive remarks" (in other words, a joke or two) about the SP-1 expedition (in which Farikh himself had taken part). In combination with other marks on his record, this helped lead to Farikh's imprisonment.[49]

Even heroes of the first rank had to tread lightly. As Mikhail Gromov noted after Stalin's death, "you were summoned to the Leader and, when you went, you did not know whether you were going to get a cross on your chest or a cross in the ground."[50] All the same, most managed to squeak through the terror. Despite accusations of profiteering and "bourgeois" behavior brought against him by Vodopianov and other rivals, Mavriki Slepnev continued to rise through GUSMP's ranks.[51] Ilya Mazuruk, who apparently had few scruples about abandoning his colleagues to the purges, kept his own record spotless to avoid the terror himself. His meticulousness showed in April 1938, when he received an odd piece of mail from abroad. The letter came from a man claiming to be Mazuruk's long-lost father, now living in a Polish hospital. The man had seen Mazuruk's name in the newspapers after the North Pole landing and recognized the young pilot as his son, separated from him during the Russian Civil War. According to the letter, Mazuruk also had two sisters still alive in Warsaw and Lvov. The mysterious writer entreated Mazuruk to make contact with him, gushing, "my beloved son Iliusha, I ask you with all of my heart to write and send a photograph, which I will kiss with tears of happiness, as if it were really you." Far from being visited by similar transports of joy, Mazuruk, mindful of the consequences of communicating with relatives outside the country, was horrified. He immediately turned the letter over to the authorities and disavowed any intention to answer it, genuine or not.[52] Why such a callous course of action? The risks posed to Mazuruk by the letter were very real, and his vehement rejection of it was simply an act of self-preservation: cynical and, in Mazuruk's case, successful.

Further exacerbating the impact of the purges on Glavsevmorput's central apparatus were the great aerial catastrophes of 1937 and 1938. The first was the failure of Levanevsky's transpolar flight to America in August 1937. Almost immediately after Levanevsky's airplane, the N-209, went missing, the fault-finding began. Only days after the incident, Sergei Bergavinov fired off a letter to Molotov, attempting to deflect any blame that might come GUSMP's way. Bergavinov pointed out that, at the last minute, Levanevsky had been spotted throwing out key pieces of equipment — skis, sleeping bags, extra rations, an inflatable raft, and, most important, the spare radio — in an effort to lighten his airplane. Therefore,

Levanevsky himself, not Glavsevmorput, bore the guilt for whatever predicament the crew found itself in when the N-209 went down.[53] Also, a scapegoat for the affair was found in the person of Mikhail Voznesensky, radioman at the Rudolf Island station. Voznesensky was accused of falling asleep at his post and thereby disrupting radio transmissions between the N-209 and the SP-1 station, which was forwarding vital weather data to the airplane. In light of Voznesensky's "obvious mental disturbance," the death sentence originally handed down to him was commuted to twenty years of hard labor.[54] Whether this satisfied the public is unknown. But behind the scenes at GUSMP, the controversy was anything but settled.

The situation grew worse during the attempt to locate Levanevsky and his missing crew. The search lasted from August 1937 to March 1938, continuing through the winter. Pilots from the United States and Canada—including James Mattern, who had been saved by Levanevsky four years earlier, and Sir Hubert Wilkins, famous for attempting the first submarine voyage to the North Pole— joined Soviet aviators in scanning the polar seas for signs of the lost aircraft. The mission ended in agonizing failure. Not only did eight months of flying fail to locate any trace of the N-209 or its crew, but the expedition also resulted in several serious accidents and caused bitter infighting within Glavsevmorput.[55]

The event that brought the problems associated with the Levanevsky search into sharpest relief was the N-212 incident. On the morning of 14 March 1938, the four-plane air group operating out of the Yagodnik airfield, near Arkhangelsk— the N-210, piloted by wing commander Boris Chukhnovsky; the N-211, flown by Mikhail Babushkin; the N-212, under Yakov Moshkovsky; and Fabii Farikh's N-213—took off, heading out over the White Sea. During liftoff, Moshkovsky's N-212 veered out of control and nudged Babushkin's aircraft, causing it to crash into the ocean ice, where it exploded in a huge fireball. Twelve people were killed or injured; among the dead was Babushkin, one of the USSR's first and most famous Arctic pilots. Babushkin was given a hero's burial in Novodevichy Cemetery; years later, he was further honored by having a metro station in northern Moscow named after him.[56]

Unsurprisingly, the primary target of the three-and-a-half-month investigation that followed was the unfortunate Moshkovsky, who, only shortly before, had earned his laurels as a junior pilot on the SP-1 expedition. Moshkovsky insisted that a malfunction in his aircraft's left motor had caused him to swerve into Babushkin's plane. The Politupravlenie and the NKVD, looking instead for an admission of sabotage, badgered him mercilessly. Over time, Moshkovsky admitted that he had indulged in three or four glasses of wine—and gotten less than two hours of sleep—the night before the accident but continued to deny that he had acted with malice. However, combined with testimony from one of the squadron's navigators that Moshkovsky had quarreled with Babushkin on several occasions, any sign of impropriety was enough to seal the aviator's fate. Moshkovsky was the first to be prosecuted for the N-212 incident, along with his co-pilot and the commander of GUSMP's White Sea air detachment.[57]

Moshkovsky's guilt or innocence, however, was only the beginning. The N-212 affair was a painful revelation of how divisive the Levanevsky search—and, by this point, Arctic flying in general—had become. The denunciations issuing forth from the Yagodnik airfield were venomous beyond belief.[58] The easily depressed Farikh was to blame, because his mood infected the entire squadron. B. A. Pivenshtein, the senior Party official in the region, was at fault for not properly supervising the group. Both Moshkovsky and Chukhnovsky were said to have fought with Babushkin shortly before his death. The latter, commenting that "chance episodes do not occur in the realm of polar aviation," made much of the fact that Marshal Mikhail Tukhachevsky, executed as an enemy of the people the summer before, had personally congratulated Moshkovsky after the SP-1 mission. Chukhnovsky also hinted that Mark Shevelev, head of GUSMP's Polar Aviation Administration, was possibly a wrecker.

The criticisms of Chukhnovsky were even more blistering. The wing commander was rumored to have had close ties with aircraft designer Andrei Tupolev, who had been placed under arrest the year before. One of Glavsevmorput's most senior pilots, Chukhnovsky was now judged, on account of his age, to have been a poor choice to fly in the mission, much less to occupy a command position. Finally, in an especially vicious attack, Vodopianov, Molokov, Mazuruk, Ivan Spirin, and Anatoly Alexeev sent a letter to Otto Shmidt condemning Chukhnovsky as an utterly failed leader. Incredibly, their main argument consisted of the fact that Chukhnovsky had revealed himself as a "sodomite" (*pederast*) in September 1937, just after the search operation began. According to the authors of the letter, Chukhnovsky's homosexuality "discredited him completely," both as a Soviet pilot and as an authority figure.[59]

Whether Chukhnovsky actually was gay and became a victim of the virulent homophobia that characterized Stalinist society, or whether the letter sent by Vodopianov and his compatriots merely represented an attempt to bring him down in the most humiliating way possible, is not known. What is clear is that the letter found its way into the hands of NKVD head Yezhov and that Chukhnovsky was reprimanded (although not punished as severely as Moshkovsky). The final verdict of the inquest, completed in June 1938, was that the N-212 incident had resulted from efforts by wreckers to carry on the perfidious work of Sergei Bergavinov, Eduard Krastin, and Nikolai Yanson—all of whom, by now, had been purged as traitors to GUSMP and the Soviet Motherland.[60]

Even successful operations, such as the retrieval of the Papaninites in February 1938, were plagued by setbacks. Not only did the crew of the dirigible USSR-V-6 perish during the effort to reach the floating station, but the entire rescue was placed in danger by the crews of the *Taimyr* and *Murman*. In what was described by the Arctic myth as a friendly race, the two ships were locked in a fierce competition to reach Papanin's station first. Pilot Ivan Cherevichny, who took part in both the North Pole landing and the retrieval of the Papaninites, later told a Politupravlenie panel that the two vessels' selfish hunt for glory had created "an unhealthy situation" and severely jeopardized the whole mission.[61] Luckily for GUSMP, the successful return of the heroes from the frozen seas of the Arctic obscured those facts, at least from the public.

The event that most rocked aviation circles in the USSR was the death of Chkalov in December 1938. Although not technically related to Glavsevmorput's work, the tragedy was popularly connected with Arctic affairs in the public mind, and official fallout from the affair had an indirect impact on the agency's fortunes. Officially, Chkalov's death was attributed to saboteurs. Ever since the accident, other theories have abounded, and, following the late 1980s, several have gained popular currency as possible explanations. The most commonly-held views are based either on Baidukov's assertion that aviation engineer Nikolai Polikarpov put the prototype of his new airplane into production too early, or on the long-standing rumor that Stalin had Chkalov killed because the "Greatest Pilot of Our Time" had openly voiced his opinion that Bukharin and Alexei Rykov should not have been found guilty at the third Moscow show trial.[62] Whatever the case—and the question remains open—the incident triggered a full-scale witchhunt in the Soviet aviation community. Among the many people arrested or temporarily taken into custody were N. M. Kharlamov, head of the Central Aero-Hydrodynamic Institute, and aeronautical designers V. M. Petliakov and V. M. Miasishchev. Andrei Tupolev, already in the hands of the authorities, was questioned as well. Even though the event took place as the purges were beginning to wind down, a good number of lesser figures were also accused of having a part in Chkalov's death.[63]

Overall, the highest levels of Glavsevmorput's leadership came under the gun. One of the first to go was Rudolf Samoilovich. Samoilovich's personal profile was hardly advantageous: he was Jewish, came from a "bourgeois" background, spoke German fluently, and had many acquaintances in Europe. He had also worked with possessive loyalty to guard the scientists in his institute from investigation and arrest; in defending so many individuals suspected of being enemies of the people, Samoilovich damaged his own reputation beyond repair. His open rivalry with Shmidt further lessened his chances for survival. Samoilovich was arrested in autumn 1937, after returning from the *Sadko*'s high-latitude drift; rumor has it that he was taken into custody while walking off the ship. In 1940, he was shot. Samoilovich's place at the VAI was taken by his assistant, Vladimir Vize, who narrowly escaped prosecution himself for his "bourgeois" origins and ties to relatives in Poland and Germany—not to mention his close relationship with Samoilovich. In June 1938, leadership of the VAI passed to Pyotr Shirshov, recently returned from the SP-1 expedition. Vize survived and continued to work for GUSMP, but many others were not so lucky; Shirshov conducted a massive purge of the institute, firing sixty-two of its top personnel (including Obruchev) and having ten of them arrested (including Urvantsev).[64]

Another central body hit hard by the purges was the Political Administration. In October 1937, Politupravlenie head Sergei Bergavinov was arrested and executed as an enemy of the people. This was due partly to the great freeze that took place in 1937, but it also had to do with being at the center of too many power struggles and working too closely with the apparatus of terror; after all, before his own death, Bergavinov had sent more than his share of people to the GULAG and the execution chamber. Bergavinov's arrest sent shock waves through the entire agency. All of the administration's seven territorial administration heads were arrested. Moreover, Bergavinov had been a powerful patron to hundreds of Glavsevmorput personnel, all of whom now hurried to deny any link whatsoever with their erstwhile mentor. In a particularly pathetic attempt to disassociate himself, Politupravlenie officer I. O. Serkin, one of Bergavinov's closest colleagues, wrote the Party Central Committee, assuring it that "I was never in any way connected to Bergavinov or his affairs."[65] The bald-faced lie fooled no one, and Serkin, like many other administration cadres, met the same fate as his former chief. Bergavinov's place was taken by L. Y. Belakhov, who presided over the Politupravlenie until 1940.

An especially dangerous position during the purge years was that of deputy head of Glavsevmorput. S. S. Ioffe had been replaced without consequences before the purges began. But Georgy Ushakov, Eduard Krastin, and Nikolai Yanson each came to grief after serving as Shmidt's deputy. Ushakov was fired, then arrested. Krastin was arrested in autumn 1937; he subsequently perished. Yanson, arrested in June 1938, died in prison. For Yanson, who had worked so hard to encourage the use of forced labor as an economic tool, falling victim to the terror was a classic case of being hoist by one's own petard. With the removal of Krastin and Yanson, a new generation of deputies came to power in 1938–1939, including Mark Shevelev, Ivan Papanin, and Ernst Krenkel.

Finally, the maelstrom caused by the purges began to affect Shmidt himself. As Glavsevmorput's chief, Shmidt had reaped many rewards for his agency's successes. At the same time, it was on his shoulders that the responsibility for GUSMP's failures rested. And, as 1937 drew to an end, Shmidt's star was on the wane. Funding for his second North Pole station, the SP-2, was cut abruptly by Sovnarkom.[66] In February 1938, Shmidt's presence in the media coverage of the SP-1 retrieval was conspicuously minimal. Although he was not completely excluded, Shmidt found himself shunted aside in photographs and newsreels—certainly not treatment to which he was accustomed.

Shmidt's situation grew worse in 1938. Amid GUSMP's violent paroxysms of criticism and self-criticism, Shmidt was, increasingly often, the target of unfavorable comments and outright denunciations. He was widely blamed for the shipping disasters of 1937; had he not diverted so many aircraft to support his precious SP-1 expedition, some argued, GUSMP might have been able to send out enough ice-reconnaissance flights to avoid the great freeze-up. Shmidt also took flak for his handling of the Levanevsky search, especially after the N-212 incident. The decision to extend the search past autumn 1937 had been enormously unpopular among Glavsevmorput pilots, and now they were vindicated in their protests: not only had the search itself failed, but it had killed more pilots. In May 1938, the aviators wrote Shmidt to remind him of their repeated objections and warnings. L. Y. Belakhov, the new Politupravlenie head, joined in criticizing Shmidt; in June he forwarded the pilots' letter to NKVD headquarters, appending a private note to say that "I tried to warn Shmidt about the possible complications that could result from such a poorly thought out plan, but he refused to listen."[67] All of this, of course, was somewhat unfair, given the tremendous pressure the regime had placed on Shmidt to find the N-209 at all costs.

As months passed, queries regarding Shmidt became more pointed—and more dangerous. Throughout 1938, the notion that Shmidt himself might be a wrecker—since so many incidents that could be construed as sabotage were taking place under his stewardship—came near to being openly broached. In April, at an open conference of GUSMP's Party leaders, one Budtolaev, head of a Murmansk ship-construction brigade, raised awkward questions. Addressing the assembly, Budtolaev stated that "I do not like Comrade Shmidt's picture that 'all was well' before the end of 1937" and expressed skepticism that Shmidt could have appointed so many individuals who had turned out to be wreckers without being aware of their treachery. Budtolaev's remarks were heard briefly, then shouted down. Later, he rose again to put them forth a second time, at which point Shmidt gave an infuriated reply: "Comrade Budtolaev, your slanderous aspersions have already been discussed and censured. You have been repudiated for your calumny, yet you insist on bringing it before us again, when it has already had its chance to be evaluated."[68]

Shmidt could quash individuals like Budtolaev, but other voices—many of them quite forceful—had similar things to say. In October 1938, the Politupravlenie sent the following report to Stalin:

> it must be noted not only that Comrade Shmidt displays inappropriate liberalism with regard to the disruption of Glavsevmorput's system by enemies of the people but that he has, on his own authority, protected an entire array of enemies who are even now carrying out their undermining work. Shmidt has repeatedly ignored the many signals sent to him by lower-level Party organizations about the debilitating activities of these scoundrels.[69]

The implication was clear: Shmidt was incapable of dealing with the flagrant crimes taking place in his agency—and might even be one of the wrongdoers himself. Even the most trivial facts about Shmidt or his career could now be interpreted as having a sinister side. His ancestry was Baltic German (though his family had been in Russia for generations). He spoke German and had many foreign contacts in Europe and America.[70] Even the case of the Wrangel mammoth came back to haunt him—was it not Shmidt who had appointed Petrov and Shuvalov, allowing them to toss such a tempting red herring in front of GUSMP?

Long before the end of 1938, the embattled Shmidt was nearing the breaking point. Even the foreign press had begun to notice that he was working under incredible strain. In April, a *Newsweek* article about Glavsevmorput's ongoing icebreaker crisis noted that Shmidt, "perhaps the most respected man in the Soviet Union," had been accused of "self-satisfaction and conceit."[71] Two months later, during a personal interview with Shmidt, an English reporter brought up GUSMP's recent problems with the authorities. Replying that "Bolshevik criticism is not in the habit of mincing words," Shmidt assured him that the reprimands Glavsevmorput had received from the government were nothing out of the ordinary—and, moreover, "the only way to learn from mistakes."[72] What Shmidt did not tell the British newsman was that his relationship with Stalin, described by one scholar as "perpetually tense," was growing steadily worse.[73] Certainly the Politupravlenie was doing little to keep the relationship healthy. In May, Belakhov circulated a memo that labeled Shmidt "rebellious" and made mention of the "fact" that "Comrade Shmidt quite often speaks in malicious tones about the

Communist Party and the Central Committee"; the principal addressees were none other than Yezhov and Stalin.[74]

By year's end, Shmidt was hopelessly beleaguered. Charges of incompetence and whispered accusations of criminal complicity were coming from all directions and with greater frequency, and Shmidt was now facing the threat of a palace coup. Ivan Papanin, who had become the deputy head of Glavsevmorput that summer, was preparing to move against his superior for the top spot in the agency. When Shmidt and Papanin had first begun working together, their relationship had been friendly, but both men were too strong-willed for one to be content to remain under the other for long. In early 1938, Papanin had the upper hand: after returning from the SP-1 expedition, he was the nation's leading hero, while Shmidt was growing more vulnerable with every passing week. For over six months, Papanin laid the groundwork for his attack against Shmidt. In the winter of 1938–1939, he struck.

By this time, there was much less to fight over than there had been before. Structurally speaking, Glavsevmorput itself had fallen on hard times; as described below, its functions and powers were severely scaled back in August 1938. All the same, GUSMP was still a prize worth having. One of the first signs that Papanin was on the march involved the defection to his camp of certain individuals who had previously been loyal to Shmidt. These included Pyotr Shirshov, Mark Shevelev, and Ernst Krenkel. Shirshov had already risen to the directorship of the VAI by joining his fortunes with Papanin's. Shevelev and Krenkel would later be rewarded with nominations as Glavsevmorput's deputy heads—the former in March 1939, the latter in October 1940.[75]

Papanin then stepped up his attack by lodging various complaints against Shmidt. Mild at first, they grew increasingly serious and, by early 1939, potentially life threatening. In one of the final blows, Yevgeny Fedorov, presumably at Papanin's behest, denounced Shmidt in the most damning fashion possible. On 3 February, Fedorov informed the Politupravlenie that, nearly a year before, Shmidt had put the SP-1 retrieval in grave danger. According to Fedorov's testimony, Shmidt had knowingly used flawed navigational data in planning the recovery operation. As the SP-1 station had approached its rendezvous point with the *Taimyr* and *Murman*, Fedorov had made sure to wire the outpost's present coordinates, as well as those of its projected position, to GUSMP headquarters. But Shmidt chose to ignore those coordinates, substituting his own instead. In his report, Fedorov insisted that his numbers had been the correct ones and that Shmidt had erred grievously in not using them. For the time being, Fedorov did not raise the issue of whether Shmidt had acted with ill intent. But he did leave the question open—just in case.[76]

With accusations like this dogging Shmidt, the stakes of the game were growing too high, and he bowed out. On 4 March 1939, Shmidt resigned his post as head of Glavsevmorput, along with all claims to any other positions in the agency. That same day, Ivan Papanin, with Mark Shevelev as his deputy, became the new leader of GUSMP. Papanin was confirmed in his position by Sovnarkom and the Politburo; he would serve in that capacity until his retirement in 1946.[77]

The details surrounding Shmidt's resignation—including the question of whether it can even be called that—remain murky. Did Shmidt leave GUSMP because he wanted to, or was he fired from his post? How did he avoid being imprisoned or even executed? Some factors indicate that Shmidt's departure was at least partially intentional. Shmidt was a restless individual and had already fulfilled his dream of reaching the North Pole. Was he bored—or at least frustrated—with his work in Glavsevmorput, which, during his final months there, involved more bookkeeping and bureaucracy than exploring?[78] Shmidt's health was also a consideration; since the inflammation of his lungs during the *Cheliuskin* expedition, his physical condition had never returned completely to normal. He was fit enough to go to the pole in 1937 but not fit enough to continue roaming through the Arctic indefinitely.

Still, if Shmidt's decision to leave Glavsevmorput was voluntary, it can only have been partially so. By March 1939, he had already spent a year and a half in frightful danger. Shmidt was a potential victim of the purges in more ways than one. His class origins were anything but proletarian. He had been a Menshevik before coming over to the party of Lenin. Worse yet, during his stint with Narkompros in the 1920s, he had, on more than one occasion, sided with Trotskyite policy lines. He was personally friendly with several cultural and artistic figures who disappeared during the 1930s, including author Isaak Babel and playwright Vsevolod Meyerhold. Rumor has it, in fact, that Shmidt, along with a circle of noted actors and writers, was briefly considered as a target by the NKVD on the basis of confessions extracted by torture from Babel in May 1939.[79] With all this on Shmidt's record, being the head of an agency beset with disasters, or facing the innuendos spread by underlings jealous of his position, seemed almost superfluous. By the end of 1938, and certainly by the beginning of 1939, Shmidt needed a way out of Glavsevmorput, and he needed it quickly—before he was forced out against his will.

It seems, therefore, that Shmidt brokered a safe exit for himself by leaving GUSMP when and how he did. Whether he was fired or left on his own is secondary to the fact that he did it gracefully. How he had the wherewithal to do so—whether he was saved by his fame, had some incriminating information that gave him leverage with the authorities, or was blessed by tremendous luck—is unknown. Whatever the case, Shmidt became vice-president of the Academy of Sciences and continued his work on the *Great Soviet Encyclopedia*. Not everything, however, went smoothly. When the icebreaker that was to have been named after him was finally built in 1940, it was commissioned instead as the *Mikoyan*.[80] In March 1942, Shmidt was eased out of the vice-presidency of the Academy of Sciences, supposedly after clashing with Vladimir Komarov, his direct superior. The same year, Shmidt was removed as editor-in-chief of the *Great Soviet Encyclopedia*, although he remained on its board until 1947.[81]

Still, Shmidt's scientific career continued to prosper, even if the luster of his fame dimmed somewhat. He served in several institutes within the Academy of Sciences, including the Institute of Geography; the Institute of Geophysics, which he headed; the Institute of Theoretical Geophysics, which he united with the Institute of Seismology; the Cosmogony Commission; and the Institute for the Study of the Evolution of the Earth, which he established. He became the editor of the Academy's geophysical publications and founded the journal *Nature*. Shmidt also worked with the physics faculty at Moscow State University, both in the geophysics department and as the university's chaired professor in the study of the evolution of the earth. His later writings on planetary studies and the origins of the earth are still standard fare for Russian schoolchildren.

So, in the end, Shmidt lived through the purges—against all odds—and the rest of the Stalinist era as well. When he died in 1956, just short of his sixty-fifth birthday, Shmidt had outlived his old master by three years. But Shmidt did more than survive. Along with a distinguished legacy of service to the Soviet state, he left behind a powerful image—that of the bold explorer, striding confidently across the Arctic expanses—that would serve the Russians for decades as a symbol of pride and triumph.

A New Primacy in the North: Dalstroi and the Demotion of GUSMP·

In spring 1936, an article in America's *Literary Digest* referred to GUSMP as "a special pet of the Soviet Government."[82] Two years later, any Glavsevmorput worker coming across such a remark in the press would have responded with a snort of sour derision. By then, Glavsevmorput was under attack from all quarters, not least from above. The Stalinist regime was anything but pleased with its "special pet," and, before 1938 came to an end, the government had gutted the agency, turning it into a shadow of its former self.

At the same time, GUSMP had yet another threat to cope with: Dalstroi, the NKVD's Main Administration for Construction in the Far North, which had transformed itself from a tiny mining trust on the bleak shores of the Sea of Okhotsk into a vast enterprise that was eager to carve out a larger jurisdiction for itself in the Arctic. Dalstroi had been a constant rival to Glavsevmorput since the establishment of both agencies in the early 1930s; only by late 1937 was it strong enough to press its claims effectively. As its larger opponent was crippled by the purges, Dalstroi took the fight to GUSMP with vigor. The results were decisive. When the government divested Glavsevmorput of its economic and administrative duties, the lion's share of those functions went to Dalstroi, making it the new power in the North.

The Emerging Dominion: The Origins of Dalstroi

Dalstroi was created in November 1931 by the Council of Labor and Defense and placed directly under the jurisdiction of the secret police; in 1938, it formally became part of the GULAG system. Dalstroi's task was to mine and ship the deposits of gold that geologists had located near the Kolyma headwaters during the 1920s. Its primary means of accomplishing the goals set for it was forced labor, and, over time, the Dalstroi prison camps became notorious as the harshest and deadliest in the entire Soviet penal system.

Located in some of the most unsettled territory on earth, Dalstroi had much to do before it could begin mining. Its first step was to build a port on the Okhotsk coastline, at the natural harbor of Nagaevo, as well as a settlement some distance inland. This new headquarters was Magadan, the gateway to Kolyma that author and GULAG survivor Varlam Shalamov called "the moorage of Hades." Next came a highway to the river port of Seimchan, 100 miles north of Magadan. Now Dalstroi was joined with the rest of the USSR in two ways. First, by the Sea of Okhotsk, which linked Magadan with Vladivostok and the Trans-Siberian Railway; second, by the Kolyma River, which flowed north from Seimchan into the Arctic Ocean.

All this was a prelude to the real work to come: harvesting the Kolyma gold. At the outset, Dalstroi was forced to fight off certain rivals. Free prospectors (*starateli*) had been working in the Russian North for decades; they were outlawed during the First Five-Year Plan period, but most were co-opted by the state as contract workers by 1932.[83] There was also Alexander Serebrovsky's *Glavzoloto*. How the two agencies settled questions of territory and jurisdiction remains nebulous, but what is certain is that, as the decade passed, Glavzoloto's presence in northeastern Siberia steadily decreased.[84]

Dalstroi's work from 1931 to 1937 was characterized by rapid growth and, by all accounts, surprisingly minimal repression. Although the agency's initial exertions took a severe toll on prison laborers, conditions improved after its gold-mining operations were in place. Dalstroi's first leader, Eduard Berzin, appears to have been unique among prison-camp administrators in his handling of inmates.[85] Berzin's priority was economic productivity, not political persecution or indiscriminate torment. He treated his prisoners as assets and lobbied for special permission to allow his charges a number of privileges normally unimaginable in a Soviet prison camp. Prisoners received wages for their labor. They received ample rations and warm clothing. Alcohol and card playing were not prohibited, and prisoners were allowed to send and receive mail. Those who worked well were promised reduced sentences.[86] Vladimir Petrov, a six-year inmate of the camps, attests that "Berzin's camp was unquestionably the best in the USSR, both in its regime, with the lowest mortality rates, and in the cultural level of its administration."[87] A woman in the Dalstroi typing pool called Berzin a man "whom everyone loved and referred to as though he were their own father" (not only was this something of an exaggeration, but the typist's admiration did not keep her from helping to prepare the 500-page denunciation used later in Berzin's arrest).[88]

Berzin's relatively humane treatment of his labor force, as well as his administrative skills, helped Dalstroi grow into one of the regime's most lucrative investments; as early as November 1934, the agency started to overfulfill its production plan.[89] But the Berzin era was not fated to last; in 1937, Dalstroi suffered a cataclysmic purge that changed the nature of the agency for the next twenty years. In June 1937, Stalin denounced Dalstroi's "coddling of prisoners."[90] In October, Berzin was arrested and taken to Moscow; he was executed in November 1939, on charges of having spied for the Japanese army. In the meantime, the NKVD thoroughly razed Dalstroi's entire apparatus. And with the purge came a new work ethic. Once the most liberal outfit in the Soviet prison-camp system, Dalstroi was transformed into a brutal machine designed as much for deliberate oppression as it was for economic rationale.

The history of Dalstroi from late 1937 onward encompasses almost two decades of the most savage repression in Soviet history. Berzin's successors cut rations, increased workloads, and gave common criminals free rein to persecute political prisoners. Still, Dalstroi's gold-mining enterprises prospered and grew. After World War II, over 100 camps were under the agency's control. Whatever proportion of them were operational during the 1930s, it was high enough for Dalstroi to produce gold in great quantities. By the mid-1930s, the Kolyma basin was reportedly turning out 20,000 kilograms of gold per year. Even under the harsh conditions following Berzin's arrest, production continued to climb, as Dalstroi squandered human lives with wanton prodigality to boost its output. By the decade's end, Dalstroi was said to have been producing one-fourth of the USSR's entire gold yield: 74.5 of 320 tons. Over time, the Kolyma operations helped raise the Soviet Union's share in worldwide gold production from 26 percent to a staggering 40 percent.[91]

By 1939, Magadan had grown from a bleak, windswept outpost into a boomtown of 70,000 free workers.[92] The city was a modern El Dorado—albeit one with a decidedly unattractive underside. Only a few years later, the sight of Magadan was impressive enough to elicit the following reaction from visiting U.S. foreign-policy specialist Owen Lattimore:

> Magadan is the domain of a remarkable concern, the Dalstroi (Far Northern Construction Company), which can be roughly compared to a combination Hudson's Bay Company and TVA. It constructs and operates ports, roads, and railroads, and operates gold mines and municipalities, including at Magadan, a first-class orchestra and a good light-opera company.[93]

Lattimore has since been criticized for being so gullibly charmed. But he could only report on what he had been shown, and Magadan was no Potemkin village. The trappings of civilization simply hid the grim realities that lay just out of sight.

The fact that normal, everyday life could coexist alongside—in fact, depend upon and interrelate with—such suffering and barbarity says much about the nature of state power in Stalin's USSR. Indeed, Magadan's existence can be taken as an emblem of what Stalinism meant for Soviet society as a whole. Luckily, although Dalstroi survived Stalin, it did not do so for long. In 1957, as part of Nikita Khrushchev's general effort to scale back the GULAG apparatus, the agency was dissolved. Twenty years of horror finally came to an end—but not before leaving hundreds of thousands, if not more, dead.[94]

Glavsevmorput and Dalstroi

It was impossible that Glavsevmorput and Dalstroi, the most important actors in the Arctic realm, would not develop some kind of relationship. Early on, Dalstroi depended heavily upon GUSMP for its supply and transport needs. In principle, Magadan and Nagaevo could be reached and provisioned by means of the Trans-

Siberian Railway, with an extension by sea from Vladivostok. But the Trans-Siberian was constantly overworked, while the Sea of Okhotsk was ice free only two-thirds of the year. Moreover, Dalstroi possessed few ships of its own.

However, Berzin was not one to allow his agency to remain at such a logistic disadvantage. Before his arrest, Berzin labored to eliminate Dalstroi's need for Glavsevmorput's services. Although complete self-sufficiency was hardly possible in the barren Kolyma basin, Dalstroi managed to establish a productive base and reduce substantially its need to import goods.[95] In addition, Berzin gathered a seagoing fleet of at least seven ships to carry both prisoners and supplies. On the rivers, Dalstroi employed the Kolyma-Indigirka River Fleet (KIRP), which included motorboats and barges. With the construction of Ambarchik, at the mouth of the Kolyma, Dalstroi was able to cut out the long and arduous voyage around the Chukchi Peninsula. Finally, Siberia's growing air-traffic network linked Magadan with Vladivostok and Khabarovsk, the Far East's largest aviation hubs. Before Berzin's ouster, Dalstroi became responsible for over 60 percent of its own transport and supply.[96]

So, released in large part from its reliance on GUSMP, and prospering economically, Dalstroi was poised to challenge its faltering neighbor directly. Officially, the relationship between the two was cordial. In "Kolyma Today," for example, journalist Max Zinger depicted hearty Glavsevmorput explorers and earnest Dalstroi workers (free laborers, of course) cheerfully chatting during a GUSMP expedition along the Kolyma. Vasily Molokov, commanding the aerial part of the mission, spoke expansively about his eagerness to assist in the work of his "colleagues" in Dalstroi. Glavsevmorput even took the trouble to provide the Dalstroi contingent with a crate of lemons to guard against scurvy—free of charge.[97] Such comradely cooperation, however, was a product of Zinger's literary fancy. By the mid-1930s, the rivalry had already begun.

The foremost point of contention involved simple geography. Although the extent of Dalstroi's territorial spread has never been determined precisely, it was certainly making inroads into lands that Glavsevmorput considered its own. By 1937–1938, Glavsevmorput was unable to hold off the interloper: it was weakening and its territory shrinking while Dalstroi was growing stronger.

When GUSMP was deprived of its economic and political might in August 1938, Dalstroi was the principal beneficiary, as described below. Dalstroi then unloaded the bulk of its transport network—especially KIRP—onto GUSMP. Having triumphed decisively in this long bout of bureaucratic Darwinism, Dalstroi no longer needed to maintain its state of semiautarky. For that matter, it was no longer necessary for Dalstroi to concern itself with the mundane details of transport at all.[98] Instead, Glavsevmorput, having been vanquished, found that much of its new work involved meeting the needs of its former opponent—a humiliating end indeed.

The Fall: Glavsevmorput in Disgrace

As upsetting as the later stages of the purges—not to mention Dalstroi's encroachments on its territories—were for Glavsevmorput, the Arctic giant had a far more serious problem: the official displeasure of the regime. Government dissatisfaction mounted steadily during the first three quarters of 1938 and proved the decisive factor in bringing down GUSMP.

The state took serious disciplinary action in spring 1938. On 28 March, the Council of People's Commissars held a plenary session to deal with GUSMP's string of recent failures. Since the beginning of 1937, Sergei Bergavinov had tried to anticipate criticism from above by castigating the agency before the regime could do so. In a series of editorials entitled "Light and Darkness in the Work of Glavsevmorput," Bergavinov balanced severe self-criticism with reminders of GUSMP's many achievements.[99] By March 1938, however, Bergavinov was dead, and the authorities had lost their willingness to listen to apologist rhetoric. That month, Sovnarkom deemed GUSMP's work unsatisfactory on all counts; it attributed the agency's disappointing efforts to poor organization, "self-satisfaction," and wrecking. Sovnarkom ordered Glavsevmorput to cleanse itself of the "doubtful elements" within its apparatus; it also cautioned that strict measures would follow if GUSMP did not mend its ways quickly.[100]

In effect, the March session was not a warning but a death knell for the agency. No amount of effort could bring about the improvements that Sovnarkom had called for, and definitely not in the time allotted. Therefore, five months later, on 10 August, GUSMP suffered its final downfall. With Molotov presiding, Sovnarkom called for the thorough reorganization of Glavsevmorput and, in the process, stripped it completely of its "continental duties." The results for GUSMP were devastating. The former overlord of the Arctic lost all its economic and administrative functions, as well as its autonomous status. On 29 August, Glavsevmorput was placed under the newly created People's Commissariat of Marine Transport (earlier that summer, Narkomvod was split into two bodies: the People's Commissariat of Marine Transport and People's Commissariat of River Transport). Thereafter, GUSMP was to be responsible solely for transport along the Northern Sea Route.[101]

In the meantime, dozens of commissariats and administrations moved in on Glavsevmorput's possessions. Profiting most from GUSMP's misfortunes was Dalstroi. The Kolyma trust had already been grasping successfully at Glavsevmorput's enterprises for some time. In May 1938, for example, Dalstroi wrested away from Glavsevmorput all geological facilities and prospecting rights in the Chukotka region.[102] After GUSMP's formal downfall, the process of seizing its assets became even easier. Although STO's Economic Council initially parceled off Glavsevmorput's enterprises to a number of agencies, Dalstroi managed to absorb most of them in the months that followed.[103] It would be impractical to spell out in detail how all of GUSMP's assets were split up and, without access to classified information, impossible to trace exactly how Dalstroi grew as a result.[104] What is certain is that Dalstroi built its own empire—which eventually grew to a territory "four times the size of France" and included the infamous mining complexes of Norilsk and Vorkuta—up from the ruins of Glavsevmorput.[105] Any more detail than that is likely to remain cloudy for some time to come.

For GUSMP, of course, this was a shocking comedown. Once the master of the North, it was now an ordinary cog in an even more ordinary transport ministry. In

March 1939, at the Eighteenth Party Congress, Molotov outlined clearly what the state and Party wanted from the new Glavsevmorput: "by the end of the Third Five-Year Plan, to turn the Northern Sea Route into a normally functioning waterway."[106] It was the agency's old motto—and a worthy, vital task. But for an agency that was accustomed to glory and heroics, it was a depressingly prosaic assignment.

In the final analysis, what should one make of GUSMP and the trials it experienced in 1937–1939? In terms of the many lives lost or ruined as the great purges pounded away at Glavsevmorput, what happened to it was a great calamity. Bureaucratically, however, the question is less easily answered. Although GUSMP was punished unjustly—slapped down with bloodshed and repression by the government because unreasonable expectations were not met—it is arguable that what was done to GUSMP *had* to be done, institutionally speaking. Glavsevmorput's hypercentralized structure was flawed from the beginning. In the verdict of Arctic scholar Terence Armstrong, GUSMP was a behemoth that "grew rapidly, became complicated and unwieldy in structure, and tried to do too much"; concomitantly, "there was plenty of inefficiency and stupidity in administration, as one might expect in a mushroom growth of such complexity."[107]

In other words, something needed to be done about GUSMP's form. And what better than to scale back its size and function, until it was in the shape best suited to allow it to do what it was most qualified to do? First and foremost, GUSMP was a scientific-research and transport agency; everything else was excess weight. The reforms of 1938 trimmed away that excess and put Glavsevmorput back on its original track. Painful as it may have been, this was the rational thing to do—although it could and should have been accomplished in a far less brutal fashion. But the actual retooling, in and of itself, was no catastrophe. Glavsevmorput survived, continued to operate, and, in many respects, improved its performance. If there is a tragedy attached to the agency's fate—beyond the human suffering—it lies not in GUSMP's loss of suzerainty over the Arctic. Instead, it lies in the fact that it was Dalstroi—along with the GULAG as a whole—that rose up to exert its baleful influence over the Soviet North.

Conclusion

Epilogue

Though reduced in its fortunes after the tribulations of 1937 and 1938, Glavsevmorput was not altogether undone. It was still operational, however sharply its functions and privileges had been truncated. And, considering the fate of KSMP before it, GUSMP's mere survival was, in and of itself, a victory of sorts. Moreover, as battered and weakened as the changes of 1938 and 1939 left Glavsevmorput, they did compel the agency to become more streamlined, better organized, and more efficient.

Glavsevmorput began its slow process of recovery before the decade came to an end. In 1939, which was declared by Papanin to be the Arctic's "first year of truly normal commercial exploitation," ten ships made a complete traversal of the Northern Sea Route, and freight turnover exceeded GUSMP's plan by 26 percent.[1] To put a flourish on the year's work, the icebreaker *Stalin*—the new pride of the Soviet icebreaker fleet—traveled through the route not once but twice, accomplishing the first one-season double run of the Northeast Passage in history.

The following year proved successful as well. On 13 January 1940, the icebreaker *Sedov*, captained by Konstantin Badigin, returned to port. The long-suffering *Sedov*, the last ship to be freed after the great freeze of 1937, had been at sea for 812 days. It steamed into safe harbor under the protection of the *Stalin*, which GUSMP had dispatched to bring the lost vessel home.[2] Over the previous two and a half years, the authorities had attempted to create a second *Cheliuskin* epic out of the *Sedov*'s voyage by depicting it as another Soviet transformation of catastrophe into triumph. The public, however, found the "adventures" of the *Sedov* dull, and the episode proved disappointing as a public-relations campaign. All the same, having the *Sedov* back in service was a great boost for Glavsevmorput, and the ship's return helped start the year auspiciously. By the end of 1940, Papanin would make the claim that GUSMP had overfulfilled its transport plan for the year by 10 percent.[3] In addition, Soviet icebreakers—as part of the guarded cooperation between Germany and the USSR during the twenty-two months following the Nazi-Soviet Pact—guided the German raider *Komet* through the Northern Sea Route in a record twenty-one days.[4] To judge by appearances, the disasters of 1937 had been overcome, and it was proclaimed in winter 1940 that normalcy had been restored throughout GUSMP's territory.

As if to affirm this, Glavsevmorput staged the last of its prewar exploits the following spring. In a mission lasting from 5 March to 11 May 1941, pilot Ivan Cherevichny and navigator Valentin Akkuratov, both junior members of the SP-1 expedition in 1937, flew to the so-called Pole of Relative Inaccessibility (*Polius nedostupnosti*). Designated as such by explorer Vilhjalmur Stefansson, the Pole of Relative Inaccessibility, located approximately 450 miles away from the North Pole itself, was at one time considered the most difficult spot to reach in the circumpolar wilderness, due both to its distance from any solid land mass and the peculiarities of pack-ice movement in the region. Cherevichny and Akkuratov made several reconnaissance flights to scout out the region in April, then touched down at "the pole" in May.[5] There was, of course, no time left for further heroics in the Arctic. Only a month after Cherevichny's and Akkuratov's expedition, the USSR found itself at war with Nazi Germany.

Militarily, the Arctic proved to be a comparatively minor front for the USSR. Economically and logistically, however, the Northern Sea Route was critical, both for its role in keeping the European and Asiatic parts of the country linked and as one of the arteries by which the Soviets received vital Lend-Lease aid from their American allies. Months before the outbreak of hostilities, Glavsevmorput had labored to prepare the route for combat. During 1940 and 1941, ships were armed, island bases were fortified, shore batteries were constructed, and military vessels were assigned to protect the expanding coastal infrastructure.[6] Despite having to cope with surprisingly heavy combat conditions, Glavsevmorput, with Papanin at its helm the entire time, performed capably. In its efforts to provide freedom of movement in the North for goods, supplies, and personnel, not to mention the Soviet Navy, GUSMP led forty-one convoys along the Northern Sea Route between 1941 and 1945. Of the 792 ships that took part in those convoys, only 62 were lost. In addition, Glavsevmorput vessels made 1,471 trips down the Siberian rivers, moving 4 million tons of supplies southward to collection points in the sub-Arctic.[7] On the whole, GUSMP executed its duties admirably, and the Kremlin recognized its efforts by decorating many of its personnel and honoring the agency itself. As Glavsevmorput's leader, Papanin was awarded his second Hero of the Soviet Union medal and promoted to the rank of rear admiral in the Soviet Navy. In 1946, Papanin retired as the head of GUSMP but remained active in the field of polar exploration—as sponsor and mentor—until his death in 1986, his ninety-second year.

During the late 1940s, scientific work in the Arctic began again in earnest. A new generation of scholars and explorers came to the forefront of GUSMP and the Arctic Institute, including A. A. Afanasev, Vasily Burkhanov, Mikhail Somov, Alexei Treshnikov, Boris Koshechkin, E. I. Tolstikov, Y. S. Libin, and others. The Soviets went on to assemble the world's largest polar aviation outfit—the yearly high-latitude air expeditions that Glavsevmorput began in 1948 included as many as thirty to forty airplanes and helicopters by the 1950s—as well as the biggest national fleet of icebreakers. In 1950, GUSMP also reinstituted the practice of establishing floating stations, larger and more complex than ever before, at the North Pole. The SP-2 party, led by Somov, included sixteen members and had a specially equipped automobile at its disposal. Four years later, Treshnikov's SP-3 and Tolstikov's SP-4 were launched simultaneously. Both were lavishly equipped, and Treshnikov's crew actually contrived to bring along a piano to entertain themselves at the pole. From 1954 to the end of the 1980s, the USSR continually maintained SP-series outposts in its Arctic waters, never failing to have at least two in operation at any given time.[8]

Glavsevmorput's years of decline came in the 1960s and 1970s. The Soviets were still going strong in the Arctic—in 1957, the USSR brought the world's first atomic icebreaker, the *Lenin*, into service, and, in 1977, the atomic icebreaker *Arktika* became the first surface vessel to reach the North Pole.[9] But scientific and transport activity in the Arctic had simply grown too extensive for GUSMP to control—or even to coordinate. The Shirshov Institute of Oceanology, the USSR Hydro-Meteorological Service, and the VAI (by now the Arctic-Antarctic Institute) were only a few of the agencies with which Glavsevmorput was now forced to share resources and responsibilities. With every passing year, GUSMP became an increasingly unimportant part of the workings of the Ministry of the Marine Fleet. Finally, in 1970, the old, tired agency was phased out altogether, to be replaced in 1971 by a much smaller Administration (*administratsiia*) of the Northern Sea Route.[10] And so, with one stroke of a pen and a minor bureaucratic shuffle, four decades of triumph and failure, innovation and folly, bravery and betrayal came to a close. Work in the Soviet Arctic would continue apace, but Glavsevmorput had forever disappeared.

Parting Thoughts

What should one make of the USSR's *Drang nach Norden*—to borrow a phrase from polar specialist Timothy Taracouzio[11]—and Glavsevmorput's part in it? Practically speaking, perhaps the most charitable thing that can be said about the Soviet Union's record in the Arctic is that it was less than consistent. Particularly during the 1930s, the USSR's drive to "sovietize" the North can be considered in the overall context of the Stalinist regime's all-consuming quest to bring about rapid, nationwide modernization. As a result, the explorers and developers of the Arctic confronted many of the same problems and dilemmas that flawed Stalin's modernizing project as a whole. To begin with, the USSR's campaign in the North was carried out in the same spirit of gigantomania that prevailed throughout the Soviet economic-administrative apparatus for over half a century. The history of GUSMP shows—as does so much else in the Soviet experience—that bigger was not necessarily better. Umbrella authority and sizable budgets were not enough to save Glavsevmorput from its clumsiness and the inherent weaknesses in its hypertrophied structure. And sheer size certainly could not help the agency to develop the delicacy of touch for which its complex and multifaceted task called.[12]

Second, GUSMP—like every other organizational body connected with economic production during the early five-year plans—faced an obstacle mentioned several times throughout this work: the unreasonable and highly, even fantastically, unrealistic demands handed down by the state. Even under ideal circumstances, what the government required of Glavsevmorput—the ability to move in the Arctic and to exploit it fully—could be achieved only in a gradual fashion.

But, as noted elsewhere, "gradual" was not a word that appeared in the Stalinist vocabulary. In combination with the repressive nature of the Soviet command economy, especially during the years of the great purges, the regime's unending refrain of "faster, faster, faster!" had a devastating impact on GUSMP's work. The Arctic giant cut corners, figuratively swept dirt under the carpet, and otherwise sacrificed quality in its operations, all in an effort to keep up with the unwavering dictates of the plan.

Finally, the entire history of Stalinist development in the North is inextricably intertwined with the great human tragedy that was the GULAG. The extent of Glavsevmorput's involvement with the USSR's wholesale utilization of unfree labor remains unclear, but its hands were by no means clean, regardless of how minor its direct role may or may not have been. The waterways that GUSMP cleared for passage were used to transport untold numbers of prisoners to mines or timber fields in the farthest reaches of Siberia. Much of the cargo carried by the agency's ships was the misbegotten fruit of those prisoners' suffering and toil. At least some elements in GUSMP's infrastructure—dormitories, roads, ports, radio stations, and more—were built by means of convict labor. One can even make the cynical observation that Glavsevmorput was, for a long while after its downfall in 1938, largely a taxi service for the GULAG. Indeed, whether the state viewed the founding of GUSMP as a potential alternative to full-scale implementation of prison labor in the North or simply as a measure complementary to it, Glavsevmorput's breakdown in the late 1930s was what provided Dalstroi and the GULAG with their opportunity to achieve dominance over the Arctic. Ultimately, the Soviet regime paid a devilish price—an unquantifiable ethical and human cost—for its advances in the North. And GUSMP footed a sizable share of that bill.

All of this (and the above list is by no means exhaustive) meant that much of the energy, enthusiasm, courage, and sheer hard work of the 1930s was squandered by inefficiency and waste, not to mention morally tainted by connection with the GULAG. During the postwar period, development and settlement in the Soviet Arctic quickened in tempo and broadened considerably in scope—but the base that Glavsevmorput left behind has proved a somewhat unsteady one on which to build. From the 1940s through the end of the Soviet era in the early 1990s, expansion in the North continued to be haphazard, plagued perpetually by shortcomings and disorganization. As the century nears its end, reports from the Russian Arctic contain a gloomy tone not dissimilar to GUSMP's dispatches from the periphery during the 1930s. More than six decades of unchecked environmental degradation—strip mining, oil spills, forest clearing, overfishing, the improper disposal of radioactive material—have ravaged the circumpolar ecosphere, perhaps beyond repair.[13] The Russian North's endangered species have been labeled "casualties of *perestroika*."[14] The native peoples of Siberia—along with the indigenous peoples of the Alaskan, Canadian, and Scandinavian Arctic—find themselves hard pressed to exist in the modern world *and* retain a sense of their traditional ethnic identities. Wildfire inflation, the collapse of the Russian mining industries, and severe food and supply shortages have paralyzed the economies of Arctic communities throughout the country and left thousands stranded in remote areas and miserable conditions. It was no exaggeration, then, when the 1995 Congress of the Union of the Far North and Polar Cities declared that, "if this state of affairs continues, the Russian North will soon begin to die."[15]

Still, in laying down any kind of developmental foundation at all in the Arctic wilderness, Glavsevmorput did accomplish something of note. After the death of Stalin, Nikita Khrushchev loosened the GULAG's stranglehold on the region, and bonus wages and premium benefits eventually replaced the prison-camp system in providing the labor force for the constantly growing number of enterprises and industries in Siberia and the North. During the Brezhnev era, foreign visitors wrote about "high-rises on the permafrost" and marveled at the number of urban centers that had been constructed in the polar hinterlands.[16] In 1980, the nonnative population of the USSR's northern territories surpassed nine million, a level of settlement that would have seemed inconceivable at the beginning of the century.[17] Despite the economic difficulties of the post-Soviet years, capital investment, much of it foreign, has continued to flow into the region, and, in June 1992, the Russians opened up the Northern Sea Route to regular international navigation and commerce. Despite the uneven nature of Russia's progress in the region, then, the Russian Arctic, for good or for ill, has been brought under the sway of the mainland. Even if it remains an area peripheral to the country as a whole, it is much less so than it was during the Stalin era—and certainly beforehand. That this is so is due in great part to what Glavsevmorput and the people who worked for it accomplished in the 1930s. And this, blemished and stained as it may be, is the agency's most enduring achievement.

Or is it? Quite arguably, GUSMP's most permanent legacy may be something less tangible: the cultural impact of the grand expeditions and epic flights that formed the basis of the Soviet Union's Arctic myth. Although the high-profile glamour of polar exploration faded after the 1930s, as advances in the North took on the character of routine technical accomplishments rather than heroic feats— and as World War II replaced the economic and industrial achievements of the 1930s as the centerpiece of the USSR's modern myth—the Arctic has never lost completely its ability to appeal to the Russian imagination. There are, of course, those who might argue that the Arctic-based culture of the high-Stalinist era is nothing more than propaganda, plain and simple. The position taken emphatically by *Red Arctic*, however, is that this is most definitely *not* the case. Instead, the Arctic myth was a complex cultural construction, laden with a variety of important meanings for twentieth-century Russia.

The Arctic myth can be viewed from a number of different angles, not all of them restricted to the Soviet context. It can be seen as a manifestation of the worldwide cultural fixation during the interwar period with aviation and other exploits associated with high-modernist technology. It can be placed in the context of the maturation and expansion of the industrial world's mass-media complex. It also fits into the general question of how twentieth-century dictatorships (and other forms of government) have used national heroes and popular-culture icons in their attempts to mobilize populations and generate mass support.

The most intriguing conclusions to be drawn from the Arctic myth, however, are those related more closely to Soviet cultural and societal issues. The *fact* that the Arctic myth played a vital role in Stalinist culture is undeniable, but the actual significance of that fact can be interpreted in a number of different ways. For a start, this work proposes that polar exploration and Arctic flying became a central, indispensable part of the socialist-realist cultural aesthetic as it emerged during the 1930s. It has been argued in *Red Arctic* that there was little else, if anything, in the real-life Soviet experience that was better suited for incorporation into the socialist-realist framework. Moreover, one can speculate further that the Arctic myth, rather than being just a subset of the socialist-realist worldview, contributed directly to the shaping of socialist realism itself. This question may prove unresolvable, but the synergy between socialist realism and the Arctic myth, as well as their evolution in tandem during the 1930s, remain interesting issues.

Studying the Arctic myth also focuses attention on the topic of cultural creation in Stalin's Soviet Union. This work has endeavored to show that the vast cultural output surrounding the polar exploits of the 1930s was not the product of an unthinking, uncritical propaganda machine driven exclusively by the state but the work of dozens of individuals and institutions, each with separate interests and perspectives. It would be rash to say that each of these actors was free to pursue his, her, or its own agenda—the Soviet cultural community operated under tight constraints, and, although the sources of the Arctic myth were myriad, the vision and the direction seem to have been primarily, if not solely, Stalin's. Nonetheless, the question of how much latitude authors, journalists, filmmakers, and others in fact had under Stalin remains open. While *Red Arctic* is unable to marshal sufficient evidence to give a definitive answer about how confining the parameters within which Soviet writers and artists worked actually were, it hopes to have furthered this line of inquiry by providing a detailed look at how one body of propaganda in particular—and a highly influential one—was designed and produced.

Last, the story of the Arctic myth has much to say about the effectiveness of Soviet propaganda and publicity campaigns. Did the media succeed in conveying to the public the material that the Stalinist regime wished it to? Did national heroes and officially sanctioned celebrities enjoy genuine popularity among Soviet citizens? In the case of the Arctic myth, the answer to both questions is yes. No man, woman, or child literate enough to read a newspaper, or with eyes and ears to see a newsreel or listen to a radio, could possibly remain unaware of his or her country's adventures in the North. And polar explorers and Arctic aviators were nothing if not appealing to a great number of ordinary people. However, whether or not Stalinist propaganda proved able to communicate the *messages* that the state desired it to, or, more to the point, to *convince* people to agree with those messages, is another matter altogether. The Arctic heroes of the 1930s inspired a tremendous amount of genuine affection and goodwill. But they also became the targets of indifference, ridicule, resentment, and disapproval. And even positive responses to polar expeditions or Arctic celebrities did not guarantee that the audience's response to the regime was positive as well. Essentially, Soviet citizens were forced to react to what the state and media put before them, but they could choose for themselves *how* to react. Did the Arctic myth help to build popular support for Stalin? The reply is a guarded yes. But it needs to be recognized that, if this was indeed the case, it was due not to a simple, Pavlovian response to the

Soviet mass media but to a much more complicated set of individual decisions and preferences—all of which shifts the Arctic myth at least partially out of the realm of propaganda and into the domain of popular culture.

In the end, perhaps the most important thing about the Arctic myth is the way in which it has been imprinted indelibly on the national memory of modern Russia. In the summer, public galas and television documentaries continue to commemorate the anniversary of Chkalov's transpolar flight to America (during the 1997 celebration of the "Stalin Route's" sixtieth anniversary, Chkalov and his flight were hailed as "the breakthrough to the twenty-first century"[18]), and schoolchildren still learn about Shmidt and Papanin in history classes. Street vendors on Moscow's Arbat hawk Soviet-era *znachki*—lapel pins and souvenir badges— bearing the images of Chkalov and Gromov (as late as 1992, Red Square's GUM, once the largest department store in the world, offered a collector's set of pins, "Stars of the Polar Seas," that featured Arctic vessels such as the *Sibiriakov*, the *Krasin*, and the *Cheliuskin*). At Izmailovsky Park, one of the capital's most popular open-air shopping venues, one young entrepreneur with packets of Stalin-era newspapers for sale mentioned that issues of *Pravda* and *Izvestiia* with front-page coverage of polar exploits were among the highlights of his stock.

More substantively, during my research in Russia I found that archivists, janitors, academicians, neighbors in my apartment building, coat-check attendants, subway commuters, librarians, and any others who happened to hear about my dissertation topic were only too happy to speak their piece about the Arctic adventures of the 1930s—and to offer up strong opinions about them in the process. Some spoke of the exploits with pride and nostalgia; "things like the *Cheliuskin* and the landing at the pole are all we have left to be proud of today," one said. A few argued that Soviet successes in the North were a vindication of Stalin and his method of rule (and, not uncommonly, used them as part of a general indictment of all the hardships Russia has faced since the collapse of communism). Conversely, others dismissed the exploits as nothing more than the pet projects of a cruel and discredited regime: one peevish interviewee remarked, "oh, all that was just part of the GULAG. Why do we need one more person singing its praises?" A bus driver with a more practical frame of mind asked me, "what does any of it matter now? My cousin in Norilsk lives without electricity and can't afford more than one meal a day. What did the *Cheliuskin* ever do for him?"

The Arctic myth's ability to prompt such a broad range of forceful reactions is a good sign that it will survive as part of the Russian mindset well into the twenty-first century. Beyond that, the varied nature of those responses reflects the difficult, often painful, attempts of Russians today to come to grips with their past, even as they prepare to face a future that portends a radical departure from that past. It is impossible for the Russians to look back on any achievement or triumph dating from the Soviet era without having first to unravel the web of moral ambiguity that is, by definition, attached to it—because that achievement was attained at the cost of innocent lives, or because it was realized only after much ineptitude and bungling, or because it served the larger purposes of one of the most brutal and repressive political regimes in history. So many things have been accomplished in Russia during the twentieth century, some of them truly great, but it is impossible to separate completely even the most glorious of them from the horrific price at which—or the horrific means *by* which—they were consummated.[19] Such is the case with the USSR's great campaign in the Arctic: as with so much else, it will, for a long time to come, remain as much a burden to the Russian memory as it is a comfort to it.

Notes

Introduction

1. The film version of *The Two Captains (Dva kapitana)* was directed by V. Vengerov and produced by Lenfil'm in 1955. The first edition of Kaverin's book appeared in 1937; a final version, expanded to include the hero's wartime experiences, was published in 1946.

2. Several works have done the same. See, for example, Yuri Slezkine, *Arctic Mirrors: Russia and the Small Peoples of the North* (Ithaca: Cornell University Press, 1994); and Franklyn Griffiths, *Arctic and North in the Russian Identity* (Toronto: University of Toronto Press, 1990). The first focuses on the Arctic's indigenous population and on questions of Soviet nationality policy; the second is a brief but wide-ranging monograph on the role of the North in Soviet culture, literature, and social psychology. *Red Arctic* is distinguished from the former by its broader perspective and from the second by its concentration on the Stalin era.

3. The Soviet literature on GUSMP and the Arctic is enormous; the most useful published sources are M. I. Belov's four-volume *Istoriia otkrytiia i osvoeniia Severnogo Morskogo Puti* (Leningrad: GUSMP, Morskoi transport, and Gidrometeoizdat, 1956–1969); and *Sovetskaia Arktika*, GUSMP's monthly professional journal (hereafter *SA*). The majority of GUSMP's (and KSMP's) papers can be found in fond 9570 of the Russian State Archive of the Economy (RGAE, formerly TsGANKh). The materials of GUSMP's Political Administration are in fond 475 of the Russian Center for the Preservation and Study of Documents of Recent History (RTsKhIDNI), formerly the Central Party Archive of the USSR). Previously, all GUSMP papers were located in the Central Archive of the Ministry of the Marine Fleet. Soviet scholars have made use of these materials in the past; to my knowledge, I am the first Westerner to do so.

Non-Russian literature on Siberia and the sub-Arctic is extensive, but only a small body of work is dedicated to the Arctic or GUSMP. This includes T. E. Armstrong, *The Northern Sea Route: Soviet Exploration of the Northeast Passage* (Cambridge: Cambridge University Press, 1952); idem, *Russian Settlement in the North* (Cambridge: Cambridge University Press, 1965); and idem, *The Russians in the Arctic* (London: Methuen, 1958); Constantine Krypton, *The Northern Sea Route and the Economy of the Soviet North* (New York: Praeger, 1956); T. A. Taracouzio, *Soviets in the Arctic* (New York: Macmillan, 1938); and C. J. Webster, "The Economic Development of the Soviet Arctic and the Sub-Arctic," *Slavonic and East European Review* 29, no. 12 (December 1950): 177–211. Although these studies are useful, they are hardly current, and the authors, for obvious reasons, had no access to archival material. Pier Horensma, *The Soviet Arctic* (London: Routledge, 1991), is the only recent treatment of the region, but in spite of its timeliness it makes no use of Russian archives. In addition, it is narrowly focused on legal, political, and technical issues.

4. The literature concerning Dal'stroi consists primarily of memoirs by camp survivors; the most famous accounts include Varlam Shalamov, *Kolyma Tales* (New York: Norton,

1980); Evgeniia Ginzburg, *Into the Whirlwind* (London: Collins and Harvill, 1967); Michael Solomon, *Magadan* (Princeton: Vertex, 1971); and Vladimir Petrov, *Soviet Gold* (New York: Farrar, Straus, 1949). A new wave of memoirs is emerging, under the auspices of the group Return; see *Resistance in the GULAG* (Moscow: Vozvrashchenie, 1992). Official Soviet literature on Dal'stroi is typically of poor or propagandistic quality, as in *Dal'stroi k 25-letiiu, 1931–1956* (Magadan, 1956); and *Magadan: Konspekt proshlego—gody, liudi, problemy* (Magadan: 1989). Dal'stroi's professional journal, *Kolyma*, is helpful in that it provides glimpses into the agency's organizational structure; the same holds true for its newspaper, *Dal'stroi* (later *Kolymskaia pravda*, then *Dal'stroevets*, then *Sovetskaia Kolyma*). The only major scholarly monograph from the West specifically dedicated to Dal'stroi is Robert Conquest, *Kolyma: The Arctic Death Camps* (London: Macmillan, 1978), although newer work is currently in progress.

5. On the GULAG, see David Dallin and Boris Nicolaevsky, *Forced Labor in Soviet Russia* (New Haven: Yale University Press, 1947); Michael Jakobson, *Origins of the GULAG: The Soviet Prison Camp System, 1917–1934* (Lexington: University Press of Kentucky, 1993); Jacques Rossi, *The GULAG Handbook* (New York: Paragon, 1992); A. I. Shifrin, *The First Guidebook to the Prison and Concentration Camps of the Soviet Union* (New York: Bantam, 1982); Aleksandr I. Solzhenitsyn, *The GULAG Archipelago, 1918–1956: An Experiment in Literary Investigation*, 2 vols. (New York: Harper and Row, 1973–1975); S. Swianiewicz, *Forced Labor and Economic Development: An Enquiry into the Experience of Soviet Industrialization* (London: Oxford University Press, 1965); and Robert Thurston, *Life and Terror in Stalin's Russia, 1934–1941* (New Haven: Yale University Press, 1996).

6. Throughout *Red Arctic*, the term "popular culture" (originally coined to describe the arts, crafts, and oral traditions of early-modern European peasants) is used elastically to include the urban commercial culture of the modern industrial era. This reflects not only the author's desire to avoid taking on the ideological baggage associated with labels like "mass culture" (the Frankfurt School's pejorative term for "low" twentieth-century culture) but also the fact that the field of cultural studies has become more flexible in its conceptions of "middlebrow" and "lowbrow" culture. In *Rethinking Popular Culture* (Berkeley: University of California Press, 1991), 3, Chandra Mukerji and Michael Schudson define popular culture simply as "the beliefs and practices, and the objects through which they are organized, that are widely shared among a population." As for the question of whether the concept of popular culture is applicable to Stalinist Russia, there is a growing consensus within Soviet studies that it is: see Robert Edelman, "The Icon and the Sax: Stites in Bright Lights," *Slavic Review* 52 (1993): 569–578; Régine Robin, "Stalinism and Popular Culture," in Hans Günther, ed., *The Culture of the Stalin Period* (New York: St. Martin's Press, 1990), 15–43; and Richard Stites, *Russian Popular Culture: Society and Entertainment since 1900* (New York: Cambridge University Press, 1992).

7. Stephen Cohen, *Rethinking the Soviet Experience* (New York: Oxford University Press, 1985), 94.

8. See Vera Dunham, *In Stalin's Time: Middleclass Values in Soviet Fiction* (Cambridge: Cambridge University Press, 1976); Christel Lane, *The Rites of Rulers: Ritual in Industrial Society—the Soviet Case* (Cambridge: Cambridge University Press, 1981); Nina Tumarkin, *Lenin Lives!: The Lenin Cult in Soviet Russia* (Cambridge: Harvard University Press, 1983); the various essays in Sheila Fitzpatrick, *The Cultural Front: Power and Culture in Revolutionary Russia* (Ithaca: Cornell University Press, 1992); and Katerina Clark, *The Soviet Novel: History as Ritual* (Chicago: University of Chicago Press, 1981). Also see Peter Kenez, *The Birth of the Propaganda State: Soviet Methods of Mass Mobilization, 1917–1929* (Cambridge: Cambridge University Press, 1985); and Kendall E. Bailes, whose *Technology and Society under Lenin and Stalin: Origins of the Soviet Technical Intelli-*

gentsia, 1917–1941 (Princeton: Princeton University Press, 1978) was one of the first monographs to make mention of the Arctic exploits of the 1930s in a cultural context and one of the original inspirations for the present work.

9. Richard Stites, *Revolutionary Dreams: Utopian Vision and Experimental Life in the Russian Revolution* (New York: Oxford University Press, 1989), vii. See Stites, *Russian Popular Culture*; Günther, ed., *Culture of the Stalin Period*; Hans Günther, *Der sozialistische Übermensch: Maksim Gor'kij und der sowjetische Heldenmythos* (Stuttgart and Weimar: J. B. Metzler, 1993); Régine Robin, *Socialist Realism: An Impossible Aesthetic* (Stanford: Stanford University Press, 1992); and Jeffrey Brooks, "Socialist Realism in *Pravda*: Read All about It!" *Slavic Review* 53 (1994): 973–991. See also Abbott Gleason et al., eds., *Bolshevik Culture* (Bloomington: Indiana University Press, 1985); Lynn Mally, *Culture of the Future: The Proletkult Movement in Revolutionary Russia* (Berkeley: University of California Press, 1990); Frank Miller, *Folklore for Stalin* (Armonk, N.Y.: M. E. Sharpe, 1990); Richard Taylor and Derek Spring, eds., *Stalinism and Soviet Cinema* (London: Routledge, 1993); and Peter Kenez, *Cinema and Soviet Society, 1917–1953* (New York: Cambridge University Press, 1992).

10. Galya Diment and Yuri Slezkine, "Introduction," in Diment and Slezkine, eds., *Between Heaven and Hell: The Myth of Siberia in Russian Culture* (New York: St. Martin's Press, 1993), 1.

11. *Sovetskii Sever*, hereafter *SoS* 2, no. 4 (October 1931): 1–6.

12. See oceanographer Artur Chilingarov, who notes in "Soviet Polar Research," *Oceanus* 34, no. 2 (Summer 1991): 41, that "almost half of all Soviet territory lies within or adjacent to the Arctic."

13. Griffiths, *Arctic and North*, 1, 11.

14. Ibid., 14.

Notes to Chapter 1

1. Background sources on polar exploration include P. D. Baird, *The Polar World* (New York: Wiley, 1965); Pierre Berton, *The Arctic Grail* (New York: Viking, 1988); Daniel Boorstin, *The Discoverers: A History of Man's Search to Know His World and Himself* (New York: Random House, 1983); R. B. Downs, *In Search of New Horizons* (Chicago: American Library Association, 1978); David Mountfield, *A History of Polar Exploration* (New York: Dial, 1974); W. E. Taylor, ed., *The Arctic World* (New York: Portland House, 1985); and *The Times Atlas of World Exploration* (New York: HarperCollins, 1991).

2. On Russian expansion into Siberia, see Belov, *Istoriia*, vol. 1; Benson Bobrick, *East of the Sun: The Epic Conquest and Tragic History of Siberia* (New York: Poseidon, 1992); R. J. Kerner, *The Urge to the Sea* (Berkeley: University of California Press, 1942); Harold Lamb, *The March of Muscovy: Ivan the Terrible and the Growth of the Russian Empire, 1400–1648* (New York: Doubleday, 1948); W. Bruce Lincoln, *The Conquest of a Continent: Siberia and the Russians* (New York: Random House, 1993); Walter McDougall, *Let the Sea Make a Noise: Four Hundred Years of Cataclysm, Conquest, War, and Folly in the North Pacific* (New York: Avon, 1993); Semen B. Okun, *The Russian-American Company* (Cambridge: Harvard University Press, 1951); John J. Stephan, *The Russian Far East: A History* (Stanford: Stanford University Press, 1994); Donald W. Treadgold, *The Great Siberian Migration* (Princeton: Princeton University Press, 1957); and Alan Wood, ed., *The History of Siberia: From Russian Conquest to Revolution* (New York: Routledge, 1991).

3. Mikhail Lomonosov, quoted in *Geografiia SSSR* (Moscow: Uchpedgiz, 1955), 319.

4. In 1818, David Buchan, with John Franklin as his lieutenant, attempted to reach the North Pole in the *Dorothea* and the *Trent*. The expedition was small, however, and got no farther than Spitsbergen.

5. On the interplay between the growth of Anglo-American mass media and the rise of polar exploration as a cultural motif in the West, see Beau Riffenburgh, *The Myth of the Explorer: The Press, Sensationalism, and Geographical Discovery* (London: Belhaven, 1993).

6. Although Cook most definitely did not reach the North Pole, confusion remains about Peary's claim to have done so. Peary had ample motive to lie: he had tried a number of times to reach the pole and faced financial ruin if his 1909 expedition failed. On his final approach to the pole, Peary took no one with him who was qualified to corroborate his navigational readings, and his log indicates that his party's return trip proceeded at the superhuman—some say impossible—pace of 45 miles per day. See Berton, *Arctic Grail*, 511–530, 551–625; Riffenburgh, *Myth of the Explorer*, 165–190; Dennis Rawlins, *Peary at the Pole: Fact or Fiction?* (Washington, D.C.: Robert Luce, 1973); and Robert M. Bryce, *Cook and Peary: The Polar Controversy, Resolved* (Mechanicsburg, Penn.: Stackpole, 1997). The National Geographic Society has presented photographic evidence in an attempt to reaffirm that Peary did indeed reach the pole (T. D. Davies, "New Evidence Places Peary at the Pole," *National Geographic* 177 [January 1990]: 44–61). Uncertainty still remains, however, and if Peary did not reach the pole, then the Soviet SP-1 expedition of 1937 was the first to do so.

7. The actual discovery of the Northwest Passage came in 1850, when Sir Robert John McClure of England, sailing from the west, reached Banks Island, the farthest point ever reached by travelers coming from the east. McClure's expedition never traveled the entire way through the passage.

8. A. Shesterikova, *Daty istorii otechestvennoi aviatsii i vozdukhoplavaniia* (Moscow: DOSAAF, 1953), 64–65; C. V. Glines, ed., *Polar Aviation* (New York: Franklin Watts, 1964), 88.

9. Diment and Slezkine, eds., *Between Heaven and Hell*, 81.

10. *SA* 3. no. 6 (June 1937): 53–56; 71–76.

11. Taracouzio, *Soviets in the Arctic*, 53–56, 70–72. Valerian Al'banov, navigator of the Brusilov expedition, recounted his adventures in *Podvig shturmana V. I. Al'banova* (Moscow, 1953).

12. Belov, *Istoriia*, 3:445–456.

13. *V. I. Lenin i Sibir'* (Novosibirsk, 1972), 64–66; *Lenin i Sever* (Arkhangelsk, 1969), 91–96; M. I. Belov, *V. I. Lenin i izuchenie Arktiki* (Leningrad: Gidrometeoizdat, 1970), 2.

14. *Morskoi transport Sovetskogo Soiuza za 50 let* (Moscow: Transport, 1967), 54–55; S. V. Slavin, *Osvoenie Severa Sovetskogo Soiuza* (Moscow: Nauka, 1982), 60; N. Voevodin, "Morskoi put' v Sibir'," *SoS* 1, no. 3 (March 1930): 69; and A. B. Margolin, "Mezhdunarodnaia interventsiia 1918–1920 godov i Severnyi morskoi put'," in *Letopis' Severa* (Moscow and Leningrad: GUSMP, 1949), 1:154–174.

15. Belov, *Istoriia*, vol. 3; Armstrong, *Russians*; and idem *Russian Settlement*; Krypton, *Northern Sea Route*; Taracouzio, *Soviets in the Arctic*; and Webster, "Economic Development."

16. L. E. Kiselev, *Partiinoe rukovodstvo khoziaistvennym i kul'turnym stroitel'stvom v avtonomykh okrugakh Severa RSFSR, 1917–1941* (Tomsk, 1989); V. A. Zibarev, ed., *Partiinye organizatsii Sovetskogo Severa* (Tomsk, 1980); *Administrativno-territorial'noe delenie Soiuza SSR, 1917–1929* (Moscow: NKVD, 1929); and *Administrativno-territorial'noe delenie Sibiri* (Novosibirsk, 1966).

17. The "small peoples" included twenty-six ethnic groups but not tribes like the Komi or Sakha (Iakut), who were more numerous and considered less backward. See James Forsyth, *A History of the Peoples of Siberia: Russia's North Asian Colony, 1581–1990* (Cambridge: Cambridge University Press, 1992); and Slezkine, *Arctic Mirrors*.

18. The Committee of the North (*Komitet sodeistviia malym narodnostiam severnykh okrain*) has been treated most thoroughly by Slezkine, *Arctic Mirrors*. The committee's papers are located in fond 3977, in the State Archive of the Russian Federation (GARF, formerly TSGAOR).

19. V. P. Timoshenko, *Ural v mirokhoziaistvennykh sviazakh, 1917–1941* (Sverdlovsk: Ural'skoe otdelenie Akademii nauk, 1991); and the papers of *Narkomtorg*, in the Central State Archive of the Russian Federation (TSGA RSFSR), fond 410.

20. S. V. Slavin, *Promyshlennoe i transportnoe osvoenie Severa SSSR* (Moscow: Ekonomizdat, 1961), 102–118.

21. *Soiuzzoloto* eventually passed from VSNKh to the People's Commissariat of Finance, then the People's Commissariat of Heavy Industry, at which point it became *Glavzoloto*. See the journals *Sovetskaia zolotopromyshlennost'* and *Zolotaia promyshlennost'*; A. P. Serebrovskii, *Zolotaia promyshlennost'*, 2 vols. (Moscow: Nauka, 1935); and John Littlepage and Demaree Bess, *In Search of Soviet Gold* (New York: Harcourt Brace and Company, 1937).

22. *Lenin i Sever*, 145–146; Taylor, *Arctic World*, 233–235; and V. A. Vasnetsov, *Pod zvezdnym flagom "Persei"* (Leningrad: Gidrometeoizdat, 1974), and idem, *Povesti Severnykh morei* (Leningrad: Gidrometeoizdat, 1977).

23. The VAI is now the Arctic-Antarctic Scientific-Research Institute; see V. Strugatskii, *K poliusam Zemli: Rasskazy iz muzeia Arktiki i Antarktiki* (Leningrad: Lenizdat, 1984).

24. For KSMP's bureaucratic history, see RGAE, fond 9570, opis' 1, delo 24, listy 2–3; Belov, *Istoriia*, 3:448–464; Taracouzio, *Soviets in the Arctic*, 174–178; and Krypton, *Northern Sea Route*, 26–27.

25. Holland Hunter, *Soviet Transportation Policy* (Cambridge: Harvard University Press, 1957); Krypton, *Northern Sea Route*, 160; R. W. Davies et al., eds., *The Economic Transformation of the Soviet Union, 1913–1945* (Cambridge: Cambridge University Press, 1994), 158–181; S. V. Bernshtein-Kogan, *Vnutrennyi vodnyi transport* (Moscow: Transpechat', 1927); and idem, *Osnovnye problemy transporta SSSR i perspektivy ego razvitiia* (Moscow: Transpechat', 1929); and RGAE, f. 210 (Bernshtein-Kogan's personal fond).

26. On the debate, see Bernshtein-Kogan, *Osnovnye problemy*, 37–44; RGAE, f. 9570, op. 1, dd. 92, 226; E. T. Krenkel', *RAEM Is My Call-Sign* (Moscow: Progress, 1978), 143.

27. Recently, Byrd's claim to have been the first to fly over the pole has been called into question, based on evidence from his own personal diaries. See *Maclean's* (20 May 1996): 35; and the *New York Times*, 9 May 1996, 10 May 1996, and 12 May 1996.

28. After 1921, Canada and Britain claimed joint custody over Vrangel' Island, and explorer Vilhjalmur Stefansson established a small settlement there. After landing on Vrangel' in 1924, the Soviets contested the British claim for two years. In 1926, the USSR served notice that it was assuming control over all lands in the Arctic Ocean, discovered or undiscovered, between 32°4' 35" E and 168°49' 30" W (Krenkel', *RAEM Is My Call Sign*, 107). Ushakov, acting as the USSR's plenipotentiary on Vrangel', placed the British and Canadian settlers under arrest and expelled them. Vrangel's remote location made it the site of several marathon expeditions. Ushakov's party remained on the island from 1924 to 1929; his successor, Aref Mineev, stayed there from 1929 to 1934.

29. N. N. Sibirtsev and V. Itin, *Severnyi morskoi put' i Karskie ekspeditsii* (Novosibirsk, 1936).

30. Maurice Parijanine, *The Krassin* (New York: Macauley, 1929); E. A. Mindlin, *Na Krasine* (Moscow and Leningrad: ZIF, 1929); A. Garri, *L'dy i liudi* (Moscow, 1928); Claudio G. Segré, *Italo Balbo: A Fascist Life* (Berkeley: University of California Press, 1987); and *Podvig vo l'dakh* (Russian State Archive of Film and Photo Documents [RGAKFD] 1-21054).

31. *Summary of the Fulfillment of the First Five-Year Plan for the Development of the*

National Economy of the USSR (Moscow: State Planning Commission, 1933), 167, 239, 249.

32. M. Ilin [Il'ia Marshak], *New Russia's Primer: The Story of the Great Plan* (Boston: Houghton Mifflin, 1931), 125–126, 132.

33. RGAE, f. 9570, op. 1, d. 369, l. 151; d. 434, l. 269; d. 465, ll. 2, 22, 30.

34. Slavin, *Promyshlennoe*, 115–116; and L. E. Kiselev, *Sever raskryvaet bogatstva* (Moscow: Mysl', 1964), 11–12.

35. *Summary*, 24–25, 176–177.

36. Ibid., 173–175. The "special expedition" was Otto Shmidt's voyage in the *Sibiriakov*.

37. *Administrativno-territorial'noe delenie Sibiri*, 117–120.

38. "Postanovlenie SNK SSSR i TSK VKP(b) o l'gotakh dlia naseleniia Dal'nevostochnogo kraia" (11 December 1933), and "Postanovlenie SNK SSSR i TSK VKP (b) o l'gotakh dlia naseleniia Vostochno-Sibirskogo kraia" (5 February 1934), both in *KPSS v rezoliutsiiakh i resheniiakh s"ezdov, konferentsii i plenumov TsK, 1898–1986* (Moscow: Politizdat, 1986), 6:98–99, 146–147; and *Pravda*, 12 December 1933 and 6 February 1934.

39. Armstrong, *Russian Settlement*, 166–167; RTSKhIDNI, f. 475, op. 1, d. 1, ll. 142–145; RGAE, f. 9570, op. 2, d. 89, ll. 78–79; GARF, f. 5408, op. 1, d. 6, ll. 39–45.

40. RGAE, f. 9570, op. 1, d. 36, l. 16.

41. "Postanovlenie STO o rabote Komseveroputi i peredache ego GUSMP," in *Sobranie zakonov i rasporiazhenii SSSR* 1, no. 21 (1933), par. 124 (hereafter *SZR SSSR*). Regarding production, the government was particularly upset that KSMP had fulfilled only 39 percent of its quotas for fishing, 20 percent for harvesting sea animals, and 42 percent for canned goods.

Notes to Chapter 2

1. Krenkel', *RAEM Is My Call-Sign*; B. Gromov, *Pokhod "Sibiriakova"* (Moscow: Sovetskaia literatura, 1934); and *Dva okeana* (RGAKFD 1-9679).

2. Ruth Gruber, *I Went to the Soviet Arctic* (New York: Simon and Schuster, 1939), vii–x.

3. "Postanovlenie o sozdanii Glavsevmorputi" (1873), SNK SSSR, 17 December 1932; RGAE, f. 9570, op. 2, d. 1, l. 7; and *SZR SSSR*, I, no. 84 (1932), par. 522.

4. Harry P. Smolka, *Forty Thousand against the Arctic* (New York: Morrow, 1937), 20–23.

5. *Letopis' Severa* (Moscow: Mysl', 1975), 7:15.

6. Glavsevmorput' was almost certainly Shmidt's brainchild; M. I. Belov, the USSR's premier Arctic scholar, indicates that this was so (*Istoriia*, 4:95–105). Stalin, however, received the credit in public; Shmidt himself was prudent enough to declare at the time that "GUSMP was created on the personal suggestion of Comrade Stalin" (Archive of the Academy of Sciences [ARAN], f. 496, op. 1, d. 197, l. 1).

7. The literature pertaining to Shmidt is quite large; see *Otto Iul'evich Shmidt: Zhizn' i deiatel'nost'* (Moscow: Nauka, 1959); G. V. Iakusheva, *Otto Iul'evich Shmidt—entsiklopedist* (Moscow: Sovetskaia entsiklopediia, 1991); N. F. Nikitenko, *Otto Iul'evich Shmidt* (Moscow, 1992); I. I. Duel', *Liniia zhizni* (Moscow: Politizdat, 1977); E. P. Podvigina, *Akademik i geroi* (Moscow: Gospolitizdat, 1960); and O. Iu. Shmidt, *Sobranie sochinenii* (Moscow: Nauka, 1960). Regarding Shmidt's work with Narkompros, see Sheila Fitzpatrick, *The Commissariat of Enlightenment* (Cambridge: Cambridge University Press, 1970); and James McClelland, "The Utopian and the Heroic: Divergent Paths to the Communist Educational Ideal," in Gleason et al., eds., *Bolshevik Culture*, 114–127. Shmidt was also an influential figure in Soviet cultural circles; along with his first wife, Vera Fedorovna, he played an important role in the importation of Freudian theory into the USSR (A. Etkind, *Eros nevozmozhnogo* [St. Petersburg: Medusa, 1993]).

8. People's Commissar of Justice Nikolai Krylenko also participated in this expedition. During the trip, he set a Soviet mountaineering record by climbing unaccompanied to 22,605 feet; he also arrogated to himself the privilege of naming the peaks of the Pamir range after Bolshevik notables, much to the dismay of the Russian Geographical Society. Krylenko's travel log was published in *Izvestiia* from August to November 1928. ARAN, f. 496, op. 2, d. 197; and Arkadii Vaksberg, *Stalin's Prosecutor: The Life of Andrei Vyshinsky* (New York: Grove Weidenfeld, 1991), 136–138.

9. Krenkel', *RAEM Is My Call-Sign*, 215; Nikolai Kondakov, interviewed by the author, 13 March 1992.

10. "Postanovlenie STO o rabote Komseveroputi i peredache ego GUSMP," 11 March 1933, *SZR SSSR* I, no. 21 (1933), par. 124.

11. RGAE, f. 9570, op. 2, d. 36, l. 288.

12. Kiselev, *Sever raskryvaet*, 21, states that GUSMP started with 29,195 people, before the bulk of KSMP's former personnel joined up. RTskhIDNI, op. 1, d. 5, ll. 38–46, shows that well over 100,000 people were employed by the agency in 1936. RTskhIDNI, f. 475, op. 1, d. 6299, l. 299, details how the number of GUSMP's manual laborers grew from 7,500 in 1933 to almost 30,000 by 1936.

13. One important exception involves precious metals. Dal'stroi took over the gold-mining enterprises along the Kolyma river basin; by the end of the decade, it had squeezed GUSMP out of the most lucrative source of income in the Arctic, expanded throughout northeastern Siberia, and become GUSMP's deadliest rival.

14. RTskhIDNI, f. 475, op. 1, d. 1, ll. 49–50. Emphasis in the original.

15. RTskhIDNI, f. 475, op. 1, d. 1, ll. 86–92.

16. "Postanovlenie SNK SSSR i TSK VKP (b) o meropriatiiakh po razvitiiu Severnogo morskogo puti i Severnogo khoziaistva," 20 July 1934, in *KPSS v rezoliutsiiakh*, 6:170–175; *Pravda*, 3 August 1934; *Izvestiia*, 3 August 1934; and RTskhIDNI, f. 17, op. 3, d. 949, ll. 72–81.

17. RTskhIDNI, f. 475, op. 1, d. 1, ll. 49–50; and RGAE, f. 9570, op. 2, d. 10, ll. 9–10, 17–31.

18. *SA* 3, no. 2 (February 1937): 14–23.

19. RTskhIDNI, f. 475, op. 1, d. 5, ll. 38–46.

20. RGAE, f. 9570, op. 2, d. 49, l. 366.

21. RGAE, f. 9570, op. 2, d. 33, ll. 202, 207–208.

22. RGAE, f. 9570, op. 2, d. 33, ll. 156–158.

23. "Postanovlenie SNK SSSR ob organizatsii Glavsevmorputi," 28 January 1935, RGAE, f. 9570, op. 2, d. 33, ll. 156–158, 202–208; *SZR SSSR* I, no. 7 (1935), par. 59; and "Postanovlenie SNK SSSR o Glavsevmorputi," 22 June 1936, *SZR SSSR* I, no. 36 (1936), par. 532–536.

24. V. A. Obruchev, *Zemlia Sannikova* (Moscow: Nauka, 1990).

25. N. N. Kondakov, interviewed by the author, 13 March 1992; on Samoilovich, see Z. M. Kanevskii, *Direktor Arktiki* (Moscow: Politizdat, 1977), and idem, *Vsia zhizn'—eksped-itsiia* (Moscow: Mysl', 1982).

26. Krenkel', *RAEM Is My Call-Sign*, 107–110.

27. Baird, *Polar World*, 211–212.

28. *Vtoroi piatiletnii plan razvitiia narodnogo khoziaistva SSSR (1933–1937 gg.)*, 2 vols. (Moscow: Gosplanizdat, 1934); *The Second Five-Year Plan for the Development of the National Economy of the USSR* (Moscow: Cooperative Publishing Society of Foreign Workers in the USSR, 1936); *Itogi vypolneniia vtorogo piatiletnego plana razvitiia narodnogo khoziaistva SSSR* (Moscow: Gosplanizdat, 1939).

29. J. N. Westwood, "Transport," in Davies et al., eds., *Economic Transformation of the Soviet Union*, 176–179.

30. *Second Five-Year Plan*, 336.

31. *Vtoroi piatiletnii plan*, 1:25–30, 261–273; 2:154–161, 174–193; *Itogi*, 44–46.

32. Eugene Zaleski, *Stalinist Planning for Economic Growth, 1933–1952* (Chapel Hill: University of North Carolina Press, 1980), 181–193.

33. *Second Five-Year Plan*, 662–671. Note that Obruchev's son Sergei became one of GUSMP's most respected Arctic geologists.

34. RGAE, f. 9570, op. 2, d. 6, ll. 253–260.

35. Swianiewicz, *Forced Labor and Economic Development*, 15.

36. RTsKhIDNI, f. 9570, op. 1, d. 1, ll. 202–206; d. 2, l. 76.

37. RTsKhIDNI, f. 9570, op. 1, d. 12, ll. 62, 66. The first copy has the secret measure blanked out.

38. John L. Scherer and Michael Jakobson, "The Collectivisation of Agriculture and the Soviet Prison Camp System," *Europe-Asia Studies* 45 (1993): 537.

39. Jakobson, *Origins of the GULAG*, 128–131.

40. John Tierney, "How to Get to Mars (and Make Millions!)," *New York Times Magazine*, 26 May 1996, 20–25.

41. P. V. Orlovskii, "Rol' gidrografii v osvoenii Severnogo Morskogo Puti," *SA* 3, no. 1 (January 1937): 23; N. I. Evgenov, "Lotsii Severnykh morei," in *Za osvoenie Arktiki* (Leningrad: GUSMP, 1935), 417; G. Gurari, "Nashe kapital'noe stroitel'stvo," *SA* 2, no. 1 (January 1936): 139; and I. M. Bashmakov, "Maiachno-lotsmeisterskaia sluzhba v Karskom more," *SA* 2, no. 9 (September 1936): 102.

42. L. V. Shelepin, "Rabota poliarnykh stantsii," in *Za osvoenie Arktiki*, 154.

43. S. A. Bergavinov, "Politotdely Severnogo Morskogo Puti," *SA* 2, no. 1 (January 1937): 19; and A. I. Levichev, "Nekotorye voprosy Sovetskoi torgovli na Krainem Severe," *SA* 3, no. 4 (April 1937): 22.

44. RGAE, f. 9570, op. 2, d. 95, l. 238.

45. V. N. Tarasenkov, "Obskii Sever i ego ekonomika," *SA* 3, no. 5 (May 1937): 78.

46. "Postanovlenie SNK SSSR i TsK VKP(b) o l'gotakh dlia naseleniia Dal'nevostochnogo kraia," 11 December 1933, and "Postanovlenie SNK SSSR i TsK VKP (b) o l'gotakh dlia naseleniia Vostochno-sibirskogo kraia," 5 February 1934, both in *KPSS v rezoliutsiiakh*, 6:98–99, 146–147.

47. Krenkel', *RAEM Is My Call-Sign*, 93.

48. RGAE, f. 9570, op. 1, d. 112, ll. 3–15. Farther to the east, KIRP worker Fedor Shirnov noted that the conditions were similar along the Kolyma, even among free workers. See the journal entry under his name in Véronique Garros, Natalia Korenevskaya, and Thomas Lahusen, eds., *Intimacy and Terror: Soviet Diaries of the 1930s* (New York: New Press, 1995), 69, 79, 89–90.

49. Gruber, *I Went to the Arctic*, 141–142.

50. A. Iu. Libman, "Samolet na sluzhbe Severnogo Morskogo Puti," *SA* 3, no. 2 (February 1937): 42.

51. N. I. Mikhalev, "Grimasy snabzheniia i torgovli na Krainem Severe," *SoS* 5, no. 1 (January-February 1934): 46.

52. RTsKhIDNI, f. 475, op. 1, d. 8, ll. 82–91.

53. Stephan, *Russian Far East*, 197–198. Almost 27,000 women responded to the call, although most settled well below the Arctic Circle.

54. RTsKhIDNI, f. 475, op. 1, d. 8, ll. 47–62, 82–91; op. 2, d. 883, l. 215.

55. Gruber, *I Went to the Arctic*, 147.

56. E. K. Fedorov, *Polar Diaries* (Moscow: Progress, 1983), 142–143.

57. Krenkel', *RAEM Is My Call-Sign*, 58–70.

58. RTsKhIDNI, f. 475, op. 1, d. 5, ll. 29–31.

59. RTsKhIDNI, f. 475, op. 1, d. 16, ll. 78–81.

60. RTsKhIDNI, f. 475, op. 1, d. 5, ll. 25–26; d. 15, ll. 22–30.

61. *Sovetskii Sever* (23 February 1934): 2.

62. RTSKhIDNI, f. 475, op. 1, d. 8, ll. 32–46.

63. S. A. Bergavinov, "O razvertyvanii sovetskoi torgovli na Krainem Severe," *SA* 3, no. 2 (February 1937): 5–13.

64. Mikhalev, "Grimasy snabzheniia," 49.

65. Slezkine, *Arctic Mirrors*, 1. For an excellent study of the Nivkhi and their relationship with Russia throughout the twentieth century, see Bruce Grant, *In the Soviet House of Culture: A Century of Perestroikas* (Princeton: Princeton University Press, 1995).

66. RTSKhIDNI, f. 475, op. 2, d. 321, l. 237; P. E. Terletskii, "Sostav naseleniia Krainego Severa," *SA* 2, no. 11 (November 1936): 36; "Natsional'noe raionirovanie Krainego Severa," *SoS* 1, no. 7–8 (July–August 1930): 13; P. Ustiugov, "Puti sovetskogo stroitel'stva na Krainem Severe," *Sovetskoe stroitel'stvo* (March 1931): 141.

67. Slezkine, *Arctic Mirrors*, 152.

68. RTSKhIDNI, f. 475, op. 1, d. 1, ll. 149–150.

69. Taracouzio, *Soviets in the Arctic*, 263–272; Armstrong, *Russian Settlement*, 166–167; and Slezkine, *Arctic Mirrors*, 158.

70. Slezkine, *Arctic Mirrors*, 148.

71. Ilin, *New Russia's Primer*, 2.

72. Obruchev, *Zemlia Sannikova*, passim.

73. Slezkine, *Arctic Mirrors*, 11.

74. RGAE, f. 9570, op. 2, d. 33, ll. 43–44. The Chukchi also received a number of Orders of the Red Star.

75. GARF, f. 3977, op. 1, d. 529, l. 12; d. 740, ll. 4–5; d. 936, l. 66.

76. Many of the ethnographers who argued for the "soft" line were purged during the 1930s (Slezkine, "From Savages to Citizens: The Cultural Revolution in the Far North, 1928-1938," *Slavic Review* 51 [1992]: 52–76).

77. RTSKhIDNI, f. 475, op. 2, d. 106, ll. 89–94.

78. *SoS* 3, no. 3 (April 1932): 94.

79. RGAE, f. 9570, op. 2, d. 95, l. 162.

80. Taracouzio, *Soviets in the Arctic*, 311; Grant, *In the Soviet House of Culture*, 97–98.

81. Kiselev, *Partiinoe rukovodstvo*, 146–168; also I. O. Serkin, "Ob oshibkakh Obdorskogo politotdela," *SA* 3, no. 10 (October 1937): 9–15, in which GUSMP's Obdorsk Political Department falsified records in order to claim Khanty and Mansi tribespeople on its payroll.

82. *Polar Times* 7 (October 1938): 41.

83. Shmidt, "Bol'sheviki zavoevaiut Arktiku," *Pravda*, 1 February 1935; Kiselev, *Sever raskryvaet*, 21; Zibarev, *Partiinye organizatsii*, 28.

84. V. G. Bogoroz-Tan, "Religiia kak tormoz sotsstroitel'stva sredi malykh narodnostei Severa," *SoS* 3, no. 1–2 (January–February 1932): 142–157.

85. RTSKhIDNI, f. 475, op. 1, d. 6, ll. 50–55.

86. T. Semushkin, *Chukotka* (Moscow, 1941), 176–182; Slezkine, "Savages," 61–63.

87. Sergei Tretiakov, "Ushakov, the Soviet Columbus," *Living Age* 348 (March–August 1935): 237–242; A. I. Mineev, *Ostrov Vrangelia* (Moscow and Leningrad: GUSMP, 1946), 65–72.

88. RGAE, f. 9570, op. 2, d. 49, l. 214; GARF, f. 3977, op. 1, d. 973, l. 4.

89. P. G. Smidovich, "Nashi zadachi na Severnykh okrainakh," *SoS* 3, nos. 1–2 (January–February 1932): 48.

90. RTSKhIDNI, f. 475, op. 1, d. 8, ll. 32–46.

91. Krypton, *Northern Sea Route*, 16.

92. RTSKhIDNI, f. 475, op. 1, d. 12, l. 144.

93. Armstrong, *Russian Settlement*, 166–167.

94. Taracouzio, *Soviets in the Arctic*, 226–227.

95. O. Iu. Shmidt, *Osvoenie Severnogo morskogo puti i zadachi sel'skogo khoziaistva Krainego Severa* (Moscow and Leningrad: Nauka, 1937).

96. P. V. Orlovskii, "Sel'skoe khoziaistvo na Krainem Severe vo vtoroi piatiletke," *SoS* 4, no. 1 (January–February 1933): 17, 23.

97. A. D. Smirnov, "Nashe sel'skogo khoziaistvo," *SA* 3, no. 9 (September 1937): 49.

98. N. M. Ianson, "Plan raboty Glavsevmorputi v 1937 godu," *SA* 3, no. 2 (February 1937): 17–18, 22.

99. "Postanovlenie SNK SSSR i TSK VKP(b) o l'gotakh dlia naseleniia Dal'nevostochnogo kraia," 11 December 1933, and "Postanovlenie SNK SSSR i TSK VKP(b) o l'gotakh dlia naseleniia Vostochno-sibirskogo kraia," 5 February 1934, and "Postanovlenie TSK VKP(b) i SNK SSSR o meropriatiiakh po organizatsionnomu i khoziaistvennomu ukrepleniiu kolkhozov i pod"emu sel'skogo khoziaistva Severnykh raionov," 1 January 1936, in *KPSS v rezoliutsiiakh*, 6:98–99, 146–147, 310–312.

100. I. V. Alimov and V. V. Berezin, "Rechnoi transport Glavsevmorputi v navigatsiiu 1937 goda," *SA* 3, no. 4 (April 1937): 77.

101. Libman, "Samolet na sluzhbe," 42.

102. *Vozdushnye puti Severa* (Moscow, 1933), 112, 449, 482; the State Archive of the Sverdlovsk Oblast' (GASO), f. 241, op. 3, d. 371.

103. O. Iu. Shmidt, *Nashi zadachi v 1936 godu* (Leningrad: GUSMP, 1936), 3.

104. GUSMP's involvement with the Dudinka-Noril'sk railroad, whose history is a grim one, is unclear. The railroad was built by GULAG prisoners and was created to utilize more efficiently the labor of the convicts working in the Noril'sk mines. Glavsevmorput seems to have had no formal responsibilities regarding the railroad, but this is uncertain.

105. Alimov and Berezin, "Rechnoi transport Glavsevmorputi," 85; Shmidt is cited in Ianson, "Plan raboty Glavsevmorputi," 21.

106. Shmidt, *Nashi zadachi*, 6, 8, 20–21.

107. Westwood, "Transport," 181.

Notes to Chapter 3

1. Gromov, *Pokhod "Sibiriakova"*; Krenkel', *RAEM Is My Call-Sign*; *Dva okeana*; and S. A. Seleznev, *Ledovyi kapitan* (Arkhangelsk, 1969).

2. The amount of material on the *Cheliuskin* "epic" is staggering. Along with the extensive coverage in *Pravda* and *Izvestiia*, see Krenkel', *RAEM Is My Call-Sign*; B. Gromov, *Gibel' "Cheliuskina"* (Moscow: Goslitizdat, 1936); *Dnevniki Cheliuskintsev* (Moscow: Pravda, 1934); *Pokhod "Cheliuskina"* (Moscow: Pravda, 1934); *Kak my spasali Cheliuskintsev* (Moscow: Pravda, 1934); A. V. Liapidevskii, *Cheliuskintsy* (Moscow and Leningrad: Detizdat, 1938); M. E. Zinger, *Geroi Sovetskogo Soiuza* (Moscow: Ogonek, 1934); S. Mogilevskaia, *Lager' na l'dine* (Moscow: Detizdat, 1935); *Po sledam Cheliuskinskoi epopei* (Magadan, 1986); *The Voyage of the Cheliuskin* (New York: Macmillan, 1935); *Chelovek, spasshi 39 zhiznei* (Moscow: Radiokomitet, 1938); *Geroi Arktiki* (RGAKFD 1-4981); *Kryl'ia nad l'dom* (RGAKFD 1-25083); and *Odisseia "Cheliuskina"* (RGAKFD 1-9650).

3. Krenkel', *RAEM Is My Call-Sign*, 170–179.

4. *Voyage of the Cheliuskin*, 5–6.

5. Academician Sigurd O. Shmidt, son of Otto Shmidt, indicates that this was indeed the case. Interviewed by the author, 7 April 1992.

6. RGAE, f. 9570, dd. 37–40.

7. Dallin and Nicolaevsky, *Forced Labor in Soviet Russia*, 127–129. Note that most his-

torians consider the number of prisoners said to have been aboard the *Dzhurma* to be greatly exaggerated.

8. The common translation of *Ne sdadimsia*; a better rendition would be "We Shall Not Yield," since the title came from the last line of Tennyson's *Ulysses* ("to strive, to seek, to find, and not to yield"), a poem whose connection with polar exploration is long-standing. *Ulysses* was written to commemorate the death of John Franklin in 1847, and the final line was inscribed on the tombstone of Robert Scott. The hero of Kaverin's *The Two Captains* makes the phrase his personal motto.

9. Krenkel', *RAEM Is My Call-Sign*, 224.

10. Ibid., 232.

11. Edward Kasinec, "Schmidt and the American Press: A Note" (unpublished bibliographic essay).

12. V. A. Durov, *Russkie i sovetskie boevye nagrady* (Moscow: Lenin State Historical Museum, 1990), 66, 76–77.

13. On the cultural importance of aviation in the history of the West, see Joseph Corn, *The Winged Gospel: America's Romance with Aviation, 1900–1950* (New York: Oxford University Press, 1983); Joseph Corn and Brian Horrigan, *Yesterday's Tomorrows: Past Visions of the American Future* (New York: Summit Books, 1984); Modris Eksteins, *The Rites of Spring* (New York: Anchor Books, 1990); Peter Fritzsche, *A Nation of Fliers: German Aviation and the Popular Imagination* (Cambridge: Harvard University Press, 1992); Le Corbusier, *Aircraft* (London: The Studio, 1935); Segré, *Italo Balbo*; and Robert Wohl, *A Passion for Wings: Aviation and the Western Imagination, 1908–1918* (New Haven: Yale University Press, 1994).

14. Bailes, *Technology and Society*, 381–406; Peter Nisbet, "The Response to Science and Technology in the Visual Arts," in Loren Graham, ed., *Science and the Soviet Social Order* (Cambridge: Harvard University Press, 1990), 341–358; Clark, *Soviet Novel*, 120–139; Robert Kilmarx, *A History of Soviet Air Power* (New York: Praeger, 1962); A. Ia. Egorov and V. P. Kliucharev, *Grazhdanskaia aviatsiia SSSR* (Moscow: Sotsekgiz, 1937); *Grazhdanskaia aviatsiia SSSR, 1917–1967* (Moscow: Transport, 1967); *Kryl'ia sovetov: Literaturno-estradnyi sbornik* (Moscow: Iskusstvo, 1939); Flora Leites, ed., *Stalinskie sokoly: Sbornik stikhov* (Moscow: Khudozhestvennaia literatura, 1939); Shesterikova, *Daty istorii*; *Soviet Aviation* (Moscow and Leningrad: State Art Publishers, 1939).

15. *Grazhdanskaia aviatsiia SSSR, 1917–1967*, 108. Until July 1936, when the USSR joined the International Aviation Federation, these records were unofficial.

16. William Odom, *The Soviet Volunteers: Modernization and Bureaucracy in a Public Mass Organization* (Princeton: Princeton University Press, 1973), 3, 60–82. Osoaviakhim's papers are in GARF, ff. 7577, 8355.

17. In one of the decade's worst aviation disasters, the *Maxim Gorky* crashed on 18 May 1935, after colliding with a young pilot's training craft above Moscow's Central Aerodrome. Forty-nine people were killed; all were buried at Novodevich'e Cemetery, and the families of the victims each received 10,000 rubles from the government.

18. *Velikii letchik nashego vremeni* (Moscow: OGIZ, 1939); I. K. Avramenko, *Gordye Stalinskie sokoly: Ukazatel' literatury k godovshchine pereletov Moskva-Severnyi polius-Severnaia Amerika* (Leningrad, 1938); G. F. Baidukov, *Pervye perelety cherez Ledovityi okean* (Moscow: Detskaia literatura, 1987), and idem, *Russian Lindbergh: The Life of Valery Chkalov* (Washington, D.C.: Smithsonian, 1991); V. P. Chkalov, et al., *Dva pereleta* (Moscow: Voenizdat, 1938), and idem, *My eshche prodolzhim Stalinskii marshrut* (Moscow: Gosizdat, 1938); O. E. Chkalova, *Valerii Pavlovich Chkalov* (Gorky, 1981); I. S. Rakhillo, *Rasskazy o Chkalove* (Moscow: Detizdat, 1960); Mikhail Kalatozov's feature film *Valerii Chkalov* (1941); *Po Stalinskomu marshrutu* (RGAKFD 1-4934); *SSSR-SShA* (RGAKFD

1-26649); *Moscow–Vancouver: 1937* (Moscow: Novosti, 1987); and Von Hardesty, "Soviets Blaze Sky Trail over Top of World," *Air and Space/Smithsonian* 2, no. 5 (December 1987–January 1988): 48–54.

19. Baidukov, *Russian Lindbergh*, 51–59.

20. Hardesty, "Soviets Blaze Sky"; Krenkel', *RAEM Is My Call-Sign*, 297–298.

21. Baidukov, *Pervye perelety*; A. S. Danilin, *Cherez Severnyi polius—s mirovym rekordom* (Moscow: DOSAAF, 1981); *Po Stalinskoi trasse* (Moscow: Molodaia gvardiia, 1937); M. M. Gromov, *Cherez vsiu zhizn'* (Moscow: Molodaia gvardiia, 1986); N. P. Kamanin, *Letchiki i kosmonavty* (Moscow: Politizdat, 1971); E. I. Riabchikov and S. Shul'man, *Gromov* (Moscow: Molodaia gvardiia, 1937); *Stalinskaia trassa* (Moscow: Partizdat, 1937); Mark Friedlander and Gene Gurney, *Higher, Faster, and Farther* (New York: Morrow, 1973), 236; and *Po Stalinskoi trasse* (RGAKFD 1-4132).

22. Krenkel', *RAEM Is My Call-Sign*, 251.

23. Iu. P. Sal'nikov, *Zhizn', otdannaia Arktike* (Moscow: Politizdat, 1984); S. A. Levanevskii, *Moia stikhiia* (Rostov, 1935); and *Po Stalinskomu puti* (RGAKFD 1-3811).

24. M. V. Vodop'ianov, *Rasskaz o moei zhizni* (Moscow: Sovetskii pisatel', 1937); V. I. Artamanov, *Zemlia i nebo Vodop'ianova* (Moscow: Politizdat, 1991); V. S. Molokov, *My vypolnili svoi dolg—vot i vse!* (Moscow: Molodaia gvardiia, 1935), and idem, *Rodnoe nebo* (Moscow: Voenizdat, 1977); I. P. Mazuruk, *Nasha aviatsiia* (Leningrad: Detizdat, 1940), and, with Antarctic explorer A. A. Lebedev, *Nad Arktikoi i Antarktikoi* (Moscow: Mysl', 1991).

25. V. I. Akkuratov, *Led i pepel* (Moscow: Sovremennik, 1984), and idem, *Na novykh trassakh* (Moscow and Leningrad: GUSMP, 1941); P. G. Golovin, *Kak ia stal letchikom* (Moscow and Leningrad: Detizdat, 1938); S. T. Morozov, *Krylatyi sledopyt Zapoliar'ia* (Moscow: Mysl', 1975); I. T. Spirin, *Rasskazy letchika* (Moscow and Leningrad: Detizdat, 1939); and V. D. Zaluzhnyi, *Shturman ledovogo pereleta* (Rostov, 1976).

26. Krenkel', *RAEM Is My Call-Sign*, and idem, *Chetyre tovarishcha* (Moscow: Progress, 1978).

27. Fedorov, *Polar Diaries*; Boris Gorbatov, *Petr Petrovich Shirshov* (Moscow: OGIZ, 1938).

28. I. D. Papanin, *Led i plamen'* (Moscow: Politizdat, 1978); idem, *Na poliuse* (Moscow and Leningrad: Detizdat, 1939); idem, *Zhizn' na l'dine* (Moscow: Mysl', 1966); V. Vishevskii, *Geroi Sovetskogo Soiuza Ivan Dmitrievich Papanin* (Moscow: OGIZ, 1938); and I. D. Papanin (Moscow: Planeta, 1990).

29. Krenkel', *RAEM Is My Call-Sign*, 295.

30. In addition to works already cited, see S. A. Bergavinov, *Arktika i polius zavoevany!* (Moscow: Partizdat, 1937), and idem, *Polius nash!* (Moscow: Partizdat, 1937); L. K. Brontman, *Na vershine mira* (Moscow and Leningrad: Detizdat, 1938), and idem, *On the Top of the World* (London: Victor Gollancz, 1938); *Desiat' mesiatsev na dreifuiushchei stantsii "Severnyi polius"* (Moscow: OGIZ, 1938); Z. M. Kanevskii, *Borot'sia i iskat'!* (Leningrad: Gidrometeoizdat, 1979); A. I. Mineev, *Zachem my organizovali ekspeditsiiu Papanina* (Moscow and Leningrad: GUSMP, 1946); S. T. Morozov, *Oni prinesli kryl'ia v Arktiku* (Moscow: Mysl', 1979); *Ekspeditsiia na Severnyi polius* (RGAKFD 1-13526); *Na Severnom poliuse* (RGAKFD 1-4111); *Papanintsy* (RGAKFD 1-2683); and *Severnyi polius zavoevan nami!* (RGAKFD 1-4167).

31. This gesture was more than symbolic; it signaled that the Soviets could now dictate how territorial claims in the Arctic would be administered. Since there was no land at the pole to claim, the USSR served notice that it was putting into effect the "sector" method of determining jurisdiction over the Arctic. Imaginary lines were to be drawn from the pole to the eastern and western edges of each Arctic nation's coastline; each would then claim

the "region of attraction" between the lines. This scheme was proposed during the 1920s by V. L. Lakhtin ("Prava Soiuza SSSR v Arktike," *Rabochii sud* [1928]: 1,135). Since it assigned over half the Arctic to the USSR, the rest of the world was hesitant about the sector method. After the North Pole landing, however, the international community moved toward adopting it (*Polar Times* 5 [October 1937]: 3).

32. Sadly, Shmidt's wife Vera died in July 1937, soon after his return from the pole. By contrast, both Shirshov and Fedorov became new fathers while they were at the pole.

33. Papanin, *Led i plamen'*, 144.

34. "Four Men and a Dog," *Time*, 31, no. 7 (14 February 1938): 51.

35. RGAE, f. 424, op. 1, d. 73, ll. 1–43; an SP-2 outpost was eventually established, but not until 1950.

36. Friedlander and Gurney, *Higher, Faster, and Farther*, 310.

37. L. K. Brontman and L. Khvat, *Geroicheskii perelet "Rodiny"* (Moscow: OGIZ, 1938); and *Tri geroini* (RGAKFD 1-4188).

38. The circumstances surrounding Chkalov's death are discussed in chapter 6; on his funeral, see chapter 4.

39. "Moscow to Miscou," *Time* 33, no. 19 (8 May 1939): 56; *New York Times*, 26–30 April 1939; V. K. Kokkinaki, *Kak my leteli* (Rostov, 1939); L. K. Brontman, *Vladimir Kokkinaki* (Moscow: Voenizdat, 1939); B. Gorbatov, *Vladimir Konstantinovich Kokkinaki* (Moscow: OGIZ, 1938); *Moskva-SShA* (RGAKFD 1-3840); and *Slava Stalinskim sokolam!* (RGAKFD 1-4193).

40. Both events are explained in more detail in the conclusion.

41. Incidentally, it was during the Spanish Civil War that the USSR realized it had focused too heavily on long-distance flying. As overenthusiastic proponents of air-power theory, the Soviets neglected the production of fighter aircraft; this error became apparent in Spain, as Messerschmitts and Fiats overwhelmed outdated Polikarpovs. See aircraft designer Aleksandr Iakovlev (whose slant on the story is somewhat biased), in Seweryn Bialer, ed., *Stalin and His Generals* (New York: Pegasus, 1969), 86–88, 166–171, 377–383.

Notes to Chapter 4

1. Clark, *Soviet Novel*, 146–147.

2. For a sample, see the works cited in the introduction. Studies that take similar approaches to cases besides that of the USSR include Michael Cherniavsky, *Tsar and People: Studies in Russian Myths* (New Haven: Yale University Press, 1961); Jay W. Baird, *The Mythical World of Nazi War Propaganda, 1939–1941* (Minneapolis: University of Minnesota Press, 1974), and idem, *To Die for Germany: Heroes in the Nazi Pantheon* (Bloomington: Indiana University Press, 1990); Frank Golsan, ed., *Fascism, Aesthetics, and Culture* (Hanover, N.H.: University Press of New England, 1992); Eric Hobsbawm and Terence Ranger, eds., *The Invention of Tradition* (Cambridge: Cambridge University Press, 1983); David I. Kertzer, *Ritual, Politics, and Power* (New Haven: Yale University Press, 1988); and Sean Wilentz, ed., *Rites of Power: Symbolism, Ritual, and Politics since the Middle Ages* (Philadelphia: University of Pennsylvania Press, 1985).

3. Bernard Cohn, "Representing Authority in Victorian India," in Hobsbawm and Ranger, eds., *Invention of Tradition*, 173.

4. Jack Zipes, *The Brothers Grimm: From Enchanted Forests to the Modern World* (New York: Routledge, 1988), 24–25.

5. Mark Bassin, "Turner, Solov'ev, and the 'Frontier Hypothesis': The Nationalist Signification of Open Spaces," *Journal of Modern History* 65, 3 (September 1993): 1–17, and idem, "Geographical Determinism in Fin-de-siècle Marxism: Georgii Plekhanov and

the Environmental Basis of Russian History," *Annals of the Association of American Geographers* 82, 1 (Spring 1992): 3–22; Ian Matley, "The Marxist Approach to the Geographical Environment," *Annals of the Association of American Geographers* 56 (1966): 97–111.

6. Leon Trotsky, *The Russian Revolution* (New York: Doubleday, 1959), 1.

7. Douglas Weiner, *Models of Nature: Ecology, Conservation, and Cultural Revolution in Soviet Russia* (Bloomington: Indiana University Press, 1988), 229–231.

8. Ibid., 22–24.

9. Stites, *Revolutionary Dreams*, 52–58, 145–164; Clark, *Soviet Novel*, 99–113, 241–250, and idem, "Little Heroes and Big Deeds: Literature Responds to the First Five-Year Plan," in Sheila Fitzpatrick, ed., *Cultural Revolution in Russia, 1928–1931* (Bloomington: Indiana University Press, 1978), 189–203.

10. John McCannon, "To Storm the Arctic: Soviet Polar Expeditions and Public Visions of Nature in the USSR, 1932–1939," *Ecumene* 2, no. 1 (January 1995): 15–31.

11. *Geroi Sovetskogo Soiuza Otto Iul'evich Shmidt* (Moscow: Radiokomitet, 1938), 3.

12. *SA* 4, no. 8 (August 1938): 7–10.

13. *Izvestiia*, 14 April 1934.

14. Smolka, *Forty Thousand against the Arctic*, 169.

15. Miller, *Folklore for Stalin*, 37, 125; and James von Geldern and Richard Stites, *Mass Culture in Soviet Russia* (Bloomington: Indiana University Press, 1995), 290.

16. This image adorns a 50-kopek postage stamp issued in 1934 (RGAE, f. 9570, op. 2, d. 39, l. 12), as well as the cover of M. V. Vodop'ianov's *Polius* (Moscow and Leningrad: GUSMP, 1939).

17. On the psychological and cultural importance of height and high ground, see Simon Schama, *Landscape and Memory* (New York: Knopf, 1995), 385–513; Tom Wolfe, *The Right Stuff* (New York: Bantam, 1983), 55–64; and John MacAloon, ed., *Rite, Drama, Festival, Spectacle* (Philadelphia: ISHI, 1984), 209–215.

18. Brontman, *Top*, 236.

19. Miller, *Folklore for Stalin*, 37–47, 144–146; *Velikii letchik*, 278–280; *Kryl'ia sovetov*, 49–50, 62–63, 137–44; D. Kedrin, "Skazka pro Beluiu Vedmed' [sic] i pro Shmidtovu Borodu," in Leites, ed., *Stalinskie sokoly*, 156–160.

20. *Pravda*, 22 May 1937; "Severnyi polius zavoevan!" *SA* 3, no. 6 (June 1937): Bergavinov, *Arktika i polius zavoevany!*.

21. Krenkel', RAEM *Is My Call-Sign*, 193.

22. *Dnevniki Cheliuskintsev*, 251–286; *Voyage of the Cheliuskin*, 194.

23. M. E. Zinger, *Lenskii pokhod* (Leningrad: Lenizdat, 1934), 47; K. S. Badigin, *Na morskikh dorogakh* (Arkhangelsk, 1985), 64.

24. For cases of psychological trauma brought on by polar night in the Russian Arctic, see L. M. Starokadomskii, "K izucheniiu vliianiia Arktiki na psikhiku," RGAE, f. 245, op. 1, d. 59.

25. Badigin, *Na morskikh dorogakh*, 31.

26. G. A. Ushakov, *Po nekhozhenoi zemle* (Leningrad: Gidrometeoizdat, 1990), 241–242.

27. G. A. Ushakov, *Ostrov metelei* (Leningrad: Gidrometeoizdat, 1990), 81.

28. M. V. Vodop'ianov, "Snova nad poliusom," *SA* 4, no. 3 (March 1938): 67–72.

29. Lewis Mumford, *Technics and Civilization* (New York: Harcourt Brace and World, 1963), 286.

30. Clark, *Soviet Novel*, 93–103; the term comes from Leo Marx's classic, *The Machine in the Garden: Technology and the Pastoral Ideal in America* (New York: Oxford University Press, 1968).

31. Clark, *Soviet Novel*, 102–103, 202–207; Jeffrey Brooks, *When Russia Learned to*

Read: Literacy and Popular Literature, 1861–1917 (Princeton: Princeton University Press, 1985), 116–117, 150.

32. Ushakov, *Ostrov metelei*, 44–45.

33. *Voyage of the Cheliuskin*, 213.

34. M. E. Zinger, *Pobezhdennoe more* (Moscow: Sovetskaia Aziia, 1932), 41; ARAN, f. 496, op. 1, d. 183, l. 2.

35. B. Gromov, *Gibel' Arktiki* (Moscow: Molodaia gvardiia, 1932), 32.

36. Mogilevskaia, *Lager' na l'dine*, 163; Molokov, *My vypolnili svoi dolg*, 58.

37. *Izvestiia*, 1 January 1938.

38. Smolka, *Forty Thousand against the Arctic*, 20–23; and Farley Mowat, *The Siberians* (Toronto: Bantam, 1970), 221.

39. In a way, the Soviets' discursive treatment of the Arctic resembled the way in which nineteenth-century Russians exoticized their southern frontiers. The stark mountains and ravines of the Caucasus, for instance, were seen to be as much a foe as the military forces the Russians faced. But that same terrain was also part of the captivating romantic appeal attested to by writers like Lermontov, Pushkin, and Tolstoy. My thanks to Richard Stites for this observation; also see Katya Hokanson, "Literary Imperialism, *Narodnost'*, and Pushkin's Invention of the Caucasus," *Russian Review* 53 (1994): 336–352.

40. Brontman, *Top*, 182.

41. Ibid., xi–xiii.

42. Barry Lopez, *Arctic Dreams: Imagination and Desire in a Northern Landscape* (New York: Scribner's, 1986), 252.

43. Zipes, *Brothers Grimm*, 43.

44. Gruber, *I Went to the Arctic*, 236.

45. M. V. Vodop'ianov, *Na kryliakh v Arktiku* (Moscow: Geograficheskaia literatura, 1954), 5.

46. Brontman, *Top*, 191.

47. *Kak my spasali Cheliuskintsev*, 113; Levanevskii, *Moia stikhiia*, 17–18.

48. Robert Service, "The Shooting of Dan McGrew," in Martin Gardner, ed., *Best Remembered Poems* (New York: Dover, 1992), 154. Emphasis in the original.

49. Krenkel', RAEM *Is My Call-Sign*, 72–73.

50. Cited in A. M. Gor'kii et al., eds., *Belomorsko-Baltiiskii kanal imeni Stalina* (Moscow: ZIF, 1934), 209–212.

51. *Moscow News*, 17 October 1942; the Russian State Archive of Literature and Art (RGALI), f. 1501, op. 1, d. 151, l. 18.

52. Peter Knox-Shaw, *The Explorer in English Fiction* (New York: St. Martin's Press, 1986), 10–11; Edward Said, *Orientalism* (New York: Pantheon, 1978).

53. Lopez, *Arctic Dreams*, 278.

54. *Pravda*, 13 January 1934.

55. *My iz Igarki* (Moscow and Leningrad: Detizdat, 1938). See chapter 5 for the darker realities behind the book.

56. Of the town's population of 12,000 to 15,000, approximately 2,300 were school-age children (Gruber, *I Went to the Arctic*, 81–83).

57. *My iz Igarki*, 6, 191–219.

58. *Pravda*, 20 July 1935.

59. *Pravda*, 7 December 1932.

60. The following portrait is compiled from the many sources cited in chapter 3.

61. Paul Zweig, *The Adventurer* (New York: Basic Books, 1974), 226–234.

62. *SA* 2, no. 11 (November 1936), 12–16.

63. Brontman, *Top*, 140.

64. Ibid., 154.

65. This point also provides an answer to a frequently asked question: did the Arctic become a "Wild East" for the Soviets in the way that the Western frontier did for the United States? There are similarities, but there is also an overriding difference. While Americans reveled (and continue to revel) in the individualistic, "rough-and-ready" aspects of the cultural myth of the West (even in instances where a specific narrative is about the imposition of law and order), Soviet authorities regarded disorder and individualism with disapproval. Hence, the Arctic myth, in great contrast to America's Western saga, filtered out as much as possible anything that was both wild *and* positive.

66. RGALI, f. 2177, op. 1, d. 57, ll. 3–6.

67. M. V. Vodop'ianov, "Novogodniaia mechta," *Pravda*, 1 January 1938.

68. M. E. Kol'tsov, "Naidennaia rodina," *Pravda*, 19 June 1934. Famous for his dispatches from Spain (he is thought to have been one of Stalin's operatives in the civil war there) and his cameo appearance as the character "Karkov" in Hemingway's *For Whom the Bell Tolls*, Kol'tsov was one of *Pravda*'s best writers, as well as the honorary commander of the USSR's "Agitational Escadrille." He was sent to the GULAG in 1937; he died in 1942.

69. ARAN, f. 496, op. 1, d. 169, l. 7.

70. Papanin, *Na poliuse*, 6.

71. Liapidevskii, *Cheliuskintsy*, 4.

72. Mazuruk, *Nasha aviatsiia*, 3.

73. Papanin, *Na poliuse*, 4–5; Vishevskii, *Geroi Sovetskogo*, 1.

74. Molokov, *My vypolnili svoi dolg*, 22–25.

75. Veniamin Kaverin, *The Two Captains* (Moscow: Raduga, 1989), 101–104.

76. Stites, *Revolutionary Dreams*, 170–171; Wohl, *Passion for Wings*, 144–153, 157–178, 269; *Poema o kryl'iakh: Zapiski aviatorov* (Moscow: Sovremennik, 1988), 92–98; V. A. Moiseev, *Plemia Ikara* (Kiev: Veselka, 1986); Leites, ed., *Stalinskie sokoly*, 12–14; Scott Palmer, "On Wings of Courage: Public 'Air-Mindedness' and National Identity in Late Imperial Russia," *Russian Review* 54 (1995): 209–226.

77. Even poet Aleksandr Pushkin—revered by the Soviets as a national bard—found his way into the Arctic myth. It is no accident, for example, that the Cheliuskinites were said to have enjoyed reading from their volume of Pushkin more than any other entertainment at Camp Shmidt. The Papaninites also made great mention of how they whiled away the hours at the SP-1 outpost with Pushkin's poetry.

78. V. Iu. Vize, *Lomonosov i Severnyi morskoi put'* (Moscow: Molodaia gvardiia, 1946), 4; V. A. Perevalov, *Lomonosov i Arktika* (Moscow: GUSMP, 1949); O. Iu. Shmidt, "Lomonosov —velikii uchitel'," *Pravda*, 15 April 1940.

79. *Popular Science* 138, no. 5 (May 1937): 25; *Polar Times* 8 (March 1939): 14.

80. *Po sledam Cheliuskinskoi epopei*, 188.

81. M. V. Vodop'ianov and G. K. Grigor'ev, *Povest' o ledovom komissare* (Moscow: Geograficheskaia literatura, 1959), 45–47.

82. Stites, *Revolutionary Dreams*, 145–170, 180–188.

83. American Wiley Post was also the recipient of Soviet assistance; when he and Australia's Harold Gatty flew around the world in 1931, the USSR allowed them to travel through Siberia. In addition, the Moscow Air Club gave a large party in their honor. This was a kind gesture but, as Post wryly noted, a less than helpful one, since it meant that he and Gatty had to fly to Sverdlovsk the following morning with vodka-induced hangovers (Friedlander and Gurney, *Higher, Faster, and Farther*, 219–23).

84. Edward Rickenbacker, *Rickenbacker: An Autobiography* (Englewood Cliffs, N.J.: Prentice Hall, 1967), 378–381.

85. ARAN, f. 496, op. 1, d. 251, ll. 7–9.

86. *Pravda* and *Izvestiia* voiced this possibility in summer 1937, as did A. Klemin, a reporter for *Scientific American*. In 1939, a Soviet scientist seriously proposed digging a tunnel beneath the Bering Straits to connect the two continents (*Komsomol'skaia pravda*, 1 January 1939).

87. RGAE, f. 9570, op. 2, d. 36, ll. 279–280.

88. *Pravda*, 18 June 1934.

89. *New York Times*, 25 June 1937.

90. Hardesty, introduction to Baidukov, *Russian Lindbergh*, 5–10.

91. Bailes, *Technology and Society*, 405–406.

92. According to the USAF Museum, fourteen air-mail pilots died in spring 1934 alone. The *New York Times* covered this crisis extensively from February to April, as did *Pravda* and *Izvestiia*, which, with ill-disguised smugness, contrasted it to the triumph of the *Cheliuskin* rescue.

93. The transpolar flights also contrasted with Germany's greatest aviation disaster of the decade: the burning of the dirigible *Hindenburg* in May 1937.

94. The FAI was the only international sports organization the USSR chose to join before World War II (James Riordan, *Sport and Soviet Society* [Cambridge: Cambridge University Press, 1977], 142).

95. Gruber, *I Went to the Arctic*, 67–69.

96. *Polar Times* 5 (October 1937): 6. Given Shmidt's yearly appearances as Grandfather Frost, the Russian version of Santa Claus, it is interesting to see how both the United States and the USSR closely connected important holiday symbols with the North Pole.

97. *Polar Times* 5 (October 1937): 2.

98. Sergei Tretiakov, "Ushakov, the Soviet Columbus," *Living Age* 348 (March–August 1935): 242.

99. *Velikii letchik*, 145–146; Baidukov, *Pervye perelety* 159.

100. Zaluzhnyi, *Shturman ledovogo pereleta*, 115.

101. RGAE, f. 9570, op. 2, d. 104, l. 4; d. 105, ll. 34, 48–50. Mattern did not try to profit from the rescue mission, as the Soviets claimed. During the search, Mattern damaged one aircraft and lost another; Republic simply wanted to recoup its sizable financial loss.

102. *Geroi Arktiki*.

103. Krenkel', *RAEM Is My Call-Sign*, 288; Vishevskii, *Geroi Sovetskogo*, 17; RGAE, f. 262, op. 1, d. 37, ll. 7–8.

104. Slogans found in *Krasnaia zvezda* during spring 1939.

105. "Rech' tovarishcha Papanina na XVIII s"zede VKP(b)," *SA* 5, no. 4 (April 1939): 89–94.

106. Gorbatov, *Kokkinaki*, 7.

107. G. F. Baidukov, "Razgrom fashistskoi eskadry (fantaziia budushchei voine)," *Pravda*, 19 August 1938.

108. *Krasnaia zvezda*, 1 January 1939; *Izvestiia*, 1 January 1938.

109. Clark, *Soviet Novel*, 124–129; Günther, *Sozialistische Übermensch*; and Rufus Mathewson, *The Positive Hero in Russian Literature* (Stanford: Stanford University Press, 1975).

110. Stites, *Revolutionary Dreams*, 52–58, 145–164; Clark, *Soviet Novel*, 99–113, 241–250, and idem, "Little Heroes," 189–203.

111. Stites, *Russian Popular Culture*, 67.

112. Matthew Cullerne Brown, *Art under Stalin* (New York: Holmes and Meier, 1991), 92.

113. Clark, *Soviet Novel*, 47–48, 151–152; Brooks, *When Russia*, 24, 31.

114. Miller, *Folklore for Stalin*; Felix Oinas, "Folklore and Politics in the Soviet Union," *Slavic Review* 32 (1973): 45–58.

115. *Komsomol'skaia pravda*, 31 December 1935; *Newsweek*, 11, no. 5 (11 April 1938): 17; ARAN, f. 496, op. 2, d. 311, l. 1.

116. Kaverin, *The Two Captains*, 268–269.

117. Brontman and Khvat, *Geroicheskii perelet "Rodiny,"* 62.

118. Wohl, *Passion for Wings*, 279–282; Lisa Bloom, *Gender on Ice: American Ideologies of Polar Expeditions* (Minneapolis: University of Minnesota Press, 1993); Mary Cadogan, *Women with Wings: Female Flyers in Fact and Fiction* (London: Macmillan, 1992); and, especially, Karen Petrone, "Gender and Heroes," in Sue Bridger, ed., *The Swing of the Pendulum: Women's Experience of Change in East Central Europe and the Former USSR* (New York: Macmillan, 1997).

119. RTSkhIDNI, f. 475, op. 2, d. 446, l. 1.

120. Zweig, *Adventurer*, 34–35.

121. Clark, *Soviet Novel*, 15–24.

122. A more accurate (if less convenient) translation of *stikhiinost'* is "elemental spontaneity," derived from *stikhiia*, which means "elements" and carries connotations of the untamed natural world (tapping discursively into the earlier-discussed themes regarding nature).

123. Clark, *Soviet Novel*, 15–24.

124. Nietzsche's influence on Maksim Gor'kii, the founder of socialist realism, is detailed in Günther, *Sozialistische Übermensch*, and Clark, *Soviet Novel*, 152–155.

125. Brontman, *Kokkinaki*, 4.

126. Krenkel', *RAEM Is My Call-Sign*, 361.

127. Kaverin, *The Two Captains*, 389.

128. *SA* 2, no. 3 (March 1936): 56.

129. Vodop'ianov, *Na kryl'iakh*, 175. This story appears in a number of memoirs. Dzerdzeevskii's "cowardice" was spotlighted only for rhetorical purposes and in a good-natured way. He acted with good judgment in delaying the flight, he was respected by the members of the expedition, and he received the same commendations as his compatriots.

130. Z. M. Kanevskii, *Zagadki i tragedii Arktiki* (Moscow: Znanie, 1991), 136–149.

131. S. Nagornyi, "Geroi," *Literaturnaia gazeta*, 15 December 1939, cited in Clark, *Soviet Novel*, 139.

132. Fedorov, *Polar Diaries*, 212.

133. *Pravda*, 18 June 1934.

134. See Molokov's memoir, *My vypolnili svoi dolg—vot i vse!*, 20.

135. Krenkel', *RAEM Is My Call Sign*, 108.

136. Gromov, *Gibel' Arktiki*, 3–4.

137. Brontman, *Top*, 29–30.

138. *Velikii letchik*, 81.

139. L. A. Kudrevatykh, *S Valeriem Chkalovym* (Moscow: Pravda, 1958), 18–19. During the 1930s, the NKVD's corps of border guards (*pogranichniki*) were widely regarded (or at least propagandized) as being among the USSR's most prestigious military units.

140. Clark, *Soviet Novel*, 255–260.

141. Krenkel', *RAEM Is My Call Sign*, 101.

142. *Otto Iul'evich Shmidt*, 342–344; *Voyage of the Cheliuskin*, 3.

143. *SA* 1, no. 1 (August 1935): 6.

144. Vasnetsov, *Povesti Severnykh morei*, 70–74.

145. *Voyage of the Cheliuskin*, 169–182. All quotations in the following paragraph come from this excerpt.

146. *Otto Iul'evich Shmidt*, 276.

147. Vodop'ianov, *Povest'*, 166–171; idem, *Polius*, 52–54; and idem, "Polius nash," *SA* 3, no. 6 (June 1937): 44–52.

148. *SA* 2, no. 3 (March 1936): 28.

149. Krenkel', *RAEM Is My Call-Sign*, 29–30; Vodop'ianov, *Na kryl'iakh*, 78–107.

150. Clark, *Soviet Novel*, 124–129.

151. *Kryl'ia sovetov*, 69–75.

152. *SA* 5, no. 3 (April 1939), 89–94.

153. Bown, *Art under Stalin*, 98–99.

154. Along with the heroes' memoirs, see *SA* 5, no. 12 (December 1939): 17–33; Brontman, *Kokkinaki*, 18, 30–32; G. F. Baidukov, *Vstrechi s tovarishchem Stalinym* (Moscow and Leningrad: Detizdat, 1940); and Aleksandr Fadeev, ed., *Vstrechi s tovarishchem Stalinym* (Moscow: OGIZ, 1939).

155. I. D. Papanin, "Nezabyvaemye vstrechi," in Fadeev, ed., *Vstrechi*, 34.

156. V. Grizodubova, "Drug i uchitel'," in Fadeev, ed., *Vstrechi*, 179.

157. *Izvestiia*, 18 August 1938.

158. Chkalov et al., *Dva pereleta*, 10–11.

159. *Pravda*, 11 August 1936; *Velikii letchik*, 128–129. Excepting a front-page photo in *Pravda* (26 June 1937) of Stalin kissing Shmidt after the SP-1 triumph, this was the only time Stalin was depicted in such a close embrace with anybody in the USSR's flagship newspapers. This observation was made by Jeffrey Brooks at the 1994 National Convention of the American Association for the Advancement of Slavic Studies (Philadelphia, PA), in a paper entitled "The Representation of Science and Technology in the Central Soviet Press, 1917–1939."

160. "Nash otets," *Izvestiia*, 18 August 1938.

161. *Pravda* and *Izvestiia*, 17–20 December 1938; *Pokhorony V. P. Chkalova* (RGAKFD 1-6655); RTSKhIDNI, f. 17, op. 3, d. 1004, ll. 119, 174.

162. *Pravda*, 11 April 1934.

163. Brontman, *Top*, 241.

164. Cited in Von Geldern and Stites, eds., *Mass Culture in Russia*, 234–235.

165. *Pravda*, 23 July 1936.

166. I. V. Stalin, "Speech to the First All-Union Conference of Stakhanovite Workers," 17 November 1935. Cited in Fitzpatrick, *Cultural Front*, 183.

167. Clark, *Soviet Novel*, 36–41; Robin, *Socialist Realism*, passim.

168. Liapidevskii, *Geroi Arktiki*, 1.

169. Vodop'ianov, *Mechta*, 15–16.

170. *Pravda*, 24 June 1937.

Notes to Chapter 5

1. *Podvig vo l'dakh*.

2. Kenez, *Cinema*, 145, notes that Stalin "personally saw and approved every single film exhibited in the Soviet Union. . . . He suggested changes, altered titles, and recommended topics."

3. Aleksandr I. Solzhenitsyn, *The First Circle* (New York: Bantam, 1969), 98–99.

4. *Pravda*, 11 August 1936; *Pravda*, 26 June 1937.

5. Dmitri Volkogonov, *Stalin: Triumph and Tragedy* (Rocklin, Calif.: Prima, 1992), 260–261.

6. RTSKhIDNI, f. 17, op. 3, d. 972, l. 55; d. 970, l. 7; literally hundreds of Politburo agenda slots were reserved for similar issues.

7. RTSKhIDNI, f. 17, op. 3, d. 907, l. 29/5; d. 910, l. 1; d. 947, ll. 9/18, 51/41; d. 948, ll. 50/32,

80/63; d. 949, ll. 119/100, 194/177; d. 950, l. 26; d. 962, l. 16; d. 982, l. 48; d. 983, l. 349; d. 987, l. 27; d. 989, l. 8; d. 990, ll. 565, 715, 861, 927; d. 997, l. 244; d. 1019, l. 104.

8. Wolfe, *Right Stuff*, 98.

9. *Pravda*, 26 June 1937.

10. *My iz Igarki*, 11.

11. Originally, Igarka's kulaks were sentenced only to five years' exile. But without internal passports, they had no right to travel and were, in effect, banished to the Arctic permanently (Gruber, *I Went to the Arctic*, 183–192).

12. *I proshloe vygliadit snom* (Sergei Miroshnichenko, 1987).

13. Smolka, *Forty Thousand against the Arctic*, 186–189.

14. *My iz Igarki*, 13.

15. Smolka, *Forty Thousand against the Arctic*, 206.

16. Gruber, *I Went to the Arctic*, 183–192.

17. Dallin and Nicolaevsky, *Forced Labor in Soviet Russia*, 223.

18. Gor'kii, et al., *Belomorsko-Baltiiskii kanal imeni Stalina*; the Politburo met in October 1933 to discuss the book's sale and distribution (RTSKhIDNI, f. 17, op. 3, d. 931, l. 78/42).

19. Jakobson, *Origins of the GULAG*, 128–131.

20. Solzhenitsyn, *GULAG Archipelago*, 241; Dallin and Nicolaevsky, *Forced Labor in Soviet Russia*, 189; Ronald Hingley, *Russian Writers and Soviet Society, 1917–1978* (New York: Random House, 1979), 140.

21. Volkogonov, *Stalin*, 182–183, 196; Vaksberg, *Stalin's Prosecutor*, 77; Robert Conquest, *The Great Terror: A Reassessment* (New York: Oxford University Press, 1990), 236, 396; Robert McNeal, *Stalin: Man and Ruler* (New York: New York University Press, 1988), 186–187, 205; and Robert Tucker, *Stalin in Power* (New York: Norton, 1990), 285, 321–330, 565.

22. Anton Antonov-Ovseenko, *The Time of Stalin* (New York: Harper and Row, 1983), 219.

23. Bailes, *Technology and Society*, 381, 389–391.

24. RTSKhIDNI, f. 17, op. 3, d. 970, l. 7; d. 990, ll. 583, 670; d. 1000, l. 195; d. 1011, l. 72; d. 1012, l. 221; f. 643, op. 1, d. 2, ll. 39–40; and f. 475, op.1, d. 28, l. 65.

25. *Po sledam Cheliuskinskoi epopei*, 224; Kasinec, "Schmidt and the American Press"; S. O. Shmidt, interviewed by the author, 7 April 1992.

26. RTSKhIDNI, f. 475, op. 2, dd. 438, 446. The VSKhV's official opening was delayed until August 1939, although parts of the exhibition went into operation earlier.

27. RTSKhIDNI, f. 475, op. 2, dd. 89, 164, 764, 790.

28. David Gelernter, *1939: The Lost World of the Fair* (New York: Free Press, 1995), 342, 352–353; and H. Bruce Franklin, "America as Science Fiction: 1939," in George Slusser et al., eds., *Coordinates: Placing Science Fiction and Fantasy* (Carbondale and Edwardsville: Southern Illinois University Press, 1983).

29. I am grateful to Lynne Viola for bringing to my attention one of the Soviet pavilion's English-language pamphlets (*USSR: New York World's Fair, 1939*).

30. Rosalinde Sartorti, "Stalinism and Carnival," in Günther, ed., *Culture of the Stalin Period*, 44–65; D. J. K. Peukert, *Inside Nazi Germany* (New Haven: Yale University Press, 1987), 188–189; Lane, *Rites of Rulers*, 23, 239; Golsan, ed., *Fascism, Aesthetics, and Culture*, 1–37; MacAloon, ed., *Rite, Drama, Festival, Spectacle*; James Mayo, *War Memorials as Political Landscape* (New York: Praeger, 1988); and Peter Cohen's 1995 documentary, *The Architecture of Doom*.

31. Littlepage and Bess, *In Search of Soviet Gold*, 239.

32. Juri Jelagin, *Taming of the Arts* (New York: Dutton, 1951), 74.

33. I. Gronskii, *Iz proshlego: Vospominaniia* (Moscow: Izvestiia, 1991), 127–129. I am indebted to Matthew Lenoe for bringing this episode to my attention.

34. *Pechat' SSSR za sorok let, 1917–1957* (Moscow, 1957), 107–108, 123.

35. *Pokhod "Cheliuskina"; Dnevniki Cheliuskintsev; Kak my spasali Cheliuskintsev.* On the origins of the *Trekhtomnik*, see Krenkel', RAEM *Is My Call-Sign*, 253; and *SA* 1, no. 1 (August 1935), 39–42.

36. RTSkHIDNI, f. 17, op. 3, d. 949, l. 119/100; d. 950, l. 26.

37. "Cheliuskintsy v Leningrade," *Literaturnaia gazeta*, 26 June 1934.

38. S. T. Morozov, *L'dy i liudi* (Moscow: Molodaia gvardiia, 1979); I. Sokolov-Mikitov, *Severnye rasskazy* (Moscow, 1939).

39. K. S. Badigin, *Skvoz' veter. Morskie rasskazy* (Moscow: Znanie, 1965); and idem, *Povesti* (Moscow: Detizdat, 1970).

40. V. A. Obruchev, *Plutoniia* (Moscow: Nauka, 1990); and idem, *Zemlia Sannikova*.

41. V. A. Obruchev, "Zavoevanie tundry" and "Solntse gasnet," in *Puteshestviia v proshloe i budushchee: Nauchno-fantasticheskie proizvedeniia* (Moscow: Nauka, 1961).

42. V. A. Obruchev, "Proisshestvie v Neskuchnom sadu," in *Puteshestviia*, 33–41. The story first appeared in the journal *Koster* (November 1940); on its real-life inspiration, see chapter 6.

43. Zinger, *Pobezhdennoe more*, 5–6.

44. M. E. Zinger, *Severnye rasskazy* (Moscow: Sovetskii pisatel', 1938), 96–108, and idem, *Rasskazy starogo poliarnika* (Moscow: Detgiz, 1959), 20–29.

45. Kaverin, *The Two Captains*; and idem, *Dva kapitana* (Moscow: Molodaia gvardiia, 1951). The idea for the novel, inspired by Kaverin's interviews of a real Arctic pilot, originated in 1936. The first version was completed in 1937; the second was published in *Koster* from 1938 to 1940. Kaverin added a second volume to cover his hero's wartime adventures; the final version was published in 1946 (RGALI, f. 1501, introductory notes).

46. Edward Brown, *Russian Literature since the Revolution* (Cambridge: Harvard University Press, 1982), 75–76; Hingley, *Russian Writers and Soviet Society*, 193–194.

47. RGALI, f. 1501, op. 1, d. 151, ll. 16, 18.

48. *Soviet Photography: An Age of Realism* (New York: Greenwich House, 1984), 96, 202, 211–220, 238–239, 253–262.

49. Richard Taylor and Derek Spring, "Introduction," and Peter Kenez, "Soviet Cinema in the Age of Stalin," both in Taylor and Spring, eds., *Stalinism and Soviet Cinema*, ix, 70.

50. Kenez, *Cinema*, 132; Maya Turovskaya, "The 1930s and 1940s: Cinema in Context," in Taylor and Spring, eds., *Stalinism and Soviet Cinema*, 42.

51. Turovskaya, "The 1930s and 1940s," 42.

52. *Podvig vo l'dakh.*

53. Kenez, *Cinema*, 160–166; and *Sovetskie khudozhestvennye fil'my*, vol. 2 (Moscow: Iskusstvo, 1961).

54. Kanevskii, *Vsia zhizn'—ekspeditsiia*, 44, and idem, *Borot'sia i iskat'!*, 101.

55. For information about Arctic porcelains, my thanks to Karen Kettering.

56. Stephen White, *The Bolshevik Poster* (New Haven: Yale University Press, 1988); *Istoriia strany v plakate* (Moscow: Panorama, 1993).

57. Reshetnikov's cartoons are most easily viewed in *Otto Iul'evich Shmidt*.

58. Mark Hopkins, *Mass Media in the Soviet Union* (New York: Pegasus, 1970), 94.

59. *Chelovek, spasshii 39 zhiznei; Geroi Sovetskogo Soiuza Otto Iul'evich Shmidt*; A. V. Liapidevskii, *Geroi Arktiki* (Moscow: Radiokomitet, 1940).

60. RTSkHIDNI, f. 475, op. 2, d. 764, l. 8.

61. ARAN, f. 496, op. 2, d. 592, ll. 1–4; d. 602, ll. 1–4; d. 603, l. 1; d. 607, l. 1.

62. Miller, *Folklore for Stalin*; Oinas, "Folklore and Politics"; Robin, "Stalinism and Popular Culture"; Vladimir Tolstoy, *Russian Decorative Arts, 1917–1937* (New York: Rizzoli, 1990); and David Elliot, *New Worlds: Russian Art and Society, 1917–1937* (New York: Rizzoli, 1986).

63. Miller, *Folklore for Stalin*, 8.

64. Oinas, "Folklore and Politics," 47.

65. Peukert, *Inside Nazi Germany*, 175. On the political uses of folklore, see Jack Zipes, *Breaking the Magic Spell: Radical Theories of Folk and Fairy Tales* (Austin: University of Texas Press, 1979); Baird, *Nazi War Propaganda*, and idem, *To Die for Germany*; Christa Kamenetsky, "Folklore and Ideology in the Third Reich," *Journal of American Folklore* 90 (1977): 168–178, and idem, "Folklore as a Political Tool in Nazi Germany," *Journal of American Folklore* 85 (1972): 221–235; and Richard Dorson, *Folklore and Fakelore* (Cambridge: Harvard University Press, 1976).

66. Tumarkin, *Lenin Lives!* 92.

67. Miller, *Folklore for Stalin*, 57–58.

68. Ibid., 64–65.

69. Ibid., 78–79, 145–146; *Velikii letchik*, 278–280.

70. Miller, *Folklore for Stalin*, 68–69, 129.

71. Ibid., 70.

72. Ibid., 78, 144–145.

73. Ibid., 123.

74. Ibid., 37, 121.

75. *Komsomol'skaia pravda*, 24 June 1937; Miller, *Folklore for Stalin*, 37, 125; Von Geldern and Stites, eds., *Mass Culture in Soviet Russia*, 287–291 (direct quotations come from this translation).

76. Tolstoy, *Russian Decorative Arts*, 378–379, 400–403; Smolka, *Forty Thousand against the Arctic*, 282; V. V. Senkevich, "Sovremennost' v fol'klore narodov Severa," *SA* 3, no. 11 (November 1937): 105.

77. In order, the verses are from Leites, ed., *Stalinskie sokoly*, 199 (allegedly from a collective farm in the Ves'egonskii region); *SA* 3, no. 11 (November 1937): 101–102 (said to be from the Balashorskii region); *SA* 2, no. 4 (April 1936): 54 (reportedly by Elena Ryvina, a peasant woman from the Leningrad region); *SA* 2, no. 4 (April 1936): 54 (reputedly from a machine-tractor station in the Lower Volga region).

78. Robin, "Stalinism and Popular Culture," 28–31; Oinas, "Folklore and Politics," 52.

79. Baidukov, *Russian Lindbergh*, 271.

80. Brontman, *Top*, 235.

81. Smolka, *Forty Thousand against the Arctic*, 67–72; Jelagin, *Taming of the Arts*, 213–217.

82. GARF, f. 5446, op. 82, d. 51, l. 52; RTSKhIDNI, f. 475, op. 2, d. 289, ll. 1–3. My thanks to Sheila Fitzpatrick for making me aware of the first item.

83. *Komsomol'skaia pravda*, 31 December 1935; *Newsweek*, 11, no. 15 (11 April 1938): 17; ARAN, f. 496, op. 2, d. 311, l. 1.

84. Krenkel', *RAEM Is My Call-Sign*, 147.

85. *Literaturnaia gazeta*, 6 November 1934.

86. *Kul'turnaia zhizn' v SSSR, 1928–1941: Khronika* (Moscow: Nauka, 1976); Etkind, *Eros nevozmozhnogo*; and Iakusheva, *Otto Iul'evich Shmidt*, 21–27.

87. Vaksberg, *Stalin's Prosecutor*, 200–201.

88. ARAN, f. 496, op. 2, dd. 590, 599; op. 3, d. 294.

89. ARAN, f. 496, op. 3, d. 293, l. 2.

90. ARAN, f. 496, op. 2, d. 595; op. 3, dd. 293, 325.

91. ARAN, f. 496, op. 2, d. 600.

92. M. V. Vodop'ianov, *Mechta pilota* (Moscow: Molodaia gvardiia, 1937) 1–6; *Mechta* (Moscow: Iskusstvo, 1937) is the prose version.

93. RTSKhIDNI, f. 475, op. 1, d. 16, ll. 38–39.

94. ARAN, f. 496, op. 2, d. 311, ll. 1–5.

95. RTSKhIDNI, f. 475, op. 1, d. 6, ll. 73–74; d. 28, ll. 55–58; ARAN, f. 496, op. 2, d. 311, ll. 1–5.

96. RTSKhIDNI, f. 475, op. 1, d. 16, ll. 38–39; d. 28, ll. 55–58.

97. Papanin, *Na poliuse*, 32–33.

98. Fedorov, *Polar Diaries*, 205.

99. RTSKhIDNI, f. 475, op. 1, d. 28, ll. 55–58.

100. RTSKhIDNI, f. 475, op. 1, d. 21, ll. 22–23.

101. James Thurber, "The Greatest Man in the World," in *The Thurber Carnival* (New York: Harper and Row, 1945), 154–160.

102. Kudrevatykh, *Valeriem Chkalovym*, 3.

103. For some thought on this matter, see the introduction to Kenez, *Birth of the Propaganda State*.

104. ARAN, f. 496, op. 1, d. 187.

105. Rakhillo, *Rasskazy o Chkalove*, 62–63.

106. *Soviet Aviation*, no page numbers given.

107. Smolka, *Forty Thousand against the Arctic*, 95.

108. Ibid.

109. RGAKFD 1–2526; *Izvestiia*, 8 December 1937; *I. D. Papanin*, 198; V. P. Kataev, "Rainbow Flower," in Miriam Morton, ed., *A Harvest of Russian Children's Literature* (Berkeley: University of California Press, 1968), 92–99.

110. Felicity Ann O'Dell, *Socialization through Children's Literature: The Soviet Example* (Cambridge: Cambridge University Press, 1978), 161–162.

111. *Izvestiia*, 5 December 1937.

112. M. Alekseev's *Drachuny*, in Sheila Fitzpatrick, *Stalin's Peasants: Resistance and Survival in the Russian Village after Collectivization* (New York: Oxford University Press, 1994), 272.

113. Kenez, *Cinema*, 133; Turovskaya; "The 1930s and 1940s," in Taylor and Spring, eds., *Stalinism and Soviet Cinema*, 42.

114. Edmund Wilson, *The Thirties* (New York: Farrar, Straus, Giroux, 1980), 559–561.

115. All three quotations from Jelagin, *Taming of the Arts*, 225–226. Speaking of young people, O'Dell, *Socialisation*, 161–162, makes the similar point that, "in many ways, Papanin is a counter-balance to the less attractive heroes with whom children were presented [in 1938]."

116. Mikhail Bakhtin, *Rabelais and His World* (Bloomington: Indiana University Press, 1984), passim.

117. *Pravda*, 18 June 1934.

118. Ibid.

119. *Pravda*, 24 May 1937; *Pravda*, 22 June 1937.

120. *Stalinets*, 22 July 1934; RGAE, f. 9570, op. 2, d. 39, ll. 120–124.

121. RTSKhIDNI, f. 475, op. 2, d. 764, l. 7.

122. Krenkel', *Chetyre tovarishcha*, 116.

123. L. V. Uspenskii, *Ty i tvoe imia* (Leningrad: Lenizdat, 1962), 456–457.

124. G. Titov, "Rasskazyvaet German Titov," in *Russian: Reading for Meaning* (New York: Harcourt, Brace, and World, 1967), 48–49.

125. M. I. Tsvetaeva, *Stikhotvoreniia i poemy* (New York: Russica, 1986), 3:179, 486.

126. L. K. Chukovskaia, *Sofiia Petrovna* (Moscow: Moskovskii rabochii, 1988), 24–28.

127. RGAE, f. 9570, op. 2, dd. 37, 39, 46. Also see the journal of Arctic worker Fedor Shirnov, who describes his reaction to the news of the *Cheliuskin's* sinking as follows: "We all felt our legs buckle under us, we just sat there in shock. . . . With all this calamity, all of us forgot about our own predicament, and all we could think of was them

[sic] people out on the ice and was [sic] they going to get rescued." Shirnov's enthusiasm for the Soviet regime is evident throughout his diary. Moreover, he actually sent his journal to Stalin himself, with the following dedication written on the last page: "I hope this work I've done/Will be of use to everyone./Barely literate I may be/But I've composed this diary,/Fifty years of notes herein/I send on to the Kremlin/to the Great Stalin. Comrade Stalin, You is [sic] dear to us all. THE END." See Garros, et al., eds., *Intimacy and Terror*, 84–85, 95–97.

128. RGAE, f. 9570, op. 2, d. 37, ll. 194–195; ll. 176–178, 227; ll. 174–175.

129. Gruber, *I Went to the Arctic*, 27.

130. Most of these letters are in ARAN, f. 496, op. 3, d. 364.

131. ARAN, f. 496, op. 3, d. 394, ll. 8–9.

132. *Komsomol'skaia pravda*, 27 April 1936.

133. Both citations come from "Andrei Stepanovich Arzhilovsky," in Garros et al., eds., *Intimacy and Terror*, 161–162.

134. A. A. Akhmatova, *V to vremia ia gostila na zemle* (Moscow: Cosmopolis, 1991), 196.

135. Nadezhda Mandelstam, *Hope against Hope: A Memoir* (New York: Atheneum, 1976), 289.

136. Vladimir Voinovich, *Pretender to the Throne* (New York: Farrar, Straus, Giroux, 1981), 308.

137. Fazil Iskander, *Sandro of Chegem* (New York: Vintage, 1983), 332.

138. Vassily Aksyonov, *The Burn* (New York: Vintage, 1985), 202–203. Also note Iu. M. Pezhemskii's 1991 television spoof *Pokhod tovarishcha Chkalova*, in which Soviet pilots land at the pole and make the earth spin backward. My thanks to Karen Petrone for bringing this item to my attention.

139. Central State Archive of Historical-Political Documents (TSGAIPD, formerly the Leningrad Party Archive), f. 25, op. 5, d. 47, l. 18. Thanks to Lesley Rimmel for bringing this story to light.

140. RTSKhIDNI, f. 475, op. 1, d. 1, ll. 104–105. According to Lesley Rimmel and Sarah Davies, similar versions appeared in other areas, such as the Kronstadt region (TSGAIPD, f. 25, op. 5, d. 2291, l. 21), Moscow, and Novosibirsk.

141. TSGAIPD, f. 24, op. 2g, d. 149, ll. 66–66ob. Cited in Sarah Davies, "Propaganda and Popular Opinion in Soviet Russia, 1934–1941" (Ph.D. diss., Oxford University, 1994).

142. Jacques Ellul, *Propaganda: The Formation of Men's Attitudes* (New York: Knopf, 1972), v, xiii, xvii, 11.

143. Cited in the introduction to Mukerji and Schudson, eds., *Rethinking Popular Culture*, 15.

144. Shearon Lowery and Melvin L. DeFleur, *Milestones in Mass Communications Research* (New York: Longman, 1983), 233–266, 296–357.

145. Alex Inkeles and Raymond Bauer, *The Soviet Citizen* (Cambridge: Harvard University Press, 1959), 183.

146. Ellul, *Propaganda*, 14.

147. Kenez, *Birth of the Propaganda State*, 253.

Notes to Chapter 6

1. ARAN, f. 496, op. 1, d. 191, l. 30.

2. Roberta Manning, "The Soviet Economic Crisis of 1936–1940 and the Great Purges," in J. Arch Getty and Roberta Manning, eds., *Stalinist Terror: New Perspectives* (New York: Cambridge University Press, 1993), 116–141.

3. RGAE, f. 9570, op. 2, d. 89, ll. 126–127.

4. A. I. Arikainen, *Skvoz' l'dy Arktiki* (Moscow: Znanie, 1982), 9; L. K. Davydov, "Vskrytie rek arkticheskoi i subarkticheskoi zony SSSR," *Problemy Arktiki* 2, no. 3 (January 1939): 24–31.

5. RGAE, f. 9570, op. 2, d. 189, ll. 126–127.

6. Ianson, "Plan raboty," 14–23.

7. S. A. Bergavinov, "Razvernem Stakhanovskoe dvizhenie v Arktike," *SA* 2, no. 3 (March 1936): 44.

8. Ianson, "Plan raboty," 14–23.

9. N. M. Ianson, "Tret'ia piatiletka Glavsevmorputi," *SA* 3, no. 9 (September 1937): 10–20.

10. A. Chikovani, "Vyzvat' bogatstva Severa k zhizni," *SA* 3, no. 12 (December 1937): 102.

11. Stephan, *Russian Far East*, 200–208; Robert Weinberg, "Purge and Politics in the Periphery: Birobidzhan in 1937," *Slavic Review* 52 (1993): 13–27.

12. On the purges, begin with Conquest, *Great Terror*; Merle Fainsod, *Smolensk under Soviet Rule* (New York: Vintage, 1958); J. Arch Getty, *Origins of the Great Purges: The Soviet Communist Party Reconsidered, 1933–1938* (Cambridge: Cambridge University Press, 1985); Getty and Manning, eds., *Stalinist Terror*; Amy Knight, *Beria: Stalin's First Lieutenant* (Princeton: Princeton University Press, 1993); Roy Medvedev, *Let History Judge* (New York: Vintage, 1971); Solzhenitsyn, GULAG *Archipelago*; Thurston, *Life and Terror in Stalin's Russia*; and Vaksberg, *Stalin's Prosecutor*.

13. Many of these younger cadres were members of the *vydvizhentsy*, the generation of technocrats educated during the Cultural Revolution of 1928–1931, then promoted extremely rapidly (for obvious reasons) during the purge years.

14. Solzhenitsyn, GULAG *Archipelago*, 1:60–66.

15. RTsKhIDNI, f. 475, op. 1, d. 5, ll. 29–31.

16. RTsKhIDNI, f. 643, op. 2, d. 1, l. 41.

17. RTsKhIDNI, f. 475, op. 1, d. 11, ll. 14, 33–34, 52–54; d. 1, ll. 104–110.

18. RTsKhIDNI, f. 475, op. 1, d. 9, ll. 218–219.

19. RTsKhIDNI, f. 643, op. 2, d. 6, ll. 30–34.

20. "Po-bol'shevistski provesti navigatsiiu," *SA* 4, no. 6 (June 1938): 17–22.

21. RTsKhIDNI, f. 475, op. 1, d. 5, ll. 221–223.

22. RTsKhIDNI, f. 475, op. 1, d. 10, l. 166.

23. RTsKhIDNI, f. 475, op. 1, d. 16, ll. 88–89.

24. Solzhenitsyn, GULAG *Archipelago*, 2:644–645.

25. Fedorov, *Polar Diaries*, 53; Mineev, *Ostrov Vrangelia*, passim.

26. RTsKhIDNI, f. 475, op. 1, d. 8, ll. 244–248.

27. RTsKhIDNI, f. 475, op. 1, d. 9, ll. 199, 201–206.

28. Krenkel', RAEM *Is My Call-Sign*, 58–70.

29. All citations from RTsKhIDNI, f. 475, op. 1, d. 9, ll. 188–206; d. 10, ll. 2–3.

30. Serkin, "Ob oshibkakh," 9–15.

31. RTsKhIDNI, f. 475, op. 1, d. 5, ll. 176–178.

32. RTsKhIDNI, f. 475, op. 1, d. 6, ll. 50–55; d. 10, ll. 9–12; regarding a similar outbreak on the Taimyr, see d. 10, ll. 15–19.

33. "Uroki Semenchukovshchiny," *SA* 2, no. 7 (July 1936): 3–7; "S protsessa nad Semenchukom," *SA* 2, no. 8 (August 1936): 63–83; Mineev, *Ostrov Vrangelia*, 172–181; A. Ia. Vyshinskii, *Protiv Semenchukovshchiny* (Moscow: OGIZ, 1936), and idem, *Sudebnye rechi* (Moscow: Iuridicheskaia literatura, 1948), 250–255.

34. Gruber, *I Went to the Arctic*, 149–150.

35. Vaksberg, *Stalin's Prosecutor*, 74–76, argues that the Semenchuk case was also a dress rehearsal for the Moscow show trials, a way of grooming Vyshinskii for the limelight: "had such a case not actually occurred, it would have been concocted." Otherwise, Vyshinskii was not the logical choice to prosecute Semenchuk. First, he had little experience with murder cases. Second, since the Semenchukovshchina was tried by the RSFSR Supreme Court, normal procedure would have called for the Procurator of the RSFSR, not the USSR, to act on behalf of the state.

36. Obruchev, "Proisshestvie"; in an afterword, Obruchev describes the actual events of 1937–1938 but in a light-hearted manner, omitting the details of the punishments that followed (whether he was aware of those details is unclear).

37. RTSkhIDNI, f. 475, op. 1, d. 16, ll. 378–404.

38. Kanevskii, *Zagadki*, 5.

39. RTSkhIDNI, f. 475, op. 1, d. 1, ll. 15–18; Kanevskii, *Zagadki*, 5.

40. RTSkhIDNI, f. 475, op. 1, d. 10, ll. 226–234; and the March 1937 issues of *Sovetskaia Arktika* and *Vodnyi transport*.

41. RTSkhIDNI, f. 475, op. 1, d. 10, ll. 43, 56–57; RGAE, f. 237 (Krasinskii's personal fond).

42. RTSkhIDNI, f. 475, op. 1, d. 1, ll. 11, 19–20.

43. RTSkhIDNI, f. 475, op. 1, d. 2, ll. 273–76.

44. RTSkhIDNI, f. 475, op. 1, d. 25, ll. 231–242. How many of the seven deaths were due to natural causes is unclear.

45. RTSkhIDNI, f. 475, op. 1, d. 11, ll. 247–255; d. 14, ll. 101–102.

46. RTSkhIDNI, f. 475, op. 1, d. 2, ll. 365–367; d. 4, ll. 79, 169–170; d. 7, ll. 32–33, 74, 354–355; d. 8, ll. 138–146.

47. Vyshinskii, *Protiv Semenchukovshchiny*, 5; Solzhenitsyn, GULAG *Archipelago*, 1:596–597, and *First Circle*, 71.

48. RTSkhIDNI, f. 475, op. 1, d. 27, ll. 80–85.

49. RTSkhIDNI, f. 475, op. 1, d. 16, ll. 106–108; and Kanevskii, *Zagadki*, 5.

50. Vaksberg, *Stalin's Prosecutor*, 262.

51. RTSkhIDNI, f. 643, op. 2, d. 6, ll. 169–170.

52. RTSkhIDNI, f. 475, op. 1, d. 16, ll. 174–175.

53. RTSkhIDNI, f. 475, op. 1, d. 6, l. 71.

54. *Polar Times* 8 (March 1939): 13.

55. RGAE, f. 9570, op. 2, dd. 104, 105; RTSkhIDNI, f. 475, op. 1, dd, 15, 16, 19, 21; f. 17, op. 3, dd. 990/661, 990/668, 990/804, 990/846, 992/35, 997/165, 1004/100.

56. RGAE, f. 262 (Babushkin's personal fond); RTSkhIDNI, f. 17, op. 3, d. 999.

57. RTSkhIDNI, f. 475, op. 1, d. 19, ll. 222–239.

58. RTSkhIDNI, f. 475, op. 1, d, 15, ll. 13–17; d. 16, l. 140; d. 19, ll. 222–239; d. 21, ll. 44–181.

59. RTSkhIDNI, f. 475, op. 1, d. 15, ll. 13–17.

60. RTSkhIDNI, f. 475, op. 1, d. 21, ll. 64–181.

61. RTSkhIDNI, f. 475, op. 1, d. 16, ll. 366–377.

62. In "Esli govorit' vsiu pravdu," *Vozdushnyi transport*, 10–17 December 1988, Baidukov argues that, because Polikarpov was rushing to produce the I-180 before Stalin's birthday, there were several design defects in the airplane Chkalov took up on 15 December. This theory is borne out by the fact that the next prototype killed a second pilot in February 1939. Sergei Taranov, in "Valery Chkalov: Did He Have to Die?" *Moscow News*, 18 March 1989, advances the theory that Chkalov was murdered by Stalin because of his political opinions. Igor Chkalov, the pilot's son, concurs with Taranov, noting that, during the third show trial, Chkalov told Vyshinskii himself that he believed the accused to be innocent. According to the younger Chkalov, Vyshinskii laughed at the pilot, saying, "Naive, that's what you are, Valerii Pavlovich!" (Vaksberg, *Stalin's Prosecutor*, 342 n 21).

63. Bialer, *Stalin and His Generals*, 168–169; Medvedev, *Let History Judge*, 228; Conquest, *Great Terror*, 93, 231, 238; RTSkhIDNI, f. 17, op. 3, dd. 1004/119, 1004/174, 1008/70.

64. On Samoilovich and the VAI, see RTSkhIDNI, f. 475, op. 1, d. 15, l. 229; d. 25, ll. 111–118; and Kanevskii, *Direktor Arktiki*, and idem, *Vsia zhizn'—ekspeditsiia*. Shirshov's career flourished; the Central Oceanographic Institute still bears his name today. All the same, he came to a sad end. According to Vadim Mokievskii and Valentina Mokievskaia (interviewed by the author, 9 March 1992), Shirshov's wife, an actress, was arrested in 1949 and died shortly after. Shirshov himself died in 1953, allegedly of grief.

65. RTSkhIDNI, f. 475, op.1, d. 6, l. 12.

66. RGAE, f. 424, op. 1, d. 73.

67. RTSkhIDNI, f. 475, op. 1, d. 15, ll. 13–17; d. 21, ll. 150–156.

68. RTSkhIDNI, f. 475, op. 1, d. 15, ll. 246–251.

69. RTSkhIDNI, f. 475, op. 1, d. 15, ll. 203–206; for further criticism, see d. 23, ll. 373–384.

70. This became a typical complaint; see, for example, RTSkhIDNI, f. 475, op. 1, d. 16, l. 36.

71. *Newsweek* 11, no. 15 (11 April 1938).

72. ARAN, f. 496, op. 2, d. 311, l. 1.

73. Iakusheva, *Otto Iul'evich Shmidt*, 39–44.

74. RTSkhIDNI, f. 475, op. 1, d. 15, ll. 22–30.

75. Despite this, the three men—especially Krenkel'—remained personally friendly to Shmidt.

76. RTSkhIDNI, f. 475, op. 1, d. 24, ll. 129–130.

77. RTSkhIDNI, f. 17, op. 3, d. 1007, l. 17.

78. This possibility is put forward by S. O. Shmidt (interviewed by the author, 7 April 1992).

79. Tucker, *Stalin in Power*, 575; Vaksberg, *Stalin's Prosecutor*, 199–200. Others supposedly named in this transparently bogus charge include authors Valentin Kataev, Leonid Leonov, Vsevolod Ivanov, Lidiia Seifullina; actor and stage producer Solomon Mikhoels; and legendary filmmaker Sergei Eisenshtein. Along with Nikolai Ezhov's wife, Evgeniia Solomonovna, Shmidt and these others were alleged to have smuggled secrets regarding military aircraft to the West via French author and aviator André Malraux.

80. Even the builders of the ship started a campaign to keep the icebreaker from being named after Shmidt; the workers of the André Marty ship-building factory petitioned the Politupravlenie to name the icebreaker the *Voroshilov* (RTSkhIDNI, f. 475, op. 1, d. 29, ll. 81–82).

81. Iakusheva, *Otto Iul'evich Shmidt*, 25.

82. "Piercing the Arctic," *Literary Digest* 121, no. 18 (2 May 1936): 15.

83. Littlepage and Bess, *In Search of Soviet Gold*, 68–82, 125–127; Mowat, *Siberians*, 264–266; M. M. Khatylaev, *Zolotopromyshlennost' Iakutii, 1923–1937* (Iakutsk, 1972), and idem, *Zolotodobyvaiushchaia promyshlennost' Vostochnoi Sibiri, 1917–1925* (Iakutsk, 1983).

84. On Glavzoloto, see its professional journal, *Sovetskaia zolotopromyshlennost'*; and GARF, f. 7679, op. 1. Serebrovskii was arrested in 1937 and executed in 1943.

85. The fact that several Latvians named Berzin worked for the Soviet regime has prompted some cases of mistaken identity. Dal'stroi's Berzin is not Reingold Berzin, as in Conquest's *Kolyma* (an error that has been repeated widely). Neither is he Ian Karlovich Berzin, as several biographical dictionaries claim. During this period, Ian Berzin headed the GRU (Soviet military intelligence), recruited the spy Richard Sorge, and led the Soviet military presence in Madrid during the Spanish Civil War. For him to have run Dal'stroi as well would have made him quite busy indeed.

86. Petrov, *Soviet Gold*, 179–185; Conquest, *Kolyma*, 43–45.

87. Petrov, *Soviet Gold*, 185, 230.

88. *Resistance in the GULAG*, 69–70.

89. RTSKhIDNI, f. 17, op. 3, d. 954, l. 1.

90. Conquest, *Kolyma*, 45–46.

91. Jakobson, *Origins of the GULAG*, 128–131; Conquest, *Kolyma*, 234–239; Erich Thiel, *The Soviet Far East: A Survey of Its Physical and Economic Geography* (London: Methuen, 1957), 199.

92. Conquest, *Kolyma*, 108.

93. Owen Lattimore, "New Road to Asia," *National Geographic* 86 (1944): 657. Incidentally, Lattimore's description of Magadan bears a striking resemblance to that in Aksyonov's *The Burn*, 222–223.

94. The most widely quoted figure regarding Dal'stroi's death toll is Conquest's estimate of three million, or "one thousand people for every ton of gold" (*Kolyma*, 14–16, 110, 214–230). However, this calculation is based largely on guesswork; a more reliable number will have to wait until concrete, archive-based research is possible.

95. Krypton, *Northern Sea Route*, 107.

96. Ibid., 55.

97. M. E. Zinger, "Kolyma segodnia," *SA* 2, no. 10 (October 1936): 50–62.

98. RGAE, f. 9570, op. 2, dd. 709, 2900.

99. S. A. Bergavinov, "Svet i teni v rabote Glavsevmorputi," *SA* 3, no. 1 (January 1937): 1–16.

100. "O rabote Glavsevmorputi za 1937 god (V Sovete Narodnykh Komissarov Soiuza SSR)," *SA* 4, no. 5 (May 1938), 21–24; RTSKhIDNI, f. 17, op. 3, d. 997, l. 1.

101. "Postanovlenie Sovnarkoma SSSR ob uluchshenii raboty Glavnogo upravleniia Severnogo morskogo puti ot 29 avgusta 1938 goda," *Pravda*, 10 August 1938.

102. Belov, *Istoriia*, 4:545.

103. RGAE, f. 9570, op. 2, d. 709; Belov, *Istoriia*, 4:546.

104. On GUSMP's dissolution, see RGAE, f. 9570, op. 2, dd. 709, 2200; RTSKhIDNI, f. 17, op. 3, d. 997, l. 1; d. 1002, l. 33; d. 1003, l. 152; d. 1009, l. 101.

105. Dallin and Nicolaevsky, *Forced Labor in Soviet Russia*, 59–61, 115–119; Conquest, *Kolyma*, 40.

106. *SA* 5, no. 4 (April 1939): 38–60.

107. Armstrong, *Northern Sea Route*, 57–64.

Notes to Conclusion

1. I. D. Papanin, "Partiino-khoziaistvennyi aktiv Glavsevmorputi," *SA* 6, no. 1 (January 1940): 18–29.

2. Badigin, *Tri zimovki*; V. Kh. Buinitskii, *812 dnei v dreifuiushchikh l'dakh* (Moscow and Leningrad: GUSMP, 1940); L. Khvat and M. Chernenko, *Geroicheskii dreif "Sedova"* (Moscow: OGIZ, 1939); and *Sedovtsy* (RGAKFD 1–4218).

3. I. D. Papanin, "Itogi 1940 goda i zadachi navigatsii 1941 goda," *SA* 7, no. 4 (April 1941): 1–24.

4. Armstrong, *Russians*, 80–89.

5. Akkuratov, *Led i pepel*, and idem, *Na novykh trassakh*; also Armstrong, *Russians*, 51–52.

6. Unsurprisingly, information on GUSMP's military preparations is scanty. Glavsevmorput' trained army and navy personnel in Arctic flying and navigation; in addition, GUSMP pilots assisted in organizing supply and transport during the 1939–1940 Winter War against Finland, as well as in evaluating the performance of aircraft and pilots in cold-

weather conditions during the USSR's last major military exercise in December 1940 and January 1941. Bialer, *Stalin and His Generals*, 143; RTsKhIDNI, f. 643, op. 2, d. 43, ll. 1–43.

7. Along with Belov, *Istoriia*, vol. 4, the best work on the wartime Arctic is Iu. P. Pribyl'skii, *Sovetskii Sever v gody Velikoi Otechestvennoi Voiny* (Tomsk, 1986). In addition, the memoirs of most polar heroes include coverage of their wartime actions. Also see V. S. Boiko, *Kryl'ia Severnogo flota* (Murmansk, 1976); Armstrong, *Russians*, 98–101; Bobrick, *East of the Sun*, 445–447; "German Attacks on Shipping along the Northern Sea Route, 1942–1944," *Polar Record* 6 (1956): 822–826; Herbert Ringold, "Lifeline to the USSR," in Glines, ed., *Polar Aviation*, 92–103; the USAF Museum; and the Arctic-Antarctic Museum, which prominently profiles the most dramatic military episode in the Soviet Arctic—the August 1942 attack of the heavy cruiser *Admiral Scheer* on Dikson Island.

8. For postwar work, see V. F. Burkhanov, *New Soviet Discoveries in the Arctic* (Moscow: Foreign Languages Publishing House, 1956); V. L. Kvint and N. M. Singur, *Nad nami poliarnaia zvezda* (Moscow: Sovetskaia Rossiia, 1984); Lebedev and Mazuruk, *Nad Arktikoi*; M. V. Viakhirev, *V kraiu purgi i l'dov* (Leningrad: Gidrometeoizdat, 1985); Strugatskii, *K poliusam Zemli*; Chilingarov, "Soviet Polar Research"; A. F. Treshnikov, "Polar Exploration," in Taylor, ed., *Arctic World*; *Times Atlas of World Exploration*, 228–230; and D. Shparo and A. Shumilov, *K poliusu!* (Moscow: Molodaia gvardiia, 1987).

9. The USSR failed to win the distinction of being first to reach the pole underwater. When the *Leninskii Komsomolets* made its way to the pole in 1962, it trailed the U.S.'s *Nautilus* by four years.

10. T. E. Armstrong et al., *The Circumpolar North: A Political and Economic Geography of the Arctic and Sub-Arctic* (London: Methuen, 1978), 60.

11. Taracouzio, *Soviets in the Arctic*, 246.

12. Joan DeBardeleben and John Hannigan, eds., *Environmental Security and Quality after Communism* (Boulder, Colo.: Westview Press, 1995), 1–6, discusses the detrimental effects of gigantomania in the Soviet productive sphere, particularly with regard to agencies involved with science and the environment. Arguing lightheartedly in favor of funding a trip to Mars privately—rather than placing NASA in charge of it—John Tierney makes the astute point in the *New York Times Magazine* that large state agencies have only rarely presided successfully over the business of exploration.

13. Jon Bowermaster, "The Last Front of the Cold War," *Atlantic Monthly* 273, no. 11 (November 1993): 36–45; and Peter Gizewski, "Military Activity and Environmental Security in the Arctic," in DeBardeleben and Hannigan, eds., *Environmental Security and Quality*, 25–41.

14. *WWF Focus* 17, no. 5 (September–October 1995): 1; Irina Pokrovskaia, "The Arctic: Once a Challenge to Conquer, Now a Challenge to Conserve," *Russian Conservation News*, 2 January 1995.

15. Reported by Russian Television (RTV), 18 October 1995; and the Open Media Research Institute, 19 October 1995.

16. Hedrick Smith, *The Russians* (New York: Ballantine, 1976), 435; and Mowat, *Siberians*, passim.

17. Griffiths, *Arctic and North*, 1, 11.

18. *Moscow Tribune*, 19 June 1997; *Segodnia*, 19 June 1997.

19. Nina Tumarkin's moving essay, "The War of Remembrance," in Richard Stites, ed., *Culture and Entertainment in Wartime Russia* (Bloomington: Indiana University Press, 1995), 194–207, discusses how Russians in the 1990s have coped with this same "war of memory" as they reevaluate their perceptions of the central event of Stalinist history: World War II.

Select Bibliography

Since *Red Arctic* attempts to include a number of different stories within its pages, it necessarily draws upon an extremely broad range of materials. The organization of this bibliography may, therefore, require some explanation. To avoid forcing children's poetry to stand shoulder-to-shoulder with graphite-mining statistics—to take just one example—I have grouped my sources into what are intended to be logical categories. First is a listing of the archives and museums in which I conducted research or from which important materials are taken. Then follow the various periodicals. I consulted in depth (with few exceptions, I have not cited individual articles); films, radio broadcasts, and television programs devoted to the Russian Arctic (most films come from Moscow's Russian State Archive of Film and Photo Documents and are identified by their catalog codes; others, as well as television programs, are cited normally, with director and year of release); reference works and unpublished materials; and works dedicated to the general history of exploration and aviation. The largest section, naturally, includes materials connected directly or indirectly to Siberia or the Russian Arctic. General sources on Russia and the USSR come next. The bibliography ends with a selection of studies related to culture and mass media.

By subdividing the bibliography, I hope to have made it easier to locate a specific work—and to understand what role it played in my research—than it would be if all sources were lumped together indiscriminately. Obviously, some works may not fall neatly into one category or another. Where, for instance, to put Solzhenitsyn's *The GULAG Archipelago*, which is about the USSR as a whole, but also says much about the Soviet North in particular? After some reflection, I have placed it in the section on the Russian Arctic. By contrast, *The First Circle*, also by Solzhenitsyn, is found among general works on Russia. Most of the categorization, however, is more straightforward, and readers should be able to find their way around the bibliography with a minimum of trial and error.

Archives and museums

Archive of the Russian Academy of Sciences (ARAN), Moscow.
Arctic and Antarctic Museum. Arctic-Antarctic Scientific-Research Institute, St. Petersburg.
Central State Archive of Historical-Political Documents (TSGAIPD, formerly the Central Party Archive of Leningrad), St. Petersburg.
Central State Archive of the Russian Federation (TSGA RSFSR), Moscow.
Hoover Institution on War, Revolution, and Peace. Stanford University, Palo Alto, California.
Russian Center for the Preservation and Study of Documents of Recent History (RTSKhIDNI, formerly the Central Party Archive of the USSR), Moscow.
Russian State Archive of the Economy (RGAE, formerly the Central State Archive of the People's Economy, TSGANKh), Moscow.

Russian State Archive of Film and Photo Documents (RGAKFD, formerly the Central State Archive of Film and Photo Documents, TSGAKFD), Krasnogorsk.

Russian State Archive of Literature and Art (RGALI, formerly the Central State Archive of Literature and Art, TSGALI), Moscow.

State Archive of the Russian Federation (GARF, formerly the Central State Archive of the October Revolution, TSGAOR), Moscow.

State Archive of the Sverdlovsk Oblast' (GASO), Ekaterinburg.

State Archive of the Tiumen' Oblast' (GATO), Tiumen'.

United States Air Force Museum. Wright-Patterson AFB, Dayton, Ohio.

Periodicals

Air and Space/Smithsonian

Arktika (VAI)

Biulleten' Arkticheskogo Instituta SSSR (VAI)

Dal'stroi

Izvestiia

Kolyma (Dal'stroi)

Komsomol'skaia pravda

Krasnaia zvezda

Literary Digest

Literaturnaia gazeta

Living Age

Moscow Tribune

Narodnoe khoziaistvo SSSR

National Geographic

Newsweek

New York Times

Ob'-Irtyshskii vodnik (Tobol'sk)

Oceanus

Polar Geography

Polar Record

Polar Times

Popular Science

Pravda

Problemy Arktiki (VAI)

Russian Conservation News

Scientific American

Severnaia Aziia (later *Sovetskaia Aziia*)

Severnyi morskoi put' (GUSMP)

Smithsonian

Sobranie zakonov i rasporiazhenii SSSR

Sovetskaia Arktika (GUSMP)

Sovetskaia Iakutiia (Iakutsk)

Sovetskaia zolotopromyshlennost' (People's Commissariat of Heavy Industry)

Sovetskii Sever (Committee of the North)

Sovetskii Sever (Tiumen')

Sovetskoe stroitel'stvo

Time

Tobol'skii Sever (Tobol'sk)

Trudy Morskogo Nauchnogo Instituta (*Plavmornin*)

Ural'skii rabochii (Sverdlovsk)

Vodnyi transport (People's Commissariat of Water Transport)

Voenno-istoricheskii zhurnal

Vozdushnyi transport

Zolotaia promyshlennost' (People's Commissariat of Non-Ferrous Metallurgy)

Films, television, and radio

The Architecture of Doom. Peter Cohen, 1995.

Axelbank, Herman. Motion Picture Collection. Hoover Institution on War, Revolution, and Peace. Videotape 11.

Chelovek, spasshii 39 zhiznei. Moscow: Radiokomitet, 1938.

Dva kapitana. V. Vengerov, 1955.

Dva okeana. RGAKFD 1-9679.

Ekspeditsiia na Severnyi polius. RGAKFD 1-13526.

Geroi Arktiki. RGAKFD 1-4981.

Geroi Sovetskogo Soiuza Otto Iul'evich Shmidt. Moscow: Radiokomitet, 1938.

I proshloe vygliadit snom. Sergei Miroshnichenko, 1987.

K belomu piatnu Arktiki. RGAKFD 1-6767.
Kryl'ia nad l'dom. RGAKFD 1-25083.
K tsentru Arktiki. RGAKFD 1-16301.
Kurs Nord. Petr Novitskii, 1929.
Liapidevskii, A. V. *Geroi Arktiki.* Moscow: Radiokomitet, 1940.
Moskva-SShA. RGAKFD 1-3840.
Na Severnom poliuse. RGAKFD 1-4111.
Odisseia "Cheliuskina". RGAKFD 1-9650.
Papanintsy. RGAKFD 1-2683.
Podvig vo l'dakh. RGAKFD 1-21054.
Pokhod tovarishcha Chkalova. Iu. M. Pezhemskii, 1991.
Pokhorony V. P. Chkalova. RGAKFD 1-6655.
Po Stalinskoi trasse. RGAKFD 1-4132.
Po Stalinskomu marshrutu. RGAKFD 1-4934.
Po Stalinskomu puti. RGAKFD 1-3811.
Realms of the Russian Bear: The Arctic Frontier. The Nature Conservancy, 1992.
RGAKFD 1-2526. Newsreel of Ufa children playing "Cheliuskinites."
Sedovtsy. RGAKFD 1-4218.
Semero smelykh. Sergei Gerasimov, 1936.
Severnyi polius zavoevan nami! RGAKFD 1-1467.
Slava Stalinskim sokolam! RGAKFD 1-4193.
SSSR-SShA. RGAKFD 1-26649.
Stalin's Arctic Disaster: The Voyage of the Cheliuskin. CineNova, 1996.
Tri geroini. RGAKFD 1-4188.
Valerii Chkalov. Mikhail Kalatozov, 1941.

Reference works and unpublished materials

Administrativno-territorial'noe delenie Sibiri. Novosibirsk, 1966.
Administrativno-territorial'noe delenie Soiuza SSR, 1917–1929. Moscow: NKVD, 1929.
Administrativno-territorial'noe delenie Soiuznykh respublik. Moscow: Vlast' Sovetov, 1937.
Administrativno-territorial'noe delenie SSSR. Moscow: Vlast' Sovetov, 1934.
Davies, R. W., J. M. Cooper, and M. J. Ilic. *Soviet Official Statistics on Industrial Production, Capital Stock, and Capital Investment, 1928–1941.* Birmingham, UK: University of Birmingham Press, 1991.
Geografiia SSSR. Moscow: Uchpedgiz, 1955.
Gilbert, Martin. *Atlas of Russian History.* New York: Dorset Press, 1985.
Itogi vypolneniia pervogo piatiletnego plana razvitiia narodnogo khoziaistva SSSR. Leningrad: Standartizatsiia i ratsionalizatsiia, 1934.
Itogi vypolneniia vtorogo piatiletnego plana razvitiia narodnogo khoziaistva SSSR. Moscow: Gosplanizdat, 1939.
Kasinec, Edward. "Schmidt and the American Press: A Note." Unpublished manuscript.
KPSS v rezoliutsiakh i resheniiakh s"ezdov, konferentsii i plenumov TsK, 1898–1986. 15 vols. Moscow: Politizdat, 1983–1989.
Kul'turnaia zhizn' v SSSR, 1928–1941: Khronika. Moscow: Nauka, 1976.
Morskoi transport Sovetskogo Soiuza za 50 let. Moscow: Transport, 1967.
Pechat' SSSR za sorok let, 1917–1957. Moscow, 1957.
Pervyi vsesoiuznyi s"ezd Sovetskikh pisatelei: Stenograficheskii otchet. Moscow, 1934.
Rechnoi transport za 50 let Sovetskoi vlasti. Moscow: Transport, 1967.
The Second Five-Year Plan for the Development of the National Economy of the

USSR. Moscow: Co-operative Publishing Society of Foreign Workers in the USSR, 1936.

Smits, Rudolf, ed. *Half a Century of Soviet Serials, 1917–1968*. 2 vols. Washington, D.C.: Library of Congress, 1968.

Sovetskie khudozhestvennye fil'my: Annotirovannyi katalog. 4 vols. Moscow: Iskusstvo, 1961.

Sovetskii rechnoi transport, 1917–1941. Moscow: Mysl', 1987.

Summary of the Fulfillment of the First Five-Year Plan for the Development of the National Economy of the USSR. Moscow: State Planning Commission, 1933.

Toniaev, V. I. *Geografiia vnutrennykh vodnykh putei SSSR*. Moscow: Transport, 1972.

Tremaine, Marie. *Arctic Bibliography*. 16 vols. Washington, D.C.: Government Printing Office, 1953–1975.

Tretii piatiletnii plan razvitiia narodnogo khoziaistva Soiuza SSR (1938–1942 gg.). Moscow: Gosplanizdat, 1939.

Vodnyi transport SSSR za 15 let. Moscow and Leningrad: Gostransizdat, 1932.

Vsia Sibir' i Dal'nii Vostok: Spravochnaia kniga na 1926 god. Moscow and Leningrad: Promizdat, 1926.

Vtoroi piatiletnii plan razvitiia narodnogo khoziaistva SSSR (1933–1937 gg.). 2 vols. Moscow: Gosplanizdat, 1934.

Materials on aviation and exploration

Angelucci, Enzo. *Rand McNally Encyclopedia of Military Aircraft*. New York: Military Press, 1990.

Armstrong, T. E., George Rogers, and Graham Rowley. *The Circumpolar North: A Political and Economic Geography of the Arctic and Sub-Arctic*. London: Methuen, 1978.

Baird, P. D. *The Polar World*. New York: Wiley, 1965.

Berton, Pierre. *The Arctic Grail*. New York: Viking, 1988.

Bloom, Lisa. *Gender on Ice: American Ideologies of Polar Expeditions*. Minneapolis: University of Minnesota Press, 1993.

Boorstin, Daniel. *The Discoverers: A History of Man's Search to Know His World and Himself*. New York: Random House, 1983.

Bryce, Robert M. *Cook and Peary: The Polar Controversy, Resolved*. Mechanicsburg, Penn.: Stackpole, 1997.

Cadogan, Mary. *Women with Wings: Female Flyers in Fact and Fiction*. London: Macmillan, 1992.

Davies, T. D. "New Evidence Places Peary at the Pole." *National Geographic* 177, no. 1 (January 1990): 44–61.

Downs, R. B. *In Search of New Horizons*. Chicago: American Library Association, 1978.

Egorov, A. Ia., and V. P. Kliucharev. *Grazhdanskaia aviatsiia SSSR*. Moscow: Sotsekgiz, 1937.

Friedlander, Mark P., and Gene Gurney. *Higher, Faster, and Farther*. New York: Morrow, 1973.

Glines, C. V., ed. *Polar Aviation*. New York: Franklin Watts, 1964.

Grazhdanskaia aviatsiia SSSR, 1917–1967. Moscow: Transport, 1967.

Grazhdanskaia aviatsiia SSSR v dokumentakh partiinykh, gosudarstvennykh i pravitel'stvikh organov. Moscow: Vozdushnyi transport, 1982.

Kilmarx, Robert A. *A History of Soviet Air Power*. New York: Praeger, 1962.

Lopez, Barry. *Arctic Dreams: Imagination and Desire in a Northern Landscape*. New York: Scribner's, 1986.

Mountfield, David. *A History of Polar Exploration*. New York: Dial, 1974.

Odom, William E. *The Soviet Volunteers: Modernization and Bureaucracy in a Public Mass Organization.* Princeton: Princeton University Press, 1973.

Rawlins, Dennis. *Peary at the Pole: Fact or Fiction?* Washington, D.C.: Robert Luce, 1973.

Rickenbacker, Edward. *Rickenbacker: An Autobiography.* Englewood Cliffs, N.J.: Prentice Hall, 1967.

Shesterikova, A. *Daty istorii otechestvennoi aviatsii i vozdukhoplavaniia.* Moscow: DOSAAF, 1953.

Simpson-Housley, Paul. *Antarctica: Exploration, Perception, and Metaphor.* London: Routledge, 1992.

Taylor, W. E., ed. *The Arctic World.* New York: Portland House, 1985.

Tierney, John. "How to Get to Mars (and Make Millions!)." *New York Times Magazine.* 26 May 1996.

The Times Atlas of World Exploration. New York: HarperCollins, 1991.

V. I. Lenin i Sovetskaia aviatsiia: Dokumenty, materialy, vospominaniia. Moscow: Voenizdat, 1979.

Vozdushnye puti Severa. Moscow, 1933.

Materials on Siberia and the Russian Arctic

Akkuratov, V. I. *Led i pepel.* Moscow: Sovremennik, 1984.

———. *Na novykh trassakh.* Moscow and Leningrad: GUSMP, 1941.

Altunin, E. V. *Kryl'ia nad Magadanom.* Moscow, 1968.

———. *Kryl'ia Severa.* Magadan, 1976.

———. *Kryl'ia Sibiri.* Irkutsk, 1981.

———. *Ocherki istorii grazhdanskoi aviatsii Vostochnoi Sibiri i Dal'nego Vostoka, 1923– 1945.* Irkutsk: Znanie RSFSR, 1986.

Arikainen, A. I. *Skvoz' l'dy Arktiki.* Moscow: Znanie, 1982.

Armstrong, T. E. *The Northern Sea Route: Soviet Exploitation of the Northeast Passage.* Cambridge: Cambridge University Press, 1952.

———. *Russian Settlement in the North.* Cambridge: Cambridge University Press, 1965.

———. *The Russians in the Arctic.* London: Methuen, 1958.

Artamanov, V. I. *Zemlia i nebo Vodop'ianova.* Moscow: Politizdat, 1991.

Avramenko, I. K. *Gordye Stalinskie sokoly: Ukazatel' literatury k godovshchine pereletov Moskva-Severnyi polius-Severnaia Amerika.* Leningrad, 1938.

Badigin, K. S. *Na morskikh dorogakh.* Arkhangelsk, 1985.

———. *Povesti.* Moscow: Detizdat, 1970.

———. *Skvoz' veter. Morskie rasskazy.* Moscow: Znanie, 1965.

———. *Tri zimovki vo l'dakh Arktiki.* Moscow: Molodaia gvardiia, 1950.

Baidukov, G. F. *Pervye perelety cherez Ledovityi okean.* Moscow: Detskaia literatura, 1987.

———. *Russian Lindbergh: The Life of Valery Chkalov.* Translated by Peter Belov. Washington, D.C.: Smithsonian, 1991.

———. *Vstrechi s tovarishchem Stalinym.* Moscow: Detizdat, 1938.

Belov, M. I. *Istoriia otkrytiia i osvoeniia Severnogo Morskogo Puti.* 4 vols. Leningrad: GUSMP, Morskoi transport, and Gidrometeoizdat, 1956–1969.

———. *Po sledam poliarnykh ekspeditsii.* Leningrad: Gidrometeoizdat, 1977.

———. *Put' cherez Ledovityi okean: Ocherki iz istorii otkrytiia i osvoeniia Severnogo morskogo puti.* Morskoi transport, 1963.

———. *V. I. Lenin i izuchenie Arktiki.* Leningrad: Gidrometeoizdat, 1970.

Bergavinov, S. A. *Arktika i polius zavoevany!* Moscow: Partizdat, 1937.

———. *Polius nash!* Moscow: Partizdat, 1937.

Bernshtein-Kogan, S. V. *Osnovnye problemy transporta SSSR i perspektivy ego razvitiia.* Moscow: Transpechat', 1929.

——. *Vnutrennyi vodnyi transport.* Moscow: Transpechat', 1927.

Bobrick, Benson. *East of the Sun: The Epic Conquest and Tragic History of Siberia.* New York: Poseidon, 1992.

Boiko, V. S. *Kryl'ia Severnogo flota.* Murmansk, 1976.

Bowermaster, Jon. "The Last Front of the Cold War." *Atlantic Monthly* 273, no. 11 (November 1993): 36–45.

Brontman, L. K. *Na vershine mira.* Moscow and Leningrad: Detizdat, 1938.

——. *On the Top of the World.* London: Victor Gollancz, 1938.

——. *Vladimir Kokkinaki.* Moscow: Voenizdat, 1939.

Brontman, L. K., and L. Khvat. *Geroicheskii perelet "Rodiny".* Moscow: OGIZ, 1938.

Buinitskii, V. Kh. *Vladimir Iul'evich Vize.* Leningrad, 1969.

——. *812 dnei v dreifuiushchikh l'dakh.* Moscow and Leningrad: GUSMP, 1940.

Burkhanov, V. F. *New Soviet Discoveries in the Arctic.* Moscow: Foreign Languages Publishing House, 1956.

Chkalov, V. P., G. F. Baidukov, and A. V. Beliakov. *Dva pereleta.* Moscow: Voenizdat, 1938.

——. *My eshche prodolzhim "Stalinskii marshrut".* Moscow: Gosizdat, 1938.

Chkalova, O. E. *Valerii Pavlovich Chkalov.* Gorky, 1981.

Conquest, Robert. *Kolyma: The Arctic Death Camps.* London: Macmillan, 1978.

Dallin, David J., and Boris Nicolaevsky. *Forced Labor in Soviet Russia.* New Haven: Yale University Press, 1947.

Dal'stroi k 25-letiiu, 1931–1956. Magadan, 1956.

Danilenko, V. F. *Kryl'ia Dal'nego Vostoka.* Khabarovsk, 1972.

Danilin, A. S. *Cherez Severnyi polius—s mirovym rekordom.* Moscow: DOSAAF, 1981.

Desiat' mesiatsev na dreifuiushchei stantsii "Severnyi polius". Moscow: OGIZ, 1938.

Diment, Galya, and Yuri Slezkine, eds. *Between Heaven and Hell: The Myth of Siberia in Russian Culture.* New York: St. Martin's Press, 1993.

Dnevniki Cheliuskintsev. Moscow: Pravda, 1934.

Duel', I. I. *Liniia zhizni.* Moscow: Politizdat, 1977.

Dvorniak, V. *Istoriia Dal'nevostochnogo parokhodstva.* Moscow, 1962.

Fadeev, A. A., ed. *Vstrechi s tovarishchem Stalinym.* Moscow: OGIZ, 1939.

Fedorov, E. K. *Polar Diaries.* Moscow: Progress, 1983.

Forsyth, James. *A History of the Peoples of Siberia: Russia's North Asian Colony, 1591–1990.* Cambridge: Cambridge University Press, 1992.

Garri, A. *L'dy i liudi.* Moscow, 1928.

Golovin, P. G. *Kak ia stal letchikom.* Moscow and Leningrad: Detizdat, 1938.

Gorbatov, B. *Petr Petrovich Shirshov.* Moscow: OGIZ, 1938.

——. *Vladimir Konstantinovich Kokkinaki.* Moscow: OGIZ, 1938.

Gor'kii, A. M., L. L. Averbakh, and S. G. Firin, eds. *Belomorsko-Baltiiskii kanal imeni Stalina.* Moscow: Istoriia zavodov i fabrik, 1934.

Grant, Bruce. *In the Soviet House of Culture: A Century of Perestroikas.* Princeton: Princeton University Press, 1995.

Griffiths, Franklyn. *Arctic and North in the Russian Identity.* Toronto: University of Toronto Press, 1990.

Gromov, B. *Gibel' Arktiki.* Moscow: Molodaia gvardiia, 1932.

——. *Gibel' "Cheliuskina".* Moscow: Goslitizdat, 1936.

——. *Pokhod "Sibiriakova".* Moscow: Sovetskaia literatura, 1934.

Gromov, M. M. *Cherez vsiu zhizn'.* Moscow: Molodaia gvardiia, 1986.

Gruber, Ruth. *I Went to the Soviet Arctic*. New York: Simon and Schuster, 1939.

Hardesty, Von. "Soviets Blaze Sky Trail over Top of World." *Air and Space/Smithsonian* 2, no. 5 (December 1987—January 1988): 48–54.

Horensma, Pier. *The Soviet Arctic*. London: Routledge, 1991.

I. D. Papanin. Moscow: Planeta, 1990.

Iakusheva, G. V. *Otto Iul'evich Shmidt—entsiklopedist*. Moscow: Sovetskaia entsiklopediia, 1991.

Istoriia Chukotki. Moscow: Mysl', 1989.

Istoriia pol'skikh, russkikh, i sovetskikh poliarnykh issledovanii: Materialy III Pol'sko-Sovetskogo Simpoziuma po istorii nauk o zemle, 25–30 sentiabria 1978. Wroclaw: Polish Academy of Sciences, 1982.

Jakobson, Michael. *Origins of the* GULAG: *The Soviet Prison Camp System, 1917–1934*. Lexington: University Press of Kentucky, 1993.

Kak my spasali Cheliuskintsy. Moscow: Pravda, 1934.

Kamanin, N. P. *Letchiki i kosmonavty*. Moscow: Politizdat, 1971.

———. *Starty v nebo*. Moscow: DOSAAF, 1976.

Kanevskii, Z. M. *Borot'sia i iskat'! Razmyshleniia o professii poliarnika*. Leningrad: Gidrometeoizdat, 1979.

———. *Direktor Arktiki*. Moscow: Politizdat, 1977.

———. *L'dy i sud'by*. Moscow: Znanie, 1973.

———. *Vsia zhizn'—ekspeditsiia*. Moscow: Mysl', 1982.

———. *Zagadki i tragedii Arktiki*. Moscow: Znanie, 1991.

Kaverin, V. A. *Dva kapitana*. Moscow: Molodaia gvardiia, 1951.

———. *The Two Captains*. Moscow: Raduga, 1989.

Kerner, R. J. *The Urge to the Sea*. Berkeley: University of California Press, 1942.

Khatylaev, M. M. *Zolotodobyvaiushchaia promyshlennost' Vostochnoi Sibiri, 1917–1925*. Iakutsk, 1983.

———. *Zolotopromyshlennost' Iakutii, 1923–1937*. Iakutsk, 1972.

Khvat, L. *Amerikanskie vstrechi*. Moscow: OGIZ, 1938.

Khvat, L., and M. Chernenko. *Geroicheskii dreif "Sedova"*. Moscow: OGIZ, 1940.

Kiselev, L. E. *Partiinoe rukovodstvo khoziaistvennym i kul'turnym stroitel'stvom v avtonomykh okrugakh Severa* RSFSR, *1917–1941*. Tomsk, 1989.

———. *Sever raskryvaet bogatstva*. Moscow: Mysl', 1964.

Kokkinaki, V. K. *Kak my leteli*. Rostov, 1939.

Krenkel', E. T. *Chetyre tovarishcha*. Moscow: Khudozhestvennaia literatura, 1940.

———. RAEM *Is My Call-Sign*. Moscow: Progress, 1978.

Kryl'ia sovetov: Literaturno-estradnyi sbornik. Moscow: Iskusstvo, 1939.

Krypton, Constantine. *The Northern Sea Route and the Economy of the Soviet North*. New York: Praeger, 1956.

Kublitskii, G. I. *Velikaia rechnaia derzhava*. Moscow: Ministerstvo rechnogo flota SSSR, 1952.

Kudrevatykh, L. A. *S Valeriem Chkalovym*. Moscow: Pravda, 1958.

Kvint, V. L., and N. M. Singur. *Nad nami poliarnaia zvezda*. Moscow: Sovetskaia Rossiia, 1984.

Lamb, Harold. *The March of Muscovy: Ivan the Terrible and the Growth of the Russian Empire, 1400–1648*. New York: Doubleday, 1948.

Lattimore, Owen. "New Road to Asia." *National Geographic* 86 (1944): 641–676.

Lebedev, A. A., and I. P. Mazuruk. *Nad Arktikoi i Antarktikoi*. Moscow: Mysl', 1991.

Leites, Flora, ed. *Stalinskie sokoly: Sbornik stikhov*. Moscow: Khudozhestvennaia literatura, 1939.

Lengyel, Emil. *Siberia*. New York: Random House, 1943.

Lenin i Sever. Arkhangelsk, 1969.

Letopis' Severa. 11 vols. Moscow: Mysl', 1949–1990 (published by GUSMP, 1949; by Geograficheskaia literatura, 1957 and 1962).

Levanevskii, S. A. *Moia stikhiia*. Rostov, 1935.

Liapidevskii, A. V. *Cheliuskintsy*. Moscow and Leningrad: Detizdat, 1938.

Lincoln, W. Bruce. *The Conquest of a Continent: Siberia and the Russians*. New York: Random House, 1993.

Littlepage, John D., and Demaree Bess. *In Search of Soviet Gold*. New York: Harcourt, Brace and Company, 1937.

Magadan: Konspekt proshlego—gody, liudi, problemy. Magadan, 1989.

Mazuruk, I. P. *Nasha aviatsiia*. Moscow and Leningrad: Detizdat, 1940.

McCannon, John. "Positive Heroes at the Pole: Celebrity Status, Self-Promotion, and the Stalinist Myth of the Arctic, 1932–1939." *Russian Review* 56 (1997): 346–365.

———. "To Storm the Arctic: Soviet Polar Expeditions and Public Visions of Nature in the USSR, 1932–1939." *Ecumene* 2 (1995): 15–31.

McDougall, Walter A. *Let the Sea Make a Noise: Four Hundred Years of Cataclysm, Conquest, War, and Folly in the North Pacific*. New York: Avon, 1993.

Mindlin, E. A. *Na Krasine*. Moscow and Leningrad: ZIF, 1929.

Mineev, A. I. *Ostrov Vrangelia*. Moscow and Leningrad: GUSMP, 1946.

———. *Zachem my organizovali ekspeditsiiu Papanina*. Moscow: OGIZ, 1938.

Mogilevskaia, S. *Lager' na l'dine*. Moscow: Detizdat, 1935.

Moiseev, V. A. *Plemia Ikara: Povest'-khronika*. Kiev: Veselka, 1986.

Molokov, V. S. *My vypolnili svoi dolg—vot i vse!* Moscow: Molodaia gvardiia, 1935.

———. *Rodnoe nebo*. Moscow: Voenizdat, 1977.

Morozov, S. T. *Krylatyi sledopyt Zapoliar'ia*. Moscow: Mysl', 1975.

———. *L'dy i liudi*. Moscow: Molodaia gvardiia, 1979.

———. *Lenskii pokhod*. Moscow: Molodaia gvardiia, 1934.

———. *Oni prinesli kryl'ia v Arktiku*. Moscow: Mysl', 1979.

Moscow—Vancouver: 1937. Moscow: Novosti, 1987.

Mowat, Farley. *The Siberians*. Toronto: Bantam, 1970.

My iz Igarki. Moscow and Leningrad: Detizdat, 1938.

Na kraiu nebe. Khabarovsk, 1976.

Nikitenko, N. F. *O. Iu. Shmidt*. Moscow, 1992.

Nikolaeva, A. G., and V. I. Sarankin. *Sil'nee l'dov*. Moscow: Morskoi transport, 1963.

Obruchev, S. V. *Po goram i tundram Chukotki: Ekspeditsiia 1934–1935 gg*. Magadan, 1974.

Obruchev, V. A. *Plutoniia*. Moscow: Nauka, 1990.

———. *Puteshestviia v proshloe i budushchee: Nauchno-fantasticheskie proizvedeniia*. Moscow: Nauka, 1961.

———. *Zemlia Sannikova*. Moscow: Nauka, 1990.

Okun, Semen B. *The Russian-American Company*. Cambridge: Harvard University Press, 1951.

Ostrovskii, Z. T. *Nad vechnymi l'dami*. Moscow and Leningrad: Gosizdat, 1929.

Otto Iul'evich Shmidt: Zhizn' i deiatel'nost'. Moscow: Nauka, 1959.

Papanin, I. D. *Led i plamen'*. Moscow: Politizdat, 1978.

———. *Na poliuse*. Moscow and Leningrad: Detizdat, 1939.

———. *Zhizn' na l'dine*. Moscow: Mysl', 1966.

Parijanine, Maurice. *The Krassin*. New York: Macauley, 1929.

Perevalov, V. A. *Lomonosov i Arktika*. Moscow: GUSMP, 1949.

Petrov, Vladimir. *Soviet Gold*. New York: Farrar, Straus, 1949.

Podvigina, E. P., and L. K. Vinogradov. *Akademik i geroi*. Moscow: Gospolitizdat, 1960.

Podvig shturmana V. I. Al'banova. Moscow, 1953.

Poema o kryl'iakh: Zapiski aviatorov. Moscow: Sovremennik, 1988.

Pokhod "Cheliuskina". Moscow: Pravda, 1934.

Popov, V. T. *Severnyi morskoi put' v filatelii*. Murmansk, 1990.

Po sledam Cheliuskinskoi epopei. Magadan, 1986.

Po Stalinskoi trasse. Moscow: Molodaia gvardiia, 1937.

Pribyl'skii, Iu. P. *Sovetskii Sever v gody Velikoi Otechestvennoi Voiny*. Tomsk, 1986.

Problemy Severa. 23 vols. Moscow: Nauka, 1958–1988.

Rabochii klass i krest'ianstvo natsional'nykh raionov Sibiri. Novosibirsk, 1974.

Rakhillo, I. S. *Rasskazy o Chkalove*. Moscow: Detizdat, 1960.

Resistance in the GULAG. Moscow: Vozvrashchenie, 1992.

Riabchikov, E. I., and S. Shul'man. *Gromov*. Moscow: Molodaia gvardiia, 1937.

Rossi, Jacques. *The* GULAG *Handbook*. New York: Paragon, 1992.

Sal'nikov, Iu. P. *Zhizn', otdannaia Arktike*. Moscow: Politizdat, 1984.

Scherer, John L., and Michael Jakobson. "The Collectivisation of Agriculture and the Soviet Prison Camp System." *Europe-Asia Studies* 45 (1993): 533–546.

Seleznev, S. A. *Ledovyi kapitan*. Arkhangelsk, 1969.

Semushkin, T. *Chukotka*. Moscow: Sovetskii pisatel', 1941.

Serebrovskii, A. P. *Zolotaia promyshlennost'*. 2 vols. Moscow and Leningrad: Nauka, 1935.

Shalamov, Varlam. *Kolyma Tales*. New York: Norton, 1980.

Shifrin, A. I. *The First Guidebook to the Prison and Concentration Camps of the Soviet Union*. New York: Bantam, 1982.

Shmidt, O. Iu. *Nashi zadachi v 1936 gody*. Leningrad: GUSMP, 1936.

——. *Neopublikovannye pis'ma O. Iu. Shmidta*. Minsk: Nauka i tekhnika, 1976.

——. *Osvoenie Severnogo morskogo puti i zadachi sel'skogo khoziaistva Krainego Severa*. Moscow and Leningrad: Nauka, 1937.

——. *Sobranie sochinenii*. Moscow: Nauka, 1960.

Shparo, D., and A. Shumilov. *K poliusu!* Moscow: Molodaia gvardiia, 1987.

Sibirtsev, N. N., and V. Itin. *Severnyi morskoi put' i Karskie ekspeditsii*. Novosibirsk, 1936.

Slavin, S. V. *Osvoenie Severa Sovetskogo Soiuza*. Moscow: Nauka, 1982.

——. *Promyshlennoe i transportnoe osvoenie Severa SSSR*. Moscow: Ekonomizdat, 1961.

Slezkine, Yuri. *Arctic Mirrors: Russia and the Small Peoples of the North*. Ithaca: Cornell University Press, 1994.

——. "From Savages to Citizens: The Cultural Revolution in the Far North, 1928–1938." *Slavic Review* 51 (1992): 52–76.

Smolka, Harry P. *Forty Thousand against the Arctic: Russia's Polar Empire*. New York: Morrow, 1937.

Sokolov-Mikitov, I. *Severnye rasskazy*. Moscow: Khudozhestvennaia literatura, 1939.

Solomon, Michael. *Magadan*. Princeton: Vertex, 1971.

Solzhenitsyn, Aleksandr I. *The* GULAG *Archipelago, 1918–1956: An Experiment in Literary Investigation*. 2 vols. New York: Harper and Row, 1973–1975.

Soviet Aviation. Moscow and Leningrad: State Art Publishers, 1939.

Spirin, I. T. *Rasskazy letchika*. Moscow and Leningrad: Detizdat, 1939.

Stalinskaia trassa. Moscow: Partizdat, 1937.

Stephan, John J. *The Russian Far East: A History*. Stanford: Stanford University Press, 1994.

Strugatskii, V. *K poliusam Zemli: Rasskazy iz muzeia Arktiki i Antarktiki*. Leningrad: Lenizdat, 1984.

Swianiewicz, S. *Forced Labor and Economic Development: An Enquiry into the Experience of Soviet Industrialization*. London: Oxford University Press, 1965.

Taracouzio, T. A. *Soviets in the Arctic*. New York: Macmillan, 1938.

Thiel, Erich. *The Soviet Far East: A Survey of Its Physical and Economic Geography*. London: Methuen, 1957.

Timoshenko, V. P. *Ural v mirokhoziaistvennykh sviazakh, 1917–1941*. Sverdlovsk: Ural'skoe otdelenie Akademii nauk, 1991.

Treadgold, Donald W. *The Great Siberian Migration*. Princeton: Princeton University Press, 1957.

Trudy dreifuiushchei ekspeditsii Glavsevmorputi na ledokol'nom parokhode "G. Sedov". Moscow and Leningrad: GUSMP, 1940.

Urvantsev, N. N. *Na Severnoi Zemle*. Leningrad: Gidrometeoizdat, 1969.

——. *Otkrytie Noril'ska*. Moscow: Nauka, 1981.

Ushakov, G. A. *Ostrov metelei*. Leningrad: Gidrometeoizdat, 1990.

——. *Po nekhozhenoi zemle*. Leningrad: Gidrometeoizdat, 1990.

Vasnetsov, V. A. *Pod zvezdnym flagom "Persei"*. Leningrad: Gidrometeoizdat, 1974.

——. *Povesti Severnykh morei*. Leningrad: Gidrometeoizdat, 1977.

Velikii letchik nashego vremeni. Moscow: OGIZ, 1939.

Viakhirev, M. V. *V kraiu purgi i l'dov*. Leningrad: Gidrometeoizdat, 1985.

V. I. Lenin i Sibir'. Novosibirsk, 1972.

Vishevskii, V. *Geroi Sovetskogo Soiuza Ivan Dmitrievich Papanin*. Moscow: OGIZ, 1938.

Vize, V. Iu. *Lomonosov i Severnyi morskoi put'*. Moscow: Molodaia gvardiia, 1946.

Vodop'ianov, M. V. *Mechta*. Moscow: Iskusstvo, 1937.

——. *Mechta pilota*. Moscow: Molodaia gvardiia, 1937.

——. *Na kryl'iakh v Arktiku*. Moscow: Geograficheskaia literatura, 1954.

——. *Polius*. Moscow and Leningrad: Detizdat, 1939.

——. *Rasskaz o moei zhizni*. Moscow: Sovetskii pisatel', 1937.

——. *Rasskazy letchika*. Gorky, 1953.

——. *Vynuzhdennaia posadka*. Moscow: Iskusstvo, 1943.

Vodop'ianov, M. V., and G. K. Grigor'ev. *Povest' o ledovom komissare*. Moscow: Geograficheskaia literatura, 1959.

Voskoboinikov, V. M. *Zov Arktiki*. Moscow: Molodaia gvardiia, 1975.

The Voyage of the Cheliuskin. New York: Macmillan, 1935.

Vyshinskii, A. Ia. *Protiv Semenchukovshchiny*. Moscow: OGIZ, 1936.

Webster, C. J. "The Economic Development of the Soviet Arctic and the Sub-Arctic." *Slavonic and East European Review* 29, no. 12. (December 1950): 177–211.

Wood, Alan, ed. *The History of Siberia: From Russian Conquest to Revolution*. New York: Routledge, 1991.

Zaluzhnyi, V. D. *Shturman ledovogo pereleta*. Rostov, 1976.

Za osvoenie Arktiki. Leningrad: GUSMP, 1935.

Zhikharev, N. A. *Ocherki istorii Severo-Vostoka RSFSR*. Magadan, 1961.

Zibarev, V. A., ed. *Partiinye organizatsii Sovetskogo Severa*. Tomsk, 1980.

Zinger, M. E. *Geroi Sovetskogo Soiuza*. Moscow: Ogonek, 1934.

——. *Lenskii pokhod*. Leningrad: Lenizdat, 1934.

——. *Pobezhdennoe more*. Moscow: Sovetskaia Aziia, 1932.

——. *Rasskazy starogo poliarnika*. Moscow: Detgiz, 1959.

——. *Severnye rasskazy*. Moscow: Sovetskii pisatel', 1938.

——. *Shturm Severa*. Moscow and Leningrad: Khudozhestvennaia literatura, 1932.

——. *U tainikov Severa*. Moscow: Ogonek, 1929.

Zubov, N. N. *V tsentre Arktiki*. Moscow and Leningrad: GUSMP, 1948.

Russian/Soviet culture, economics, and politics

Akhmatova, A. A. *V to vremia ia gostila na zemle*. Moscow: Cosmopolis, 1991.

Aksyonov, Vassily. *The Burn*. New York: Vintage, 1985.

Antonov-Ovseenko, Anton. *The Time of Stalin: Portrait of a Tyranny*. New York: Harper and Row, 1983.

Bailes, Kendall E. *Technology and Society under Lenin and Stalin: Origins of the Soviet Technical Intelligentsia, 1917–1941*. Princeton: Princeton University Press, 1978.

Bassin, Mark. "Geographical Determinism in Fin-de-siècle Marxism: Georgii Plekhanov and the Environmental Basis of Russian History." *Annals of the Association of American Geographers* 82 (1992): 3–22.

——. "Turner, Solov'ev, and the 'Frontier Hypothesis': The Nationalist Signification of Open Spaces." *Journal of Modern History* 65 (1993): 473–511.

Benn, David W. *Persuasion and Soviet Politics*. Oxford: Blackwell, 1989.

Bialer, Seweryn, ed. *Stalin and His Generals*. New York: Pegasus, 1969.

Billington, James. *The Icon and the Axe: An Interpretive History of Russian Culture*. New York: Vintage, 1966.

Bown, Matthew Cullerne. *Art Under Stalin*. New York: Holmes and Meier, 1991.

Brooks, Jeffrey. "Socialist Realism in *Pravda*: Read All about It!" *Slavic Review* 53 (1994): 973–991.

——. *When Russia Learned to Read*. Princeton: Princeton University Press, 1985.

Brower, Daniel. "Imperial Russia and Its Orient: The Renown of Nikolai Przhevalsky." *Russian Review* 53 (1994): 367–381.

Brown, Edward J. *Russian Literature since the Revolution*. Cambridge: Harvard University Press, 1982.

Cherniavsky, Michael. *Tsar and People: Studies in Russian Myths*. New Haven: Yale University Press, 1961.

Chukovskaia, L. K. *Sofiia Petrovna*. Moscow: Moskovskii rabochii, 1988.

Clark, Katerina. "Little Heroes and Big Deeds: Literature Responds to the First Five-Year Plan." In Sheila Fitzpatrick, ed., *Cultural Revolution in Russia, 1928–1931*. Bloomington: Indiana University Press, 1978.

——. *The Soviet Novel: History as Ritual*. Chicago: University of Chicago Press, 1981.

Conquest, Robert. *The Great Terror: A Reassessment*. New York: Oxford University Press, 1990.

Davies, R. W., Mark Harrison, and S. G. Wheatcroft, eds. *The Economic Transformation of the Soviet Union, 1913–1945*. Cambridge: Cambridge University Press, 1994.

DeBardeleben, Joan, and John Hannigan, eds. *Environmental Security and Quality after Communism*. Boulder, Colo.: Westview Press, 1995.

Dunham, Vera. *In Stalin's Time: Middleclass Values in Soviet Fiction*. Cambridge: Cambridge University Press, 1976.

Durov, V. A. *Russkie i sovetskie boevye nagrady*. Moscow: Lenin State Historical Museum, 1990.

Edelman, Robert. "The Icon and the Sax: Stites in Bright Lights." *Slavic Review* 52 (1993): 569–578.

Elliot, David. *New Worlds: Russian Art and Society, 1917–1937*. New York: Rizzoli, 1986.

Etkind, A. *Eros nevozmozhnogo*. St. Petersburg: Medusa, 1993.

Fainsod, Merle. *Smolensk under Soviet Rule*. New York: Vintage, 1958.

Fitzpatrick, Sheila. *The Commissariat of Enlightenment*. Cambridge: Cambridge University Press, 1970.

——. *The Cultural Front: Power and Culture in Revolutionary Russia*. Ithaca: Cornell University Press, 1992.

————. *Stalin's Peasants: Resistance and Survival in the Russian Village after Collectiviza-tion*. New York: Oxford University Press, 1994.

Garrand, John, and Carol Garrand. *Inside the Soviet Writers' Union*. New York: Free Press, 1990.

Garros, Véronique, Natalia Koronevskaya, and Thomas Lahusen, eds. *Intimacy and Ter-ror: Soviet Diaries of the 1930s*. New York: New Press, 1995.

Getty, J. Arch. *Origins of the Great Purges: The Communist Party Reconsidered, 1933–1938*. New York: Cambridge University Press, 1985.

Getty, J. Arch, and Roberta Manning, eds. *Stalinist Terror: New Perspectives*. New York: Cambridge University Press, 1993.

Ginzburg, Evgeniia. *Into the Whirlwind*. London: Collins and Harvill, 1967.

Gleason, Abbott, Peter Kenez, and Richard Stites, eds. *Bolshevik Culture*. Bloomington: Indiana University Press, 1985.

Graham, Loren R., ed. *Science and the Soviet Social Order*. Cambridge: Harvard Univer-sity Press, 1990.

Gronskii, I. *Iz proshlego: Vospominaniia*. Moscow: Izvestiia, 1991.

Günther, Hans. *Der sozialistische Übermensch: Maksim Gor'kij und der sowjetische Heldenmythos*. Stuttgart and Weimar: J. B. Metzler, 1993.

Günther, Hans, ed. *The Culture of the Stalin Period*. New York: St. Martin's Press, 1990.

Hingley, Ronald. *Russian Writers and Soviet Society, 1917–1978*. New York: Random House, 1979.

Hokanson, Katya. "Literary Imperialism, *Narodnost'*, and Pushkin's Invention of the Cau-casus." *Russian Review* 53 (1994): 336–352.

Hopkins, Mark W. *Mass Media in the Soviet Union*. New York: Pegasus, 1970.

Hunter, Holland. *Soviet Transportation Policy*. Cambridge: Harvard University Press, 1957.

Ilin, M. [Il'ia Marshak]. *New Russia's Primer: The Story of the Great Plan*. Boston: Houghton Mifflin, 1931.

Inkeles, Alex. *Public Opinion in Soviet Russia: A Study in Mass Persuasion*. Cambridge: Harvard University Press, 1967.

Inkeles, Alex, and Raymond Bauer. *The Soviet Citizen: Daily Life in a Totalitarian Soci-ety*. Cambridge: Harvard University Press, 1959.

Iskander, Fazil. *Sandro of Chegem*. New York: Vintage, 1983.

Istoriia strany v plakate. Moscow: Panorama, 1993.

Jelagin, Juri. *Taming of the Arts*. New York: Dutton, 1951.

Karachun, D., and V. Karlinskii. *Pochtovye marki SSSR, 1918–1968*. Moscow: Sviaz', 1969.

Kenez, Peter. *The Birth of the Propaganda State: Soviet Methods of Mass Mobilization, 1917–1929*. Cambridge: Cambridge University Press, 1985.

————. *Cinema and Soviet Society, 1917–1953*. New York: Cambridge University Press, 1992.

Knight, Amy. *Beria: Stalin's First Lieutenant*. Princeton: Princeton University Press, 1993.

Kotlyar, A. *Newspapers in the USSR: Reflections and Observations of a Soviet Journalist*. New York: Research Program on the USSR, 1955.

Lane, Christel. *The Rites of Rulers: Ritual in Industrial Society—The Soviet Case*. Cam-bridge: Cambridge University Press, 1981.

Mally, Lynn. *Culture of the Future: The Proletkult Movement in Revolutionary Russia*. Berkeley: University of California Press, 1990.

Mandelstam, Nadezhda. *Hope against Hope: A Memoir*. New York: Atheneum, 1976.

Mathewson, Rufus. *The Positive Hero in Russian Literature*. Stanford: Stanford University Press, 1975.

Matley, Ian. "The Marxist Approach to the Geographical Environment." *Annals of the Association of American Geographers* 56 (1966): 97–111.

McNeal, Robert. *Stalin: Man and Ruler.* New York: New York University Press, 1988.

Medvedev, Roy A. *Let History Judge.* New York: Vintage, 1971.

Miller, Frank. *Folklore for Stalin.* Armonk, N.Y.: M. E. Sharpe, 1990.

Morton, Miriam, ed. *A Harvest of Russian Children's Literature.* Berkeley: University of California Press, 1968.

O'Dell, Felicity Ann. *Socialisation through Children's Literature: The Soviet Example.* Cambridge: Cambridge University Press, 1978.

Oinas, Felix J. "Folklore and Politics in the Soviet Union." *Slavic Review* 32 (1973): 45–58.

Palmer, Scott. "On Wings of Courage: Public 'Air-Mindedness' and National Identity in Late Imperial Russia." *Russian Review* 54 (1995): 209–226.

Petrone, Karen. "Gender and Heroes." In Sue Bridger, ed., *The Swing of the Pendulum: Women's Experience of Change in East Central Europe and the Former USSR.* New York: Macmillan, 1997.

Popkin, Cathy. "Chekhov as Ethnographer: Epistemological Crisis on Sakhalin Island." *Slavic Review* 51 (1992): 36–51.

Riordan, James. *Sport in Soviet Society.* Cambridge: Cambridge University Press, 1977.

Robin, Régine. *Socialist Realism: An Impossible Aesthetic.* Stanford: Stanford University Press, 1992.

Russia: A Complete and Thoroughly Illustrated Album for the Stamps of Russia. New York: Minkus, 1972.

Smith, Hedrick. *The Russians.* New York: Ballantine, 1976.

Sokolov, Y. M. *Russian Folklore.* Detroit, 1971.

Solzhenitsyn, Aleksandr I. *The First Circle.* New York: Bantam, 1969.

Soviet Photography: An Age of Realism. New York: Greenwich, 1984.

Spiridonova, Lidiia. "Gorky and Stalin (According to New Materials from A. M. Gorky's Archive)." *Russian Review* 54 (1995): 413–423.

Stites, Richard. *Revolutionary Dreams: Utopian Vision and Experimental Life in the Russian Revolution.* New York: Oxford University Press, 1989.

———. *Russian Popular Culture: Entertainment and Society since 1900.* New York: Cambridge University Press, 1992.

Stites, Richard, ed. *Culture and Entertainment in Wartime Russia.* Bloomington: Indiana University Press, 1995.

Tarkhanov, Alexei, and Sergei Kavtaradze. *Architecture of the Stalin Era.* New York: Rizzoli, 1992.

Taylor, Richard, and Derek Spring, eds. *Stalinism and Soviet Cinema.* London: Routledge, 1993.

Thurston, Robert. *Life and Terror in Stalin's Russia, 1934–1941.* New Haven: Yale University Press, 1996.

Tolstoy, Vladimir. *Russian Decorative Arts, 1917–1937.* New York: Rizzoli, 1990.

Tsvetaeva, M. I. *Stikhotvoreniia i poemy.* 3 vols. New York: Russica, 1983.

Tucker, Robert C. *Stalin in Power: The Revolution from Above, 1929–1941.* New York: Norton, 1990.

Tumarkin, Nina. *Lenin Lives! The Lenin Cult in Soviet Russia.* Cambridge: Harvard University Press, 1983.

Uspenskii, L. V. *Ty i tvoe imia.* Leningrad: Lenizdat, 1962.

Vaksberg, Arkadii. *Stalin's Prosecutor: The Life of Andrei Vyshinsky.* New York: Grove Weidenfeld, 1991.

Voinovich, Vladimir. *Pretender to the Throne*. New York: Farrar, Straus, Giroux, 1981.

Volkogonov, Dmitri. *Stalin: Triumph and Tragedy*. Rocklin, Calif.: Prima, 1992.

von Geldern, James, and Richard Stites, eds. *Mass Culture in Soviet Russia*. Bloomington: Indiana University Press, 1995.

Vyshinskii, A. Ia. *Sudebnye rechi*. Moscow: Iuridicheskaia literatura, 1948.

Weinberg, Robert. "Purge and Politics in the Periphery: Birobidzhan in 1937." *Slavic Review* 52 (1993): 13–27.

Weiner, Douglas. *Models of Nature: Ecology, Conservation, and Cultural Revolution in Soviet Russia*. Bloomington: Indiana University Press, 1988.

White, Stephen. *The Bolshevik Poster*. New Haven: Yale University Press, 1988.

Zaleski, Eugene. *Stalinist Planning for Economic Growth, 1933–1952*. Chapel Hill: University of North Carolina Press, 1980.

General materials on culture and mass media

Adams, Percy G. *Travel Literature and the Evolution of the Novel*. Lexington: University Press of Kentucky, 1983.

Baird, Jay W. *The Mythical World of Nazi War Propaganda, 1939–1945*. Minneapolis: University of Minnesota Press, 1974.

———. *To Die for Germany: Heroes in the Nazi Pantheon*. Bloomington: Indiana University Press, 1990.

Bakhtin, Mikhail. *Rabelais and His World*. Bloomington: Indiana University Press, 1984.

Battersby, Martin. *The Decorative Thirties*. New York: Whitney Library of Design, 1988.

Corn, Joseph. *The Winged Gospel: America's Romance with Aviation, 1900–1950*. New York: Oxford University Press, 1983.

Corn, Joseph, and Brian Horrigan. *Yesterday's Tomorrows: Past Visions of the American Future*. New York: Summit Books, 1984.

Dorfman, Ariel, and Armand Mattelart. *How to Read Donald Duck: Imperial Ideology in the Disney Comic*. New York: International General, 1975.

Dorson, Richard. *Folklore and Fakelore*. Cambridge: Harvard University Press, 1976.

Eksteins, Modris. *Rites of Spring: The Great War and the Birth of the Modern Age*. New York: Anchor Books, 1990.

Ellul, Jacques. *Propaganda: The Formation of Men's Attitudes*. New York: Knopf, 1972.

Franklin, H. Bruce. "America as Science Fiction: 1939." In George E. Slusser, Eric S. Rabkin, Robert Scholes, eds., *Coordinates: Placing Science Fiction and Fantasy*. Carbondale and Edwardsville: Southern Illinois University Press, 1983.

Fritzsche, Peter. *A Nation of Fliers: German Aviation and the Popular Imagination*. Cambridge: Harvard University Press, 1992.

Gelernter, David. *1939: The Lost World of the Fair*. New York: Free Press, 1995.

Golsan, Richard, ed. *Fascism, Aesthetics, and Culture*. Hanover, N.H.: University Press of New England, 1992.

Green, Martin. *Dreams of Adventure, Deeds of Empire*. New York: Basic Books, 1979.

Hobsbawm, Eric, and Terence Ranger, eds. *The Invention of Tradition*. Cambridge: Cambridge University Press, 1983.

Kamenetsky, Christa. "Folklore and Ideology in the Third Reich." *Journal of American Folklore* 90 (1977): 168–178.

———. "Folklore as a Political Tool in Nazi Germany." *Journal of American Folklore* 85 (1972): 221–235.

Kertzer, David I. *Ritual, Politics, and Power*. New Haven: Yale University Press, 1988.

Knox-Shaw, Peter. *The Explorer in English Fiction*. New York: St. Martin's Press, 1986.

Le Corbusier [Charles Eduoard Jeanneret-Gris]. *Aircraft*. London: The Studio, 1935.

Lowenthal, Leo. *Literature and Mass Culture*. New Brunswick, N.J.: Transaction Books, 1984.

Lowery, Shearon, and Melvin L. DeFleur. *Milestones in Mass Communications Research*. New York: Longman, 1983.

MacAloon, John, ed. *Rite, Drama, Festival, Spectacle*. Philadelphia: Institute for the Study of Human Issues, 1984.

Marx, Leo. *The Machine in the Garden: Technology and the Pastoral Ideal in America*. New York: Oxford University Press, 1968.

Mayo, James M. *War Memorials as Political Landscape*. New York: Praeger, 1988.

Mukerji, Chandra, and Michael Schudson, eds. *Rethinking Popular Culture*. Berkeley: University of California Press, 1991.

Mumford, Lewis. *Technics and Civilization*. New York: Harcourt Brace and World, 1963.

Peukert, D. J. K. *Inside Nazi Germany: Conformity, Opposition, and Racism in Everyday Life*. New Haven: Yale University Press, 1987.

Riffenburgh, Beau. *The Myth of the Explorer: The Press, Sensationalism, and Geographical Discovery*. London: Belhaven Press, 1993.

Said, Edward. *Orientalism*. New York: Pantheon, 1993.

Schama, Simon. *Landscape and Memory*. New York: Knopf, 1995.

Segré, Claudio G. *Italo Balbo: A Fascist Life*. Berkeley: University of California Press, 1987.

Wilentz, Sean, ed. *Rites of Power: Symbolism, Ritual, and Politics since the Middle Ages*. Philadelphia: University of Pennsylvania Press, 1985.

Williams, Rosalind. *Notes on the Underground: An Essay on Technology, Society, and the Imagination*. Cambridge: MIT Press, 1990.

Wilson, Edmund. *The Thirties*. New York: Farrar, Straus, Giroux, 1980.

Wohl, Robert. *A Passion for Wings: Aviation and the Western Imagination, 1903–1918*. New Haven: Yale University Press, 1994.

Wolfe, Tom. *The Right Stuff*. New York: Bantam, 1983.

Zipes, Jack. *Breaking the Magic Spell: Radical Theories of Folk and Fairy Tales*. Austin: University of Texas Press, 1979.

———. *The Brothers Grimm: From Enchanted Forests to the Modern World*. New York: Routledge, 1988.

Zweig, Paul. *The Adventurer*. New York: Basic Books, 1974.

Index

Academy of Sciences, 15, 21, 23, 35, 130, 158, 167–168

Aeroarctic. *See* International Society for the Study of the Arctic by Means of Airships

Afanasev, A. A., 175

Agitational Escadrille, 69, 197n68

agriculture, 31, 40, 54–55. *See also* collectivization; reindeer

air transport, 26–27, 30–31, 36–37, 49, 55–58, 69, 146–149, 171

Akhmatova, Anna, 141

Akkuratov, Valentin, 175

Aksyonov, Vassily, 141, 209n93

alcoholism and narcotics abuse, 48–49, 52, 54, 152

Alexeev, Anatoly, 73, 162

All-Union Agricultural-Economic Exhibition (VSKHV), 116–117, 129, 201n26

All-Union Arctic Scientific-Research Institute (VAI, Arctic Institute), 24–27, 35–36, 39–42, 53, 87, 116, 159, 163, 166, 175–176, 186n23

All-Union Trust of the Gold Industry (Soiuzzoloto), 23, 186n21. *See also* Main Administration of the Gold and Platinum Industries

Amundsen, Roald, 17, 26, 29, 60, 73

Andree, Salomon, 26

Andreev, Andrei, 108

Andrews, Roy Chapman, 67

Antonov-Ovseenko, Vladimir, 114

Arctic Coal-Mining Company (Arktikugol), 22, 37–38, 48, 153–155

Arctic Institute. *See* All-Union Arctic Scientific-Research Institute

Arctic myth. *See* socialist realism

Arktika, 176

Armstrong, Terence, 173, 182n3

Aseev, Nikolai, 119, 130

aviation, as cultural symbol, 9, 68–72, 93, 95, 97–98, 125, 127, 178, 192n13

Aviation Day (18 August), 68–69, 72, 94, 96

Babel, Isaak, 167

Babushkin, Mikhail, 62–63, 78, 161–162

Badigin, Konstantin, 85, 120, 174

Baevsky, Ivan, 66, 159–160

Baidukov, Georgy, 70–71, 98, 127–128, 163, 207n62

Bailes, Kendall, 96, 115, 183–184n8

Bakhtin, Mikhail, 137

Barents, Willem, 13

BBK. *See* White Sea-Baltic Sea Canal

Bedny, Demian, 119

Belakhov, L. Y., 164–166

Beliakov, Alexander, 70–71, 127–128

Belomor. *See* White Sea-Baltic Sea Canal

Belov, M. I., 182n3, 187n6

Bergavinov, Sergei, 37, 39, 43, 50, 158, 160, 162–163, 172

Beria, Lavrenty, 108

Bering, Vitus, 15, 93. *See also* Great Northern Expedition

Berman, Matvei, 44

Bernshtein-Kogan, Sergei, 25

Berzin, Eduard, 169–171, 208n85

Bobrov, Alexei, 66–67, 159–160

bogatyr, as cultural symbol, 99, 102, 126, 133. *See also* folklore

Bogoraz-Tan, Vladimir, 50

Briandinsky, Alexander, 79

Brontman, Lazar, 74, 76, 119

Brusilov, Georgy, 19, 93–94, 185n11

Bukharin, Nikolai, 131, 150, 163

Burkhanov, Vasily, 175

Byrd, Richard, 26, 73–74, 186n27